ENDORSEMENTS

"This is an important book about a golden moment in the history of Theatre for Young Audiences in the United States. From 1936-1943 Junior Programs operated an ambitious national touring program that brought high quality theatre, opera and ballet to millions of young people, their families, schools and communities. It was a time, not so different from our own when the rise of fascism, political turmoil and an impending war, threatened the very foundations of Democracy. Lancourt meticulously chronicles the principles of social justice that inspired the company's *"Credo"*, their innovative production processes, and the astonishing organizational structure that mobilized thousands of volunteers and local partnerships in small towns and large cities alike. Junior Programs embraced many of the same values that we espouse in the world of TYA today: artistic excellence, community activism, educational relevance and a commitment to diversity and inclusion. Their legacy provides inspiration for us to recognize that the performing arts experiences for, with and about young people can be so much more than entertainment... they can be life changing!"

—**Suzan Zeder**,
President, Board of Trustees,
The Childrens Theatre Foundation of America

"Lancourt's book is an extremely valuable read for TYA scholars and practitioners today because we must draw on so many lessons from Junior Programs' past: the power of activating theatre beyond simply a means of entertainment, towards a more just and equitable future for our young people. Junior Programs' commitment to using theatre as an educational tool for young audiences' development all across America is more crucial now than ever. This text opens a window for the reader into an extraordinary time in American TYA history, as we are faced with similar challenges in today's society."

—**Sara Morgulis**,
Executive Director, TYA/USA

"Joan Lancourt's masterfully researched book is a treasury of insights into Junior Programs, an early twentieth-century theatre for young audiences. Their educational partnerships and productions, which range across theatre, ballet, and opera, offered a model for pedagogy and practice that should be an inspiration to educational theatres across the United States. *More than Entertainment: Democracy and the Performing Arts* is essential reading for scholars of 20th century American theatre and artists who believe in the theatre's ability to shape and change society."

—**Noe Montez**,
Associate Professor of Theatre Studies, Emory University

"Junior Programs was a bold, innovative and visionary initiative to bring the performing arts to young people in communities across the United States. It is also an excellent early example of effective community engagement. Their approach, based on foundational American values of participatory democracy, diversity, equal access, social solidarity, civic activism, social and economic justice, relied on the creation of a local Sponsoring Committee in every community in which they performed. Field secretaries, acting in the best tradition of grassroots organizing, identified potential partners from civic clubs, schools, local government, religious institutions, local businesses, libraries, and neighborhood associations, and guided the formation of the sponsoring committees. This infrastructure of activist volunteers selected the productions, and were responsible for raising the financial resources, securing the venue, orchestrating the publicity, and managing ticket sales as well as all the logistics related to the local performance. Empty seats were a rarity! Junior Programs accomplished all this at a time when democratic principles and institutions were under attack, domestically and internationally. Today, with these same anti-democratic forces in ascendance, grassroots organizers, youth workers, educators, librarians, clergy and civic activists as well as theater artists have much to learn from this remarkable enterprise – "preparing the next generation for full citizenship in a democratic society."

—**Lee Staples**,
Professor Emeritus, Boston University School of Social Work; author of Roots to Power: A Manual For Grassroots Organizing

"This book is an important documentation of Junior Program's pioneering programs. It chronicles a highly successful strategy with strong relevance to issues facing the field of TYA today. With its multifaceted approach, Junior Programs was extremely successful at addressing issues such as autocracy, racism, and xenophobia. And it is well documented that exposure to the arts, especially to quality theatre, has the ability to influence the perceptions, attitudes, and even behaviors of its youthful audience."

—**Moses Goldberg**,
Retired Artistic Director, Stage One: The Louisville Children's Theatre.

"Given today's politics, and the danger we face of losing our democracy, the messages in *Doodle Dandy of the U.S.A.* are as relevant today as they were in 1942. We have the divide and conquer strategies of the bullies, the enablers letting "black clouds gather" to threaten our freedom, and collective citizen action as a countervailing force. It's all our current day saga. It's a prescient piece of theater, a call to vigilance, and a warning of the cost of doing nothing. Kudos to Junior Programs."

—**Benny Sato Ambush**,
Artistic Director, Venice Theatre, Fla.

"Joan Lancourt's fascinating history of Junior Programs, Inc. is the forgotten story of a highly successful professional touring theatre company that formed innovative partnerships with schools and communities across the nation, using theater, opera and ballet as a catalyst to introduce children to the excitement of cultural, racial and ethnic diversity, and to deepen the entire K-12 educational curriculum. Lancourt's tale is more than history: it is an inspiring vision of the power of theatre to fan the flames of democracy for the next generation. If only all today's school activities had such rich and diverse outcomes."

—**Jeffrey Benson**,
K-12 teacher, administrator and author of "10 Steps for Managing Change in Schools: How do we take initiatives from goals to actions?" and "Improve Every Lesson Plan with SEL."

"*More Than Entertainment: Democracy and the Performing Arts* recovers for us seemingly forgotten wisdom. Children are born to learn through engagement with the world, and to be members of communities. Junior Programs reminds us that our survival as free people depends on adults taking special care to shape opportunities for children to learn to be citizens of democratic communities. As a public-school classroom teacher, assistant principal and principal for 28 years, I've seen American education get caught in the trap of dismissing the performing arts in pursuit of test scores. Tests don't help children make sense of the world they live in, school partnerships with the performing arts do."

—**Joshua Frank,**
Educator, administrator, and President of Equity Intersection,
an educational nonprofit

More Than Entertainment:
Democracy and the Performing Arts

JUNIOR PROGRAMS, Inc.
(1936-1943)
Pioneers of Theater for Young Audiences

Joan Lancourt

MEDIA.COM

More Than Entertainment:
Democracy and the Performing Arts

JUNIOR PROGRAMS, Inc. (1936-1943)
Pioneers of Theater for Young Audiences

Copyright © 2025 by Joan Lancourt

All rights reserved.
No part of this book may be reproduced in any form
or by any means—whether electronic, digital, mechanical, or otherwise—
without permission in writing from the publisher, except by a reviewer,
who may quote brief passages in a review.

The views and opinions expressed in this book
are those of the author and do not necessarily reflect the official policy or
position of Illumify Media Global.

Published by
Illumify Media Global
www.IllumifyMedia.com
"Let's bring your book to life!"

Paperback ISBN: 978-1-964251-08-0
Library of Congress Control Number: 2024915164

Typeset by Art Innovations (http://artinnovations.in/)
Cover by Debbie Lewis

Printed in the United States of America

To My Father
whose love, creative and artistic spirit,
commitment to social justice, equity and fairness
infused not only his life and work,
but mine as well.

*Empathy and respect for others
are at the heart of both democracy and the performing arts.*

CONTENTS

List of Illustrations xv
Acknowledgments xviii
Preface xix

I. SETTING THE STAGE 1
    The Context of Their Times 8
    Rethinking Childhood and Education 9
    The Evolution of the Theater for Young Audiences 10
    The Larger Theater Landscape 12
    The Federal Theatre Project 15

II. MORE THAN ENTERTAINMENT 20
    The Founding of Junior Programs, Inc. 20
    The Junior Programs Leadership Team 24
        Dorothy L. McFadden 24
        Saul Lancourt 27
    The Junior Programs Credo 30
    Junior Programs and Democracy 33
    Junior Programs and The Other 37
    A More Vibrant Form of Education 41
    The Secret Sauce: Community Engagement and
    Organizational Infrastructure 43
    The Junior Programs, Inc. Companies 46
    Junior Programs' Overarching Commitments 48

III. THE PRODUCTIONS:
PART I—THE JUNIOR PROGRAMS PLAYERS 53
    Personal Factors 54
    The Racial Justice Challenges of the Time 55

The Plays 66
  The Reward of the Sun God 66
  Run, Peddler, Run 76
  The Emperor's Treasure Chest 85
  The Adventures of Marco Polo 94
  Doodle Dandy of the U.S.A. 118

IV. THE PRODUCTIONS:
PART II—THE JUNIOR PROGRAMS OPERA &
JUNIOR PROGRAMS BALLET COMPANIES 139

The Junior Programs Opera Company 139
  Hansel and Gretel 145
  The Bumble Bee Prince 152
  Jack and the Beanstalk 162
The Junior Programs Ballet Company 174
  Pinocchio 178
  The Princess and the Swineherd 184
  The Adventures of Puck 186
  Robin Hood 191

V. THE EDUCATIONAL INNOVATIONS 203

The Junior Programs Approach to Education 203
  Educational Partnerships 206
  Parental Education 210
An Overview of the Correlated Curriculum
Study Units (CCSUs) 211
  The Junior Programs Players Correlated Curriculum
  Study Units (CCSUs) 217
    The Reward of the Sun God 218
    Run, Peddler, Run 221
    The Emperor's Treasure Chest 223
    The Adventures of Marco Polo 235
    Doodle Dandy of the U.S.A. 240

The Junior Programs Opera Correlated Curriculum
Study Units (CCSUs) 248
    Hansel and Gretel 248
    The Bumble Bee Prince 249
The Junior Programs Ballet Correlated Curriculum
Study Units (CCSUs) 251
    The Adventures of Puck 251
    Robin Hood 253
Junior Programs' Synthesis of Education and the Performing Arts 257

VI. THE ORGANIZATIONAL INNOVATIONS 260

Local Sponsoring Committees 261
The Junior Programs Local Sponsoring Committees' Organization
and Promotion Booklet 268
The Production Process 286
    Step 1: Finding Appropriate Material 286
    Step 2, 3, and 4: Production 288
    Step 5: Rehearsals 289
    Step 6: Previews 291
    Step 7: Bookings 291
    Step 8: Field Secretaries 292
    Step 9: Touring 294
    Step 10 and 11: Educational Materials 294
On the Road with Junior Programs 296
Finances and Fundraising 303

VII. THE JUNIOR PROGRAMS LEGACY 309

The Post–World War II Years 309
A Legacy of Learning 312
    The Primacy of Audience Development 312
    Reframing the Performing Arts – An Expanded Role for
    Children's Theaters in a Democracy 315
    The Power of Partnerships I – The Role of the Performing Arts
    in Education 318

The Power of Partnerships II – The Role of the Performing Arts in the Community 322
Reframing the Role of the Performing Arts in Addressing Racism 327
Junior Programs' Artistic Innovations 332
    Making Opera and Dance Accessible..333
    The Synthesis of Story, Dance, and Song...335
    The Commitment to Authenticity..336
    Sets to Fit Every Performance Space 337
The Legacy of Leadership 338

VIII. APPENDIX I: PARTIAL RECONSTRUCTION OF JUNIOR PROGRAMS TOURING SCHEDULE 341

IX. BIBLIOGRAPHY 350

Primary Sources... 350
Additional Sources 350

Endnotes... 361
About the Author 394
Index.. 396

LIST OF ILLUSTRATIONS

1. Junior Programs Players Announcement Flyer for *Reward of the Sun God* (Lancourt's personal papers) 66
2. Junior Programs Players Announcement Flyer for *Run, Peddler, Run* (Lancourt's personal papers) 77
3. The Junior Programs Mascot: Joop the Giraffe Teaches Children Good Audience Behavior (Lancourt's personal papers) *93*
4. Junior Programs *The Adventures of Marco Polo*—Act I, Venice. Set Design by Kenneth MacClelland (Author's personal collection) 100
5. Junior Programs *The Adventures of Marco Polo*—Act I and Prologue to Act II, The Great Map of the Polo's Journey to Cathay. Set Design by Kenneth MacClelland (Lancourt's personal papers) 107
6. Junior Programs *The Adventures of Marco Polo*—Act II, The Throne Room of Kublai Khan, Set Design by Kenneth MacClelland (Author's personal collection) 111
7. Junior Programs *The Adventures of Marco Polo*— Costume Design for Act II (Author's personal collection) 114
8. Junior Programs *The Adventures of Marco Polo*— Costume Design for Act II (Author's personal collection) 115
9. Junior Programs *Doodle Dandy of the U.S.A.*—USO Hunter College Program Flyer (Lancourt's personal papers) 119
10. Junior Programs *Doodle Dandy of the U.S.A.*—The "Seeograph," Act I, Scene 1 Thomas Jefferson (Alfred Allegro), Doodle Dandy (Sam Steen), Humphrey Dumphrey (Leon Kahn), and Benjamin Franklin (Blake Ritter). (*Doodle Dandy of the U.S.A.*, 12) 122
11. Junior Programs *Doodle Dandy of the U.S.A.*—Doodle Dandy (Sam Steen) and his Lucky Star (Barbara Gaye). (*Doodle Dandy of the U.S.A.*, 23) 125
12. Junior Programs *Doodle Dandy of the U.S.A.*—Doodle Dandy (Sam Steen) at the High School Play (*Doodle Dandy of the U.S.A.*, 89) 129

13. Junior Programs Opera *Hansel and Gretel*—
Gingerbread House and Witch's Oven, Hansel (Marion Selee)
and Gretel (Cecile Sherman) (Lancourt's personal papers)............................. 145
14. Junior Programs Announcement Flyer for *Pinocchio* and
Hansel and Gretel (Lancourt's personal papers). 149
15. Junior Programs Opera—Book Cover for *The Bumble Bee Prince,* Illustration
by Sheilah Beckett (Saul Lancourt, Garden City Publishing Co., Inc.,
New York, 1940. Author's personal collection)... 152
16. Junior Programs Opera *Jack and the Beanstalk*—Jack (Alma Milstead)
and his Cow (Tom Williams and Ford Ogden)
on the Way to Market (JP Scrapbooks) 165
17. Junior Programs Opera *Jack and the Beanstalk*—The Road to the
Giant's Castle, Jack (Alma Milstead), the Princess (Cecile Sherman),
and the Giant (Howard Laramy) (Lancourt's personal papers)...................... 166
18. Junior Programs Ballet Announcement Flyer for *Pinocchio*
(Lancourt's personal papers) 178
19. Junior Programs Ballet *Robin Hood*—Robin (Edwin Strawbridge)
and His Merry Band of Archers (JP Scrapbooks)... 194
20. Junior Programs Ballet *Robin Hood*—Robin (Edwin Strawbridge) at
the Queen's Court Tournament (Lancourt's personal papers) 200
21. Junior Programs Coloring Contest for *The Bumble Bee Prince,*
Illustration by Carroll B. Colby (Lancourt's personal papers) 276
22. Junior Programs Coloring Contest for *Robin Hood,* Illustration by
Sheilah Beckett (Lancourt's personal papers) 278

ACKNOWLEDGEMENTS

Writing a book is both an intellectual and an emotional endeavor. It involves long stretches of solitude, of sorting and connecting, hearing the words in your head, pouring them onto the page, changing, cuttting, clarifying, revising, and polishing. But ultimately, success is knowing that what you have written—your message or purpose—has been heard and understood by those who read what you have written. Achieving that kind of success requires feedback, a foil against which to test your thinking, another perspective to challenge you, to push you to go deeper or wider, to lighten up, to warn you about a stone wall up ahead. Of course, it's wonderful to hear the "Wow, this is really good!" But often, it's the interrogations, the thoughtful questions, and the suggestions (even the ones you don't take) that are most helpful in being able to clearly communicate the story you are trying to tell. I'm grateful to have had both kinds of feedback, encouragement and support—from family, friends, and colleagues old and new.

First and foremost, I am so deeply grateful to my brother, Dr. Jerold Lancourt for his unwavering support, and his thoughtful and multiple readings of the manuscript. His praise *and* his challenges helped me think more deeply about what I wanted to say. I'm also grateful for his help with internet searches, and for his photographic expertise in preparing the pictures that appear in the book. I also want to thank several friends and colleagues. Benny Sato Ambush, Artistic Director of the Venice Theater in Venice, Florida, was an early supporter, and his continued encouragement, his historical perspective on Black theater, and his help in connecting me with others in the TYA field was invaluable. Noe Montez, Associate Professor of Theatre Studies, Emory University, provided substantive guidance, offering sage advice to "widen the scope" of my research beyond that of a simple case study, and suggesting additional academic resources. Bill Marx, editor of *the arts fuse*, an independent, curated, on-line journal of arts criticism, not only provided encouragement, but the opportunity to publish an early article based on the book, an invaluable exercise in focusing my thinking. Finally, my gratitude goes to Lee Staples, Professor Emeritus, Boston University School of Social Work, a long-time friend, and community organizing colleague. His close reading of the manuscript and unparalleled expertise in all things "community" helped validate several of Junior Programs' unique achievements.

There were also two wonderful mentors whom I have only met on Zoom. Jonathan Shmidt Chapman, former Executive Director of TYA-USA helped fill me in on the current challenges facing the field of children's theater and made it clear that the story of Junior Programs was important and would fill a significant gap in the history of TYA. In Moses Goldberg, former Artistic Director of Stage One: The Louisville Children's Theatre, I felt like I had found a kindred spirit. His books were infused with the same ethos and animating principles that had infused Junior Programs, and I am so grateful for the gift of his time and insights shared during multiple zooms. He was an invaluable sounding board for questions about TYA trends, themes, and directions, and, after reading the manuscript and various chapter revisions, his continued encouragement helped keep me focused on the finish line.

And special thanks go to my editor, Shelby Brewster, whose broad knowledge of the performing arts, editorial skills, probing questions, and feminist reader's eye helped fill in omissions and smooth the rough edges of the manuscript; and to Illumify Media, who made the publishing process as painless as possible.

PREFACE

I grew up in a theater-centric family. After a short post World War II stint managing for Mike Todd, my father, Saul Lancourt, took over the Joe Leblang theater interests for the next two plus decades, first managing Broadway's 48th Street Theater, and then Leblang's, one of the three major theater ticket brokers in New York City. Our lives were scheduled around what was happening on Broadway. Mealtimes, even vacations, were dictated by the success or failure of plays on and off the Great White Way.

However, whenever my father spoke of his life's achievements, Junior Programs, Inc., the children's theater company he helped establish in 1936 with Dorothy McFadden, took center stage. Together, they were determined to use the performing arts to educate the children of the United States, an education filled with teaching cultural values, social equality, and, in the run-up to WWII, the importance of protecting our democracy and freedom. As artistic and production director of Junior Programs that was his great hope—to tap the entertainment inherent in the performing arts to educate the next generation. The play, *Doodle Dandy of the U.S.A.*, which he wrote and directed, was specifically created to teach children about democracy, and about the important role every member of the young audience would need to play if democracy was to survive and flourish. *Doodle,* as he would refer to it, was his answer to fascism, and to his hope that the performing arts would play a significant role in bringing us all closer to achieving the American dream. *Doodle* opened at Broadway's Belasco Theatre in December 1942, and then went on tour, reaching children in cities and towns the length and breadth of the country. The play was dedicated to me before I was born: "To Joan Ellen, who was on the way, and of whom I was thinking when I wrote: *Freedom's a child straight and strong, Playin' in the sun the whole day long."* (*Doodle Dandy of the U.S.A.*, Saul Lancourt, Musette Publishers, New York, 1943, un-numbered page). One of my earliest memories is of looking at a photograph of me, at about the age of three, holding the published book of the play with its picture of Doodle Dandy prancing across the red, white, and blue cover.

Doodle was the culmination of Junior Programs' astonishing seven-year record of successfully introducing live theater, opera, and dance to four million children in every part of the nation. Nevertheless, despite their almost unqualified success—artistically, socially, educationally, and organizationally—in 1943, the company was forced to close. For so many individuals and institutions, including Junior Programs, when the United States entered WWII, things were forever changed.

The reasons for Junior Programs' closure were threefold. First, many of its professional actors, singers, and dancers were being drafted. Second, as a touring company, the ability to obtain gas and tires—for scenery trucks, for the transportation of the actors and for the buses required in each city or town to transport local children to performances—was severely hampered by the rationing of rubber and then gas. And finally, as local sponsoring organizations shifted their focus to the urgency of direct "war work," maintaining a steady stream of bookings and fund raising became unsustainable. Like so many things that war disrupts, the individuals involved were forced to move on to other endeavors, and the story of Junior Programs' stellar achievements faded from view.

My father continued to talk about *Doodle* from time to time, but he, too, had moved on to other business aspects of the theater. Many years after his death in March 2002, in a spree of organizing papers and files, I sat down one day and started reading through several albums of news clippings, photos, and company papers he had kept as mementos. I had browsed through them before, mostly looking at the pictures. This time, as I actually read the reviews, I was captivated by the vision, the creativity, and the success of the whole Junior Programs enterprise. It seemed to dance across the by now yellowed, half-crumbling pages of newsprint in much the same way that Doodle himself had leaped and flitted across so many stages. Searching the internet for more information, I found only one history of children's theater that briefly referred to Junior Programs as the "crowning achievement" in children's theater of that time. (*Historical Guide to Children's Theatre in America,* Nellie McCaslin, Greenwood Press, New York, 1987, p. 25). This further piqued my curiosity. Why had nothing more been written about their extraordinary accomplishments? And given their repeated successes, why hadn't Junior Programs been revived after the war? But I had waited too long! There was no one still alive who could answer those questions. I had other questions, too: about specific productions, about the *zeitgeist* of the times, and about how Junior Programs had mobilized the resources to enable three separate companies—opera, drama, and ballet—to undertake extended nationwide tours for seven years. I also wanted to know what they had learned about the performing arts as a vehicle for educating children, and, most of all, about what had made them so successful.

With these questions swirling in my head, I recalled my father mentioning that when Junior Programs closed, they had donated all their files—boxes of news clippings, photos, production and educational materials, and organizational records—to the drama department of the New York Public Library, now the Billy Rose Theatre Division at Lincoln Center. It had been almost eighty years. Were those files and papers, the story of their innovations and all they had learned, still there—like Sleeping Beauty, hidden away? I wrote to enquire, and to my joyful relief, the library responded rather quickly. Indeed, they had the Junior Programs, Inc. Scrapbooks—thirteen boxes of them. It seemed almost a miracle!

I arranged to go to New York, arriving at the library with my computer and my curiosity. Holding my breath, as I opened that first box, a frisson went through me that I will never forget. It was as if, instead of being given to the library, the boxes had been given to the one-year-old me for safe-keeping. My brush with "time travel" was about to begin. Arriving each morning when the library opened, I poured through the boxes, running across Broadway for a quick lunchtime sandwich, and then returning until the library closed each evening.

From first to last, the content of the boxes detailed the overwhelmingly positive response of children across the country—to what they saw on stage, and to the astonishingly detailed correlated educational units that accompanied most of the productions. When children enjoy an activity, they want more of it; and when that activity is fun, they remember it. The Scrapbooks are a testament to the fact that the young audiences wanted more, and that Junior Programs, year after year, fulfilled their desires. It also became clear that during their seven years of touring, Junior Programs had learned a thing or two about how to engage a youthful audience. This included how best to communicate with children on issues of serious import—issues like democracy, diversity, and the need for inclusion. It also was clear that the staff, artists, and leaders of Junior Programs were true pioneers, working to forge a new theatrical and educational genre, a robust, fully professional adult performing arts company focused specifically on addressing the needs of young audiences. In the spirit of true pioneers, they brought that new genre to hundreds of communities across the country, many of which had never had the opportunity to attend live theater, opera, and dance. Junior Programs' pioneering work also identified many of the core issues facing the fledgling genre—issues of access, community engagement, artistic innovation, and social, economic, and racial equity—issues that still present major challenges to today's TYA companies and practitioners.

After immersing myself in their work and searching for additional information to fill in the inevitable gaps in the records, it became increasingly obvious that this pioneering company had much to tell us. This book is a record of what I learned about their work; and the lessons they learned still resonate today—if we are willing to listen.

I. SETTING THE STAGE

Both the nation and the performing arts are in a state of crisis. On the metaphorical national stage, American democracy is experiencing a crisis of sustainability, with the country struggling to retain its democratic structures in the face of forces determined to destroy them. On the actual regional and local stages, the performing arts are also encountering sustainability challenges, in part due to the post-COVID reluctance of the aging, primarily white adult audience to return to the theaters in sufficient numbers. Numerous reasons for both crises exist, but thus far, efforts to address either have been inadequate.

Enter from the wings, stage left, *Wei Ji,* an imposing Chinese character who represents "Crisis." In each hand, he carries a magnifying glass. Through one, we see the dangers he brings with him; but through the other, we can see the opportunities, shadowy though they at first may be. *Wei Ji* is one of the many symbols of Tao wisdom in which everything has two sides, in this case, wherever there is danger, there is also opportunity—if we choose to look for it.[1] *Reframing* the crisis in this way, shifts the problem-solving energy. Instead of an energy-draining struggle to tinker around the edges of a dysfunctional system, the search for possible opportunities can unleash a powerful and innovative collaborative synergy. This approach has the potential for transformative adaptations—the kind needed to *create* the desired future rather than simply react to a deteriorating present.

By viewing the crisis of a diminishing audience through *Wei Ji*'s magnifying glass of opportunity, we see that for decades, insufficient attention has been paid to the *intentional* development of a broader, younger, more diverse audience base. True, the field of theater for young audiences (TYA)—the subset of the performing arts focused on the development of the next generation of theater goers—has been doing yeoman's work. Nevertheless, the current predicament suggests there is an opportunity for TYA to play a far more central role in the overall ecology of the performing arts.

Long the stepchild of the larger theater world, if regional theaters are to ensure a sufficient and steady flow of future audiences, we need a more intentional, robust partnership between adult regional and local theaters and TYA theaters. Theaters for young audiences are an essential part of the foundation on which we can build a more lasting solution to this key facet of the current audience problem. Clearly, there is opportunity here!

But what possible relationship is there between the performing arts and the currently precarious state of American democracy? Again, *Wei Ji*'s lens for magnifying opportunity reveals a hidden-in-plain sight connection. Peering more closely through the opportunity lens, we see an auspicious bit of serendipity—the rediscovery of Junior Programs, Inc. (1936–43), one of the most successful early pioneers of adult professional theater for children. According to their *Credo,* Junior Programs' raison d'être as a national touring company was to *use the performing arts not simply to develop the audiences of tomorrow, but to prepare that next generation for the role it would inevitably need to play in the preservation and sustainability of the nation's democracy.* This book is the story of how their work embodied that mission—to bring us closer to America's ideals and aspirations.

In addition to making the connection between the crisis in audience development and that occurring in the nation's democracy, Junior Programs is also an example of two additional opportunities. The first is of a company whose *modus operandi* was to continually *reframe* as opportunities the many challenges they faced. Becoming a true democracy is, after all, an unfinished experiment. The second is that their story offers today's performing artists a legacy of core principles and guidelines for success.

While there are clearly many differences between then and now, there are also numerous similarities. Then, as now, on the national stage, democracy in the United States faced a series of external and internal threats. The Depression had left indelible scars, and the rapidly growing fear of communism and fascism were looming ominously on the horizon. Successive waves of immigration to our shores had brought men, women, and children whose cultures, religions, and skin colors differed from those of our founding fathers, further complicating the detrimental legacy of the US brand of Black enslavement. There was also a shift taking place in the nation's view of the importance of childhood as a protected and developmentally important period, and the performing arts had already been drafted as a means of helping wave after wave of immigrant children learn English and ease the process of assimilation. Finally, with the exception of the occasional productions of *Peter Pan*, *The Wizard of Oz,* or a holiday extravaganza, the economic concerns of commercial theaters were, then and now, focused primarily on the entertainment tastes of a largely white, upper-middle-class, and elite adult audience.

Today, on the national stage, we are faced with the trifecta of climate change, repeated challenges to our democracy, and racism, coupled with our efforts to negotiate the rocky, uncharted, post-pandemic paths to a "new normal." Democracy, as we are painfully discovering anew, can never be taken for granted. Tune in to any news program or online social media forum and you will find ample and frightening evidence of its fragility. On January 6, 2022, the one-year anniversary of the assault on the US Capitol in Washington, DC, President Joe Biden told the people of the United States that democracy was in serious jeopardy.[2] We are learning that our democracy is not magically self-sustaining: it requires constant nourishment and nurturing if we are to keep the ever-present forces of fascism and chaos at bay. In the iconic words of Arthur Miller, "attention must be paid."[3] For too many foundational issues in our current society—and for too long—our attention has been elsewhere: on the pursuit of individual success, on immediate gratification, on the false gods of neoliberal meritocracy, on a profligate destruction of natural resources, and on technology as the prime remedy for our lack of stewardship of life on this planet Earth. The result has been an increase in the degrees of inequality and inequity, both social, economic, and political, which have polarized the nation more than at any time since the Civil War. That in some measure, this is a consequence of the persistent and too-often intentional failure to address the underlying issues of enslavement and racism, their concomitant economic inequities, and our penchant for *othering* those whose skin color or ethnic origins are unlike those of the original white European colonists, is an irony not easy to dismiss.

If we are to have any real hope of preserving our democratic form of government, we must confront and address these issues. If we are to be successful, we must renew and increase our commitment to the youth of the nation—*all of them*—by preparing every one of them to be lifelong learners, able to defend their democracy in all its complexity, making it, in practice, a democracy inclusive of *all*. In a speech on November 2, 2022, President Biden again reiterated, "Nothing is guaranteed about democracy in America. Every generation must defend it, protect it, preserve it, choose it . . . It's a choice, a decision of the people."[4]

It is in this context that the rediscovery of the Junior Programs story can help remind us that when it comes to sustaining a democratic nation, the children are the future. The myriad tasks and acts of constant vigilance will fall to them. If they are not fully prepared and ready, if they fail, then we will lose the soul of our nation. However, if they are to succeed, we must be far more intentional than we have been in providing them with the empathy, knowledge, skills and understanding of what it takes to sustain a democracy in a nation of great diversity. We must use every means at our disposal to instill a broad constellation of democratic values in their minds and hearts—values of diversity, empathy, inclusion, compromise, listening, equity, equality, and civic engagement. Like the air they breathe, democracy must become something without which they cannot live. From its earliest days, Junior Programs embodied this essential focus, and they understood that, if they were to succeed, the performing arts would need to become "more than entertainment."

Inculcating inclusive democratic values in the youth of a nation as diverse as ours is no easy task. Our youth are an eclectic lot, consisting of numerous races, classes, ethnicities, genders, sexual preferences, abilities, and learning styles. The results of a 2014 World Values survey about democracy offer cause for concern. When US respondents born after 1980 were asked how essential it was to live in a democratically governed country, only 30% rated it at the upper end of a 1-10 scale.[5] Given the current environment, it seems likely that success in protecting and sustaining our democracy is going to require more than the traditional pedagogy of textbooks, courses and lectures, homework assignments, debates, and field trips to our nation's capital. Success requires that we leave no stone unturned, that all those responsible for preparing the next generations for these responsibilities become more creative, innovative, adaptive, and flexible than ever before. The Junior Programs story is especially relevant now because they left few stones unturned. They broke the old molds that were steeped in "the way we've always done things." Their model embodied a set of core values, chief among them the belief in and a commitment to a broadly inclusive democracy that reflected the richness of the nation's diversity, and they also remind us that the performing arts can and should be a major player in achieving that goal.

Three additional factors contributed to their steady stream of successes, each of which offer lessons for current consideration. First, was the *genuine respect they felt for their young audiences*. "No connoisseur is better able to evaluate good theatre and criticize the false and shoddy than the child . . . a youthful audience [is] the hardest to please and the quickest to show their disapproval of anything second-rate . . . Children are really the most discriminating of all audiences, because they are the original actors . . . They are forever play-acting themselves, playing house, cowboys and Indians, in fact, anything that momentarily stimulates the imagination" (Floral Park, NY, *Gateway,* Jan 26, 1939).

Second, was their development of *significant partnerships with leading educators of the day, and with the local school systems* in the cities and towns in which they performed. Then, as now, the involvement of professional performing arts organizations with mainstream educational systems—if they focused on educational systems at all—primarily emphasized educating children in the various aspects of the performing arts: drama, music, dance, acting, playwriting, or costume and set design. Junior Programs, however, appears to have been unique in their commitment to using the performing arts not only to educate children about the arts, but also as a catalyst to supplement the entire standard K-12 educational curricula. This was accomplished by creating a suite of *correlated curriculum study units* (CCSUs) for most of their productions. These units were designed to augment and enrich a broader range of classes—from history, political science, social studies, geography, science and literature to physical education, shop, home economics, and everything in between. Thus, their *educational partnerships* provided local frontline K-12 teachers in multiple disciplines with a suite of age-appropriate pedagogical units. Designed by leading educators, the units enhanced the traditional curricula by connecting each subject-matter department to the specific focus of a Junior Programs' production. Junior Programs saw no conflict between theater as an art form and theater as an educational undertaking. They pursued both outcomes in tandem, and by all accounts, succeeded in creating a model that seamlessly integrated the two.

The third factor contributing to their success, again with implications for today, was the importance they placed on developing *vibrant partnerships with the local communities in which they performed*. Through these partnerships, they created a nationwide network of local sponsoring organizations and individuals, many of whom volunteered their time, skills, and energies, thereby providing local administrative, marketing, sales, and logistical support for each Junior Programs production. This enabled them to sustain a nationwide touring schedule with a relatively small New York–based staff. These robust and substantive partnerships with a broad network of active and engaged community sponsors ensured that Junior Programs was in continuing conversation with a diverse array of communities across the country. Indeed, the fact that there were seldom empty seats for their performances suggests that the productions they offered were well tuned to communities' needs.

Their model was also based on a belief that the performing arts themselves would be immeasurably enriched by the creativity of the diverse cultures inherent in a nation of immigrants. They also believed the arts were not only an essential element in the daily life of a civilized society but that it had a unique ability to contribute to the education of the next generation in its broadest, deepest sense. These values and beliefs informed the way Junior Programs did their work. For seven successful years, their three companies—the Junior Programs Opera, the Junior Programs Players, and the Junior Programs Ballet—set out on extensive nationwide tours, performing in cities and towns in every part of the country, ultimately offering twelve fully mounted professional productions of the highest quality to audiences of four million children. Their numerous successes were brought to an untimely end when the WWII draft robbed them of their performers, and the rationing of gas and rubber tires made continued touring impossible.

One of the values of knowing our historical roots is that it puts present struggles into a larger context. In a sense, knowing we stand on the shoulders of those who came before—and *learning from their successes and failures*—and knowing others will stand on our shoulders in the future engenders a sense of continuity and connection that invests our current struggles with a deeper meaning and purpose. The current issues of accessibility, equity, diversity, inclusivity, respect for young people, community engagement, artistic and pedagogical excellence, innovation, and inspiration, as well as the larger issues of sustaining democracy and developing the next generations of theater audiences, are all a continuation of the path pioneered by Junior Programs. So, too, are the ways in which they reached deep into the smaller cities and towns of America, where they planted some of the early seeds for today's network of regional children's theaters.[6]

Similarly, their artistic innovations, their many forms of engagement with local communities, and their optimistic belief that the performing arts could be a powerful element in all aspects of a child's education, especially in the arena of social justice, are still key criteria for success. And above all, the way their *Credo* linked the performing arts with a *sense of responsibility to the next generation as the future of democracy* offers today's performing arts practitioners and educators a sense of hope, as part of a larger mission, inspired by a set of principles to guide current and future efforts. Their understanding of the power of live performance to inspire and encourage children to develop an expansive empathy, and of the potential of the performing arts as a critical component for the flowering of democracy in a civil society rather than solely as entertainment, has never been more urgently needed. The rediscovery of their story provides a vivid example of an early effort to address these issues and forge a deeper connection between the performing arts, youthful development, and the needs of the larger society. That its efforts were successful in contributing to the foundation of a new theatrical field—a nationwide theater for young audiences—offers inspiration and encouragement.

Junior Programs identified and opened a door to a set of artistic, social, political, and educational ventures at a time when most performing artists were unaware such a door even existed. Junior Programs also knew the performing arts had something unique to offer in terms of addressing important social concerns, and that it could and should be a player in helping to reshape our society. The story of their boldness, their multi-faceted creativity, their inclusiveness, and their flexibility and willingness to experiment deserves our respect and attention. So too, their inventiveness and refusal to be constrained by the past or by the status quo. But above all, it was their on-going ability to *reframe*—to see problems as opportunities—that deserves further study. And their success strongly suggests that we put what they learned to good use as we continue to develop and explore what TYA has to offer—to children, to their educational process, to adult theater, to communities, and to the nation.

With the record of their achievements newly brought to light, it is now possible to fill in a major gap in TYA's origin story, and to examine the ways in which Junior Programs addressed a set of issues and threats that were similar to the ones we face today. However, to appreciate their achievements, an overview of the context in which they operated is useful. The sections which follow provide brief summaries of the political zeitgeist of their time, the growing shift in thinking related to our understanding of childhood and its developmental needs, the shape and state of the adult commercial theater of the time, the early beginning of a theater for young audiences, and the influential but short-lived existence of a concurrent experiment, the Federal Theatre Project.

The Context of Their Times

In *Alice in Wonderland*, Lewis Carroll—a master teller of stories for children—has the King direct the White Rabbit to "Begin at the beginning . . . and go on till you come to the end: then stop."[7] If we follow Carroll's advice and look for the beginning of the Junior Programs story, we find ourselves in the 1920s and '30s, in the immediate aftermath of the Great Depression—a time of economic, political, and social upheaval and strife, in some ways not too dissimilar to current circumstances. Like today, the thirties were also a time of deep divisions in the US body politic over the legitimate roles of government and labor in a capitalist society. There was a growing anti-communism fanning the flames of fear pitted against the waves of immigrant labor struggling to free themselves from industrial exploitation so they, too, could taste the fruits of democracy and experience a measure of economic security—in other words, live "the American Dream." And, as always, there was the racism that has haunted that dream since the beginning.

The Depression, and these roiling national conflicts, led to the growth of the labor movement and a spate of government programs, many of which have become so much a part of the fabric of our personal and national lives most of us cannot imagine life without them: Social Security, the Federal Home Loan Program, the GI Bill, the National Labor Relations Act, and many more. Despite the inherent racism at the heart of some of these programs,[8] it was initiatives such as these that provided the scaffolding and the safety net which, at the time, very possibly saved the American democratic experiment from failure.

Junior Programs' recognition that the performing arts offered a creative medium for imbuing young people with the ideals and spirit of democracy surfaced in the crucible of the 1930s. It was catalyzed by a fusion of several streams of emerging thought and experience: first, a fundamental shift in society's view of children; second, a deeply expanded understanding of the nature of human development and the related educational processes; and third, the use of the performing arts as a powerful medium in the educational and developmental processes of childhood socialization.

Rethinking Childhood and Education

In a reaction to the excesses of the Industrial Revolution, we find a growing shift from a view of the child as an economic producer (i.e., child labor) to the concept of "childhood" as a protected period of human growth, education, and development.[9] The Victorian, upper-middle-class concept of childhood innocence was slowly extended to working-class children. With that extension, there grew a sense of civic responsibility that sought to shield children from too early an entry into the industrial workforce. This shift in perspective was both dramatic and nuanced, captured first in an 1893 speech by Samuel Gompers, president of the American Federation of Labor. In it, he argued for the imperative of saving our children from being forced into wage slavery "in their infancy." "Give them the sunshine of the school and playground instead of the factory . . . [and] more of the opportunities to cultivate our better natures."[10] From statements such as this, Gompers clearly believed social and economic change needed to begin with children, and that "the child figures as the developing American to whom democratic educational opportunities must be offered."[11]

These insights were further developed in John Spargo's warning in *The Bitter Cry of the Children* (1906). Spargo, an early leader in the Socialist Party of America, spoke of the "peril to a young and growing nation embodied in the stunted forms of its laboring children."[12] It was not only the children, but "even more important . . . is the thought that civilization itself is imperiled when children are dwarfed physically, mentally, and morally by hunger, heavy toil, and unwholesome surroundings."[13] In 1908, Indiana senator Albert Beveridge, in his introduction to *The Cry of the Children* by Bessie Van Vorsts, wrote "When our people know that more than a million American children are dying of overwork or being forever stunted and dwarfed in body, mind and soul; when they know that we are pouring into the body of our citizenship two hundred and fifty thousand degenerates (at the very lowest estimate) every year who have clouded minds and a burning hatred of the society that has wronged them, and that they have the ballot in their hands . . . we may hope for an end of this national disgrace."[14] This shift in how US society thought about its children and childhood led to a spate of child labor laws, and the National Child Labor Commission's mission incorporated the idea that applying a combination of "knowledge and science to social problems" would yield significant social benefits.[15]

This view was reinforced by other emerging trends fueled by the growing impact of the Freudian view of child development and the significant influence of John Dewey's pragmatic focus on the whole child. From Dewey's perspective, education was not simply a passing on of information, but a prime means of inculcating democratic values.[16] Dewey offered a critique of the Darwinian worldview by asserting the importance of considering social conditions and the values of everyday life in the context of education. His child-centered approach challenged the traditional curriculum-centered methods that viewed the child as an empty vessel and the educational process as one focused on the child's acquisition of what others already knew. Dewey's perspective connected child, school, and society, wherein school was a place for "compassionate imagination, creative expression, and civic self-governance," a place to learn and experiment with democracy, and to adapt successfully to an ever-changing world.[17] For Dewey, "the success or failure of democracy rests on education," an education that "open[s] the road and point[s] the way to new and better experiences."[18] To succeed in that role, school needed to become a micro-community, a place to develop habits of problem solving, and, as such, "it is incumbent upon society to make education its highest political and economic priority."[19]

These shifts in thinking about childhood and education, coupled with a growing awareness of the need to assist immigrant communities in adapting to life in America led to further creative thinking from a growing number of social welfare advocates working to improve conditions in immigrant neighborhoods across the country.

The Evolution of the Theater for Young Audiences

Not long after Gompers's recognition of the importance of allowing children the time needed to "cultivate their better natures," and remarkably congruent with Dewey's educational precepts, Jane Addams and Laura Dainty of Hull House, a Chicago settlement house, founded the Hull-House Players based on their belief that "good plays performed by amateurs could have a 'salutary influence on the community.'"[20] In 1903, social worker Alice Minnie Herts founded the Children's Educational Theatre in New York, the first theater designed specifically for children, "to make our thousands of immigrant children better citizens; to educate them; to develop their sympathies and their characters; to give them the best possible sort of good time, and to counteract the evil and sordid influences of tenement and factory."[21] Herts, in a subsequent book, documents the enormous emotional, developmental, and social benefits derived by children's active use of and involvement in all aspects of theatrical performance-making, up to and including its use in the prevention of delinquency and crime.[22]

From these earliest stirrings, the growth of TYA proceeded somewhat haphazardly. There were productions for children in many small, primarily amateur community theaters and recreation centers throughout the country. In this context, the many chapters of the Association of Junior Leagues of America were a major force in supporting theater for children. They viewed theater as meeting "a fundamental need of human beings. It allows them to enter worlds larger than their own, [and] *to encounter people different from themselves* [emphasis added]."[23] Additionally, there was "educational theater" in which the children were directly involved in what Winifred Ward, a Northwestern University professor and founder of the Children's Theatre of Evanston in 1925, called participant-centered "creative dramatics."[24] The King-Coit School of Acting and Design, founded in 1923 in New York City, was a similar endeavor.[25]

In the early 1920s, the New York City Association of Teachers of English enlisted Clare Tree Major, an English actress, to dramatize several literary works in the high school curriculum, such as *Little Women* and *Hans Brinker*. Major had formed one of the first adult professional companies focused on productions for children—the *Threshold Players*.[26] Also a touring company, she created what was likely the first partnership with public school teachers when she agreed to provide the Association of Teachers of English with additional materials coordinated with the state's high school English curriculum. However, unlike the broadly inclusive Junior Programs' CCSUs, Major's materials focused primarily on the literary aspects and merits of the English curriculum.[27] There were also a handful of geographically based professional children's theaters in the early 1930s, such as Adrienne Morrison's Children's Players in New York City[28]; the Atlanta Children's Theatre, whose focus was entertainment;[29] the Children's Civic Theatre of Chicago[30]; the East Bay Children's Theatre in Oakland, California[31]; the Heckscher Children's Theatre in New York[32];

the Old Globe Theatre in San Diego,[33] and the Goodman Theatre for Children in Chicago offering adaptations of familiar folk and fairy tales.[34] In the early 1930s, several universities also began to offer productions suitable for children as part of their drama department curricula, including Boston's Emerson College Children's Theatre, focused on presenting well-known classics, Mills College (California), and Syracuse University (New York).[35]

Thus, by the early 1930s, we can identify the "beginnings" to which Lewis Carroll alluded. From this earliest stage, the idea of using theater and other performing arts to catalyze and contribute its emotional, intellectual, and experiential power to engage children in their education was being explored in various ways. As I have written elsewhere, it is worth remembering that theater has been part of the democratic process since the sixth century BCE:

> The citizens of Athens regularly gathered in their amphitheaters and used drama as the collective means for interrogating and considering how well—or poorly—their democracy expressed their social, civic, and political values. Regrettably, since then, theater and democracy have traveled widely divergent paths, to the detriment of both. Still, the primal connection has not been forgotten. In a 2018 TED talk, Oskar Eustis of New York's Public Theater . . . [recalled] this intimate relationship when he argued that theater supplied the three basic tools of democratic citizenship: a stage for the collision of competing ideas; a format that creates community; and a form of storytelling that engenders empathy.[36]

Thus, we can see that the use of the dramatic form to explore and strengthen democracy has roots that reach deep into the foundation of Western civilization. In the chapters which follow, we will identify the several ways in which Junior Programs' approach to TYA connected theater to the practice of democracy by using the three basic tools Eustis mentions.

The Larger Theater Landscape

By the early years of the twentieth century, theater had become as much business as show. The first three decades saw the building of eighty theaters in New York City.

I. SETTING THE STAGE

Broadway may have been the beating heart of the American theatrical world, but for the rest of the country, going to the theater was dependent on a reliable stream of theatrical touring companies. These tours were controlled by a cadre of competing booking agents. During the closing years of the 1890s, booking agents Marc Klaw and Abraham Lincoln Erlanger controlled a string of theaters that crisscrossed the country. In 1896, the Klaw and Erlanger Exchange, initially a stabilizing force in the booking of shows available for touring, became the Theatrical Syndicate and, for a time, dominated the business end of show business. There were several organizations, however, that challenged their dominance, and by the 1920s, the powerful Shubert Brothers organization had won control of the industry.[37]

A bird's-eye view of the US commercial entertainment industry chronicles an inexorable shift from vaudeville as the primary form of theatrical entertainment to a steady flow of mostly unmemorable theatrical fare. This was punctuated by what we might now call "the classics": an adaptation of *The Wizard of Oz* in 1902; Maude Adams in *Peter Pan* in 1905; in 1907, Ziegfeld's first *Follies*. In 1910, Fanny Brice came on the scene; in 1916, Ziegfeld featured Will Rogers; and in 1917, Eddie Cantor. *Abie's Irish Rose* played 2,327 performances in 1922, and in 1933, *Tobacco Road* began its seven-year run.[38] By the 1920s, musical theater had emerged as a major American genre, written by the likes of Jerome Kern, Oscar Hammerstein II, Richard Rodgers and Lorenz Hart, George M. Cohan, Cole Porter, and George and Ira Gershwin. Standing on the shoulders of Franz Lehár's American debut of *The Merry Widow* (1907), Victor Herbert's *Naughty Marietta* (1910), and Sigmund Romberg's *The Student Prince* (1924), these composers created a new, distinctly American musical form. In 1927, the form, having always been a crowd-pleaser, launched Kern and Hammerstein's *Showboat,* a production that, despite its openly racist stereotypes, seamlessly integrated music, song, and dance for the first time in a way that opened the door to an endless stream of popular musical and dramatic entertainments.[39]

In the actors' circle, there were stars such as the Barrymores, Sarah Bernhardt, Fred and Adele Astaire, Paul Robeson, the Marx Brothers, Mae West, Alfred Lunt and Lynn Fontanne, Katharine Cornell, Helen Hayes, and Ethel Merman. Threaded through this array of popular entertainment fare was a group of playwrights—theatrical innovators who might be termed the "serious" theater people. Eugene

O'Neill was prolific, beginning in 1916 with *Bound East for Cardiff*, followed by *Beyond the Horizon, The Emperor Jones, Anna Christie, The Hairy Ape, All God's Chillun Got Wings, Desire Under the Elms, Strange Interlude, Mourning Becomes Electra*, and, in 1933, *Ah Wilderness!* There were plays by Maxwell Anderson, George S. Kaufman, Elmer Rice, Robert Sherwood, and a steady stream of George Bernard Shaw and Henrik Ibsen. In 1934, Lillian Hellman's *The Children's Hour* debuted, and 1935 saw Clifford Odets's *Waiting For Lefty*, followed by *Awake and Sing!* and *Paradise Lost*, and Langston Hughes's *Mulatto*, all of which addressed serious social and political issues of the time.[40]

During this period, in reaction to what they experienced as constraints in the commercial theater in terms of form, subject, and style, a dissatisfied group of theater artists broke away from Broadway. They formed several small group theaters—what came to be known as Off-Broadway and Off-Off-Broadway. In 1915, the Washington Square Players produced Ibsen, Shaw, and Chekhov; by 1919 they had morphed into the Theatre Guild. The Neighborhood Playhouse pioneered Off-Broadway fare, and *Folksbiene* (1915), the Yiddish Arts Theatre (1918), and the Jewish Arts Theatre (1919) attested to the vibrancy of an audience for a distinctly Jewish theater. The Actors' Theatre was founded in 1922; the Civic Repertory Theatre of Eva Le Gallienne and New Playwrights Theatre were formed in 1926; and in 1931, Harold Clurman's Group Theatre was founded. In 1923, the Moscow Arts Theatre arrived in New York and, with its director Konstantin Stanislavski, made an indelible and lasting impression on American theater's acting style and theatrical training.[41] There were also groups such as The Theatre Union, (1933 to 1937), a professional workers theatre in New York.[42] Nevertheless, the need to fill the seats in those eighty New York venues and the nationwide string of regional theaters every season with moneymaking productions became the driving force of the industry.

In addition, and impossible to ignore from a business standpoint, was the inexorable competition from the growing film industry. In 1905, the first motion-picture theater opened in Pennsylvania. In 1912, a series of mergers led to the creation of Universal Pictures, and Mack Sennett's Keystone Kops films gained popularity. By 1914, Paramount Pictures had been formed as a distributor of films for numerous independent production companies, and in 1915, D. W. Griffith's *Birth of a Nation* premiered. Hollywood became ground zero for American moviemaking. In 1914,

Sam Lucas, in *Uncle Tom's Cabin*, became the first Black actor to play a lead role. By 1921, Charlie Chaplin and Rudolf Valentino were stars. Rin Tin Tin made his Hollywood debut in 1922, and in 1924, Columbia Pictures and Metro Goldwyn Mayor were formed, followed by a steady stream of popular stars including Lon Chaney, Harold Lloyd, and Buster Keaton. In 1927, *The Jazz Singer* launched the "talkies," Greta Garbo and Clara Bow became national icons, and in 1928, Walt Disney gave the nation Mickey Mouse. In 1929, the stock market crashed, but the film industry introduced Technicolor. By the 1930s, Boris Karloff and Bela Lugosi began the "monster craze," followed by King Kong, Laurel and Hardy, and the Marx Brothers, all becoming familiar household names.[43] Radio also became another form of popular entertainment. In the 1920s, Westinghouse offered the first radio programming, a move designed to increase the sale of radios. By the mid-twenties, three hundred plus commercial stations had formed, and networks of local stations were created to share the cost of programming. Radio, too, became big business. The Radio Corporation of America (RCA) and the National Broadcasting Company (NBC) were formed, and entertainment programming offered *Amos 'n Andy*, *The Shadow*, and *Abbott and Costello*, along with FDR's popular *Fireside Chats*.[44]

Clearly, both society and the theater world were in a state of flux. The need to absorb a vast and diverse immigrant population, the growing pains of theater not only as an art form but as an industry, and the competition posed by the multiple new entertainment technologies of film and radio all created an increasing sense of social, political, and economic instability. It was onto this stage that the famous, and ultimately infamous, Federal Theater Project appeared.

The Federal Theatre Project

Launched into the sea of new and swirling social currents in child development, education, and democracy, as well as the rough-and-tumble tensions between industry and labor, was one of President Franklin Delano Roosevelt's signature programs: the Works Progress Administration (WPA). Designed to get the country back to work as quickly as possible after the onset of the Great Depression, the WPA provided jobs (rather than simple monetary relief) in a broad range of fields—from the construction of roads, parks, public buildings, and electrification projects to a Writers Project collecting and documenting slave narratives, as well as various public arts projects for visual artists. In 1935, a small piece of that larger national effort became the Federal Theatre Project (FTP), which aimed to put theater people back to work. The FTP was conceived as noncommercial theater, in distinct contrast to the larger theatrical scene which had become a highly commercial venture centered in New York City. The FTP challenged the prevailing theatrical scene not only in terms of its elite ticket pricing model, pegging FTP ticket prices at a broadly accessible five to twenty-five cents, but in terms of subject matter and production style. Until the advent of the FTP, Broadway theater and its related touring companies were primarily a playground for the elite and upper-middle classes. According to C. W. E. Bigsby, the prevailing approach was a "celebration of bourgeois individualism and the display of a new technological sophistication." With its romantic emphasis on the individual, it showcased upward mobility, a cult of heroes, and a star system.[45]

The FTP was none of these. It was focused on serving a more populist audience, and it was committed to offering a different kind of theatrical fare. It was charged with employing thousands of out-of-work theater people; there was no star system; and the audience was to include the ordinary working people of America. It was also "uncensored," said Harry Hopkins, head of the WPA; and, unusual for the time, the FTP produced plays specifically written for young audiences.[46]

Headed by Hallie Flanagan, former director of Vassar's Experimental Theatre, the FTP was committed to providing American audiences, most of whom had never attended a live performance, with not only the traditional fare of Shakespeare, Shaw, Ibsen, Chekhov, Marlowe, O'Neill, Tarkington, Anderson, Rice, Sherwood, and even a sprinkle of Pirandello and Boucicault, but with productions that stretched the form and explored new, contemporary subject matter.[47] The FTP operated from the idea that "no play should be presented that offered entertainment as its sole objective; substance and a point of view were basic requirements for scripts."[48] As a result, in addition to more traditional theatrical fare, the FTP spawned a bold, starkly dramatic format called the Living Newspaper, using it to produce a series of plays dramatizing significant issues related to working-class American life. Three of their productions provide examples of the kinds of problems they sought to explore: "*Triple-A Plowed Under* (1936), depicted the political and economic conditions affecting the farmer in the 1930s; *Injunction Granted* (1936), focused on the history of management-labor tensions in America; and *One-Third of a Nation* (1938), dramatized the atrocious living conditions in the country's slums."[49] The FTP's commitment to engaging with social and political issues also led to the creation of Negro Theatre Units, several of which produced the John Houseman/Orson Welles *"Voodoo" Macbeth* and *The Swing Mikado*, both adaptations by the Chicago Negro Theatre Unit of Shakespeare's *Macbeth* and Gilbert and Sullivan's *Mikado*, respectively.[50] The Negro Theatre Units also offered Theodore Brown's *Natural Man*, an exploration of Black masculinity in the form of the legend of John Henry and his epic contest with the steam drill,[51] and the FTP also launched *First Americans*, a series of fourteen fifteen-minute radio plays that dramatized the "history, myths and customs" of different Native American tribes.[52]

Organizationally, the FTP was the first regionally based national performing arts organization in the United States. It divided the country into five districts: New York, Boston, New Orleans, Chicago, and Los Angeles. This structure enabled the regional units to "listen" locally and to program in ways that tapped into local concerns.[53] The FTP also had a unit that read new plays by new playwrights, thereby increasing the range of options available for production. As a result, the FTP was able to offer a broad menu of productions, including new plays by Thornton Wilder and George Bernard Shaw, as well as T. S. Eliot's much-admired *Murder in the Cathedral* (1935).[54]

Until the advent of the FTP, professional theater for children had been of little interest to either the commercial business organizations that dominated Broadway, or to the off- or off-off-Broadway theaters. However, the creation of the FTP's Children's Units provided a stage on which the emerging trends in child development and education could join with the view of theater as an important and vibrant means of inculcating the values and behavioral commitments needed for a sustainable democracy. Under the aegis of the FTP, there was, a Children's Unit in New York, but there were also units in Charlotte, Greensboro, Chicago and Los Angeles, with units touring through Illinois, Indiana, and Iowa. These units performed in parks and schools, as well as more traditional venues.[55] The plays they produced ranged from classic children's stories like *Rip Van Winkle, The Emperor's New Clothes, Hansel and Gretel,* and *Pinocchio* to new plays with socially relevant contemporary stories.[56] There was, for example, the Chicago production of a new play by Charlotte Chorpenning based on the then-popular children's story *Little Black Sambo*. Her version explicitly sought to transform a degrading, racist stereotype of the African American child into a "universal" child searching for self-fulfillment—a clever, poetic, quick-witted, responsible child able to overcome his powerful assailants.[57]

It is important to note that all FTP units, especially the Negro Units, had to contend with the deeply entrenched racial politics of the time. The early 1930s was the time of the Scottsboro Boys and the 1935 Harlem riot. In 1933, there were twenty-four lynchings, fifteen in 1934, and eighteen in 1935.[58] As documented in *Dreaming America*, "all of the units struggled against racism and the perpetuation of African American stereotypes that dominated white theatrical representation of blacks." While some productions tried to portray the Black characters in a sympathetic manner, most of the plays were written by white playwrights who were "largely ignorant about the realities of African American life."[59] African Americans were traditionally portrayed through a white lens, one distorted by hundreds of years of white racism. For example, unlike the Chicago production mentioned above, "extant photos of the Cincinnati production of *Little Black Sambo* demonstrate that its black performers still wore blackface."[60] For several FTP units, the *Little Black Sambo* story was a puppet show, replete with the full range of negative caricatures: "perpetual grins against coal-black faces with wide eyes and thick red lips," ragged overalls, and bandanas, so that "before a word has been spoken, the audience has been informed by a wealth of signs as to how to read the show." With its "emphasis on minstrel characterizations—distortions of dialect, malapropisms, inversion of gender norms . . . exaggerated dance, emphasis on song and what passes for African American verbal play," these versions shifted the focus of the play to Sambo's fear of the tigers, to lying about what happened to his clothes, to stereotypical black dialect, and a concluding cakewalk while Sambo's mother Mumbo flipped pancakes.[61] When compared with the more positive Chicago version, those versions indicate the continued "denial of black inclusion into the increasingly universalized protected child . . . deserving the rights and privileges of schooling, play, decent food, and health care."[62]

In *A Letter to Santa Claus*, offered for the 1938 holiday season, the FTP produced a play that embodied the disturbing shadows of fascism, world conflict, poverty, hunger, and disillusionment that were unsettling to so many American families and communities at that time.[63] And, both fortunately and unfortunately, there was the imaginative and clever *The Revolt of the Beavers* (1937), an absolute charmer of an allegorical tale depicting a community of talking beavers (portrayed by actors on roller skates) caught up in a struggle to free Beaverland and the Beaver workforce from the evil Boss Beaver. *The Revolt of the Beavers* was fortunate because it embodied a host of complex ideas, both moral, intellectual, and political in an appealing and thoroughly engaging conceit, one fully accessible to even young children. It was unfortunate because Brooks Atkinson, theater critic of the *New York Times,* immediately labeled the production "Mother Goose Marx."[64] The result: after only seventeen performances, the production was shut down—with enthusiastic support from the popular press— because the House Un-American Activities Committee (HUAC), initially created to investigate fascist activities. thought, based on little actual evidence, that "the beavers rushing around on roller-skates, were disseminating Communism."[65] HUAC came to this conclusion despite the fact that no member of the committee actually attended a performance.

The unfortunate fate of the FTP is well documented. It had survived for a turbulent four years before succumbing to partisan politicking. In June 1939, Congress voted to defund the program, the result of an accretion of accusations that its productions were spreading communist propaganda. One anecdote sums up the level of outright ignorance and political partisanship that produced their decision: during one of Hallie Flanagan's several appearances before HUAC to defend the FTP productions, she had referred to Christopher Marlowe, one of Shakespeare's contemporaries. Congressman Joe Starnes of Alabama wanted to know who this Christopher Marlowe person was. "You were quoting from this Marlowe . . . Is he a Communist? . . . Tell us who Marlowe is, so we can get the proper references."[66]

The death of the FTP was a low point in the history of American theater. Fortunately for the children of America, there was another professional adult theater company for children that managed to avoid congressional censure. By the time the FTP disbanded, Junior Programs, Inc., founded in 1936, was well on its way to establishing itself as a nationally prominent pioneer of professional theater for children.

II. MORE THAN ENTERTAINMENT

The story of Junior Programs, Inc., is one of a deep belief in the essential link between a civilized democratic society and the performing arts, and of artists' responsibility to use their art to pass on to the next generation the fundamental values required to sustain and nourish such a society. It is a story of optimism in dark times; of a commitment to and a confidence in their collective ability to meet whatever challenges lay ahead; to break with tradition when needed; and to experiment, innovate, and learn in a continuous cycle of creativity, flexibility, and emergence. It is a story of beating the odds with an astonishing seven-year string of successes. It is a story with a legacy of lessons for today.

Devoted exclusively to producing professional performances by adults for young audiences, Junior Programs consisted of three distinct companies, all under the Junior Programs, Inc. banner: the Junior Programs Players, the Junior Programs Opera, and the Junior Programs Ballet. Their fully staged performances, however, were not the sum total of their work. Recognizing that it takes thoughtful discussion, questions, and activities to internalize and own a set of democratic social values, Junior Programs viewed their educational focus as central to their mission. From their perspective, *it was the combination of the artistic excellence of their productions and the related pedagogical materials that made their work powerful.*

The Founding of Junior Programs, Inc.

The impetus for Junior Programs came from a somewhat unexpected quarter: Maplewood, New Jersey. There, a young mother of two found herself searching in vain for the kinds of entertainment that would provide her children with not only some wholesome amusement, but with the moral, cultural, and intellectual guidance

II. MORE THAN ENTERTAINMENT

needed to prepare them for their responsibilities as future adults. Her name was Dorothy L. McFadden, and she was deeply concerned about the paucity of suitable radio, film and live programs for her children. In her view, what was needed were cultural opportunities that would provide an alternative to "the unwholesome, over-emotional, and tawdry fare which many commercial producers are offering merely for their own profit."[67]

In 1933, McFadden was an active member of the Educational Committee of the Maplewood Women's Club. One day, after a meeting, she, and several other members "were deploring the amount of time our children spent listening to radio programs which had no real value at all--and what a shame it was that they were not hearing good music or seeing any real theatre."[68] She and her friends continued to share their concerns about the "cheap and sensational" offerings, none of which focused on the developmental and intellectual needs of young audiences. There were a few commercial companies that occasionally performed a play for children, and there were amateur productions sponsored by the Association of Junior Leagues of America, but the standards of production varied widely, with many little more than mediocre; and the opportunity to attend live professional theater, music, and dance was still virtually unknown to American youth. These Maplewood conversations finally led to McFadden exclaiming, "Why can't we produce decent entertainment ourselves?"[69]

Their search for alternatives initially led them to the National Music League's professional mini-opera production of *Hansel and Gretel*. The National Music League, Inc. (NML) was a not-for-profit association for the promotion of music that sought to make an investment in America such that the "under-privileged individual has the opportunity with those more fortunate of listening to the most outstanding artists." This project was part of a larger NML effort to make musical audiences more inclusive—to attract a more diverse audience, especially more young people. "The future of America rests with the next generation, and it is our responsibility to see that our children receive the finest cultural advantages possible so that they will develop a high standard of American culture." The NML's first effort in this direction was a beautifully staged production of the Humperdinck opera, *Hansel and Gretel* developed by its Junior Programs Department. First performed on March 10, 1934, this production was acknowledged as "the most finished presentation of the opera for audiences of young people." In part with McFadden's assistance, the NML ultimately gave thirty-one performances of the opera in twenty schools to an audience of 32,000 children.[70]

The collaboration with the NML led to the creation of the Saturday Entertainment Committee, with representatives from all the Maplewood-South Orange PTAs, and to the development of a series of local programs that included not only the Humperdinck opera but the Sue Hastings Marionettes, a Beacon Hill Ensemble concert, a film on wild animals offered by the New York Zoological Park, and a magician—all performed, rent free, in the high school auditorium. The series was an enormous success. The programs cost a total of $1971.77, with ticket sales of $2219.95, generating a profit of $248.18. Numerous calls from neighboring towns eager for a similar series led McFadden to approach the NML's executive director, Lucy Milligan, who ended up hiring McFadden as a field secretary—to be paid a 10% commission on any programs she booked. McFadden's unpublished autobiography chronicles the interview with Milligan, and recounts McFadden's failure to mention that not only did she not have a car (a requirement for field secretaries), she did not know how to drive. "Can do" to the core, McFadden quickly purchased a Ford, and persuaded Eddie the Postman to teach her how to drive. She booked $10,000 worth of programs in her first year, and in her recounting of the story, she was careful to note that she never took the $1000 commission. Instead, in 1936, when she formally incorporated as Junior Programs, Inc., the NML gave the new company the rights to *Hansel and Gretel*, along with the production's scenery, lighting, and other accoutrements.[71]

Building on the initial work of the NML, McFadden's first efforts encompassed a series of ten professional stage shows specifically curated for children: one a month (with some so popular they were repeated twice), performed in the local school auditorium, and charging ten cents per child per performance. The varied nature of the programs, the availability of a "season ticket," and the commitment of the organizers to keep ticket prices low and to give free tickets to orphanages, hospitals, and those who could not otherwise afford them, attracted an unusually diverse group of children. Building on her initial efforts, ten neighboring New Jersey communities joined the effort, with McFadden organizing the "season" through the NML's Junior Programs Department. Educators soon awoke to the value of such programming and

II. MORE THAN ENTERTAINMENT

after a third year, in which the effort was joined by women's groups in several other Eastern states, McFadden decided to leave the NML.

In August 1936, she officially formed the new organization—Junior Programs, Inc. It was an educational, charitable (i.e. tax deductible) non-profit membership organization.[72] Renting an office from the Child Study Association on 57th Street, Junior Programs, Inc. retained a loose affiliation with the NML, and soon became the primary non-commercial, non-governmental, privately-funded organization dedicated to bringing the best of American cultural performances to the youngsters of America. During their first year, Junior Programs operated primarily as a booking agent. Although they had taken over the NML's production of *Hansel and Gretel*, in their earliest days, Junior Programs focused on a roster of individual performers: their repertoire included marionettes, monologists, films, and musicians.[73]

An example of one of their individual performers was the artist, Robert Alden Reaser. His *Stories in Black and White for Young People* is described in an undated Junior Programs' marketing flyer: "Skillful drawing is magical in the way it holds the attention of young people. As used by Mr. Reaser to illustrate stories, it becomes "swell fun." With piano accompaniment, a typical program offered a sketch of James McNeil Whistler, with notes on how heads were drawn, followed by some famous Whistler stories. His performance also included "La Boite a Joujoux" by Andre Helle, with music by Claude Debussy - a delightful tale of a French toyshop, with swift brush and ink drawing on a strip of paper 20 feet long." The flyer for this program also included excerpts from congratulatory letters sent to the Junior Programs office following a performance at Horace Mann High School in New York City. From the principal, we hear, "You are genuine artists, and you have a program which not only entertains, but also has real educational value. . . your program brings this spirit of joyousness." The Carnegie Foundation for the Advancement of Teaching also expressed gratitude, and according to the principal of Mamaroneck Junior High, "We saw the impossible performed in our Jr. High School assembly—a thousand students, teachers and parents spellbound by good music and drawing . . . while our "problem boys" were foremost among those who crowded eagerly around the Reasers after the recital." Another flyer announced a performance by Joan and Betty Rayner of the *Australian Children's Theatre*—"a non-profit travelling theatre taking artists of international standing to town and country children"—performing *The Princess and the Puppet Man,* a play by the Rayners based on folk tales from Denmark and Holland.[74]

The Junior Programs Leadership Team

None of Junior Programs' productions, tours, or years of success would have been possible without the talents and capabilities of both Dorothy McFadden and Saul Lancourt. Together, in what appears to have been a highly productive partnership, they were responsible for weaving together four key factors that enabled Junior Programs to successfully implement McFadden's vision. The first factor was the *ability to create professional productions of the highest quality*, productions children would repeatedly flock to see; and to design those productions so they could be mounted and performed under all manner of production conditions on an odd assortment of stages in municipal auditoriums, high school gymnasiums, and movie theaters. Second was the *creation of a fully integrated suite of correlated curriculum study units (CCSUs)* developed through partnerships not only with nationally recognized educational institutions such as the Teachers College of Columbia University, but with a vast network of local school systems and their teachers. A third factor was the *creation of an organizational distribution infrastructure* that would be able to operate with a relatively modest, centralized New York City staff to coordinate a highly decentralized, nationwide network of local volunteers able to reliably organize the myriad local activities required to deliver the productions in a successful and professional manner. And fourth, as any executive director knows, even the most dazzling programs require the *ability to raise the money* to pay for the development and distribution of the productions on a consistent basis. However, before moving on to an exploration of each of these factors, a brief sketch of the two leaders who "pulled it all together" in a way that generated a seven-year sequence of success after success is in order.

Dorothy L. McFadden

According to dozens of articles lauding her vision, McFadden was a woman in her mid-thirties who had intended to go to Vassar. Instead, she married her childhood sweetheart, James Lyman McFadden, ultimately co-founder of Madison, New Jersey's Gow-Mac Instrument Company, manufacturers of gas analysis equipment for chemists.[75] They lived in Maplewood, New Jersey, with their two children, James and Jean. McFadden was active in the local women's club and parent-teacher association, as were so many of the civic-minded middle- and upper-class wives of that time. Born in Frankfort, Germany, her parents were of German and Irish heritage. Her father, who had become a naturalized American citizen in 1898, was a senior executive for Roessler and Hasslacher, a German chemical company with an American branch that was eventually acquired by DuPont. From a privileged Presbyterian, Republican upbringing that included multiple trips to Europe, after her marriage, McFadden attended the Extension Division of the Teachers College of Columbia University. Photographs show an attractive young woman with a pleasing demeanor, but not someone you would single out of a crowd as a determined visionary, capable of successfully launching and sustaining a complex, dynamic enterprise in an almost nonexistent segment of the male-dominated theatrical world.

Her vision for Junior Programs was in part shaped by two trips she made, paid for by her father, to several European countries—one in 1937, the second in 1938.[76] While in Europe, she attended numerous performances, and met with an array of children's theater directors, classroom teachers and children in Denmark, Russia, Poland, Austria, Germany, Hungary, Czechoslovakia and France, and she was captivated by what she experienced. Their commitment to quality was striking. In Denmark, the nation's leading artists performed in the Danish National Children's Theatre, and the scenery was designed by artists from the Royal Copenhagen Opera House. In Moscow, she found the "beauty and perfection of technique of the children's theater . . . had not been exaggerated." Every play was "tested over years of performances, polished and cut and elaborated or changed in an effort to achieve perfection." She was also intrigued to learn that the content of many of the Russian productions was not focused on Soviet propaganda, but on folklore and classical material. The frequency and regularity of productions created specifically for children was also impressive. In Denmark, children attended five performances every winter; in Poland, sixty towns provided monthly concerts especially designed for children; in Russia, the children were surrounded by almost daily opportunities for cultural engagement in buildings and theaters especially organized for their artistic enjoyment. And everywhere, there were partnerships between the performing arts, the teachers, the parents, and the children themselves—with feedback solicited regularly from teachers, students, and local parent councils. There were also specially elected school committees which not only helped select the plays but ensured that the "staging and acting are artistically perfect." She soon realized that the reason the theatrical stages and concert halls in Europe had a thriving adult audience was that Europeans were trained, from their earliest days, to appreciate the finest in cultural entertainment; and she also knew that Americans could not expect their cultural heritage to survive if they gave their children no opportunity to appreciate those arts during their early habit-forming years.[77]

She returned to the US energized and fully persuaded that if the performing arts were to have an audience in the future, as a nation, we could not allow American youngsters to grow up artistically ignorant; and, based on what she had experienced during her European study tours, *"Only the best is good enough for children"* soon became the Junior Programs motto, emblazoned across programs and a broad range of marketing materials. She was also persuaded that in a democracy such as ours, in which our freedoms give us the power of choice, entertainment would be what we make it. Therefore, it was the duty of parents and teachers to provide the children of America's democracy with opportunities to build and develop what she considered to be their "naturally good taste."[78] McFadden made it clear that she "blamed adults for depraving their children's taste so that when they grow up they patronize the most inane motion pictures, vaudeville and burlesque shows. If left alone a child will instinctively enjoy beauty and good drama. It's the adult who makes a disparaging remark about the dullness of opera and makes fun of so-called 'highbrow' music and dance who influences the child to adopt the same attitude."[79] In a similar vein, the Roanoke, Virginia, *Times* (March 16, 1940) quoted her as saying, "If we as parents don't see that there are enough good things to choose from the child cannot be blamed for choosing trash."

For McFadden, Junior Programs was a labor of love: love for her own children, for whom she wanted the best in cultural experiences; love for children in general, whom she saw as nothing less than the future of America; and a love of the grand democratic experiment that was the "U. S. of A." There can be little doubt that she was a pioneer. At a time when women of her class were still primarily housewives and mothers, she worked more than full time—without pay—to make her vision a reality. At that time, dedicated "career women," especially married women, were few and

II. MORE THAN ENTERTAINMENT

far between, and McFadden claimed not to know what she thought of the "married career woman idea." But she did know "that a married woman with a big outside job has to make funny adjustments, like my hearing Jeannie's spelling and then rushing to catch the 8:20 morning train. I am very jealous of every minute I can spend with my family, [they] come first in my life" (*Motion Picture Herald*, Jun 18, 1938). Whether she thought of herself as a career woman or not, she did view her work as missionary work: "Our audiences are the theater audiences of tomorrow and liking the theater is an acquired taste. Thus, it's a kind of missionary work" (*Times*, Caspar, WY,1938). And her missionary work "inspired thousands of women everywhere with her own enthusiasm for the cultural welfare of children. Members of Parent-Teacher Associations, Women's Clubs, Junior Leagues, and teachers have organized committees in hundreds of towns and cities to bring Junior Programs entertainments to children."[80] Under her leadership, and undaunted by the magnitude of the task, her vision inspired and enlisted the support of a wide array of prominent sponsors and donors, not only from all sectors of the arts, but from educational, academic, religious, political, and philanthropic institutions. As it turns out, McFadden was also an organizational visionary, ultimately devising a nationwide organizational structure flexible enough to enable the three Junior Programs companies to grow and sustain season after season of nationwide touring (see Chapter VI).

Saul Lancourt

According to the *Brooklyn Eagle* (Dec 26, 1937), not yet thirty when he was hired by McFadden, Saul Lancourt "has been practically everything in the theatre and opera—actor, stagehand, scenic designer, dancer, electrician, stage manager, and director."[81] An undated Junior Programs' press release indicates that he trained and worked alongside luminaries such as actor Burgess Meredith, Italian baritone Eduardo Ciannelli, and actors Lloyd Nolan and Henry O'Neill. As an assistant director of the Chautauqua, and Worcester Festival Opera Companies, he worked with Metropolitan Opera stars—baritone Lawrence Tibbett, soprano Josephine Antoine, tenor Frederick Jagel, lyric soprano Helen Jepson—and many other famous names in opera. "Mr. Lancourt began his career as a piano prodigy at the age of 13. His experiences since then have been varied and extensive in all branches of entertainment. Four years ago he became associated with Junior Programs, Inc. as

Supervising Manager and Director, and excepting for his work with Chautauqua and Worcester in the summer seasons, has been devoting all of his time and energy to the ideal of raising the standards of cultural entertainment for children and young people" (Junior Programs' Biographies, n.d.). Not long into his tenure at Junior Programs, *Reader's Digest* (Jan 1939) tells us, "Saul Lancourt, has turned down offers of twice his present salary from Broadway producers. 'The bug has bitten me,' he says. 'This is more than a job. It's an adventure.'"

McFadden had made him responsible for creating, shaping, and managing all aspects of the artistic and production processes required to launch a steady stream of successful productions for Junior Programs. His job, in effect, was to ensure that, as the company motto would soon make explicit, "*Only the best is good enough for children.*" That "best" needed to be capable of touring reliably and repeatedly to an eclectic mix of cities and towns, season after season. McFadden said, "Saul was my good right hand, with all his professional skill and experience. He poured his whole life into our Junior Programs project. It never would have gotten anywhere without him. He supervised the casting of every show—operas and later spoken ballets and dramas—also the costuming, construction of scenery, lighting, [and] renting the Hertz trucks and an 8-passenger car for touring."[82]

Lancourt was born in New York City and raised by his Romanian-born mother, her three sisters, and his grandmother. His mother, a Jewish immigrant still in her teens when she arrived from Romania in 1906, worked in the garment industry. By saving her earnings, she brought her three sisters and her mother, one by one, to New York from a tiny village in Romania. Her marriage to Lancourt's father was brief, but young Saul grew up with a healthy respect for his tight-knit family of strong, independent working women, women who firmly believed in the overriding value of education, and the opportunity America provided for immigrants from all corners of the globe. Family lore has it that when it came time for the four sisters to bring their father to America, their mother, Saul's indomitable grandmother, told her husband that if he came to New York, he would have to get a job. A religious Jew from a rabbinical family, he never came.

Saul's youngest aunt had become a pianist and had married an opera singer. It was she who provided her nephew with piano lessons, and with exposure to the eclectic richness of the myriad artistic, musical, and cultural traditions available in New

York's "melting pot." To earn money for a much-coveted bicycle, young Saul secretly started giving piano lessons to his friends for nickels and dimes. When his mother discovered what he was doing, she made him return the money. Whether he ever got that bicycle is unknown, but the musical die was cast. Lancourt was also deeply influenced by the socialist/union values of his two other aunts—early organizers in the International Ladies Garment Workers Union and the Amalgamated Clothing Workers of America. These values, held by a large swath of the late-nineteenth- and early-twentieth-century waves of European immigrants, were strongly rooted in his immediate world. Fleeing fascism and religious and economic oppression, many of these immigrants were committed to doing whatever they could to ensure that the inequities of their previous existence would not be repeated in their newly adopted country. After graduating from City College in the unlucky year of 1929, he worked briefly as a high school English teacher—but it soon became clear that he needed to make a place for himself in the theatrical and musical world. He married his high-school sweetheart, Ruth Helfand, a graduate of Hunter College and daughter of socialist Russian immigrants. She became a high school biology teacher, and later an accomplished painter. Their daughter, Joan, was born in February 1942, just after the premier of Junior Programs' final production, *Doodle Dandy of the U.S.A.* Their son, Jerold—with a "J" after his maternal grandfather, Joseph—was born two years later.

An iconoclast in many ways, not the least of which was his deeply embedded belief that the five women who raised him were every bit as capable as men, and that participation in the socialist ferment of the time was an innate part of what a young man of his background did, Lancourt embodied both a reverence for the Western cultural canon and the pioneering spirit, innovative creative energy, and excitement of New York's intellectual and artistically multicultural world. Having steeped himself in the musical and operatic world during his tenure at the Chautauqua and Worcester Opera Festivals, he joined Junior Programs with a distinct vision of how to instill in children a love and appreciation of opera and the other performing arts. His vision of a lively, action-oriented, musically sound, and adventurous approach became a signature of every Junior Programs production, be it opera, dance, or drama. He was also a master negotiator and mediator, never losing his temper, and he had an intuitive sense of diplomacy—all of which served him well in the rough and tumble theatrical world of ambitious and often oversized egos. As one reviewer for the Indianapolis, Indiana, *Star* (Mar 14, 1940) pointed out, he infused dramatic action and pantomime into opera and dance, and musical rhythms and physical grace into dramas. "Directly responsible for putting into effect the ideas of Mrs. Dorothy McFadden . . . At the age of 30, he looks back on one of the strangest careers in the modern theatre and holds probably the only job of its kind in the country, that of a one-man source of children's entertainment . . . His is the only perfect score in the professional theatre with every production a greater success than its predecessor." (*Post-Search*, Bainbridge, GA, Jan 30, 1941).

Together, these two leaders brought Junior Programs to life. It is clear from numerous documents that the field staff, the various boards and advisory boards, the committees, the artists, the designers, and the educators were all engaged because they, too, believed in the Junior Programs mission and vision. Over and over, reviews and articles made it clear that everyone involved cared deeply about the artistic, cultural, and social education and development of children; that they viewed live performance as a powerful means of educating those children; and that they felt a sense of personal responsibility for offering live performance as a way of preparing children to eventually take their places as future citizens. In the run-up to WWII, there was a growing sense that Democracy with a capital D was under assault. Everyone who participated seemed to see Junior Programs as a way of doing their part to make sure "Democracy" survived. According to Gladys Swarthout, Metropolitan Opera mezzo-soprano, and chair of Junior Programs National Sponsoring Committee, "Everyone of these artists seems imbued with a joyous spirit which is the true essence of real art—a spirit which comes from generous giving of one's self to an audience that gives much back."[83] That this sense of mission was shared not only by the company's two leaders, but by so many of those involved appears to have contributed to a sense of organizational stability, a not insignificant factor in the company's ability to adapt and innovate as the need arose.

The Junior Programs *Credo*

Sometime after their 1936 incorporation, Junior Programs formally articulated their vision and mission in a *Code of Entertainment,* and a year or two later, the *Code* morphed to become a *Credo* which provided a clear statement of the company's values—values which served as the foundation and guide for their work. Their *Code* and *Credo* offer a thought-provoking window into the breadth and boldness of their mission. Both documents are noteworthy for the way they speak to their foundational

II. MORE THAN ENTERTAINMENT

belief that the performing arts have a much larger role to play in the development and maintenance of a democratic society than that of solely entertaining their audience.

The Junior Programs vision and mission were first articulated in their *Code of Entertainment*:

> For Children in A Democracy
> formulated by Junior Programs, Inc.
>
> The more the rest of the world goes mad with destruction, the more important it becomes for the children of our land to realize that life is to be lived for joy and happiness rather than for death and killing. The creation and appreciation of any peaceful art engenders a love of freedom.
>
> Believing that all arts spring from the people and flourish best in a democracy, Junior Programs, Inc., holds that all American children, regardless of race, creed, social or economic position, should have the opportunity to enjoy the finest professional performances of music, drama and ballet, performances which will evoke their wholesome laughter, develop their artistic judgment, and inculcate a love of democratic ideals.
>
> Junior Programs, Inc., is doing and will continue to do its best to make available to the children of our democracy the artistry of all races and nationalities, unclouded by bigotry, hatred and the war.
>
> If the folkway of democracy is to endure, there must be a constant nurturing of peacetime pleasures:
>
>> "Freedom needs all her poets; it is they
>> Who give her aspiration wings,
>> And to the wiser law of music sway
>> Her wild imaginings." [James Russell] Lowell.[84]

This *Code* eventually morphed into the Junior Programs *Credo*:

> In order that American children may be guided to the preservation of democracy, freedom, and the world's cultural heritage, and

realizing the important influence which recreational habits have on the character and personality development of the child, Junior Programs, Inc. has devised a Creed of Entertainment for Children in a Democracy:

SINCE music, drama and all the arts spring from the free development of the individual and therefore flourish best in a democracy,

WE BELIEVE that all American children, regardless of race, creed, or social or economic status, should have the benefit of inspiration by the finest professional artists in performance created for youth;

WE BELIEVE that these performances should arouse the children's wholesome laughter, help develop their personalities and artistic tastes, and guide them towards democratic ideals;

WE BELIEVE that the artistry of all races and nationalities undistorted by bigotry, hatred and the antagonisms of war, should be made available to all children;

WE BELIEVE that the parents, churches, the schools and communities as a whole, should be free to plan and select the entertainment which their children are to see without dictation from political or other pressure groups, and that they should be educated to this responsibility; and finally,

WE BELIEVE that a press free to evaluate and criticize such entertainment results naturally in ever higher artistic standards.

ONLY THE BEST IS GOOD ENOUGH FOR CHILDREN

The Only Non-Commercial, Non-Profit Making Organization of Its Kind - bringing the finest theatre to every child at 15-25c ticket prices, because of the generous support of an ever-growing list of contributing members.[85]

What is striking about these statements is not only the clarity and specificity of their vision, but its applicability to the multidimensional challenges still facing today's theaters for young audiences. Junior Programs' overarching goal was to use the performing arts to contribute to America's ability to *live* its aspirations—to *be* and *become* its best self—by *actively* contributing to the preparation of the next generation for its often-daunting task of carrying the mantle of democratic citizenship forward. From beginning to end, Junior Programs never faltered in their commitment to these values and aspirations.

The grandness and boldness of their vision—and the formally articulated intentionality of its commitment to social justice, to racial and ethnic equity and inclusiveness, to the importance of developing a child's artistic judgement and appreciation for the artistry of all races and nationalities, and to the ability of the performing arts to foster and inculcate a love for democratic ideals—appears to have been not only unique at that time, but timeless. In a nation of immigrants, and with the nation's continually changing demographics, it is the *world's* cultural heritage that needs sharing—then and now. It is a mission as relevant today as it was then, and it speaks explicitly to today's multicultural and multiracial needs. It also echoes John Dewey's view of the arts as an integral part of the experiential educational and democratic processes. For Dewey, the arts were "life at its fullest," an experience "so vivified and integrated as to be qualitatively distinct"—a consummate experience! In his *Art as Experience*, he "makes explicit art's natural continuities with everyday life," and seeks to "prevent its reduction to mere entertainment or "transient pleasurable excitations."[86]

It would be fascinating to know more about the process by which Junior Programs' *Code* and *Credo* were developed, but all we have are the statements themselves. Nevertheless, both stand as beacons of hope—a voice from the past with a message that continues to resonate today!

Junior Programs and Democracy

Given that preserving and sustaining American democracy was such a guiding force, and that their final production, *Doodle Dandy of the U.S.A.*, was written specifically to teach children about democracy, it seems fair to dig a little deeper into what democracy meant to Junior Programs, and how those meanings informed their work. Why did it become such a central feature of their vision and mission?

To answer that question, we need to consider the historic and political context in which they were living—to wit, the rising wave of fascism, international and domestic, and the very real threat it posed to America's still aspirational democracy. In *Letters from an American,* (May 29, 2023), historian and educator Heather Cox Richardson discussed *Army Talks,* a series of educational pamphlets on fascism published by the US War Department in 1943. She uses the March 24, 1945 pamphlet to explain:

> Fascism . . . "is government by the few and for the few." . . . Fascists "make their own rules and change them when they choose. . . . They maintain themselves in power by . . . skillful manipulation of fear and hate" . . . Americans should not be fooled into thinking that fascism could not come to America . . . First, they [the fascists] would pit religious, racial, and economic groups against one another to break down national unity. Part of that effort to divide and conquer would be a "well-planned 'hate campaign' against minority races, religions, and other groups." . . . The only way to stop the rise of fascism in the United States . . . "is by making our democracy work . . . By getting men to hate rather than to think," it prevents them "from seeking the real cause and a democratic solution to the problem . . . If we permit discrimination, prejudice, or hate to rob *anyone* of his democratic rights, our own freedom and all democracy is threatened."[87]

The key insight here is that making democracy work requires bringing people together to overcome the individual and group differences inherent in a nation of immigrants from diverse cultures, races, ethnicities, and religions. In a sense, the Greek derivation of the word democracy—*demos,* meaning *the people*, and *kratos,* meaning *power*—defines democracy as the antithesis of the US Army's explanation of fascism. For Junior Programs, it was the full and equitable participation of *all the people* in the exercise of *their power* that was required for a full and successful democracy, and it was their belief that the performing arts could play a catalytic role in embedding that aspiration in the minds and hearts of the next generation.

In "Creative Democracy—The Task Before Us," John Dewey also articulated the challenge facing the American polity as it confronted the fascist threat. Writing in his eighties, long after he had established himself as one of the leading thinkers on education, he highlighted the centrality of democracy to the educational process. "For a long period we acted as if our democracy were something that perpetuated itself automatically," requiring little more than the performance of a set of periodic "political duties" such as voting. But in the face of the Nazi threat, he emphasized his belief that a truly functional democracy required something more personal. To reap its benefits, *democracy needed to become a way of life for each person—an indelible part of their individual character, and as such, a guide to all their activities.* Being a democracy meant having "faith in the potentialities of human nature . . . irrespective of race, color, sex, birth and family, [or] of material or cultural wealth." To make democracy more than just words on paper, that faith needed to embrace a commitment to the creation of conditions which would enable every individual to realize their potential. This faith also included the belief in each person's capacity for intelligent judgement, the exercise of which involved a "day-to-day working together with others . . . Intolerance, abuse, calling of names because of differences of opinion about religion or politics . . . differences of race, color, wealth or degrees of culture are treason to the democratic way of life." Legal guarantees of civil liberties, free expression and freedom of assembly are insufficient if daily discourse is choked off by "suspicion . . . abuse . . . fear . . . and hatred." He viewed differences as "a means of enriching one's own life-experience" as well as that of others. "Experience" was a central feature of his philosophy—for it was through experience that one *learned* to interact with others in a manner congruent with democratic values and a democratic way of life. For Dewey, "experience" meant the "free interaction" of individuals with their surroundings in an educational process that enabled them to "go beyond what exists" into an exploration of future possibilities. The process of "experience" was both means and end; a way "to call into being the things that have not existed in the past." For him, "*the task of democracy is forever that of creation of a freer and more humane experience in which all share and to which all contribute* [emphasis added]."[88] This "learning through experience" was not only essential to Dewey's understanding of democracy, but to his whole approach to education. It was through the process of an experientially based education that future citizens of a democracy would learn how to live their democratic values. Democracy and education, then, were inextricably linked as fundamental processes in the creation a more genuinely free society.

In Dewey's linking of democracy, an experiential education, the arts, and his focus on the creation of "things that have not existed in the past," we can hear in the Junior Programs *Credo* more than just echoes of his beliefs. At its heart, their *Credo is* a statement of their intention to put Dewey's philosophy into practice, and to use the performing arts as an essential means to that end. In reading their *Credo,* we come away with a sense that implicitly and explicitly, it places the performing arts in what Junior Programs considered to be its rightful place—as an important actor in what appears to be a never-ending battle against fascism. For Junior Programs, it was *the gap* that still existed between the nation's democratic aspiration and the reality of the nation's immediate situation that the performing arts could and should help to address.

From their perspective, too many of *the people* were still denied the ability to exercise the *power* to influence their world, a power conferred on all citizens in a true democracy. While Black men had officially gained the right to be part of *the people* with the passage of the Fifteenth Amendment on February 3, 1870, in the ensuing sixty-six years, a web of poll taxes, literacy tests, and dozens of Jim Crow strategies by individual states to curtail the ability of Black men to vote were still preventing that right from being fully exercised. And although the 1848 Treaty of Guadalupe Hidalgo had allowed Mexicans living in US territories to become citizens, they, too, were often vigorously discouraged from exercising their right to vote. Further, in an appalling irony, Native Americans were not able to become citizens until the passage of the 1924 Indian Citizenship Act, a mere dozen years before the 1936 founding of Junior Programs. And it would be another sixteen to twenty-nine years—with the Immigration and Nationality Acts of 1952 and 1965—before people of Asian heritage would officially become part of *the people.* In 1936, even white women, having been granted the right to vote in 1920, had been part of *the people* for a mere sixteen years.[89]

But Junior Programs believed that for American democracy to succeed, people of *all* races, creeds, national origins, and social and economic statuses would need to be actively involved; and it was through their use of the performing arts, coupled with their CCSUs that they saw a way to provide *all* children with an understanding of how important it was to be inclusive and to view all kinds of diversity as an asset rather than a liability. Their goal, then, was to awaken in the hearts and minds of their young audiences the deep desire and ability to sustain and expand America's aspiration to a more fully democratic way of life.

Junior Programs and *The Other*

To achieve that goal, their productions would have to counter the steady stream of negative stereotypes emanating from Hollywood about those groups which had been historically excluded from *the people* and denied the *power* to which they were entitled. What Junior Programs would need to provide was a series of positive narratives about those marginalized groups—a kind of remedial "narrative reparations"—that would challenge the multiple strands of racism that were still a significant part of the nation's social, political, and economic every-day life. As we will see in Chapter III, this facet of their mission had an important impact on the plays they chose to commission, and with *Doodle Dandy of the U.S.A.,* they succeeded in creating a production in which democracy itself became a character—one who played a leading role, not just as an abstract idea but as an impish Puck-like sprite which inspired the entire community, *including the children,* to participate in a set of collective and collaborative actions to rid their town of its would-be dictator.

From the perspective of social and interpersonal dynamics, these negative film and radio narratives had cast virtually all marginalized groups as *the other*—a concept in which people who were visibly different from the dominant white Eurocentric American society were defined as *not belonging*. The concept of the other is an important thread through many disciplines—ranging from psychology, philosophy, ethics, sociology, and political science to gender studies, anticolonial studies, phenomenology, and critical theory. As Alison Mountz points out, the concept is not only a philosophic construct, it also may be used as both a noun and a verb. As a noun, it refers to a person or group of persons who are different from oneself. As a verb, it refers to a process of categorizing and labeling persons or groups as not belonging to the mainstream society. To *other* an individual or group of individuals is to view them as marginal, locating them outside the center of the normative social order.[90]

At the heart of the concept of the other is the positive and essential role it plays in our individual psychological and emotional ability to recognize the "not-Self"; to understand that there is another being, separate from the Self. This is not only an essential step in the human ability to define the Self, but it is key to an individual's ability to enter into meaningful relationships with another person; and it is the permeability of the boundaries between the two beings that allows for the possibility of a relationship.[91]

However, it is in the disciplines of sociology, political science, gender studies, and anticolonial studies, that the other has been more fully examined as a negative concept. In those disciplines, it refers to the process by which a dominant group defines social norms, and, once defined, any person or group which does not—or cannot—conform to those norms is seen as the other. The very existence of an alternative set of norms is seen by the dominant group as a threat to its continued dominance, or, in essence, as a challenge to the status quo. To maintain dominance, "the powers that be" must then go to *whatever lengths are necessary* to justify the negation and exclusion of the other. Typically, this has been done by characterizing the "not us" group as deficient, defective, or deviant in ways that justify their lack of inclusion in the larger polity. Rather than enabling interpersonal relationships, this definition of the other creates false binaries and unequal power relationships, putting the other into a socially subordinate category that supports the desired social exclusion.[92]

Two examples help explain how the process works. In *The Second Sex,* Simone de Beauvoir, a groundbreaking figure in feminism and women's studies, explored the ways in which men, as the historically dominant group, defined women as the other—as "not men." Men, de Beauvoir asserted, saw themselves as the essential center—a state which relegated women to that of the inessential other. Defined in this way, women become objects, often so much so that many participate in their own objectification. As objects, women are then viewed as passive, alienated, and in need of patriarchal structures to organize their lives. Repeat this assessment frequently enough, and create social, political, and economic structures that reinforce such a view, and many women begin to internalize the myth of their inferiority, thereby justifying the primacy of the male voice. Either despite or even because of this negative consequence, de Beauvoir, in *The Ethics of Ambiguity,* explores the nature of an individual's responsibility to the other, especially if that other is an oppressed group. She concluded that if she did not help that group throw off its oppressors, then she, herself, would be complicit in their oppression.[93] In one sense, Junior Programs' commitment to help create alternative narratives was an expression of de Beauvoir's sense of responsibility. Junior Programs' reparative narratives would give the other a voice—one that would help *normalize* the diversity of the excluded or marginalized groups, thereby removing the perception of them as a threat.

Another example of othering is described by Edward Said, a Palestinian anti-colonialist scholar. In his *Orientalism*, Said examines the concept of "Orientalism" as an interpretation by Western outsiders of the Arab/Islamic/Asian cultures. In Said's analysis, these foreign observers used misrepresentation, fantasy, and myths to create an imaginary geography that was deemed "exotic" and often unabashedly sexual. The "Orient" was seen as both alluring and deeply threatening to a rationally superior West. In his analysis, Said describes the ways in which the various branches of the arts played a significant and successful role in forming and disseminating these misrepresentations. Novels such as Flaubert's *Salammbo* or *Salome* described the Orient as both fascinating, and morally corrupt.[94] Ingres's painting of *The Turkish Bath*, rendered the ablutions of voluptuous harem women as overtly sensual, as did ballets such as *Le Corsair* and *Sheherazade*.[95] Over time, the collective weight of these and other myths, stemming from multiple, reenforcing artistic sources, enabled the West to consider these depictions not as fantasy, but as reality. These misrepresentations became "knowledge," and Foucault describes the way systems of knowledge serve to construct the way we see and experience the world.[96] This Orientalist pseudo-knowledge indelibly shaped the West's view of the Orient as inferior and in need of being saved from itself—a view conveniently available to the nineteenth-century European powers as justification for their colonial conquest and economic exploitation of the Oriental other. From Said's point of view, not only did Orientalism's othering shape the Western view of lands and cultures stretching from the Arab and Islamic Middle East through India, Indochina, and the Far East, it had a tremendous negative influence on how the peoples of the East saw themselves. According to Said, this damage could only be undone when those who had been othered could begin to speak for themselves.[97]

Closer to home, the process of othering still permeates many areas of US national life. In "A Brief History of the Enduring Phony Science that Perpetuates White Supremacy," Michael Ruane discusses how the pseudoscientific othering of the Black population in the US has been relentless in its efforts to keep African Americans out of the mainstream of American society.[98] Recent "critical race theory"

(CRT) scholarship also has made a compelling case that to justify the exclusion of non-white populations from economic gain, it was and is necessary for the dominant white society to other peoples of color—deeming them born deficient in intelligence, immoral or amoral, and therefore undeserving of inclusion in the social, political, or economic life of the dominant white society.[99]

With these examples as background, even a brief examination of the negative ways in which Hollywood of the 1920s and '30s repeatedly characterized the communities of color in the US serves to illustrate not only the same dynamics of othering described by de Beauvoir, Said, Ruane, and Kendi, it also suggests that Hollywood—as the voice of the dominant white, Eurocentric society—was both speaking for and influencing the ways in which the larger white society viewed communities of color—as a threat to the continuation of white dominance. During the '20s and '30s, for example, male Asians were portrayed in films as inscrutable, cunning, and sly—and incapable of speaking proper English. The character of Fu Manchu was portrayed as the "yellow peril" incarnate, while Asian women were depicted as "dragon ladies," exotic women of the night, or eager to please "China dolls."[100] Latinx men, often Mexican, were cast either as villainous bandidos, shifty, dishonest, and violent, or lazy, untrustworthy slackers, asleep under a sombrero in the mid-day sun. Latinx women were portrayed as half-breed harlots, lusty, hot-tempered, and blatantly sexual.[101] Black American men were characterized as childlike, simple-minded, grinning Sambos, idle, inarticulate "coons," or mentally inferior, threatening brutes; while Black women were either mammies, domineering Sapphires, or dangerous Jezebels.[102] The prevailing screen images of Indigenous and First Nations peoples in popular Hollywood Westerns were also damning, with endless visuals of Indigenous men galloping across the landscape uttering blood-curdling screams as they savagely killed and scalped innocent white settlers; and when they were not killing, they were portrayed as lazy, immoral, vengeful, heathen drunks.[103]

The themes that emerge from these Hollywood examples were striking. Repeated over and over again by the white film makers, these misrepresentations of the other as superstitious, gullible, weak, lazy, barbaric, and morally corrupt became "knowledge" and then "truths." Taken together, they illustrate not only the key dynamics of the othering that was a normal part of the American culture, but, as Said, de Beauvoir,

Ruane and Kendi point out, the deeply damaging effect such othering has on the self-image of the groups being othered.

While Junior Programs did not have the conceptual framework or the vocabulary we have today with which to describe the many ways the US has historically "centered whiteness" and defended "white supremacy," in aggregate, the plays they commissioned indicate that they were well aware of the negative effects of the othering being practiced by Hollywood. As a result, their willingness to challenge Hollywood's othering by providing a steady stream of productions that would show diverse cultures in a way that would *normalize and appreciate the differences* became central to their mission. Even a quick review of the plays they commissioned confirms this assessment. *The Reward of the Sun God* was a lively, action-oriented story of two appealingly precocious Indigenous Hopi children. Two additional plays—*The Emperor's Treasure Chest,* a play about a group of lively Brazilian children, and *The Adventures of Marco Polo,* which portrayed Asians in a positive light—were explicitly commissioned in the runup to WWII to counteract the prevalent othering of the South American and Asian communities. In essence, these plays were one of the earliest efforts to give those who were being othered a voice—a way in which they could begin to speak for themselves and tell their own stories.

Productions that created new, positive narratives and gave voice to those who had been othered were essential to achieving the Junior Programs mission, but as already noted, the founding of Junior Programs recognized the need to deliver more than solely entertainment. A more vibrant form of education was required to explore, amplify and reenforce the performances, and it also was essential to obtain substantive participation from the communities in which they performed. The two sections which follow offer an overview of the ways in which Junior Programs addressed these two requirements, each of which will be examined in greater detail in subsequent chapters.

A More Vibrant Form of Education

Given the prominence of the members of Junior Programs' Educational Guidance Committee, it seems likely that Junior Programs also understood that the stories children hear in their formative years possess a special power—often seeping into their unconscious to shape what and how they think, and how they behave long into adulthood. Junior Programs' understanding of the importance of providing positive alternatives to racial and cultural othering may also be responsible not only for their focus on commissioning plays with positive stories of people and communities of color, but also on the importance they accorded to the broad array of CCSUs developed by their Educational Guidance Committee.

They appear to have understood that reversing the damage done by the pervasive process of othering would require more than attendance at a single performance, no matter how appealing the story or how excellent the production. It was the performance *and* the deeper, broader exploration of any given subject matter afforded by their CCSUs, each medium feeding into and amplifying the impact of the other, that held the key. By producing numerous CCSUs to enable young people to gain a deeper and more extensive understanding of the diverse cultures that make up the rich heritage of an immigrant nation, Junior Programs would be able to show how appealing and interesting diverse cultures could be. They also would be taking advantage of this early and developmentally important time in a child's life to help them see cultural diversity as positive, normal, and non-threatening. An article by Margaret Lloyd in the *Christian Science Monitor* (May 8, 1937) underscores this commitment. In "Aims of Junior Programs, Inc.," she says, "It is the aim of . . . Junior Programs Inc. to reach the average child—with entertainment that is *deep experience instead of casual pastime* [emphasis added]—and at a purely nominal fee." Lloyd also notes that "To this end, they work with parent-teacher affiliations, women's clubs, occasionally a Junior League branch and the public schools." An *American Woman's Association Bulletin* (March 11, 1937) also describes Junior Programs' productions as "definitely designed to give the children an awareness of the attractive and interesting characteristics, histories and civilizations of other countries and races."

Today, the performing arts' engagement with various local K-12 school systems frequently takes the form of a "guest appearance" by a company or university-based teaching artist who goes into a school to educate children about some aspect of the performing arts (e.g., acting, playwriting, or the study of a specific play). Junior Programs' broader, deeper vision required more. To be sure, their CCSUs contained material focused on the performing arts, but their educational vision also included enabling other front-line teachers to use the subject matter of a given production not only as a catalyst to a deeper exploration of their specific subject matter, but as a way their subject matter could enrich a student's experience of the play. As such, they would be able to bring their subjects to life in ways that could speak more directly to each child's personal interest and reality. In other words, as a pedagogical medium, the performing arts could transport a student into a bright, compelling, engaging and curiosity-inducing world in a way that more academically oriented textbooks or lectures could not.

The Junior Programs Educational Guidance Committee enabled the company to partner with leading subject-matter experts of the day, commissioning a wide range of production-related subject and grade-specific CCSUs (e.g., history, geography, social studies, literature, physical education, shop, home economics, and political science, as well as music, dance, and drama). All were designed to be delivered by frontline subject-matter or grade-specific classroom teachers wherever Junior Programs performed. These units were provided to teachers two or three months prior to the arrival of a production and were considered by the teachers as important curriculum resources to be incorporated into their lesson plans. For Junior Programs, partnerships between the performing arts and the local K-12 schools were an important component of their view of the performing arts as a powerful educational asset; and over the years, their work with the local school systems in the cities and towns in which they performed became a unique hallmark of their approach to the development of democratic and artistic sensibilities in their youthful audiences.

The Secret Sauce: Community Engagement and Organizational Infrastructure

In addition to their educational innovations, there was yet another innovation crucial to the success of both their productions and their educational work—the creation of an organizational structure that would incorporate the active engagement of the community into every aspect of the company's work. By all accounts, the structures, and processes McFadden and Lancourt developed were well suited to the work that needed to be done. Paging through the Junior Programs documents and news clippings, it doesn't take long to understand that Junior Programs' ability to infuse their mission into their work derived, in part, from the importance of civic and community engagement as an essential ingredient in protecting and sustaining the American democratic way of life. Their highly decentralized network, which ultimately consisted of well over two hundred local sponsoring organizations, created a very cost-effective distribution infrastructure. This enabled Junior Programs to tour extensively throughout the country while maintaining a modest New York based staff of six or seven field secretaries. Further, this decentralized network served to embed in Junior Programs' structure a central tenet of an inclusive democracy—broad-based community participation enabling many of those involved to have input into the choices and decision-making of the company.

Essentially, McFadden replicated on a national scale the structures she had experienced in her local network of women's clubs and volunteer civic and community organizations. It was an effective infrastructure that kept Junior Programs close to their audiences and made it possible to schedule and administer complex twenty-to-thirty-week nationwide tours for each of the three Junior Programs companies. By incorporating local communities into the structures and processes of the organization, McFadden and Lancourt, in effect, created a two-way flow of communication that made it possible to obtain feedback from diverse communities. It is also worth noting that both leaders were frequently "out in the field," themselves; McFadden promoting Junior Programs to a broad range of potential civic sponsors, and Lancourt continually assessing the audiences' reaction to each production. These feedback loops were used to inform their choice of future productions as well as the development of the CCSUs. It also enabled them to collaborate and partner with a range of social, educational, and governmental agencies which, in the run-up to WWII, needed all the help they could get to *create the kind of broad national unity necessary for successful military mobilization*. Responsible for preparing the country for the possibility of war, these various agencies welcomed and applauded the use of the performing arts as an effective way to help address the many negative racial and ethnic stereotypes that existed throughout the nation. Thus, Junior Programs became an unexpected but welcome ally.

From their early New York headquarters at 221 West 57th Street, McFadden managed the various sponsoring boards, fundraising activities, management contracts, activities of the educational guidance board, the touring schedules, and the field secretaries. In turn, those secretaries managed the nation-wide network of local "sponsoring committees" in the two hundred plus cities and towns across the United States. From these same headquarters, Lancourt managed the production-related activities, including script and musical score development, auditioning and hiring of the performers, designers, and production crews, and rehearsals for the three Junior Programs companies.

John Martin, dance critic for the *New York Times* (Jun 23, 1940), provides a brief but descriptive summary of how the Junior Programs organization worked: "Performances are sponsored in various communities by parent-teachers associations, women's clubs, Junior Leagues, Chambers of Commerce, music clubs, Rotary, Kiwanis and Lions, and the communities served number slightly more with populations under 5,000 than with populations over 100,000, with the largest single population group lying between 25,000 and 50,000." Martin also noted, "Performers are paid Equity rates or better. Admissions average from 10-25 cents, with free seats for the underprivileged." Similarly, Walter Terry, dance critic of the *New York Herald Tribune* (Jan 12, 1941) explained, "[Educational] materials are sent on ahead to the schools, and . . . if Robin Hood is to be presented . . . the history class gets busy with a study of feudal days . . . the athletic director features . . . archery; the music instructor has his student orchestra . . . try out the music; the art department splashes paint about in the business of making posters . . . and where there is an advanced physical education department, the fundamentals of the dance activity are featured. Such a program makes the young student feel that he is really playing a part in the theater and its accompanying excitement."

This approach to what we now call community engagement—direct, personal, volunteer engagement on the part of a vast number of individuals and organizations already involved in the day-to-day life of their local communities—were the fuel that made the civic engine run.

Neither Junior Programs' artistic nor educational innovations would have been possible without McFadden's unique, volunteer organizational model as there is no way Junior Programs could have paid for all the local-level work needed to make their extensive touring schedule a reality. But virtually every city and town in the nation had its Kiwanis, Rotary and College Clubs, its Masons, its Junior League branches, PTAs, and Chambers of Commerce, and the missions of each of these organizations, in one way or another, encompassed the well-being of the community's children. In effect, McFadden had brilliantly tapped into the beating heart of America's civic life.

The Junior Programs, Inc., Companies

For the better part of their seven years, Junior Programs, Inc., was the umbrella organization for three touring companies: the Junior Programs Players, the Junior Programs Opera, and the Junior Programs Ballet. Collectively, from 1936 to 1943, the three companies produced and toured twelve fully staged productions. During much of that time, Junior Programs added a new opera, a new ballet, and a new play to the repertoire each season. Each production was developed, rehearsed, and premiered in New York City for an audience of youngsters before being sent out on increasingly longer and geographically broader national tours. A review of the Junior Programs touring schedule (see Appendix 1) indicates that many of the productions remained in the repertoire for multiple years, and that year after year, many of the cities and towns contracted for a "season" of two or three productions.

Given the gaps in company records, it is difficult to determine the exact dates of a given production's premiere. However, for their first season—1936 to 1937—the Junior Programs Opera toured the NML version of Humperdinck's classic, *Hansel and Gretel;* and the Junior Programs Ballet commissioned the nationally and internationally acclaimed dancer and choreographer, Edwin Strawbridge, to create their first narrative *dance-play,* a dance version of the children's classic, *Pinocchio.* The following season—1937 to 1938—the opera company premiered an adaptation of Rimsky-Korsakov's *Tale of the Tzar Saltan*, which they retitled *The Bumble Bee Prince*. The Junior Programs Players toured their newly commissioned play about two Hopi Native American children, *The Reward of the Sun God* by John Louw Nelson; and the ballet company added a second new dance-play, Strawbridge's adaptation of *The Princess and the Swineherd,* based on the Hans Christian Anderson fairy tale. For the 1939 to 1940 season, the Junior Programs Players launched Charlotte Perry's adaptation of *Run, Peddler, Run,* a drama about two young Irish immigrants set in the American colonial period; and the ballet company commissioned another Strawbridge dance-play based on Shakespeare's *A Midsummer's Night's Dream*, renamed *The Adventures of Puck*. During the 1940 to 1941 season, the opera company adapted a revival of the American opera, *Jack and the Beanstalk,* with music by Louis Gruenberg and lyrics by John Erskine. The Players commissioned a tale of mystery and intrigue about a group of high-spirited Brazilian children, *The Emperor's Treasure Chest* by Cecile

II. MORE THAN ENTERTAINMENT 47

Hulse Matschat; and the ballet company added a fourth dance-play choreographed by Strawbridge, *Robin Hood,* incorporating authentic medieval English music.

When the United States entered WWII in 1941, the draft and the rationing of gas and rubber made it impossible to sustain and tour three separate companies. Thus, for what turned out to be their final two seasons (1941 to 1942 and 1942 to 1943), Junior Programs combined the music, dance, and acting talents of the three companies into one seamless whole, touring first *The Adventures of Marco Polo* by Saul Lancourt, with music by Margaret Carlisle and dances choreographed by Ruth St. Denis, and finally, *Doodle Dandy of the U.S.A.*, again by Saul Lancourt, with music by Elie Siegmeister and choreography by Ted Shawn.

An article in *The Independent* (St. Petersburg, FL, Nov 1940) offers an assessment of the role Junior Programs productions played in transforming children's entertainment:

> Professional artistic entertainment specially devised for children is a phenomenon of comparatively recent origin; and the extent of its rapid progress in modern techniques and quality will be viewed in three of the six entertainments [*Robin Hood, The Bumble Bee Prince,* and *Run, Peddler, Run*] . . . during the 1940–'41 season . . . sponsored by the Children's Theater Bureau of St. Petersburg . . . Directly responsible for putting into effect the ideas of Mrs. Dorothy McFadden . . . is Saul Lancourt, production-director of the organization. At the age of 30 he looks back on one of the strangest careers in the modern theater and holds probably the only job of its kind in the country, that of a one-man source of children's entertainment.
>
> The Junior Programs Opera and Ballet companies have the longest and most extensive tours of any professional troupes in the country. The stage for children in America has now reached a point of artistic development that compares with the best in the adult theater and even surpasses it in many respects. Mr. Lancourt says, "There is no lack of the finest American artists for the stage. We choose them carefully for Junior Programs. We have also spared no efforts to devise scenery, props, lighting, and equipment for touring productions that

will reproduce on practically any auditorium stage in the country the same modern impressions that have till now been possible only in the best New York theaters."

This, and hundreds of other newspaper reviews and articles from across the country, makes it clear that the quality and entertainment value of their productions was never sacrificed as Junior Programs pursued their social, educational, and artistic goals. For each of the three companies, their commitment to artistic excellence *and* a willingness to experiment never wavered—a combination which led to several important artistic and social innovations. Nothing like the breadth and scope of Junior Programs had existed before, and their dedication to the children of the nation as the primary hope for the future clearly suggests Junior Programs be viewed—and studied—as far more than a footnote in the history of TYA.

Junior Programs' Overarching Commitments

Before exploring each of the building blocks—the high-quality productions, the correlated curriculum study units, and the community engagement needed to breathe life into the vision embodied in their *Credo*—it is worth pausing to highlight and summarize three of Junior Programs' overarching commitments which, taken together, were largely responsible for their success.

First was their intentional commitment to using the performing arts as a legitimate and viable means of preparing the next generation for full citizenship and participation in a democratic civil society. This expansive view of theater was infused with Dewey's precepts of learning through the experiential engagement of the whole child, emotional as well as intellectual. This led Junior Programs productions to emphasize a more positive view of society and offer a vision of America to which every child might aspire. They embedded this vision in a series of child-centered stories that highlighted the best aspects of human nature rather than vilifying the status quo for its failures. It was not that their stories lacked villains; there were plenty of those. Rather, the plots embodied and emphasized a more positive view of a story's characters in relation to their social and economic surroundings, and, of special import to the sustainability of a democracy, a positive view of cultures other than the dominant, white Eurocentric culture. Like Dewey, both in their stories and their overall approach, Junior Programs emphasized the essential importance of community—a perspective integral to what they offered on stage and to the organizational and educational models they developed. Finally, instead of pointing out the many ways in which society was not living up to its ideals, *Junior Programs chose to share and amplify a positive view of those who had been left out.* In this way, they managed to avoid the polemic and propagandistic accusations that were a key factor in the demise of the FTP.

Second was their commitment to accessibility, a condition necessary to achieve their first commitment. Today, accessibility, in its numerous forms, peppers the language of virtually every cultural organization. It has become the pot-of-gold at the end of the cultural arts rainbow. But for Junior Programs, and for McFadden and Lancourt, accessibility was at the core of the company's raison d'être. *All* children needed to be engaged. It is no exaggeration to say that three-quarters of a century before "access" became an artistic buzzword, one of Junior Programs' most important innovations was their understanding that the cultural heritage of the nation, in *all* its manifestations, was not, indeed, *must not be,* the province of an elite class. Rather, it belonged to everyone, in every part of the country, in every city and town, to all races and ethnicities, and to those at every economic level. For reasons that will be addressed in the following chapter, for Junior Programs, the concept of access had one significant and pragmatic limit, especially in the context of America's history of Black enslavement: almost every social and civic institution in the nation was formally and informally segregated by race. However, given that seemingly immutable fact, they appear to have pushed the concept of access as close to the limits of the possible as they dared without jeopardizing the company's physical safety.

During their seven years of existence, they were directly responsible for offering a diverse array of live performances, the focus and quality of which had never been available on such a scale to so broad a socioeconomic cross section of the country. As noted earlier, there were a handful of smaller companies, such as Clare Tree Major's touring *Threshold Players,* but cumulatively the scale of the Junior Programs tours appears to have been unprecedented, ultimately reaching an audience of four million children in every part of the nation, most of whom would never have been exposed to live performances of opera, ballet, or theater were it not for the existence of Junior Programs. By all accounts, their young audiences took to the opportunity like ducks to water. While the regionally located Children's Units of the FTP also aimed to reach a broader audience of young people, their productions were usually performed primarily in a region's main cities, or on modest regional tours; and this is largely true of the current regional children's theater model. Junior Programs, on the other hand, succeeded in touring live performances not only to major regional cities, but into the highways and byways of smalltown America (See Appendix 1).

For Junior Programs, access also had a second meaning: access to something more than the Eurocentric cultural canon. In keeping with their view of the diversity at the heart of American democracy, they took some of the earliest steps toward including in their productions of *The Reward of the Sun God, The Emperor's Treasure Chest* and *Marco Polo,* the artistic achievements of non-Western cultures.

Third was their commitment to multiple forms of innovation and learning, again, a requirement if they were to make good on their first two commitments. Despite their years of success, McFadden frequently referred to Junior Programs as an "experiment."[104] Perhaps she thought of it that way because she and Lancourt were continually confronted with a steady stream of challenges—artistic, logistic, social, and financial. It was clear from the outset that the "tried and true" simply would not get them where they wanted to be. It was, therefore, fortunate that both McFadden and Lancourt were not only visionaries but iconoclastic in their approach. At a fundamental level, they understood that cutting the prevailing models of adult entertainment down to a junior size—in somewhat the same way so many early children's portraits depict them as miniature adults—could never bring their vision to life. Instead, it required them to continually experiment and innovate in numerous ways. In a sense, they became *masters of innovation, transforming each challenge into a series of opportunities* as they learned how to creatively solve a broad array of problems. They did so repeatedly, often in ways they could not have anticipated or even imagined at the outset. Getting children to sit through operas that frequently put the most cultured adults to sleep? No problem! Junior Programs can do that! Creating high-quality sets that could be adapted to any kind of stage? No problem! Commissioning plays that showed diverse, non-white cultures in a positive light? Junior Programs can do that! Touring three companies, nationwide, with a bare-bones staff? Marry performance and a wide-ranging curriculum used by regular frontline teachers in hundreds of schools across the country? No problem. Create ballets that had children on the edge of their seats? Junior Programs can do that too! And when the necessity imposed by the impending war required them to combine three companies into one, seamlessly weaving together music, dance, and drama, with only minimal sets? Once again, no problem! In reading through the reviews and other materials, it doesn't take long to understand that their willingness to experiment, innovate, and learn was at the heart of their seven-year string of successes. Taken together, these three overlapping and interconnected commitments were fundamental to Junior Programs' story of success.

For those involved with what is now known as theater for young audiences, the questions with which Junior Programs wrestled are still very real and urgent. How best to prepare the country's young people for their role as preservers of the democratic flame? How best to stitch together the many, sometimes contradictory strands of access, inclusion, diversity, and community? How best to address deeply rooted political and social challenges, weaving artistic excellence, innovation, and respect for young audiences into an educational package designed for maximum impact? Theater for young audiences is still dedicated to addressing all these concerns. In 1936, however, the idea of using the performing arts as a solution to society's larger problems was still a somewhat amorphous gleam in the eyes of McFadden and Lancourt. There was no roadmap: they had to invent one as they went along. But luckily for the four million children who attended Junior Programs' performances, neither McFadden nor Lancourt were afraid to experiment, innovate, and learn.

A caveat before moving on: the source and date labels of many of the clippings and documents in all three sets of archival materials—the Junior Programs Scrapbooks in the Billy Rose Theatre Division of The New York Public Library, Lancourt's personal papers, and McFadden's unpublished autobiography—were either never included, have fallen out, or crumbled to a state of illegibility, often making it difficult or impossible to identify the newspapers from which a review had been clipped, or to ascertain their dates of publication. There were also numerous internal documents in the Billy Rose Junior Programs Scrapbooks collection and Lancourt's personal papers that had no specific headings. Some appeared to be publicity releases or marketing materials, others were simply a page or two of information related to a specific production or person but lacking any identification of the document from which it had come. Despite these difficulties, collectively, the materials tell a lively and compelling story. Finally, to address potential concerns as to personal bias in my assessment of Junior Programs' achievements, I have chosen to tell their story largely as it was revealed to me through the vast array of news clippings, reviews, programs, documents, and photographs, organizing and fitting quotes from the materials together like pieces of a large mosaic. Each clipping—and I have included the very few less than laudatory comments—either adds a new detail or perspective or illustrates and reinforces the consistency of their nation-wide audiences' delight—the sum-total of which adds up to their successful seven-year run.

III. THE PRODUCTIONS: PART I—THE JUNIOR PROGRAMS PLAYERS

Almost immediately, McFadden and Lancourt realized that finding performing arts material suitable for children was not going to be easy, and there is no evidence to suggest that they had any preconceived grand design for the commissioning of specific plays. Yet, when considered collectively, the five scripts commissioned by the Junior Programs Players form a remarkably comprehensive expression of the core values articulated in the company's *Credo*—to wit, *all* children, regardless of race, creed, or social and economic position, need to understand and value not only the rich diversity of the American culture, but to ensure the preservation and extension of our democracy so that it welcomes the *world's* cultural heritage. With *The Reward of the Sun God* set in an Indigenous Hopi village, with *Run, Peddler, Run* introducing issues of early Irish immigration and the oppressions of child labor, with the Brazilian setting of *The Emperor's Treasure Chest,* and a focus on China in *The Adventures of Marco Polo,* their choices provided positive portrayals of several racial and ethnic groups traditionally othered by the larger American society. And with *Doodle Dandy of the U.S.A.,* the Players directly addressed the issues related to teaching children about the importance of—and how to preserve—American democracy. The absence of a play focused on a positive view of African American children will be addressed in an upcoming section.

Given the lack of any overarching plan, one can't help but wonder how they came up with so coherent a set of choices. There was, of course, the *Credo* to guide them, but three additional influences may have been at play: McFadden's and Lancourt's personal life experiences; the racial and ethnic justice challenges of the time; and

McFadden and Lancourt's overarching sense of what was needed for the education and development of young minds.

Personal Factors

Lancourt, a first-generation Jewish American, knew what it was like to be othered. His family, having fled both religious and economic oppression, had instilled in young Saul a belief in the promise of freedom and democracy, and the hope that those freedoms would serve as a hedge against antisemitism and the myriad other forms of cultural and class discrimination.

Well past the turn of the twentieth century, New York City's Lower East Side—the first stop for many of the succeeding waves of European immigrants—was a diverse cauldron of others. The streets were filled with the sounds of different languages, different customs, different foods, and different religions. Although a shared goal was to become American, successful, upwardly mobile, and animated by a drive to make a good life for themselves and their families—made possible by the promise of democratic citizenship—there was, at the same time, an often unspoken, self-affirming belief that others had value. Certainly, this was true for the Jewish immigrants who carried that sensibility at a deep cultural and psychological level. They had always been othered, even in their countries of origin, but America offered the promise of a place that would recognize their value, a place where they could belong. As Jesse Green, current theater critic at the *New York Times*, points out, one of the things the theater does best is "to create liminal spaces that allow us to cross over into new understandings of otherness . . . [and] of all people, Jews should recognize the necessity of that." In a sense, the connection Green makes—between the ability of the performing arts to explore otherness, and the fact that it was, in some measure, the Jewish experience of having always been othered that contributed to that ability—describes the cultural sea in which Lancourt was swimming.[105]

McFadden, a Protestant, was also an immigrant, albeit of a far more affluent social and economic class. Her parents were of German and Irish ancestry, and her husband's forebears were Scots-Irish. While her parent's social and economic class may have protected her from the trials and tribulations experienced by the waves of poor Irish Catholics, it is hard to imagine she would have been sympathetic to the open discrimination and othering so many Irish Catholic and other immigrants experienced in the United States.

Thus, when taken together, it seems entirely possible that Lancourt's and McFadden's personal histories played some part in the choices they made. What they wanted the performing arts to do was to help create a level playing field—one in which those viewed by the larger society as other would finally find themselves included. This, from the perspective of the *Credo*, was a prerequisite for a successful democracy. However, for Junior Programs, inclusion was not the same as the then popular notion of assimilation. Quite the opposite. Junior Programs went to considerable lengths to show that far from wanting to erase racial, ethnic, and artistic diversity, they believed such diversity could and would enrich the American culture.

There was, however, one facet of othering that was beyond the personal experience of both McFadden and Lancourt—that based on skin color.

The Racial Justice Challenges of the Time

For people of color, the path to national belonging based on assimilation was out of reach. The color of their skin made it impossible to blend in. However, given the values made explicit in the company's *Credo,* and the growing need for nationwide unity in the buildup to WWII, it is hard to imagine that McFadden and Lancourt were not well-aware of the challenges to democracy posed by the American brand of racism. They may not have had the vocabulary we have today—of white privilege, white fragility, systemic and structural racism, appropriation and microaggressions—or the insights such a vocabulary reveals. However, the *Credo* and many of the choices McFadden and Lancourt made on behalf of Junior Programs suggest that they were aware of the need to oppose the racism embedded in the larger American culture. To do this, they would need to journey into uncharted territory, forging a path practitioners of TYA still travel today.

There are countless books detailing the history of intentional racial segregation and American immigration policy, and of the divisive and pernicious impact such policies have had on American society. A full treatment of these facets of American history is beyond the scope of this book. Nevertheless, even an overview of the oppressions faced by Black Americans, Native Americans, and Latinx and Asian American immigrants illustrates the urgent need to provide alternatives to the numerous and broadly accepted negative racial narratives.

In *Mediocre*, Ijeoma Oluo's account of Buffalo Bill's Wild West Shows lays bare the genocidal story of the relationship between the broader American culture and the Native American tribes of North America. McFadden likely didn't know that "scalping," far from being a uniquely Native American tradition, had been a European staple for two thousand years; or that the massacre of the American buffalo had been part of an intentional strategy to eliminate Indigenous peoples from the North American continent; or that the US system of national parks was created from parcels of stolen land.[106] But McFadden did know that she did not want her children to grow up believing the Hollywood myths that consistently portrayed Native Americans as bloodthirsty savages. She did not want them to believe that "the only good Indian was a dead Indian," or that Teddy Roosevelt's "violent masculinity of the West" was something to emulate.[107] Instead, as a means of countering the nation's growing internal factionalism and all-too-prevalent othering of Indigenous peoples and cultures, Junior Programs produced *The Reward of the Sun God*, a positive and admiring portrayal showing one example of a much maligned and betrayed Native American culture. It was a production respectful of the complex Hopi religion, myths, and customs. It offered a picture of the responsibilities each member of the Hopi tribe felt toward each other, and to the tribe as a whole. It depicted the reverence they felt toward their religious beliefs, and their steely, communal determination to endure and survive the most challenging privations; and it showed a culture intimately in accord with the rhythms and needs of their natural surroundings. And key to the play's success, it showed the universality of the youthful derring-do and mischief of its two young protagonists—all presented with carefully authentic costumes and correlated curriculum materials.

A second Players' production focused on yet another much maligned racial and ethnic minority, those from the countries of South America. *The Emperor's Treasure Chest* presented a positive depiction of a group of exuberant, entrepreneurial Brazilian children working together to solve the mystery of the emperor's treasure—all while tending their market stalls on the riverbanks of the bustling river port city of Pera. As in *Sun God*, the characters were attired in authentic Brazilian costumes, and the performance was punctuated with authentic songs and dances. Here, then, was Junior Programs' antidote to Hollywood's stereotypical characterization of people from Central and South America as bandits, gangsters, and lazy ne'er-do-wells. These Hollywood images and stereotypes of people of color as rapists, killers, outlaws, and loose women had become so negative that in 1922 Mexico, Honduras, and Costa Rica had banned any Hollywood film that depicted Latinx people in these ways.[108]

Like its Native American and Latinx racism, American anti-Asian hate also has a long and depressing history. Even a cursory search through the history of anti-Asian immigration policies or a quick read of "The Anti-Asian Roots of Today's Anti-Immigration Politics" offers a litany of racially based exclusions.[109] In 1875, the Page Act targeted Chinese women brought to the United States for supposedly "lewd and immoral purposes." After the Page Act, many Chinese women refused to come to the United States, and those who did were subjected to humiliating physical exams. With only a small population of women, and laws forbidding marriage outside ones' race, Chinese laborers—lured by the Gold Rush and employment building the vast network of cross-continental railroads—were unable to start families. This reinforced the image of them as irresponsible, dangerous drifters. The Chinese Exclusion Act (1882) and subsequent Geary Act (1892) extended the ban on Chinese immigration. It wasn't until 1943—ironically the year Junior Programs was forced to close—that, to ensure China's support during WWII, Chinese immigrants were permitted to obtain US citizenship. In 1907, a limit had been imposed on immigration from Japan, and these early restrictions were not repealed until 1965 after thousands of Japanese families had been summarily removed from their homes and interned in American "concentration camps" during WWII.[110]

Once again, the Junior Programs Players provided an alternative to Hollywood's view of Chinese people as cunning, servile, devious, inscrutable Orientals. With their lavish production of *The Adventures of Marco Polo,* Junior Programs depicted China, its vast and ancient culture, and its emperor, Kublai Kahn, in a positive light. As part of the play's development and the company's desire for authenticity, Lancourt did more than the usual amount of research into various aspects of China's history, enabling Junior Programs to identify specific instances of Kublai Kahn's tolerant attitude toward China's own cultural diversity. While today, such tolerance is clearly no longer the case, in *Marco Polo,* we find this spirit expressed in a scene between Kublai Khan and his advisor in which the great Khan says, "I do not want men as gifts. They are not beasts to be thrown from one place to another." In a subsequent scene, when Marco saves the emperor from a brush with death, Kublai Khan draws Marco close "so all may see how you, of one race, saved the life of one of another race. You shall be at my right hand always. Let us strive together, as people of all faiths should . . . regardless of the color of their skin, the shape of their faces, or the manner of their worship."[111]

While not specifically focused on skin color, the Players' production of *Run, Peddler, Run*, was a story depicting the early practice of indentured servitude,[112] and it offered a spirited, non-dogmatic defense of the then recent spate of child labor laws, as well as a sympathetic portrayal of two young Irish immigrants. By the late 1930s, the Depression had reduced the stream of Irish immigration to a trickle, but the othering of the primarily Catholic Irish immigrants was still very much in evidence. Catholicism had been viewed by many as incompatible with American values. There had been the anti-immigrant, anti-Catholic Bible Riots of 1844 in Philadelphia over how religion should be presented in public schools, and a series of anti-Irish secret societies had morphed into the anti-immigration Know-Nothings political movement in the mid-to late-nineteenth century.[113] This anti-Irish stance included the common refrain in help wanted ads, "No Irish Need Apply!" And popular Hollywood actors such as James Cagney, in films such as *The Public Enemy* (1931), still branded the Irish as gangsters and villains. Similarly, although the popular author James T. Farrell created the character of Studs Lonigan as a victim of the social and economic excesses of American capitalism, his series of novels portrayed Lonigan's descent into "cruelty, violence and moral degeneration," a depiction that for decades became the prevailing image of the Irish in the popular American culture.[114]

This brief overview of four of the Players' commissioned works brings us face to face with the question, "Why was there no Players production providing a positive story of Black children?" I found this absence deeply troubling. Black Americans have experienced centuries of systemic racism, exclusion, oppression, lynchings and other forms of violence. Extensive recent research, within the frame of what is now termed "critical race theory" (CRT) has pulled back the curtain on the literal and intentional whitewashing of American history and its institutions, and on the ways in which it has permeated every aspect of America's social, economic, and political life. Why, then, was there no "Black" play added to the Players repertoire?

It was also striking that, in all the Junior Programs' materials in the Billy Rose Theatre Division's collection, or in Lancourt's and McFadden's personal papers, there was no mention of whether children of color attended Junior Programs' performances.

There is a photograph of a youthful New York audience with one child who appears to be Black, but at that time, even in the North, schools were segregated, and none of the reviews or materials mentioned anything about the racial composition of Junior Programs' audiences. Even if segregated, were Black children able to sit in an auditorium balcony or the last few rows? Were they simply not invited, or not allowed to attend? Could they have been included? And if not, what would it have taken to include them? While I was not able to answer these specific questions, further research did offer three possible explanations for the lack of a play focused on Black children, and it is likely that all three were in play as Junior Programs considered the scripts they wanted to commission. First, was the widespread racial animus toward people of color, and Black people in particular. Second, because of this racial animus, there were the very real problems posed by interracial casting. In some states, there were laws or traditions that forbid a person of color on stage from even touching a white person in any way.[115] Third, there were the very real dangers inherent in any attempt to tour companies with a mixed cast, especially, but not only, in the South—and it would have been especially dangerous to tour with a production that might be interpreted as challenging the practice of racial segregation and Black inferiority.

Current works such as Nikole Hannah-Jones's *1619 Project* and Ibram X. Kendi's *Stamped from the Beginning: The Definitive History of Racist Ideas in America* document the sordid and shameful history of enslavement and segregation in the United States.[116] According to Carol Anderson's *White Rage,* racism during the 1930s and 1940s was virulent, blatant, and, in many places, unchecked and unapologetic. She provides a detailed litany of the ways in which Southern whites were determined to maintain the racist, anti-Black status quo, and the brutal and vicious lengths to which they went to counter even the smallest effort to implement any change in that status quo. Furthermore, Anderson makes it clear that the trigger for white rage was and is "black advancement."[117] Violence and the threat of violence was ever present. Lynchings continued to occur in the South during the 1930s and 1940s; schools were unapologetically segregated, even in the North. In the South and Southwest, Blacks were sometimes allowed to attend various public events such as a country fair, but only on "Colored Day." Railroads and other forms of public transportation were segregated; hotels, motels, restaurants, gas stations, water fountains, and public toilets were segregated; and well into the 1950s, there were ten thousand "sundown towns" in almost every part of the country.[118] Racial profiling by police in many parts of the country, especially, but by no means exclusively, in the South, was common. According to *The Negro Motorist Green Book*, "driving while Black" was at best anxiety producing or humiliating, and at worst downright dangerous and possibly life-threatening. The *Green Book* offers several examples of White Southern vandalism practiced on Black automobiles, just to "put them in their place," though the consequences could also be far more dire.[119]

Errol G. Hill and James V. Hatch, in *A History of African American Theatre*, provide an impressively exhaustive picture of the anti-Black racism rampant in the 1930s American theater world. After World War I, blackface minstrelsy, an extremely popular form of vaudeville entertainment that caricatured the songs and dances of slavery, began to die out. But it wasn't until the 1940s that the "NAACP demanded that they blacken up no more."[120] "Broadway policy in 1925 was to have white actors play "colored" roles in blackface in order to avoid mixed casts."[121] And if Black characters were portrayed on stage, it was primarily as lowlifes, vulgar, lewd, stupid, simple-minded, or passive.[122] Aspiring Black actors were not accepted into professional training programs, and even Black vaudevillians performed in blackface. One prominent Harlem vaudevillian, "Pigmeat" Markham, commented that "without his blackface he felt naked on stage."[123] In 1922, when Charles Gilpin, one of the few well-known Black actors, was invited to an awards dinner honoring individuals who had best served theater that year, members of the sponsoring organization, the New York Drama League, balked at "inviting a 'Negro' to the awards dinner." Gilpin ultimately agreed to a compromise: he would appear and speak, but he would not stay for the dinner.[124] In the early 1930s, for a production of the popular Black play *The Green Pastures* in Washington, DC, the nation's capital, no Black people were allowed in the audience.[125] When granting the Federal Theater Project the rights to his play *Haiti*, white Southern journalist and playwright William Du Bois (not to be confused with W. E. B. Du Bois) "stipulated that no white person should touch a black person in performance."[126] In Birmingham, Alabama, the FTP's Negro Unit "performed under extreme racist restrictions . . . [to wit] *no plays could challenge the complete segregation of the races* [emphasis added]."[127] The military was still a segregated institution, and it wasn't until 1942, with Irving Berlin's *This is the Army*, "a musical extravaganza of over 300, performed entirely by army personnel . . . [that we find] the first integrated unit in the army."[128] Even in 1946, the Broadway play, *On Whitman Avenue* "explored the powerful monied interests with a stake in maintaining the separation of the races, with one character exclaiming, "I don't know a nice way of saying you can fight for your country, but you can't live in it.""[129] Hill and Hatch do document the few scattered examples of mixed-race casting, but in the grand scheme of theatrical productions, during the first decades of the twentieth century, mixed casts were few and far between, and such productions were largely, if not entirely, local.[130]

Overall, anti-Black racism in the world of theatrical entertainment mirrored the situation in American society at large. As a touring company whose performers often spent twenty to thirty weeks of each year traveling in automobiles and trucks on back roads, frequently at night, with long periods of those tours spent crisscrossing the Southern states, the realities described in the *Green Book* could not be ignored. It doesn't take much imagination to realize the very real dangers a mixed-raced touring company would have faced. With multiple Black performers, the company would have been unable to stop to eat or go to the toilet. Gas stations might refuse to service their vehicles. Finding any kind of decent overnight accommodation would have posed insurmountable problems. In an era when many rural homes didn't even have telephones, an encounter with an unfriendly local sheriff could have been life-threatening for any Black or multi-racial group of performers. We have only to remember the unpunished murders of Chaney, Schwerner, and Goodman, the three civil rights workers committed to challenging Southern racism in 1964, to know that a mixed-race cast in a play holding a mirror up to anti-Black racism would have posed very real dangers. Given the picture painted by Hill and Hatch, with the chilling directive that "no plays could challenge the complete segregation of the races,"[131] and with Junior Programs' *Credo* making it unlikely that they would offer a play about Black children performed by white actors in blackface—and with a long list of bookings in Southern auditoriums—the fact that Junior Programs did not commission a play depicting Black children in a non-racist light becomes less surprising, though no less distressing.

That said, there may have been one Black actress in the company. In recounting to our family various stories related to touring with Junior Programs, my father sometimes referred to an incident in Washington, DC. The Players had taken the train from New York, and he mentioned a Black actress who had had to travel in a separate section of the train. Arriving in DC, she went off to a separate hotel some distance from the one in which the rest of the company was staying. One evening, she became ill. My father refused to send her back to her distant hotel alone, and insisted she take his room instead. To the hotel management's extreme consternation, he spent the night on a chair in the hotel lobby. Apparently, the manager had not wanted the scene which would have ensued had he attempted to forcibly remove her from my father's room. The story offers a tiny hint as to the kinds of problems that could occur had the company tried to tour through the small towns and byways of America at that time with a mixed-race cast.

Unfortunately, in telling the story, my father never mentioned the play's title, the actress's name, or the role she played. However, as far as I have been able to determine, Janto, the young, enslaved tavern girl in *Run, Peddler, Run*, is the only specifically Black role in any of the Junior Programs' productions. So, it is possible he may have been referring to Virginia True, the actress who played the role of Janto. I have been unable to ascertain Ms. True's race, and to cloud the issue further, in a review of the play at the Mary Washington Lyceum in Fredericksburg, Virginia, George St. Julian notes that as a northerner, True had to "brush up on her Negro accent before she does many more performances in the South" (*Free Lance Star*, Feb 7, 1940). Did such a comment mean that Ms. True was not Black, or did it mean that as a northern Black, she needed to work on her southern Black accent? At this remove, it is impossible to know!

What Do Young Minds Need?

Junior Programs was not the only company interested in using the performing arts to both entertain and address social, political, and economic issues. The FTP also embraced these issues. But there were several significant differences in the way Junior Programs approached these issues. For example, instead of focusing on the dark underbelly of capitalism's failures, they offered their youthful audience a series of positive views of children from the various communities of others. These portrayals were designed to help their young audiences see the young characters in the plays as not so very different from themselves, and to show the cultural, racial, and ethnic differences as interesting and fun—in other words, to *normalize* the other. That differences were not only interesting, but stimulating to the imagination was reenforced with each succeeding play. This in turn laid the groundwork for the inclusion necessary in a true democracy—the sense that all kinds of people belonged, and that everyone was not only entitled to participate, but that in order to *be* a democracy, everyone needed to be able to participate.

The final Players' production—Junior Programs' answer to the question, "How do you teach children about democracy?"—was *Doodle Dandy of the U.S.A.* Set in the imaginary town of Springville, and making use of folksy song and dance, *Doodle Dandy* illustrated, with humor and rollicking metaphor, the key characteristics of democracy: a community of working and middle-class citizens acting in concert to protect and ensure individual and collective freedoms. The script's mix of fantasy and reality, infused with a "we're-all-in-this-together" spirit, made it clear that a sense of inclusion, community, and collaborative collective action were key to defending against the threats to liberty and democracy posed by fascism and dictatorship. As the play's author, Lancourt also indicated in the twists and turns of the plot that *the children themselves had a significant role to play in protecting democracy.* For example, when the would-be dictator of Springville, Humphrey Dumphrey, tries to close the town's newspaper, it is one of the high school students who gathers all the other students together to put on a show demonstrating what the town must do to rid itself of Dumphrey and his determination to rob them of their civil liberties. This student "play within the play" becomes the turning point in arousing the whole town to fight back and preserve their freedoms.[132]

One could read about these problems in a textbook or article, but how much more powerful and exciting to be drawn into the stories on stage - to *experience,* even vicariously, the emotional as well as intellectual impact of an alternative way of learning about the world. With this Deweyan approach, *Doodle Dandy* directly addressed the deepening political need to solidify America's commitment to democracy, thereby strengthening and expanding the sense of national and international unity required to win a war. And with its story of successful collective action on the part of the whole town of Springville, with its songs of freedom, and dances of liberty and collective action, *Doodle Dandy* also served to draw the other four Players productions into a broader frame, one in which the normalizing of racial, ethnic, religious, and class diversity became a prerequisite to becoming a full-fledged democracy.

Junior Programs, anchored as it was in its role as an educational and cultural resource, and as a partner in a broad network of local school systems at all grade levels, framed their plays in a way that emphasized the positive aspects of the country's diverse cultures rather than the stereotypical negatives. Junior Programs' productions also consistently provided stories which embodied an aspirational set of values, beliefs, and behaviors congruent with the characteristics of democracy—stories into which all children could easily step despite their differences. In part consciously, and in part unconsciously, McFadden and Lancourt seem to have created a strategy that embodied their *Credo*. Rather than using their productions to expose, ridicule, and critique the numerous impediments to the American Dream—as the FTP did—Junior Programs' productions offered child-centered stories which spoke to, amplified, articulated, and supported a foundational set of America's social and cultural aspirations. This aspirational vision embodied the ideals of equality, fairness, and fair play, of community responsibility and solidarity, of fighting for justice, and of a positive view of racial and cultural diversity that fostered inclusivity. *Doodle Dandy* also made clear the preciousness of democracy, and the need to continually work together to preserve and extend its liberties and freedoms to everyone. According to *Doodle*, it was a fight that would never be done, and one that would always need the next generation to guard against democracy's demise.

It was this expansive perspective that appears to have resonated so deeply with the Junior Programs audiences and kept them coming back for more. It was this positive spirit that animated the Players choice of plays, each commissioned to introduce and bring to life various facets of the American Dream in a way easily absorbed and digested by children of all ages and all socioeconomic backgrounds—all embodied in stories full of action, derring-do, song, dance, and humor. In aggregate, what these five plays sought was to normalize the other, to bring different cultural strands together—not by erasing the differences, as often happened in pursuit of assimilation, but by valuing each difference and showing how it could be woven into a richer, more powerful American tapestry. Each production depicted a specific set of cultural differences in a positive light, while at the same time emphasizing shared human traits of youthful exuberance, adventurousness, curiosity, risk-taking, determination, and goodwill. Each of the plays also emphasized the power and importance of community, a theme entirely in keeping with Dewey's experiential educational philosophy, as well as with Junior Programs' belief in centering community engagement.

This essentially creative approach to social and political issues—of building up rather than just tearing down, of using the performing arts as an educational catalyst, and as partners to and resources for frontline teachers—was one of Junior Programs major innovations. The benefits to be derived from this positive approach are supported by current research into the dynamics of commitment and mobilization for social change. Many of these current studies suggest that generating active engagement is often best achieved by presenting a positive view of a desirable future, *before* focusing on the distressing current conditions in need of remedy. Potential supporters often shy away from problems they feel are overwhelming, but they are more likely to engage if they are inspired by a picture of a more desirable future they can help create.[133]

With these five productions, Junior Programs, forged the beginnings of an identifiable path leading toward a healthy more actualized democracy. Their approach encompassed both *intentionality* and *serendipity*. The intentionality was influenced in part by their sense of optimism, born of their belief in the potential of future generations, and in part by their strong belief in the performing arts ability to reinvent itself, to become a significant force shaping the nation's future citizens rather than remaining solely a source of entertainment. The remainder of this chapter provides a more detailed description and assessments of the five dramas commissioned by the Junior Programs Players. For each production, if a script was not available, I have pieced together the story of the play from available reviews, company press releases, and performance programs. Audience reactions are characterized from a broad range of newspaper reviews and articles, and I have included any "behind the scenes" information available about the production itself. I have also provided an overview of the specific social and political events and concerns to which each of the plays responded.

THE PLAYS

The Reward of the Sun God [134]

"'Reward of Sun God' Play All Children Will Like"
(Kinston, North Carolina *Free Press*, February 2, 1940)

Junior Programs Players Announcement Flyer for *Reward of the Sun God*
(Lancourt's personal papers)

The earliest of Junior Programs' commissioned plays, prepared during the 1937–38 season, was *The Reward of the Sun God*. There was a logic to this choice if we remember that Junior Programs owed its founding to one of McFadden's pet dissatisfactions—her aversion to the violent "shoot 'em up," cowboys and Indians fare pumped out by Hollywood in a seemingly endless stream. These films had been, and continued to be, formative for millions of American children—planting in their conscious and unconscious minds the notion that in the endless epic contest between good and evil, the white man was always the good guy, and the "Red Indian" was always the bad guy.

With the commissioning of *The Reward of the Sun God*, written by a well-known musician, John Louw Nelson—and, in keeping with the Junior Programs *Credo* of helping American children learn about and value cultures other than their own—the Junior Programs' Players offered a much-needed corrective to the Eurocentric view of Native Americans as primitive and savage. The *American Women's Association Bulletin* (Mar 11, 1937) noted that Junior Programs productions "are definitely designed to give the children an awareness of the attractive and interesting characteristics, histories and civilizations of other countries and races. They are presently working on a new play . . . based on a legend of the Hopi Indians. Its story of 'The Reward of the Sun God' will give children quite a different picture of American Indians than the one most children have—a picture associated with scalping and war whoops." According to the Manitowoc, Wisconsin, *Herald Times* (Feb 3, 1940), the "Manitowoc children got a new angle on 'Let's play Injun' . . . Instead of the typical 'blood and thunder' children think of in connection with Indians, there was, in 'The Reward of the Sun God,' the poetry and religion and lore that more truly typifies a people." The Hartford, Connecticut, *Times* (March 4, 1940) called it a fascinating play, a tale of two Hopi children full of authenticity and psychological insights.

While this sense of "authenticity" would not pass muster by today's standards—it was, after all, written by a white man—its positive perspective was highly innovative for its time, a result made possible by the playwright's eight-year sojourn living among the Hopi tribe of Southwest Arizona. Nelson was a former Director of Research for the Museum of American Indians in New York, and his book *Rhythm for Rain*, which served as the foundation for the play, is a chronicle of Hopi culture, religion, history, artifacts, music, and dance. It tells of the historic and devastating three-year drought during the latter part of the nineteenth century that almost annihilated the tribe. It is the "story of the Masked Gods performing dance after dance in a vain attempt to bring the rain; of children bartered for corn and water; of a thrilling struggle with hunger, thirst, pain and fear."[135] According to Nelson, it was not just the external drama of the drought that he found compelling. He also felt the deep sense of epic tragedy as they embraced their faith in the ancient gods—the symbol of life and hope to an entire race, the amassed inheritance of a thousand years.[136]

Rhythm for Rain was admired by multiple news sources. The *Saturday Review of Literature* (n.d.) commented, "It is the breath quickening record of man's struggle with his environment." The *New York Herald Tribune* (n.d.) called it, "Extraordinary in its beauty and compelling power." Praises continued in additional news outlets: "as American a book as has been written in a long time" (*Newark News*, n.d.); "a moving story of humanity," (*Dallas Morning News*, n.d.); "glows with beauty and color," (*Brooklyn Eagle*, n.d.); "John Louw Nelson has put a beating heart into the Indian and has made him vitally alive" (*New York Sun*, n.d.). Today, many of the adjectives used by the press to describe Native Americans (i.e., exotic, romantic, etc.), or the fact that it was a white man, who "put a beating heart into the Indian," would justifiably cause an outcry. However, given the pervasiveness of the negative images pumped out by Hollywood at that time, the efforts of Nelson and Junior Programs to understand and value the Hopi culture on its own terms was an important step in shifting the dominant narrative to one that would legitimate cultural diversity and belonging as an important American social value. It also made manifest Junior Programs' belief that theater could, and should, be used as an educational modality capable of helping to form not only children's understanding of those different from themselves, but to view those differences from a positive perspective.

Nelson, admired by Mrs. Oliver Harriman and Princess Pignatelli of the Junior Programs National Board, had been primarily a composer and concert artist.[137] His interest in Hopi rituals began with observing their rhythmic drum music, the pounding of their dancing feet, and their singing. He was drawn by what he heard as "echoes tapping from their ancient past." He describes them as "an insistent message summoning forth something in him as well as a calling together of the rain clouds for the mating of sky and earth." He was awed by the "masked men leaping in prayer . . . [by] the sweat oozing out of the tiny eye-holes of their masks . . . [by] their blistering feet on the stove-hot rock of the mesa crest . . . and [he] had felt its [the rain's] driving force sweeping out of the whitened east. In the face of such elemental faith and victory, what could he do but accept the sincerity and . . . courage of men who challenged the summer-burned sun and defied the up-thrust heat of the seared dry sand."[138]

These sensibilities engendered in him a deep and abiding respect for Hopi culture and its *kachinas* (Hopi gods). It is important to understand how at odds this respect was with the then-prevailing American view of Indigenous peoples. While moviegoers absorbed Hollywood's derisive stereotypes, they were likely unaware that there also existed a pervasive legal framework underpinning the view of Indians as savages—savages to whom the protections of the Constitution simply did not apply. In a *New York Times* article, Maggie Blackhawk explains that the doctrine of Manifest Destiny articulated one of America's first "forever wars," with General Andrew Jackson claiming that even "the laws of war did not apply to conflicts with savages." In 1892, Captain Richard Henry Pratt, founder of the Carlisle Indian Industrial School, justified the existence of the so-called boarding schools, little more than military-run detention camps in which Indigenous children were separated from their families, in order to "kill the Indian in him and save the man." Blackhawk goes on to describe how Native Americans were jailed for practicing their religions and were forced to become Christians. In the Supreme Court case *United States v. Rogers* (1846), Justice Taney articulated what became the Plenary Power Doctrine in which the United States could wield power over the "unfortunate race" without any constitutional limits. And this "longest war" is not over.[139] It seems unlikely that either McFadden or Lancourt knew of the complex legal infrastructure that kept the prevailing negative assumptions in place, but Nelson's positive and respectful view of the Hopi culture and religion was ideally suited to the purpose expressed in the company's *Credo*.

As would prove to be the case in its other productions, Junior Programs offered its positive perspective without any hint of preaching. The publicity for the play simply bills it as the "Adventures of a Hopi Boy and Girl," —a brother and sister—with whom any child could identify. As one reviewer from the Manitowoc, Wisconsin, *Herald Times* (Feb 3, 1940) tells us:

> The adults in the audience...noted with enthusiasm the unusually fine make-up, dramatic artistry, [and] the fine stage mechanics. But to the children it simply added up to a 'swell play'... Particularly appealing to the children was the petite *katchina*, or Hopi god, Kokozhori, played by Vi de Camp. Most of the youngsters who saw the play probably spent yesterday evening shouting "Kokozhori" to the accompaniment of much arm waving... [and] while the youngsters make enough noise to deafen ordinary ears before the play starts... the moment the curtains part there is complete and immediate silence. The children become absorbed in the play... And certainly... do not lack appreciation. It is easy to see... why artists are willing to devote their talents to children. We have seen grown-ups laugh and snicker... at entirely the wrong moments... But not the children. They sit tongue-tied and wide-eyed and appreciate everything that is presented to them.

While no script has come to light, I was able to locate a rough draft of Nelson's story, *Reward of the Sun God,* complete with his handwritten notes and edits. Coupled with the Kinston, North Carolina *Free Press* review (Feb 2, 1940) I have synthesized a synopsis of the story.[140]

Set in Mish-ong-novi, a Hopi village high on a mountain top in Arizona, we meet Hoya, a young Hopi boy standing on the roof of the sacred *kiva* (a large circular, underground room used for spiritual ceremonies). He is boasting to his sister, Mana, of his skill in the Hopi corncob racing game. During one demonstration of his prowess, the corncob accidentally falls through the rooftop opening of the sacred *kiva*. Children, however, are forbidden to enter the *kiva*. As the two siblings nervously discuss what to do, their conversation quickly establishes the importance and centrality of the *kachinas* to the Hopi way of life. But, as with all children, the forbidden is irresistible. Hoya climbs into the *kiva* to retrieve his corncob. When he reappears, holding something behind his back, Mana cannot resist a peek at what he has hidden. It is a green-headed mask with black wings—the image of the Crow Mother *Kachina*. Hoya slips the mask on, then fearfully removes it. He tells Mana that having found this head and many others in the *kiva*, he thinks that perhaps when the *kachinas* come to dance in the village, they aren't the real gods, but only Hopi men wearing these masks. Mana is frightened by his blasphemy, but her curiosity gets the better of her, and together, they begin to imitate the ceremonial dances they have observed. They are interrupted by the appearance of their older sister, Yampove. She scolds them, and tries to stop their dancing, warning them that they will bring the wrath of the gods to the village, to their family, and to their mother! Hoya protests that the gods wouldn't punish a whole village just because *he* has done something wrong. Yampove reminds him that the Hopi Way is that everything is shared—the good and the bad.

Suddenly, they hear the voices of the village chief, Mongwi, and their uncle, Letaiyo. Yampove throws her cloak over the masks. The two men, intent on entering the *kiva,* fail to see the children. A few moments later, greatly agitated, Mongwi climbs out. Distraught, the chief cries out, and many villagers come running. Mongwi tells them some sacred objects are missing, and he is to blame. "But you've done no wrong," Letaiya says. Mongwi responds that, as chief, he is responsible for everything that happens: "If one of my people has done wrong, it is I who am at fault."[141] In great consternation, the villagers leave the square. Terrified Hoya quickly returns the masks. The chief returns with their uncle and their mother, who urge him to look again for the masks. He is old; perhaps his eyesight is failing! He and Letaiya descend into the *kiva* and find the mask. A prayer of thanksgiving is said, but Hoya is beside himself with regret.

Yampove prays to the gods to be lenient: "They are still so young: their lives are like green shoots of corn that are just beginning to reach for the sun. There is wisdom in your rays, great god of sun . . . there is gentleness and mercy, oh brother of the clouds, in your arms that cradle the rain . . . let these two earn forgiveness for what they have done."[142] But how? Helping their mother with her chores is a start, but when they hear that the Sun God will visit their village the following day, fear overtakes them. The next day, the Sun God comes. His huge round mask is painted many colors, and his bright red fringe of hair is like the rays of the sun pointing in every direction. He makes four marks on the wall of their house—a sign of protection for the year to come, but the wall is old and cracked, and it begins to crumble. Distraught, the children redouble their efforts to be helpful, and pray at a little altar for Ko-ko-zho-ri. Finally, spring arrives, but the earth is parched, and the old chief calls everyone together, telling them, "We have always wanted to live in this land that others call the desert because here we can be near our gods . . . Now these gods . . . are angry because of something some one of us has done . . . [but] we must have faith in our hearts as long as there is life in our bodies."[143] But for months, there is no rain and the people become weak from hunger. Hoya and Mana say their own prayers to a small cloud overhead, but instead of bringing rain, the cloud disappears, and they are sure that this is punishment for their transgression. One day, they see the spotted body and black mask of Ko-ko-zho-ri, the Corn God. They ask for his help. He tells them if they are brave, they must go to the Land of the Shadow Spring where the Sun God sleeps and ask his forgiveness. Convinced that the drought is their fault, they follow him to the home of the Sun God, green and lush with grasses and food. However, before they can meet the Sun God, they must pass four tests. The two children passed the first three tests—for swiftness, courage, and strength. The final test, set by the Crow Mother, requires Hoya to create a song powerful and beautiful enough to bring the Sun God out of his house. After a few moments, Hoya begins to sing and dance, and Mana dances with him as any good Hopi girl would do.

> In the north a snake lies in the sun
> Holding with his tail
> The rattle to call the clouds.
> Snake of the north
> Wake to my beating drum
> Tell yellow clouds
> The Hopi must have rain.

A yellow light glows for a moment in the north as Hoya continues to sing.

> In the east
> A bear lies sleeping
> Deep in a cave
> Within the mother earth.
> Bear of the east
> Wake to my beating drum
> Tell the white clouds
> The Hopi must have rain.

Handing his little drum to one of the Mud Head gods and stretching his arms wide like the wings of an eagle soaring through the sky, Hoya begins the Hopi Eagle Dance.

> In the south
> An eagle is flying
> High in the sky
> On his journey to the sun
> Eagle of south
> Fly to my beating drum
> Tell the red clouds
> The Hopi must have rain.
> In the west
> A deer is leaping
> High on the slope
> Of the mountain of the gods
> Deer of the west
> Leap to my beating drum
> Tell the blue clouds
> The Hopi must have rain.[144]

When Hoya sings the final verse, *kachinas* of all sizes, shapes and colors come crowding into the open in front of the Sun God's house. Photographs of this scene show the elaborate costumes created for the production, based on a close study of Nelson's extensive collection of authentic *kachina* dolls. Finally, as Hoya's voice dies away, the door of the house is flung open, a flame of light bursts forth, and the Sun God appears. As he comes toward the children, he holds up his staff, and instantly the voices of all the *kachinas* are stilled.

> You have done well, Hopi boy and Hopi girl, and so you have earned the reward of the Sun God. My gift to you is the gift of joy, the joy of living in a happy land where the sun shines gently with a father's smile . . . you have made me forget my anger. Tell your people that now they can dance with faith in my will to send the clouds . . .

> Yet much time must pass before this corn may grow, and I have not forgotten that your people are starving . . . I shall send food . . . at the very instant that my sun rays touch the top of the door, but if any woman fails to clean her house. . . then instead of food, she will find it filled with cactus.[145]

Hoya and Mana stare at the great God of the Sky and see him rise higher and higher through the water of the Shadow Spring. Ko-ko-zho-ri tells them he will guide them back to their village. But when the two children climb out of the *kiva* no one believes their story. Hoya shows them the sacred gourd given him by the Mother of the Cloud, and tells them they must all clean their houses before sunrise. Finally, the villagers agree, and as day dawns, there is food and water in abundance in every house. Soon Hoya and Mana spot a little cloud, and they shout for everyone to do the Hopi Rain Dance. The cloud comes closer, grows bigger and darker, and they hear the Voice of the Storm:

> Let the smoke
> That is our breath of prayer
> Rise with our faith
> Let the meal
> that is the soul of mother earth
> Tell of our need.

They all toss pinches of sacred cornmeal toward the cloud, and Hoya pours water from the Sacred Gourd given to him during his stay in the Shadow Spring. Thunder crashes, and it begins to rain, sweeping from the sky into the faces of the Hopi men and women as they repeat the chant: "We have rain."[146]

The play concludes on an upbeat note: the children and their community have faced a daunting challenge and won the day. Further, in addition to advancing the notion that children have agency, *The Reward of the Sun God* fulfills Oskar Eustis' description of the three things theater has to offer. First, the story on stage challenges the prevailing idea of Indigenous people as "savages." Second, it is about a community, and creates in the audience a sense of community; and third, it evokes an empathic connection to the struggle of the children to be both the children they are while at the same time, learning how to become responsible adults.

There is conflicting information as to who directed the production of *The Reward of the Sun God*. One undated program in Lancourt's personal papers lists Percival Vivian, a British actor/director, and a second program lists Charlotte Chorpenning, artistic director of Chicago's Goodman Children's Theater.[147] Chorpenning was well known for writing plays focused on characters with whom her youthful audiences could easily identify, and, like the Junior Programs productions, she had a reputation for never talking down to her audience. An untitled page from Lancourt's personal papers, taken from what appears to be a Goodman Children's Theater statement about their work, comments that a child's personality is dependent on their life experience, and that continued exposure to varied plays, attractively produced and acted, serve to increase and vary a child's emotional experience. This allows them to "see through to the end experiences which might prove detrimental in actual life." Plays can "vicariously enlarge a child's circle of acquaintants, stimulate, and strengthen their sense of beauty, creativity, and imaginative abilities, and develop a readiness to accept and resist a variety of situations they would not normally encounter." The Goodman statement goes on to say, "two things are very important: that these plays be not emasculated, that they be vigorous and call on the children to face heavy odds, and second, it is also important that none of these crises leave them in fear and avoidance complexes. For that reason, all our plays at the Goodman see to it that all stirring and challenging moments are immediately followed by relaxing ones, either through beauty or laughter."[148] While the identity of *The Reward of the Sun God's* director remains unclear, Chorpenning's philosophy of children's theater was clearly compatible with that expressed in the Junior Programs *Credo*.

With the caveat that the twenty-first-century conversation regarding authenticity and cultural appropriation differs in significant ways from that of the mid-1930s, the production of *Reward of the Sun God* also provided an uncommon degree of authenticity—a goal that was to become a hallmark of Junior Programs' productions. While Kenneth MacClelland, another white man, was responsible for the scenic design, the costumes were designed by Nelson's wife who had access to his extensive collection of authentic *kachina* masks, dolls, and other Hopi clothing and artifacts. According to the *Times* (Hartford, CT, March 4, 1940), the masks, costumes, and properties used in the play were all personally supervised by the author to ensure authenticity, and many of the pieces used were from Mr. Nelson's collection or were accurate reproductions. The Hopi dances, while perhaps not as authentic as the costumes, were choreographed by Irene Marmein, a highly respected member of an avant-garde vaudeville dance group, the Marmein Dancers.[149]

In essence, then, *The Reward of the Sun God* tested a template for youthful drama that would establish the Junior Programs Players productions as a new and successful approach to children's theater. Not only did it offer a compelling, empathetic, and positive story of a widely stigmatized culture, it was a story with which any child could identify, and one that reached far beyond the desire to simply entertain its audience. It also managed to avoid a dogmatic or didactic "message" that could be construed as propaganda, while at the same time using the dramatic form to share a great deal of information about Hopi values and culture. It also set a new standard for authenticity and production quality, as well as a respectful and increasingly sophisticated approach to understanding the needs of child development. This was exemplified by Chorpenning's philosophy stressing the expansion of a child's range of lived experience through appropriately challenging situations, carefully coupled with the emotional supports required to absorb and internalize the situations in a positive way.[150] The continued development of this template, and each of its several characteristics, is evident in the productions that followed.

Run, Peddler, Run[151]

"2,000 WITNESS 'RUN, PEDDLER, RUN,' DRAMA—Wild Laughter, Shrieks, Heard As Pupils See Play"

(Ogden City, Utah, *Examiner*, January 21, 1941)

Run, Peddler, Run, continued Junior Programs' focus on the underlying theme of the other, in this instance, the ethnic and religious othering of the Irish immigrants. Despite the play's setting in the American colonial period—well before the mid-nineteenth-century Irish potato famine created an enormous wave of Irish immigration—by identifying the young hero and heroine as Irish immigrants, the story connects the audience to the history of othering faced by later waves of Irish immigration. The play also gently introduced the audience to two forms of child labor: indentured servitude and enslavement. For the most part, indentured servants were white adults (arriving either of their own free will or to work off a criminal sentence), but there were numerous instances in which a parent would "bind" or indenture their child to a colonial resident in the hope of a better life for their offspring once the period of indenture was over. The play's eleven-year-old Irish heroine, Annie Pattison, sent to an uncle in America who never comes to collect her, falls into this category. For reasons already explored, Junior Programs did not directly address the issue of African American enslavement, but by presenting both indentured servitude and enslavement in the context of child labor, *Run, Peddler, Run* underscored the growing need to consider children's developmental needs as future citizens of a democracy rather than simply as fodder for the industrial labor force.

Junior Programs Players Announcement Flyer for *Run, Peddler, Run*
(Lancourt's personal papers)

Paradoxically, the genesis of *Run, Peddler, Run* offers an example of how a rich array of resources—the kind Junior Programs' CCSUs were designed to provide to teachers—would enhance and deepen a child's educational experience. The result of a year-long project by a group of fourth-grade students from Rosemary Junior School in Greenwich, Connecticut, their educational explorations led to the development of the play. Mrs. Katherine Center, the Rosemary Junior School fourth-grade teacher described the process of the play's development. It all began when she undertook a project on town life in early America for her squirmy nine-year-old students. "There simply wasn't any material to be found accurate enough and detailed enough for the children to understand the period . . . I had to go out and find it." A friend, the "wife of the Superintendent of Schools in Groton, Conn. . . . introduced her to the musty records, yellowed with age, in the handwriting of clerks dead two hundred years."[152] She goes on to tell us, "My fourth-grade children run a Post Office for the school, selling stamps and delivering mail, so learning the history of the Post Office had real meaning for them. Because the Old Post Road wends its way through our town, we started . . . by imagining what the country was like . . . before there were any large cities or paved roads. We read letters describing the difficulties travellers [sic] had getting through the underbrush and across rivers . . . The children were permitted to pretend they were travellers [sic] in those times. One child decided to start a ferry, another became a tavern keeper. Then came questions, 'Did they really have ferries? Did they have taverns?' These questions sent us to books for accurate information."[153]

In addition to validating the existence of ferries and taverns, the students began to informally construct and act out pieces of a story. They learned, for example, that a tavern keeper's wife would provide food for the travelers. That discovery led to finding out what kind of food would be served, and then, in a home economics class, to the actual making of bread, butter, and hasty pudding. They read *Old Time Schools and School Books* by Clifton Johnson (Macmillan Company, 1917), which gave a picture of what schools were like in early America, and that it "wasn't considered necessary for girls to learn to write . . . their chief schooling, other than learning to read, was learning to cook, spin, dye, make candles, and soap, etc. They . . . experimented with all these hand processes, and this [hands-on] work brought forth great sympathy for the little 'bound-out' girl at the tavern."

Old Post Bags by Alvin F. Harlow (Appleton & Company, 1928) made it clear why the road was named the Post Road, and soon a Post Rider became a character

III. THE PRODUCTIONS: PART I—THE JUNIOR PROGRAMS PLAYERS 79

in their play. They took a trip along the Post Road which made the hills, streams, and stone markers with which the Post Rider had to contend more real. Questions led to further exploration: "If it was so hard to travel by land, why didn't they go by boat?" This raised the question of trade. "Where did they go? What did they carry? What money did they use?" They read diaries (Joshua Hempstead of New London, Connecticut) about shipping candles and horses to Barbados and bringing salt and molasses in return. A ship captain soon became a character in the play. After reading *Hawkers and Walkers in Early America* by Richardson Wright (J.B. Lippincott Company, 1927), which included an "account of two brothers and their sister coming over from Ireland and making and peddling tinware [sic] . . . an itinerant peddler appears as a character. A law that peddlers had to pay a tax when they entered Connecticut . . . intrigued the children" and became a reason to include an encounter between the Peddler and the Constable.[154]

The students also discovered that the tavernkeeper's wife probably had a bound-out girl to help her. Their drama teacher, Charlotte Perry, a well-known figure in the theater and dance world, found a book, *Bound Girl of Cobble Hill* by Lois Lenski, which told of how poor people, many of whom were adolescents, could be bound-out to work off the cost of their passage from England.[155] "Bound children were expected to obey faithfully, and, for doing work often equivalent to that of an adult, received no compensation other than their keep." (*Morning Star*, Wilmington, NC, n.d.). As the class explored the customs and mores of early-eighteenth-century colonial life, issues related to early immigration and the hardships of indentured servitude became part of their investigation. The Junior Programs marketing materials and several newspaper reviews specifically referenced the students' genuine concern for the difficulties and hardships experienced by a bound girl forced to work at an exhausting and extremely unpleasant job. Given that the bound girl was only two years older than the Rosemary students, the stark contrast between the students' own lived experience and that of the bound girl would have been difficult to overlook.

As their play developed, the students included a town meeting scene which enabled the audience to learn about some of the "customs and laws of the period," and after much discussion, the "children took sides and argued the points as though it were a real town meeting."[156] A Yale pamphlet, "Roads and Road Making in Colonial Conn.," included laws that required men to work on the highways or pay a fine, but further reading revealed that the initial amount of the fine had been set so low that people preferred to pay the fine rather than do the work![157] Perry continued to collaborate with Katherine Center, helping to lay out some more formal scenes including one with Annie's brother, "who . . . having gotten into trouble because he couldn't pay the required peddler tax . . . ultimately turns up as a highway man . . . [who] is finally helped out of his difficulty by the tavern keeper."[158] Center's project concluded with a performance of the play by her class, and so personally did the students identify with the characters that they were able to act out the plot without having to learn specific lines.

Center's account of her process is a remarkable account of how rich and engaging an educational experience can be when authentic and wide-ranging materials and activities are used as part of a holistic pedagogical experience. From the CCSUs provided by the Junior Programs Educational Guidance Committee (see Chapter V), we know that the committee's vision for the projects and the activities they commissioned incorporated many of the kinds of activities and experiences Center described. Her account of her own labor-intensive, time-consuming search for pedagogical resources was the itch the Educational Guidance Committee aimed to scratch: their goal was to provide a similar wealth of enriching resources appropriately tailored to various grade levels, and to make them available to frontline teachers in school systems wherever Junior Programs performed.

How this play came to McFadden and Lancourt's attention is unknown, but it is easy to see why Center's deeply experiential approach to learning would appeal to them: it was just the sort of pedagogy they were after. Several reviews suggest that their decision to produce *Run, Peddler, Run* was a good one. In a Greenwich, Connecticut, *Press* review (April 18, 1940), the headline notes "Peddler Cast Scores a Success." It goes on to say, "Their fast moving offering was received with delight." Unfortunately, there were few marketing materials or company documents in any of the three Junior Programs collections that could give a clear synopsis of the twists and turns of the story—and from the available reviews, there appear to have been literally twists at every turn, and a full complement of entrances and exits which kept children and adults alike on the edge of their seats.

In broad strokes, the story is one of the eleven-year-old Irish immigrant, Annie Pattison who is desperately searching for her older brother, William Pattison, an itinerant tin peddler. The setting is New London, Connecticut in 1730, and Annie's uncle fails to arrive and pay for her passage. To defray his expense, the ship's captain, the greedy Nicholas Oursell, sells Annie to the rapacious tavern keepers, Gideon Small and his mean-spirited sister, Abigail. A secondary theme finds Hannah Snood, described as a "good woman," accused of witchcraft, and there is some reference to witch's marks on some of the local cattle. The play offers a picture of life in colonial America, recreating scenes which provided interesting information about the background of our early Democracy. There were numerous plot twists, one hinging on William's inability to pay the peddler's tax, reducing him to the status of highway man. Ultimately, he is rescued by Gideon Small, and in several additional but unspecified turns, William becomes the hero. He rescues Hannah Snood from the accusation of witchcraft—a life threatening allegation in colonial America—by killing the wolf responsible for the so-called witch's marks on the cattle. And of course, a happy ending is provided when William and Annie are reunited, and he buys his sister's freedom. There was also Titus Hurlbert, a lively but skeptical selectman, Rob Roy, the postrider, Carlista Nichols, a mother, and Janto, the enslaved Black child owned by Abigail Small. Unfortunately, there was no further information as to how these characters figured into the plot.

The newspaper reviews however, all speak to a satisfied series of audiences, and it is interesting to note that the marketing of *Run, Peddler, Run* included information on how the play was developed. A Lake Forest review comments, "These children turned the clock back some 200 years and modeled their habits and lives after their colonial ancestors. They made their own soap, manufactured their own candles, sheared wool from live sheep, carded and spun the wool on genuine antique spinning wheels and wove cloth on hand looms. Out of these studies they created and acted a play on the life of American colonists at the turn of the 18th century. Now acted by professional actors, Junior Programs will bring 'Run Peddler Run' [*sic*] to Lake Forest [next February]" (Lake Forest, IL, unknown source, Apr 25, 1940).

An April 17, 1940, review (unknown source) featured the headline, "'Run, Peddlar [*sic*], Run' Pleases Adults As Well As Children." The reviewer was clear:

> That it appeals to an adult mind as well as to a child's emotions is perhaps the highest compliment that can be paid to the Junior Programs production, 'Run Peddlar [*sic*] Run' . . . [T]he play is an

ideal one for young audiences. But it is also so entertainingly presented that grown-ups found themselves extremely interested. Compactly written, presented in a professional setting, with exceptionally good lighting effects and acted in a lively fashion by a good cast, 'Run Peddlar [sic] Run' moved its eager audience to unrestrained cheers and applause . . . Edythe Wood gave a lilting performance as the ingenue, despite obvious difficulties with her brogue. It was a mistake, too, to present her in the first scene as an eleven-year-old, which she plainly isn't. Viki Weldon should be remembered for her sharp portrayal of a bitter-tongued spinster, Abigail Small, and complimented on her swift transition from the same spinster to the doubtful, stricken mother, Carlista Nichols. In William Pattison, the merry peddlar [sic], Barney Brown created a lively, and extremely noisy character, whose rapid journeys across stage gave a swifter pace to an already well-timed show . . . [and] Junior Programs are to be congratulated on this, their first production in Greenwich. They are certainly assured of a joyous welcome from the local small fry should they choose to return and it is hoped that they will.

George St. Julian of the *Free Lance Star* of Fredericksburg, VA. (Feb 7, 1940), describes the third Junior Programs production in the Mary Washington Lyceum series in George Washington Hall.

The action took place on the waterfront of New London, Conn. in 1736, the "dark age" of witches and indentured servants in America . . . The plot revolves around the struggles of the heroine, little Annie Pattison, trying to find her brother . . . In the course of the three acts, William Pattison, a very slippery peddler, manages to run to and from every important incident in the play. The part was taken by Barney Brown, and our congratulations go to Mr. Brown for so smoothly executing one of the hardest tricks of the stage, which was to take the audience away from the actual setting, by making it follow his elusive movements and his melodious voice completely off the stage to other imaginative streets and courts of New London.

It is this elusive peddler who turns out to be the hero—for he not only kills the wolf that has accounted for the witch's mark on the cattle, but also buys his sister's freedom . . . Though a trifle slow at first, the story soon gathers momentum, growing more involved and more interesting with each scene . . . While the play did not reach exalted dramatic heights, it was a well-balanced performance which maintained sustained if not enthusiastic interest. It gave to many an effective picture of the narrow-minded and superstitious nature of early New England settlers in the days when witchcraft was prevalent." St. Julian goes on to laud Edyth Wood for a "splendid portrayal of Annie Pattison . . . [and] it was generally agreed that Walter Draper's depiction of selectman Titus Hurlbut . . . was one of the high spots of the show, both in accuracy and humor . . . There was only one outstanding flaw in the entire production and that was the New England accent of Janto, a young colored slave. And I think it only fair to warn Virginia True to brush up on her Negro accent before she does many more performances in the South.

And the *World Herald* (Omaha, NB, Jan 15, 1941) tells us, "You can't have a good piece for the young folks without a suitable villain, who in this case is a combination of Gideon Small the innkeeper, his rough and cruel sister, Abigail, and a rascally double-dealing old sea captain, Nicolas Oursell. The young audience had no trouble in following the simple and light plot of the tin peddler's search for his sister, her hard lot at the tavern and the accusations of witchcraft against Hannah. As in most plays of this type practically everything depends on the acting and in this respect the company had a fine sense of the fitness of the characters and the method of playing them . . . All members of the company are young but experienced players and showed by a combination of spoken word and pantomimic effect that they understand the requirements of playing before children."

The Parkersburg, West Virginia *News* (n.d.) lauded the Junior League for sponsoring the play, singling out Tony James as Captain Nicholas Oursell: "Considered one of the most versatile Thespians in the entire cast by its [Junior Programs'] director, Saul Lancourt, Tony brings to acting the zest and gusto he used to employ on the gridiron for crashing through the heavy line." The reviewer compliments

James's extraordinary vitality and natural flair for mimicry, as well as his ability to develop his character beyond the bare bones presented by the playwright's words. And in Utah, the headline in the *Ogden City Examiner* (Jan 21, 1941) read, "2,000 WITNESS 'RUN, PEDDLER, RUN,' DRAMA Wild Laughter, Shrieks, Heard as Pupils See Play." Sponsored by the *American Association of University Women*, the play was "exceptionally well received by the audience . . . composed of grammar grade children from schools throughout the city. Drama especially written and produced for children is a comparatively new thing in this part of the country . . . [and] the enthusiasm of the audience was remarkable. There were moments of wild laughter . . . and some of breathlessly hushed suspense as the children lived along with their colonial ancestors . . . The acting was excellent and the play itself was charming . . . This group of young actors deserves much praise for the rich experiences they are bringing to children throughout the country."

Run, Peddler, Run also provides another example of Junior Programs' interest in authenticity. An undated Junior Programs' marketing piece in Lancourt's personal papers explains their efforts toward the authenticity of the costumes. According to costume designer Nettie Hopkins, "Clothes of New England colonists were mostly of a rough, homespun quality, and in but a few standard colors made from home-fashioned dyes obtained from local berries . . . The colors were usually a tawny brown, red or shadings of these . . . I knew just what dyes they used . . . because we have a place in the village of Black Point, Connecticut, just south of New London, and the same berries and vegetation . . . still grow there." The marketing materials go on to say, "In order to find out just how to clothe characters portraying . . . farmers, innkeepers, peddlers, bond servants, sailors, shipmasters and chandlers, Mrs. Hopkins [dipped into] ancient newspapers with advertisements for clothing . . . [as well as] notices offering rewards for the capture of escaped bond servants which gave detailed descriptions of the garments they were wearing." Having identified the appropriate clothing, Hopkins searched for something similar, finally deciding on a rough upholstery fabric for the contemporary garments.

By all available accounts, *Run, Peddler, Run* was an engaging adventure story crammed with high jinks, plot twists, and several hiss-worthy villains. With its appealing eleven-year-old Irish heroine, trapped into indentured servitude, the play also managed to combine amusing entertainment and education with a gentle exploration of child labor in a way that underscored the benefits of the life-changing early-twentieth-century movement to enact a broad range of child labor laws.

The Emperor's Treasure Chest[159]

"Junior Programs Presents Thriller for Youngsters In Christmas Week. . . time to mention a modern miracle."

(Virginia Boren, *Seattle Times*, n.d.)

The Players' third play, the 1940–41 season production of *The Emperor's Treasure Chest*, challenged another negative cultural trope, that of Brown immigrants from "south of the border." In his inaugural address on March 4, 1933, FDR had reversed previous administration policies toward South America, promising instead to dedicate the United States to a policy of being a "good neighbor." Key principles of this new policy were nonintervention and noninterference, especially militarily, in the political lives of US neighbors to the south. It was a time of a growing need for hemispheric unity, and the success of FDR's policy can, in part, be measured by the rapidity with which most Latin American countries rallied to the Allied cause as the clouds of WWII approached. Nonintervention saw the US withdrawal from Nicaragua, Haiti, and Cuba—except for retaining the base at Guantanamo. When Mexico expropriated foreign oil companies in 1938, the US went so far as to defend Mexico's right to do so—so long as prompt compensation was provided. FDR's approach paid off handsomely, creating a hemispheric united front against possible Axis aggression while maintaining the flow of oil, petroleum, and other raw materials necessary for the war effort.

One very important aspect of FDR's Good Neighbor Policy was its recognition of the importance of reversing the negative stereotypes that existed in the American psyche toward the people of many South American nations. As noted earlier, the popular image was one of a backward, lazy, superstitious people and the offensiveness of many Hollywood stereotypes of Latinx characters had become so blatant that the offending American films were banned by several South American countries. To counter these dysfunctional and unacceptable characterizations, a broad set of US efforts were launched. In 1939, the New York World's Fair became a place to redefine negative South American stereotypes, with many countries showcasing their vibrant cultures. An Office of Inter-American Affairs was created, with Nelson Rockefeller as its director. The office not only pressed Hollywood to hire South Americans, but strongly encouraged them to produce movies portraying South Americans in a positive way.[160]

Given Junior Programs' mission, this aspect of FDR's Good Neighbor Policy was tailor made for them. Committed to showing different races and cultures in a positive light, in 1938, they contacted Cecile Hulse Matschat to discuss the commissioning of *The Emperor's Treasure Chest*. Both McFadden and Matschat were avid gardeners and members of the *Society of Women Geographers*. Matschat, a botanist and the author of numerous books, was in the process of publishing *Seven Grass Huts: An Engineer's Wife in Central and South America* (Farrar & Rinehart, 1939), for which she won a Literary Guild award. As with *Sun God*, Junior Programs' reach for authenticity was, by today's standards, somewhat rudimentary, but at the time, even Junior Programs' imperfect efforts were a notable step forward. Like Nelson, Matschat, a white, non-Latin woman, had a more than average familiarity with the culture depicted in the play, and she spent two years working with several South American governments, the Brazilian Consulate, and a range of other Brazilian cultural resources to ensure a greater-than-normal level of authenticity.

The development of *The Emperor's Treasure Chest* was also an ideal opportunity for the company's Educational Guidance Committee whose honorary chair was Dr. W. Carson Ryan, President of the Progressive Education Association. The *New Haven Register* (n.d.) offers a description of the situation facing the nation:

> Never in our history as a nation has there been such a great need for the building up of a better international and inter-racial feeling. Since we have in the United States a melting pot[161] of peoples from all over the world, we have also all their inherited prejudices, as well as new antagonisms that have grown up within our own borders. It is more vitally important now than ever before, that we retain and strengthen our national poise, our sense of fairness and justice, our belief in the equality of man and the rights of every individual. Educators throughout the country are aware of this need and are

developing new methods, searching for new ideas, with which to build up in impressionable youth a wholesome respect for all their fellow beings. A definite program is needed . . . for it is at unexpected moments that the need for intercultural education may arise. Since a positive approach is always to be preferred, emphasis on the good qualities and on the cultural contributions of each race and nation is greatly to be desired." The article goes on to share Ryan's sense of hope: "Those of us who are concerned with a richer curriculum provision for schools are greatly interested in what is being done in connection with Junior Programs, Inc. I am myself particularly impressed with the thorough, discriminating way in which the problem of providing superior cultural entertainment, *and at the same time* stimulating creative activities, *on the part of the children themselves* [emphasis added], has been approached." The article concludes with the comment, "The Junior Programs organization, in selecting its productions to be shown to young people each season, has deliberately kept this need for intercultural education in mind, and has chosen music, stories, lectures, etc. from as many different countries and races as possible. (Chapter V provides a detailed look at the CCSU on Brazil commissioned by the Educational Guidance Committee to accompany the production.)

Virginia Boren, reviewer for the *Seattle Times* (n.d.), called the Junior Programs performance of *The Emperor's Treasure Chest* "a modern miracle."

> Not only is this organization working its miracles all over the United States, but Seattle children joyfully share in . . . the presentation of "The Emperor's Treasure Chest". . . [It is] a thrilling play of modern South America with all the romantic color of fiestas in the market place of Para, [and] an exciting hunt for hidden treasure . . . It has mystery, comedy, historic background, and gifted professional actors who have been playing before huge houses all across the continent . . . [I]t recommends itself to child audiences because it is lively and interesting, exciting and adventurous. . . and if there's anything that

can make children wide-eyed come away with a feeling that although these children are of another land they are just like children of our own country . . . Junior Programs does more than amuse your children 5 times a year! It's more than an organization to produce fine children's entertainment. It's an educational foundation, aiming to coordinate and supplement the work of the schools . . . [and] If you know any children who haven't purchased their Junior Programs season tickets, why not tuck one into their Christmas stockings? A kindhearted Seattle woman has purchased twenty of these tickets for twenty little ones at a Seattle orphanage.

In an undated document marked "Teacher Material," in Lancourt's personal papers, Junior Programs sketches out the story: "In 1889, Don Pedro, the last Emperor of the great South American country of Brazil, was forced to give up his throne and flee from his country back to Portugal. Leaving in such haste, he could take with him only a few of his most cherished possessions. The rest of his wealth was confiscated by the new Brazilian government. In the play, "The Emperor's Treasure Chest," all the costumes and scenery are absolutely true but the exciting story of the hidden treasure is just a tale of what might have happened to some of Dom Pedro's great wealth. This is the mystery. (But we won't tell you where the treasure was found—that would spoil the fun when you come to the play.)"

Additional reviews flesh out the story: At the marketplace of Para, the greatest city on the Amazon, and the rubber-shipping center, we see "a red-sailed lateen ship tied to the dock . . . dominating the center of the backdrop which showed more distant sailing vessels and tall buildings, [and] a velour drop-curtain of royal blue achieved the effect of a sky bright with sunshine. Market stalls displayed colorful merchandise of native Brazil" ('Murray Pupils Sail to Brazil via Stage,' Mimi Boteler, *The Daily Times,* no state, n.d.). There, according to Junior Programs teaching material:

[W]e find our young hero, Pedro, a boy of 10 and his girlfriends, Maria and Silvana busily tending their booths and hoping to sell many of their wares. Pedro's ambition is to become a trader on an Amazon River boat—and he spends more time wandering about among the gaily colored sails at the dock than in tending to his business. His grandmother—a huge old lady who was once a servant in the Emperor's house—scolds him roundly for not watching his stall. She is afraid that some of the valuable objects which she has displayed might be stolen. Among them are some beautiful things that the Emperor had given to Granny when he fled to Portugal—gifts that she cherished, but was now forced to sell due to the family's poverty. Pedro and his friends often amused themselves by dressing up in some of the gorgeous robes and acting out incidents in the life of the Emperor, just as Granny had described them. While they are playing, a passing trader, Jose (pronounced Ho-say) notices them. Pedro proudly shows Jose and his son, Mateo, the Emperor's belongings. Among them is an old book, written in French, which none of Pedro's family had ever been able to read. Mateo idly looks through it and reads a bit here and there, when suddenly, he realizes that it is the Emperor's diary, and that there are directions in it for finding some treasure he had left hidden. And now the excitement begins: Jose tries to buy the diary from Pedro but makes the whole family suspicious by offering to give him his whole trading ship for it. Pedro asks a newspaper man, a great friend of his, to tell him what the book says, and learns that the directions for finding the treasure are very mysterious:

> If you search in dark places, you may need a light.
> That which is hidden, may still be in sight.
> The treasure you seek, is close to your hand.
> It is red, white, and green and came from the land.

Can you guess what they might mean? Come and see the play, and watch how Pedro hides the rhyme, how Jose and Mateo steal it, how both families secretly break into an old mansion in Rio de Janeiro looking for the treasure, and what happens to them there. They have many funny adventures, with stout old Granny getting stuck in the window and the police trying to arrest them all. Be sure not to miss seeing this exciting, hilarious play of the mysterious Emperor's Treasure Chest (Junior Programs Press Release to Teachers, n.d.).

Supplementing the above description, the *Daily Times* review goes on:

> Roberta Barkley, who in real life is a slim-figured size 12, playing the role of old Granny, a monstrous fat and funny size 62. She offered the comedy relief to this most exciting mystery. Her role was the most exacting and was admirably handled with a finesse that was all very convincing as to her venerability. Granny berated her grandson for his idleness and proceeded to show him how to decorate the market stall to attract customers. Her insistence upon standing on a small stool to decorate the roof of the stall had dire results when she literally flattened Pedro, upon whom she fell . . . Before the curtains were drawn apart for the second act, the sound of gay Brazilian airs were heard . . . In this act, suspense was created with the hiding of the map in Granny's umbrella, while those sinister strangers watched unbeknown to Granny and Pedro. The youthful audience was so distressed that several called out a warning to Granny.
>
> The third act was set in an old-style mansion in Rio de Janeiro and conveyed the atmosphere of mystery necessary to the action of the play. . . [T]he hunt proceeded with great gusto. The strangers arrived first but had not succeeded in finding the treasure. Upon hearing footsteps, it became necessary for them to hide. Granny, Pedro and his girl-friends arrive, and a humorous interlude ensues when Granny attempts to climb through a window and gets stuck. To wild audience cheers, Pedro ultimately succeeds in finding the gems in the base of an old candlestick. Now wealthy, Granny and Pedro share some of the treasure with their friends.

An early headline tells us, "Good Will Shows Proposed for Children of Americas" (unknown source, n.d.). "Through the use of drama and the opera a program to help build good-will between the children of this country and their South American neighbors is to be started this Fall by Junior Programs, a non-profit educational venture . . . Thousands of boys and girls in school systems throughout the US will be shown graphically how the people of the Southern Hemisphere live. The good-will tour will follow the policy outlined by the Washington Administration to bring about better relations between North and South America . . . Cooperation is planned with the American School of the Air of the Columbia Broadcasting system which will broadcast a version of the play to school classrooms throughout the country this Fall." The partnership between Junior Programs and CBS's American School of the Air also made it possible for those children not fortunate enough to be able to see a live performance of *The Emperor's Treasure Chest* to listen to the play, which would have its radio premier on *Tales from Far and Near*, on March 13, 1941 (*CBS Student Guide*, Oct. 1940).

An article in the Greenville, South Carolina *Piedmont* (March 11, 1941) offers additional information:

> Just as swing and jazz are universally recognized as indigenous to the US, so rumba, conga, tango and other melodies and rhythms are typically native of Latin America. [*The Emperor's Treasure Chest* takes us to] carnival time in the romantic tropical port of Para, Brazil. All members of the company will sing and dance to popular airs . . . Dressed in native costume the girls in Bahianas and heavily bejeweled, the men in boots, pantaloons and open necked shirts . . . will bring to life all the tingling excitement of fiesta time beneath the Southern Cross.
>
> All music and dancing were supervised by Elsie Houston, the internationally renowned singer and authority on Latin America . . . who sings nightly at Radio City's popular Rainbow Room. Born in Brazil, she is a direct descendant of Sam Houston. For "The Emperor's Treasure Chest," she has selected 3 popular Brazilian airs, "O Le Le O La La", "Miaow Miaow", and "Florisbella". She also spent hours initiating the cast in the peculiar rhythm of carnival time in Brazil.

> This unique movement can only be described as a stiff-kneed flat-footed quiver which never stops during the entire period of the fiesta, lasting sometimes several days. The people live to this hammering rhythm walking about, talking, gesturing and even eating to its beat. It is something to be seen nowhere else in the world. Described by an authority on Brazilian music, Margaret Steward, as a "product of the Indian racial element, the Portuguese melodic element and the African rhythmic element, fused into an original and ethnical expression. With its quantities of forms, it is varied, complex and beautiful as Brazil itself, with its heterogeneous population, contrasting climates, varied and beautiful scenery and vast solitudes.

Suzanne Martin of the *Seattle Post Intelligencer* (Dec 28, 1940) described the thrilled response of four thousand children to the fanfare and fun of the story. "Yesterday's performance, sent across country by Junior Programs, Inc. so children may have worthwhile entertainment of their own . . . met the keen eye of its juvenile audience with honors. There were no hisses for the villain (an audience of Joops[162] are too polite), but an old-time stock company hero was [n]ever greeted with more cheers than Actor Barry Mahool, whose timely arrival saved the treasure hunt from complete collapse."

Another review acknowledged the play as part of a larger effort to promote the Good Neighbor Policy and felt that the youthful audience, as a result of watching an amusing play in which their South American counterparts displayed the same impulse to hunt for hidden treasure and tease and be lectured by their grandmothers as any American child, would here after lend a more sympathetic ear to the word Brazil. ("Youngsters See Life in So. America," unknown source, n.d.). The *Louisville Courier Journal* (March 1941) agreed, noting that Maria and Silvana mirrored the love any American girl would have for "finery, dancing, and gaiety . . . [while] attending their first prom with a big name band from New York."

Still another review gives us a behind the scenes glimpse of the costume created to turn the youthful Roberta Barclay into a "monstrous fat and funny old granny wearing a size 62 dress . . . her sides quivering like mountains of jelly . . . Saul Lancourt, the director, forbade the use of padding," as it would be too

III. THE PRODUCTIONS: PART I—THE JUNIOR PROGRAMS PLAYERS

Joop Club

It is the essence of Junior Programs' philosophy that AN INTERESTING PERFORMANCE WILL HOLD BOYS' AND GIRLS' ATTENTION. Audience etiquette, however, should be taught, courtesy in entering seats, removing hats, keeping feet quiet, etc.

In order to make this audience training a painless and even joyful process, Junior Programs Inc. has chosen as its mascot

Joop THE GIRAFFE

He represents the perfect audience: Can always see over others' heads, can make no sounds (no giraffe can!), rarely needs a drink of water, is friendly, happy, polite.

Every child attending a Junior Program performance automatically becomes a member of the Joop Club. In each town a child is elected as SUPER-JOOPER, the local club president, to recite the Joop Club "Rules for Audience Courtesy" and lead the Joop Club song at performances.

Joop (in life-size facsimile) will appear between the curtains before each performance!

His ear wiggling is interpreted by a member of the cast into messages of fun and hints on courtesy to the audience.

The Junior Programs Mascot: Joop the Giraffe Teaches Children Good Audience Behavior
(Lancourt's personal papers)

heavy. The solution was "the construction of a light steel skeletal structure affixed with slender springs to Miss Barkley's waist, shoulders and other parts of the body. The size 62 dress worn over that, and a special wig and face makeup complete[d] the effect ... [of] a natural-appearing feminine Falstaffian character whose comic behavior leaves an unforgettable impression." Other costumes called *bahianas*—for the carnival and fiesta in the second act—consisted of "a white blouse ornately decorated with colored ribbons and laces and full flowing ruffled skirt[s] of dark printed material overlaid with a profusion of brightly colored streamers. For jewelry, the girls wear everything they can carry, earrings, [and] chains upon chains of necklaces and bracelets. The entire jewelry ensemble makes for pleasant tinkling sound with every movement. Topping it off is a tightly bound turban . . . surmounted with a small basket of fruit. The shoes are tomankas, wooden mule-shaped shoes with bright-colored cloth at the toe" (*Tribune,* La Crosse, WI, n.d.).

Again, the Players' template proved to be a recipe for success. Entertainment, empathy, and education—all rolled into a fun-filled afternoon, supported and enriched by Junior Programs' CCSU on Brazil. Here was a portrayal of others who were interesting and adventurous; the kind of kids any American youngster would like to have as a friend and real neighbor. But the play did more than offer a window into another culture; it gave the children a way to connect with one of the larger political issues of the day—the national need to be a "good neighbor"—and it did so without being doctrinaire.

The Adventures of Marco Polo[163]

"'Marco Polo' Called the Best of Junior Programs Plays"

(Omaha, NE, unknown source, Nov 7, 1941)

Ironically, what turned out to be their penultimate production was also something of a first for Junior Programs. Typically, the three companies performed and toured separately. *Marco Polo* represented the first time Junior Programs synthesized singing, dancing, and acting into a single professional stage production, with all the dancers and singers having fully developed speaking parts. According to the *Green Bay Press Gazette* (n.d.):

> Lancourt, who created the half-historical, half-fictional plot, said this represented 'an inevitable development of the modern theater which demands a synthesis of all the interpretive arts, with

performers skilled in every talent of the stage, acting, music and the dance.' Asked for a statement with regard to the new production, Mr. Lancourt, the author . . . said: 'The Adventures of Marco Polo' will fuse the techniques developed by Junior Programs, Inc., in its opera, ballet and play productions of former years. We have found it essential for some time to use music and dancing, not as ornamental additions which stop the action, but as integral parts of the plot, actually furthering the drama. As a result of the experience gained in watching the audience's reaction to our productions of opera, narrative ballet and drama, Mrs. McFadden and I felt it would be interesting to develop an additional type of production which would make use of the best features and freedoms of each. We tried to find a name for this new form . . . but could not think of anything adequate. We have had to resort to calling 'Marco Polo' a play with music, although that hardly covers its content.

What Lancourt did not say explicitly at that time was that this new form also made a virtue of a growing necessity: many of their young male performers were being drafted, and it was no longer possible to find the well-trained professionals required for three separate companies. For many organizations, this would have been a major crisis. Junior Programs appears to have taken it in stride—just one more example of their *Wei Ji* approach to a challenge. Not only were they successful in merging the three companies, they also succeeded in transforming it into an opportunity to be artistically innovative, weaving each of the three company's artistry—drama, music, and dance—into a seamless whole. And given the glowing reviews *Marco Polo* received, they were handsomely rewarded for their efforts.

As with *The Emperor's Treasure Chest,* their choice of *The Adventures of Marco Polo* appears to have combined both their mission to use the performing arts to broaden children's understanding of other peoples and other cultures with what they understood as the political needs of the time. Despite the broad currency of Hollywood's dehumanizing stereotypes of the Chinese people as conniving, servile, and incapable of proper English pronunciation, there was a growing sympathy for China, generated by the Japanese brutality during the Nanjing Massacre in December, 1937.[164] Mindful of the possibility of needing China as an ally, FDR skirted several of the isolationist Neutrality Acts—which forbid sending American armaments to any nations at war—and began sending arms to China to enable its defense against the Japanese invasion. At that point, Roosevelt was technically not in violation of the Neutrality Acts as what soon became the Second Sino-Japanese War was still an "undeclared war."[165]

Here, then, was another opportunity for Junior Programs to create a new narrative about another much-maligned community of color, and to everyone's delight, *The Adventures of Marco Polo* became one of Junior Programs' most lavish and successful productions. Its avowed purpose, according to the *Brooklyn Eagle* (Dec 14, 1941) was to present a more positive view of "the little understood culture and civilization of China, now joined with Western Democracy in a death struggle against the forces of aggression." The Schenectady *Gazette* (Jan 24, 1942) also noted "this newest production . . . was especially planned and created to promote good will and understanding between America and China at a time when, as never before, they are vitally needed . . . An understanding of contemporary life should rest on knowledge of an earlier age," McFadden explained. "Our fight to preserve our own and China's cultural heritages can be strengthened" she went on, calling attention to how China, at the time of Marco Polo, was far ahead of medieval Europe in many ways. Marco Polo's reports of what he saw in China were almost incomprehensible to his Venetian peers. Few believed in "stones that burned and provided heat" (a lump of coal), a "floating needle that always pointed North/South" (a compass), or the writing of books using "wooden blocks that produced a page at a time" (printing). "And in the history of China we may also perceive how the progressive ideas of an enlightened monarch like Kublai Khan were often seriously threatened by forces of bigotry, [and] a narrow nationalism." The New York *Post*, (Dec 19, 1941) also quotes McFadden: "In 'Marco Polo'. . . Kublai Khan wants to open his kingdom to every race and nationality, for they all have something to offer each other. The whole theme is a plea for understanding among nations—which is not out of date, even in war time."

Indeed, research confirms that despite his long string of military conquests, Kublai Khan's transformation from Mongolian conqueror to supreme ruler included many important innovations. He understood that while one might be able to "conquer [an] empire on horseback . . . one cannot govern it on horseback." Viewed as "relatively wise and benevolent," he was known for his religious tolerance, clemency toward the conquered, and the interdependence of ruler and ruled.[166] His reign was also notable for numerous infrastructure improvements. These included an efficient postal system, the introduction of a paper currency backed by gold reserves, and a vast network of roads which fostered economic growth and expansion of trade.[167] He also supported numerous scientific advancements such as the development of several new instruments for astronomers which enabled the correction of the Chinese calendar, the construction of an observatory in Shaanxi, the introduction by Muslim scholars of Euclidean Geometry and Arabic numerals, and the creation of an Institute of Medicine in Beijing. He was also known for appointing people based on the merits of their achievements, as well as for encouraging the development of arts and literature.[168]

Again, it is important to remember how counter to the prevailing beliefs about China Junior Programs' view was at the time. Anti-Asian violence was a regular feature of the Western-American political landscape in the mid- to late 1800s: 1855 spawned the Tacoma Massacre; and in 1871 a similar massacre occurred in Los Angeles. In the late 1870s, there were "anti coolie clubs in every ward in San Francisco to protect 'free white labor' from the degrading influence of the Chinese," and in 1882, there was the Chinese Exclusion Act.[169] According to Uyehara, the Chinese represented foreigners who could never be assimilated, and these flames of fear—of the "Yellow Peril" and oriental aggression—were fanned by white labor leaders to unite a previously fragmented array of European immigrant groups by creating a cross-class, cross-cultural identification with "whiteness" with slogans such as "Keep California White." With an influx of Japanese immigrants in the early days of the twentieth century, anti-Asian bigotry was institutionalized for Asians in a way that it was not for the early German and Irish immigrants: there was the 1913 California Alien Land Act, the Immigration Act of 1924, and the infamous 1942 Executive Order 9066 which created so-called "detention camps" for all Japanese Americans. Even the liberal Supreme Court Justice Earl Warren had weighed in against civil liberties for Japanese Americans.[170]

William Vickery, the editorial secretary of the Service Bureau for Intercultural Education, a New York educational association, clearly understood the message embodied in the Junior Programs mission: "Now, as at no time since the World War [WWI], there is an acute need for developing understanding and good will among

United States peoples of diverse national and racial backgrounds. Propagandists both in this country and abroad have been trying desperately to destroy our national unity by appealing to existing hates and fears. Teachers, of course, recognize their obligations and unique opportunity to promote cooperation among ethnic groups and to combat prejudice. The crucial question is, 'How can this be done effectively?'"

From a perspective that, even in 2024, is still often considered leading edge, Vickery believed that "Intercultural education has at least two major objectives: First, it endeavors to develop in children who belong to the dominant group respect and liking for the members of minority groups. This probably can best be done by correcting false impressions based on misinformation, and by accenting that a person's being a good American has nothing to do with, say, the color of his skin or the nationality of his father. Second, it attempts to give children of minority groups the feeling that they 'belong'; that their people are helping to build an American culture, and that the more sources from which American civilization draws, the better and richer it will become. This objective requires that such children be made aware and proud of the positive contributions of their ancestors to better living, and that they be given a chance to explain and express the achievements of their groups."[171]

It was into this larger political environment that Junior Programs launched *The Adventures of Marco Polo*. In a Junior Programs press release (n.d.), titled "A Letter From Joop the Giraffe, Mascot of Junior Programs' Joop Club", we read:

> Dear Joop Club Members:
>
> Have you heard about the new show that I am bringing you this year? It's "The Adventures of Marco Polo," and it certainly is full of adventures. Marco Polo's father was an Italian merchant who sailed away before Marco was born . . . You can imagine what stories of strange lands and queer customs he had to tell Marco when he returned years later, and what wonderful gleaming jewels and gorgeous silks and unusual swords and other weapons he brought back to sell in Venice. Of course, the boy Marco immediately wanted to go back to these distant countries . . . and have some adventures of his own. And that's just what he did! In our . . . play you will see Marco first at home in Venice and then in China at the court of the wise and

III. THE PRODUCTIONS: PART I—THE JUNIOR PROGRAMS PLAYERS 99

>powerful emperor, Kublai Khan. He manages to find out about a plot against the great Khan's life and save him from his enemy. I'm sure you will want to see this exciting new . . . play and I hope you will bring your friends . . . so that there will be lots and lots of new Joop Club members to say hello to me between scenes. Here's to seeing you soon! Your friend, JOOP.

Another piece of Junior Programs marketing material (n.d.) provides a synopsis of *The Adventures of Marco Polo*:

>Many hundreds of years ago in the Italian city of Venice, a young lad of fifteen by the name of Marco Polo is not leading a very merry life. His mother is dead and his father, Nicolo Polo, a great Venetian merchant, has gone away on a trading voyage many years before, leaving Marco in care of an uncle whose name is Barto. The longer Marco's father stays away, the more Barto is convinced that Nicolo is dead and never coming back—and the worse young Marco is treated. Little by little, Uncle Barto, his shrewish wife, Christiana, and their son Nicki, take more and more power into their hands. And although they are living in the house of Nicolo Polo, they make Marco feel as if he is an outcast. Barto and his family ride about the canals of Venice in grand style while poor Marco either does all the menial tasks of the household or waits vainly on the docks, hoping that some ship will bring his father home.

>One fine day, a tall gentleman dressed in rich furs and accompanied by a very strange person whom he addresses as Ching, knocks at the door of the Polo house. It is Nicolo Polo returning from fifteen years of travel to the far corners of the earth. Although Barto and his family can hardly hide their disappointment at his return, they try to get back in his good graces by arranging a celebration in his honor. During the dancing and singing, Marco returns home, rowing the heavy golden gondola, which no one but Nicolo Polo may use. Upon finding out that Barto had intended to use it and seeing how badly Marco had been treated, Nicolo banishes Barto and his family from

Junior Programs *The Adventures of Marco Polo* Act I, Venice.
Set Design by Kenneth MacClelland
(Author's personal collection)

the house. Marco is overjoyed at his father's return and asks to be taken with him on his next journey.

Next will be shown the largest map you have ever seen and a voice will tell the story of Marco's travels from Venice across the deserts and oceans to the Empire of Kublai Khan.

You will see his image walk across the map in the exact path that Marco took hundreds of years ago . . . In the beautiful palace of Chagannor in the wonderful land of Cathay (now called China) sits Kublai Khan, the greatest Emperor the world has ever known. With him is Achmath, his vice-regent, who argues forcibly with the Emperor. He does not wish to see Marco Polo and his father received at the court. They are foreigners—of another religion—and should not be trusted, he says.

According to the unpaginated *Marco Polo* script in Lancourt's personal papers, when Achmath advises the emperor not to receive the Polos because the Tartar god Natigay is the only true god, Kublai Khan answers, "All people of good will worship the same god! They give him different names. It matters little." And as the emperor leaves, he informs Achmath that he will, indeed, receive the Polos. Achmath then conspires with Tebet—an emissary from the emperor's evil cousin, Prince Nayan—to kill the emperor. The instrument of death is to be a sword, the handle of which will be covered with a deadly poison. Tebet will perform an intricate Sword Dance, never touching the handle, and at the end of the dance will hand the sword, handle first, to the Khan. The poison is so powerful that merely touching it will kill the Khan.

In the scene which follows, Marco and Ching arrive at the palace. Achmath and Tebet try to trick Marco into violating a deeply held Tartar belief that forbids anyone from stepping on the threshold to the emperor's throne room, an act which would anger the Sun, who would then withhold his warmth. Ching knows of this belief and stops Marco, ostensibly to change his traveling shoes for appropriate soft slippers. With Marco's foot stopped in midair, Tebet tries to push Marco into stepping on the threshold, but Ching manages to push Tebet away and vaults Marco over the threshold. Tebet and Achmath leave in disgust to continue their plotting, and an exchange between Ching, Aijurac, a young court musician, and Marco sing the praises of Kublai Khan. Marco tells of seeing the wheat the emperor has sent to places experiencing famine, and of the "herds of sheep the Khan has taken from his own flocks and sent to a land stricken by drought." But Aijurac bemoans the fact that for every good deed the Khan does, Achmath, the Khan's tax collector, "takes back half for himself."

While Ching goes off to find Nicolo Polo, Aijurac throws a few pieces of coal into a small vessel. "What is that?" Marco asks, and she replies, "I keep a little fire near my lute and pipes so that the chill of the night air will not take their sweetness from them." Marco is still puzzled, commenting, "Coal? It is a black stone?" Aijurac answers, "Look into this little vessel. See the black stone grow red with heat. Feel the warmth it gives off. It will burn for hours." She puts on a pair of white gloves and puts her hand in the fire. Marco cries out, "You will burn yourself." Aijurac, handing one of the gloves to Marco, says, "The fire and heat cannot go through the cloth [asbestos]. Hold it and see for yourself." She begins to sing a sorrowful song, and when questioned by Marco, she unburdens herself, telling him of what she has overheard of Tebet and Achmath's plot. Ching returns and Aijurac goes into greater detail about the Sword Dance. Suddenly, they hear the approach of the emperor, and they hide behind an archway.

The emperor arrives, followed by Achmath. The Khan asks whether the Polos have arrived, and Marco steps forward. Kublai Khan asks if the countries of the West progress on the path of peace. "No Sire," Marco responds, "one city hates another. The evil force of war still rages." Kublai Khan counters, "It is always simple to call one's enemies 'evil.' But then again, your enemies call you 'evil.' Who then is to judge which one is really in the wrong?" Marco answers, "The Khan is much too wise for me. All I know is that [your] lands are at peace and those to the West are at continuous war." The Khan replies, "We too have our wars, Marco, and probably shall have them again—unless our children are wiser than we." "Do you think they will be?" asks Marco, and the Khan relies, "A little song I have heard them sing at their play gives me great hope . . . Aijurac, do your people know this song?" Aijurac says they do, and the Khan asks her to sing. According to the stage directions, after the first verse, it becomes a pantomime ballet with Ching playing the monkey's sons.

> Long ago at the top of a tree,
> Lived a monkey and her sons three.

III. THE PRODUCTIONS: PART I—THE JUNIOR PROGRAMS PLAYERS

> Hither and yon, to and fro
> Backwards and forwards, she watched them go.
> Forwards and backwards, from and to,
> Yon and hither, the monkeys flew.
> One fine day, the mother knew
> Her chattering sons would be lost to view.
> She gave her blessing, shed some tears,
> Wished them well, and said, "My dears,
> The world will teach you things I know,
> Learn these three rules before you go.
> Mischief comes through opening the mouth
> On matter you know nothing about.
> Be sure, my sons, your eyes to hide
> From jealous action turn aside.
> Mischief comes through lending an ear
> To unkind words you should not hear.

Achmath mocks the song: "Childish nonsense! I thank Natigay that there is still one Mongol Prince who rules his province with Tartar strength." The Khan reminds Achmath that he has forbidden him to mention Prince Nayan, and Achmath retorts, "He . . . loves you dearly. He has sent even this man, Tebet . . . as his gift to you." The Khan responds, "I do not want men as gifts. They are not beasts to be thrown from one to another." Achmath (placatingly) responds, "You are right, my Lord, Prince Nayan sends not the man but his accomplishments." With that, he commands Tebet to perform the Sword Dance.

The stage directions tell us the dance begins calmly, but soon grows wilder. "Tebet throws the sword into the ground and bends over backwards to pick it up with his teeth. As he is about to accomplish this feat, Ching and Marco dash in and begin to take part in the dance. Each time Tebet tries for the sword, they intercept him until Marco has a chance to pick it up himself . . . making certain not to touch the handle. He runs to Achmath and bowing . . . hands him the sword, handle first. Achmath recoils . . ." Kublai Khan demands to know what is going on. Achmath tries to blame the confusion on the foreigners, and Kublai Khan demands the sword, but Marco intervenes: "If the Baron will not touch it, perhaps it is wise for the Khan to do the same," Marco says softly. Now suspicious, Kublai Khan suggests that the Sword Dance be done again, without Marco and Ching's interruption. Marco tries to hand the sword first to Achmath and then to Tebet. Tebet tries to flee but Ching stops him. Marco reveals the plot, and Achmath and Tebet are taken away by Ching and the guards. Kublai Khan then commands Marco to stand beside him "so all may see how you, of one race, saved the life of one of another race. You shall be at my right hand always. Let us strive together, as people of all faiths should, and we shall yet know a golden age when all pursue their lives in tranquil calm and all share in the rich harvest of the marvels created by mankind, regardless of the color of their skin, the shape of their faces, or the manner of their worship."

Marco Polo had a message to convey—about China, about diversity and belonging, and the negative impacts of othering—although those were not the words then in use. The *Brooklyn Eagle* (Dec 29, 1942) responded to Lancourt's script: In *Marco Polo,* "his characters are either very bad or very good. There is no mistaking them, and the good ones win . . . Along the way he manages to weave a few excellent moral lessons into his tale, but they are so pleasantly dramatized that it is probable that the kiddies don't realize they are getting them. In fact, he has included some remarks on racial and religious intolerance which a lot of oldsters could take to heart these days. Marco Polo is good for everybody from 6-65. We recommend it heartily." In a similar vein, the Ridgefield, New Jersey, *Times* (n.d.) wrote, that the "prophecy of peace and love between China and Western nations provide the timeless note for [the] ending of the operetta."

Even, Walter Terry, dance critic for the *New York Herald Tribune*, characterized the story as having only "a dash or two of moral preaching." Terry, an avid promotor of the American regional dance movement, notes:

> [Lancourt] has staged the famous story in colorful fashion, and yesterday's audience of children were highly delighted with it . . . Margaret Carlisle's music is thoroughly engaging with gay tarantella music for the scene in Venice and soft oriental melodies for the episode in Cathay. Multi-colored sets, right out of a story book were provided for by Kenneth MacClelland and the costumes were as bright as one could want . . . Ruth St. Denis staged the dances . . .

and a fine job she did. The Italian dances were fleet and joyous and the Oriental numbers were as inventive and as theatrically striking as one would expect from the St. Denis hand . . . Dorothy Lysaght . . . performed Miss St. Denis's own familiar solo, 'Chinese Scarf Dance.' Miss Lysaght manipulated the whirling pattern-making scarves with dexterity and, although there were occasional hints of effort, the dance as a whole was effectively presented. First dancing honors certainly went to Charles Tate. His physical agility is something to marvel at and his command of the comic in dance movements accounts for the highlights of this production. Dale Lefler was vigorous as the treacherous dagger dancer.[172]

In a *New York Herald Tribune* article, (Jan 4, 1942) Terry pointed out the absence of didacticism: "Fun and education were neatly fused . . . [and] historically informative, yet there was nothing of the text book about them, for the producers saw to it that the pageantry of the past was reproduced in terms of exciting theater. Extensive tours carry these ballets to the towns, cities and schools of America and their importance cannot be exaggerated. The dancers of today are frequently faced with audiences' ignorance and indifference . . . Junior Programs with its Marco Polo . . . [is] helping to build the intelligent, adult dance audiences of tomorrow by acquainting children with the excitement of ballet."

Terry's "great lady" was, and still is, a dance legend, and securing her as choreographer for *Marco Polo* is an indication of the high standard of quality Junior Programs set for themselves. At that time, St. Denis was acknowledged as the foremost American authority on "dances of the Orient." She was famous in both the United States and abroad for her performances in what were considered dance masterpieces that held millions enthralled. Other reviewers recognized the significance of drawing on St. Denis's expertise to create authentic choreography: "Miss St. Denis, conceded by all dance critics as America's leading dance creator, was the founder, with Ted Shawn of the famous Denishawn school . . . She has made epoch making tours as head of her own troupe of dancers not only in Europe, but throughout China, Japan, India, Java and other Far Eastern lands . . . Her knowledge of the dances of the Orient, obtained through many years of travel and study in the Far East, was held the proper source for the creation of authentically derived dances of the court of Kublai

Khan. When Miss St. Denis and her company performed in Pekin, China, she was admired by China's greatest exponent of the dance, Mei-Lan-Fang" (*Index-Journal*, Salinas, CA, March 16, 1942).

Today, St. Denis's work is no longer viewed as authentic. In fact, it was pictures of Egyptian and Hindu mythological figures that had made an indelible impression on St. Denis that inspired her. She was captivated by the spiritual feeling these pictures engendered in her, but the dances she created were entirely divorced from their true cultural moorings and religious meanings. One critic suggests that while she was sincere in her desire to explore new dance forms, her use of Oriental gestures was detached from their authentic cultural meanings. Rather, the gestures were filtered through both her personal emotional responses, and the desire of her Western audiences for a sexualized exoticism. Nevertheless, despite this lack of authenticity, St. Denis is, rightfully, still considered one of the most important figures in the development of modern dance.[173] In addition to her work with the dancers, St. Denis also provided some of the dance costumes and music from her own private collection for the production.[174]

While *Marco Polo* provided a new synthesis of music, dance and drama, the production was also noteworthy because of Kenneth MacClelland's sets. Not simple backdrops, so wonderfully did they create a sense of place that they took on the aura of being "characters" in the play. Of note was the enormous map used at the opening of Act I and the Prologue to Act II.

The Isabella County *Times-News* (Mt. Pleasant, MI, Oct 28, 194?) provides a description:

> Perhaps the largest geography map ever seen in this city . . . accurately reproducing the features of several authentic Thirteenth Century maps depicting the world as it was then known . . . 'Marco Polo' opens with a panoramic montage, visual and aural, delineating the widespread travels over the then-known world of Marco Polo . . . In the background is the parchment picture map adapted from many of those drawn and illustrated by Europe's medieval cartographers, replete with their horrible monsters at the edge of the earth, where the sea falls off into nothingness; sailing vessels splitting the waves and wind gods in the skies with puffed cheeks ballooning the sails as

III. THE PRODUCTIONS: PART I—THE JUNIOR PROGRAMS PLAYERS 107

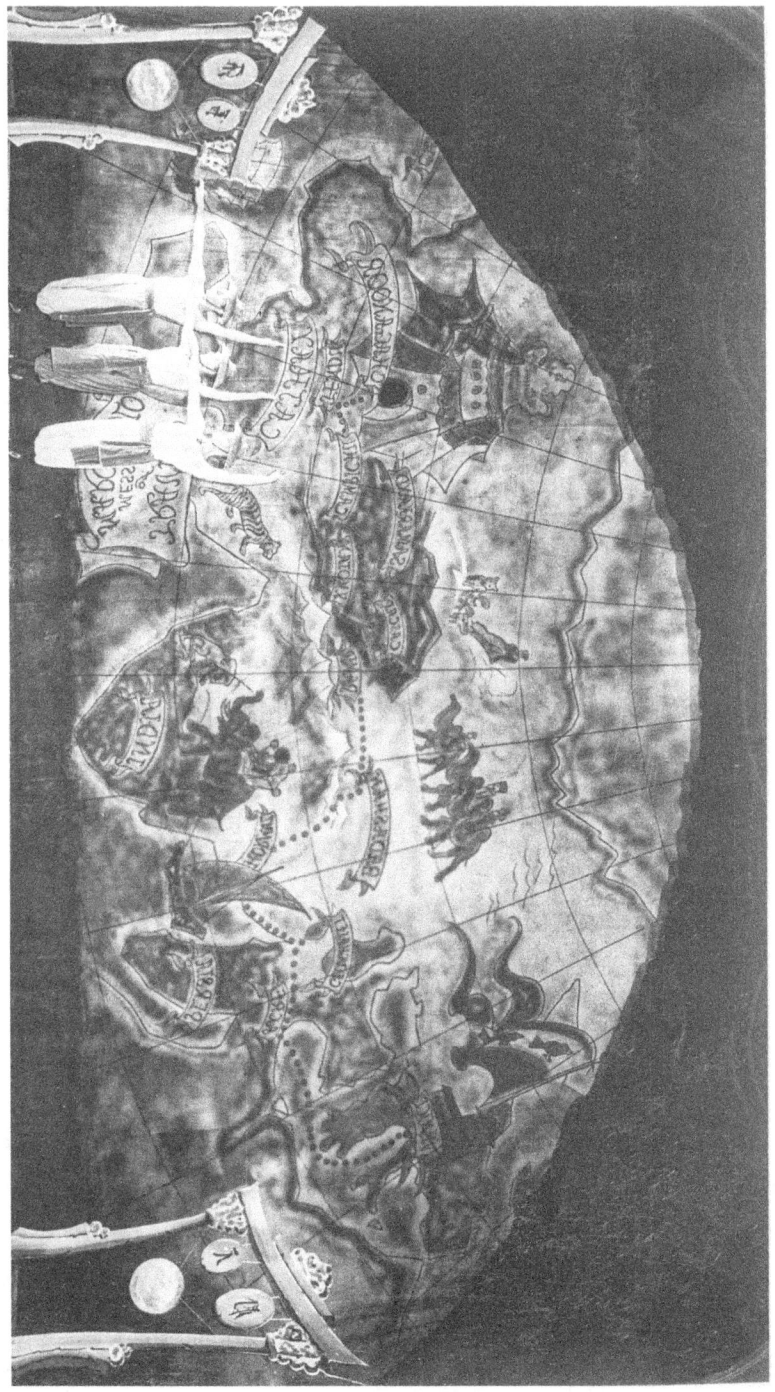

**Junior Programs *The Adventures of Marco Polo* Act I and Prologue to Act II,
The Great Map of the Polo's Journey to Cathay
Set Design by Kenneth MacClelland**
(Lancourt's personal papers)

they blew; caravans of camels over the deserts; gleaming white cities rising out of the wilderness; and people in their native costumes, Arab nomads, African blacks, brown men of India, and yellow of Cathay . . . To heighten the dramatic qualities of the cartographic display lights gleam like stars in the various areas of the Thirteenth Century world, twinkling and fading like living things as reference is made in the interludes to each of the romantic far-away places of Marco Polo's journeys in turn. A conception of the world as it was felt by the people who lived in medieval times is intensively vivified in an atmosphere created in the authentic spirit of the dark ages . . . Synthesized with a narration which sets the scene of the play and establishes its mood, a musical background composed by Margaret Carlisle furnishes the motif for a sequence of fragmentary dances each symbolizing in swift succession the coloring and spirit of the lands of Marco Polo's travels. Dancers glide around in front of the huge map that fills the entire background of the stage in graceful bodily delineations of the narrator's promise of wonders to come.

Barry Mahool, who played Nicolo Polo, also narrated the opening lines of the play, as well as the Polo's journey back to Cathay which formed the Prologue to Act II. The map appears as the house darkens, and we hear two Chinese gongs of varying pitch. Turbaned guards squat at each side of the stage where the gongs are placed. As the reverberations die away, the Narrator calls, as if through the ages:

Marco Polo _____ Marco Polo _____
Marco Polo. Great Princes, Emperors, and Kings, Dukes and Marquises, Counts and Knights and Burgesses, and people of all degrees who desire to get knowledge of the various races of mankind and of the sundry regions of the world, take this book and cause it to be read to you. For ye shall find therein all kinds of wonderful things . . . So wrote Marco Polo in the year 1298 . . . names have changed - Cathay is now China, and Persia is Iran . . . (The guards strike the gongs, the music starts and . . . the guards do a pantomime dance, describing in movement authentic to the countries mentioned - 'The Adventures of Marco

Polo.' The lights in the map chart his path across Europe and Asia.)

> [The Narrator begins the tale] High in the mountains of Tibet . . . Or making trade for the jade of Khotan . . . In a caravan thirsty and footsore . . . Siberian dogs pulled his seven sleds Through the snows of Caracoran . . . He fought . . . the robber bandits of Karauna . . .the cannibals of the isles of Zanghibar. . .He traded. . .With Moslems at the Lake of Geluchalat. . . With Idolators, Buddhists, Sensin and others . . . How did it happen that of all people, Marco Polo . . . should be the one to have . . . seen so much? To understand anything one must go back to the beginning.

The stage darkens, the map and guards disappear, and from off stage, we hear a Gondolier singing. Slowly, the lights come up, and we are in the Venetian courtyard of the house of Polo next to a canal. Silently, a gondola glides across the rear of the stage.

A similar scene with the enormous map serves as the Prologue to Act II, with the Narrator intoning, "For three years the Polos traveled." The script explains that "A light begins to glow from behind the map. As the Narrator speaks, we see the path of the Polos illuminated across Europe and Asia. The lighted portion is about eighteen inches to two feet wide. Using the ancient Chinese shadow puppet techniques, we see Nicolo, Marco Polo and Ching start the journey. They move slowly from place to place as their travels are described both musically and by THE VOICE." The narrator begins:

> Through the charted waters of the Mediterranean,
> To the great seaport of Acre,
> Then north to the cities of Armenia,
> They fished in the Lake of Geluchalat,
> Sailed the Persian Seas in a hand-sewn bark,
> To the windswept city of Hormus.
> They marched, they rode,
> They were carried, they strode,
> Camels through the desert sands,
> Hump-backed oxen through the marshes,

> Horses on the plains of Badashan.
> They fought, they traded,
> They climbed, they waded,
> Across the rivers of Pamir,
> Through the Kingdom of Cascar,
> To the noble city of Samarkand.
> Then through the greatest desert of all,
> For weeks on end fighting wind and sand,
> Toward the outposts of Cathay.
> Through cities names like ancient music,
> Campichu-Yungchang, Calachen, Tendu
> Now they make their way.
> Till at last they see the shimmering dream
> of Kublai Khan, Golden Chagannor,
> In the light of a fading day.
> (The light grows more concentrated as the figures reach Chagannor.
> All the rest fades from view. The map disappears.)

The script's description of the palace of Chagannor (as well as numerous photos of the stage sets) provides a hint of the splendor of the sets.

> A large throne set upon dais stage right. The main entrance to the room is by a circular arch stage left. The entire back wall is covered with oriental tapestry and marble columns. A gilded dragon encircles each column, the tail forming part of the support and the head taking the place of the capitol. A set of drums and gongs on each side are as far down stage as possible. The gongs are in a rack and the drums are of the kettle variety and form part of the decor. The tapestries have figures of birds and beasts and a large variety of flowers. As the curtain rises, it is early evening and the room is as yet unlit. In the half light we see the dancers seated before a drum and we hear an oriental rhythm . . . Aijuric, . . . is seated stage right with a one string lute. She is singing of the glories of Chagannor, the City of the White Pool and the delight of the Great Kublai Khan. Choi-chong is seated stage left.

III. THE PRODUCTIONS: PART I—THE JUNIOR PROGRAMS PLAYERS 111

**Junior Programs *The Adventures of Marco Polo* Act II,
The Throne Room of Kublai Khan
Set Design by Kenneth MacClelland**
(Author's personal collection)

> He beats a small drum and joins in the song, singing a verse now and then. Kublai Khan is seated on his throne. Achmath his Vice-Regent paces angrily about the room.

The response to *Marco Polo* across the country was consistent. In Omaha NE (Nov 7, 1941), the headline was "'Marco Polo' Called the Best of Junior Programs Plays." The Flushing, New York *Bayside Times* (Dec 25, 194?) featured the headline, "Adventures of Marco Polo' on Holiday 'Must' List at New Yorker Xmas Week." The *Montgomery Advertiser* (Alabama, n.d.) reported that, "a thousand or more children sat wide-eyed on the edges of their seats . . . enthralled by the wonderous journeys of Marco Polo and the splendors of the court of Kublai Khan . . . [and] the grownups . . . seemed equally pleased . . . While the show was presented especially for children, the performance in no way played down to them. With insights seldom seen in directors of performances for boys and girls, the producers . . . gave the young audience credit for good sense and artistic appreciation. They were rewarded with rapt and eager attention followed by thunderous applause."

A *New York Post* piece (n.d.), called Marco Polo a "superior children's play. Not once does it talk down to the children nor are the actors ever putting on a show for the little ones. They accept the boys and girls as their equals and together they have a fine time . . . It is excellent children's entertainment produced by those with adult minds." Robert Francis of the *Brooklyn Eagle* (n.d.) credited Lancourt with the production's success: "[I]t is to Mr. Lancourt that 'Marco Polo' owes most of its charm. He knows exactly what he is doing. He tells a simple straightforward story, never making the mistake of becoming condescending or writing down to his young audience." The *Opera News,* the classical music magazine of the Metropolitan Opera Guild (New York City, Dec 22, 1941), echoed the sentiment that *Marco Polo* "never plays down to them . . . Even in a state of war,—yes, especially in such a tense, grim atmosphere,—we must give to our youth the sanity, the relaxation, the poise which enjoyment of the best music can bring. We must nourish the artistic talents of our children so that after this period of horror, the creative genius of our nation may lead the world in all the arts." From the New Bedford, Massachusetts, *Mercury* (Oct. 3, 1941), we hear: "'The Adventures of Marco Polo' served yesterday to bring to our school children a glowing jewel of theater arts. Nothing so beautiful and rich; so significant in every line of speech and song, clash of cymbals or sound of flute, posture in dancing or well calculated movement has ever been seen here . . . From earlier productions we have come to recognize the fine contribution of Saul Lancourt . . . [and] It was a great satisfaction to have for the first time a long talk with Mr. Lancourt, for his is the mind behind much of the artistry of the presentations."

The Wisconsin *Monroe Evening Times* (Feb 18, 1942) also praised the production: "History was made easy and enjoyable for several hundred youngsters yesterday . . . It was like a wonderful dream in technicolor and with music, although no dream was ever so lavish . . . The players were gorgeously costumed in the thirteenth century styles of Venice and Cathay, but the dialogue and actions often were sassy and modern. For humorous instance, a lady of noble bearing placed two fingers between her lips and sounded a piercing street-corner whistle as she summoned a gondola . . . A gondola which actually moved across the stage was just one of the many strikingly beautiful stage appointments." In "Marco Polo Applauded" (unknown source, n.d.), the reviewer spoke highly of all aspects of the production: "From every point of interest—scenery, costumes, staging, acting, singing, dancing and story—the play was superlative juvenile entertainment. Skillfully blending one with the other, the arts of music, the dance, and acting were each employed to their full advantage to create an atmosphere, heightened emotions, and advance the plot." A *New York Post* (n.d.) piece by Mary Braggiotti offers an amusing vignette that illustrates a not uncommon audience response: In "Wyandotte, Mich., Frederic, aged seven, soberly applauded with the rest of the audience. Then, a grim, determined look on his manly little face, he mingled with the horde of young autograph seekers who trouped back stage . . . But Freddy wasn't there for any such sissy purpose as getting autographs. He strode up to the villain, who, in doublet and hose was innocently walking to his dressing room—and kicked him in the pants. That solemn duty discharged, he (Freddy. . .) felt better and joined the fun."

The *Green Bay Press Gazette* (n.d.) describes Dale Lefler as a "dashing, dark haired young man . . . gifted with an amazing versatility." A member of Ted Shawn's all-male dance company and the Roxy Theater's dance ensemble, Lefler was remembered for his ingenious interpretations of the Cat and the Crow in the dance-play *Pinocchio,* and the King and the Magician in the dance-play *The Princess and the Swineherd.* The review goes on to say: "The prodigy among these terpsichorean performers, however, is young Charles Tate, who at the age of 20 is counted one of the youngest ballet principles . . . Endowed with a superb comic

Junior Programs *The Adventures of Marco Polo* Costume Design for Act II
(Author's personal collection)

III. THE PRODUCTIONS: PART I—THE JUNIOR PROGRAMS PLAYERS 115

Junior Programs *The Adventures of Marco Polo* Costume Design for Act II
(Author's personal collection)

sense, he was the sensation of last year's Junior Programs ballet, "Robin Hood" in the roles of the jester and Friar Tuck. Tate began dancing professionally when he was 5 in his home town of Mobile, Ala., won scholarships at Ted Shawn's school, and leaped immediately into principal roles in professional ballet. In 'Marco Polo' he . . . enact[s] the part of Ching, a Chinese Sancho Panza character. His interpretation presents a rather fresh note on the spirit of the Oriental. For Ching is not *the mincing meditative Chinaman, lacking in physical vigor,* caricatured so many times in theater and motion pictures. *Rather he is a symbol of the new China—active, virile, and positive in his gait and manner* [emphasis added]." The *Star Gazetter* (Elmira, NY, Jan 29, 1942) also described Tate as a symbol of the new China. The Montgomery Alabama, *Journal* (n.d.) applauded Cecile Sherman (Aijurac), a Mobile girl, as the prima donna of the troupe. A star with the American Opera Company and New York Comique, her "rare talent for acting and a voice which has won her the best superlatives of Robert Simon of *The New Yorker* and music critics of all the metropolitan centers, Miss Sherman is one of the few artists in opera who can actually portray as well as sing her roles."

Unusual for the time, the *Press Gazette* reviewer made an interesting observation: "It might seem odd that a tall blue-eyed blond with saucy tip-tilted nose [Natalie MacDonald] enact the role of a demure Chinese dancing maiden, or that a Mobile, Alabama young man [Charles Tate] with a distinct southern drawl and a debonair New York dancer [Dale Lefler] play the roles of Chinese comic and villain respectively. Such casting would indeed have been grotesque if the performers were not three of the most promising among America's younger crop of ballet artists, recruited from the stages of New York's Metropolitan Opera, Carnegie Hall and the famous Roxy theater." Why this particular reviewer was moved to comment on the inauthentic casting is unknown, but his or her observation would certainly be in accord with today's sensibilities.

Finally, the January 10, 1942 *The Billboard*, "From Out Front" by Eugene Burr, describes his dilemma as an adult reviewing children's entertainment.

> In my dilemma I turned to a young lady of my acquaintance, Dixie Lee Brock, aged nine, and asked her to help me out by doing the Marco Polo review for me. Obviously, she's an infinitely better

III. THE PRODUCTIONS: PART I—THE JUNIOR PROGRAMS PLAYERS

judge of a show designed to appeal to children . . . She consented; and so I give you Miss Brock . . . 'The first lesson this play taught me was to be kind to one another and always tell the truth. I thought the best dancer was Dorothy Lysaght. I liked the music and the songs very much. My favorite song was *The Three Wise Monkeys*. I think it would be wonderful if every child in America could see this play, as we should love one another no matter what race or nationality.' According to Miss Brock, then, the play does its work, being enjoyable to the audience at which it is aimed. And if it gives rise in all its young auditors to the reactions noted by my reviewer, it's doing a magnificent, tragically needed job in the world today.

The reviews make it clear that if the Players' goal was to portray the people and culture of China in a positive light, *Marco Polo* was a major success. Without exception, the reviews paint a picture of a lavish production designed to spark children's imagination and awaken their curiosity, as well as offer a story with a range of positive role models—of wisdom and cross-cultural collaboration (Kublai Khan), of friendship and support (Ching), and of creativity (Aijurac and Moliu)—all brought to life in the performance itself. In tandem with the unusually comprehensive curriculum design for *Marco Polo* (see Chapter V), the live performance of the play clearly offered an appealing alternative to Hollywood's negative othering.

Doodle Dandy of the U.S.A.[175]

"Child Play Shows a Dictator, Youngsters Shout Him Down"
(*The Milwaukee Journal*, n.d.)

"Doodle Dandy Lauded as Play Building Good Citizenship"
(Nashville, Tenn. *Tennessean,* Nov 8, 1942)

In 1941, the United States officially entered WWII. According to McFadden, "all our efforts, the endless sacrifices which we shall have to make to win this war, will be useless if we do not bring up our children to be better citizens in a better world ahead . . . *Doodle Dandy will make them think about the meanings of our freedoms, [and] the responsibilities of democratic citizens. Unless they understand these, they will not be ready to take their part in making freedom work* [emphasis added] . . . Whatever we do for the good of the child of today is war work in its best sense." (*Ledger Enquirer*, Columbus, GA, Nov 5, 1942).

Gladys Swarthout, Metropolitan Opera mezzo soprano, Hollywood actress, and chair of the Junior Programs National Sponsoring Committee, and her husband, Captain Frank Chapman of the US Marine Corps, also acknowledged that in bringing music and theater to the young people of the country, the work of Junior Programs had never been as important as it was at that moment. "The armed forces realize the definite effect on morale of entertainment but, perhaps, we have not realized yet that civilian morale is equally important. Beyond this is the equally important consideration that the children to whom Junior Programs is bringing the best in entertainment, are going to be the ones in whose hands will lie the reconstruction of a shattered world. They must be trained for that responsibility in every way and the Arts must not be neglected in that training for our future is in their hands."[176]

The press release also quotes the US Office of Education concerning the importance of teaching good citizenship: *"The aim is to keep so clear the fundamental issues of the war that understanding will kindle and keep alight a flaming devotion to the cause of democratic freedom.* [emphasis added]"[177] And Albert Stoessel, a conductor and director at Julliard and a member of Junior Programs' National Sponsoring Committee, reenforced the point. "It seems to me so necessary to give our citizens of the future every possible lift in maintaining a sane and joyous

III. THE PRODUCTIONS: PART I—THE JUNIOR PROGRAMS PLAYERS

Junior Programs *Doodle Dandy of the U.S.A.* **USO Hunter College Program Flyer**
(Lancourt's personal papers)

outlook to help them in their task of building a better world. I know that Doodle Dandy will meet with great success" (*Tennessean,* Nashville, TN, Nov 8, 1942).

In searching for an appropriate follow-up to *Marco Polo,* Junior Programs had been exploring the possibility of a play focused on the life of a quintessentially American character. According to Barry Mahool, one of the company's leading actors, they had been considering three possible subjects for their next production: Walt Whitman, Thomas Jefferson, and Benjamin Franklin.[178] In an article for the *New York Times,* Lancourt shared the company's thinking: "It was a time when big words about democracy and civilization were flying faster than Lockheed Lightnings. In traveling about the country, we found our audiences completely confused by these big words . . . In treating [that] theme, we felt it best to go back to the homely fundamentals upon which our country was founded and relate these fundamentals to what might happen if some minor league Fuehrer tried to enthrone himself in a representative American community. In this way we were able to give our audiences a starting point within the realm of their own experience."[179]

Initially, Lancourt had no intention of writing the script. He had approached Thornton Wilder, but Wilder declined, saying "You did such a good job on 'Marco Polo,' why don't you write it yourself?" (*Standard Times,* New Bedford, MA, Jan 24, 1943). And, from an interview with the *Providence Sunday Journal* (Jan 17, 1943), we learn that "'Doodle Dandy' . . . was conceived after [Lancourt] had talked with thousands of young people in [the] audiences. 'I felt,' he says, 'that what they needed most was an understanding of the roots of our country and what the loss of any of our freedoms would mean to them personally. 'Doodle Dandy' will give them that idea of the homely fundamentals we are trying to protect. It's not a historical pageant—nor a hysterically patriotic appeal—it makes no mention of the war—but is rather a human story that will bring home to even the youngest audience what is meant by the 'Four Freedoms.'"[180]

The team Lancourt assembled to develop the production was impressive. Having worked with Ruth St. Denis on *Marco Polo,* he reached out to her husband, Ted Shawn, to choreograph the dance sequences for *Doodle Dandy.* Cofounder of the Denishawn Company which changed the course of dance history, Shawn's choreography for his company of all male dancers at Jacobs Pillow drew on the movements of laboring workers, Indigenous ceremonies, and other folk dances. He broke with the European dance vocabulary to develop a bold, athletic, masculine style that connected the physical and spiritual. John Martin, dance critic for the *New York Times,* called him the "first male dancer in America to achieve a position of influence and importance."[181] Sam Steen, the actor/dancer cast as Doodle Dandy, had been a member of Shawn's company, and "for the needs of this allegory, Mr. Shawn had the entire *Doodle Dandy* cast under his personal direction for a week at Jacob's Pillow in the Berkshires."[182] The two intelligent and lively dances Shawn created—the barn raising, and the bread-making dances—became poetic metaphors for the way "union of effort" leads to success, be it for building a barn or for creating a stable government.[183]

Elie Siegmeister was a quintessentially American composer, interested in developing an authentic American musical vocabulary. He was founder and director of the American Ballad Singers, pioneers in the folk music renaissance. He had set several of Langston Hughes poems to music and published a collection of *Negro Songs of Protest,* and with Olin Downes, music critic of the *New York Times,* Siegmeister assembled the well-known *Treasury of American Song.* He was an advocate of art and serious concert music for the common man, and his *American Holiday* was one of the first collections to integrate American working songs and common street tunes within an orchestral context.[184] In his approach to the score for *Doodle Dandy,* Siegmeister commented, "children's musical interests are much more mature and genuine than is generally recognized. Unfortunately, most of our children's music is still written . . . by those who believe that 'naive' and 'cute' pieces appeal to children. In inviting him to compose this score, it was generally agreed that he was not to write down to . . . children, but to write as good music as he possibly could, which adults also might enjoy. Writing for such an audience is an excellent discipline for a composer . . . [and] the aim in this play is to show that freedom has been deeply ingrained in the feelings and ideas of common Americans since the earliest times and to bring this out musically."[185]

Leo Kerz' sets for the production were also cause for comment. Gas and tire rationing meant the company could no longer transport elaborate sets from town to town. As Junior Programs had done in the past, it made necessity a spur to innovation. Instead of the elaborate sets they had designed for *Marco Polo,* to suggest the various scenes and room interiors for *Doodle Dandy* they used projections. A marketing piece from the Dramatists Play Service (n.d.) describing how a community theater could obtain the rights to the play included a description of the sets: "The sets in this play should be extremely simple . . .[the] scenes should in no case be very realistic. The

Shining Office of Freedom, Inc. should be shown practically without scenery . . . The street scenes and the 2 office scenes require only a minimum of furnishings. The high school auditorium scene is practically without a set or furniture, [and] except for the costumes of Doodle Dandy, . . . Jefferson [and] Franklin . . . clothing is modern and realistic." An Omaha, Nebraska, review (unknown source, Feb 7, 1943) added that, according to Mr. Lancourt, children would find projections more stimulating, as they allowed the action on stage to be continuous, like in the movies. No need to break the flow of action while sets were changed. Today, the use of projections to create a set or scene is common, but in 1943, it was, according to another unidentified source, a "dramatically and radically different treatment."

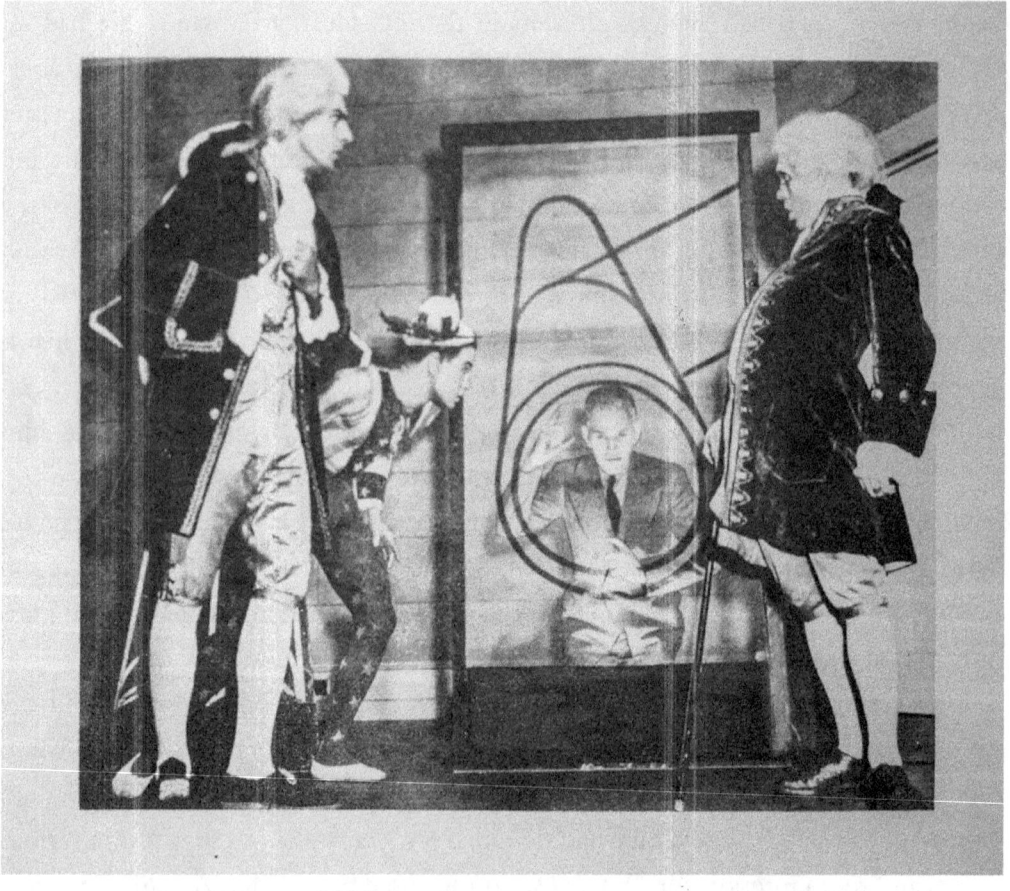

Junior Programs *Doodle Dandy of the U.S.A.* The "Seeograph" Act I, Scene 1
Thomas Jefferson (Alfred Allegro), Doodle Dandy (Sam Steen),
Humphrey Dumphrey (Leon Kahn), and Benjamin Franklin (Blake Ritter)
(Doodle Dandy of the U.S.A., 12)

Similarly innovative was the imaginative use of what today would be called "technology." In the play's first scene, children were amazed by the "Seeograph" and the "Hearograph" used by Ben Franklin and Thomas Jefferson to zero in on what was happening in Springville. The former was an unusual telescope with many lenses, tubes, dials, and meters that made it possible to "see" what was happening in any part of the world. The latter was a combination of many horns and screens that enabled the listener to "hear" a complete report of what was being said in any part of the world. Today, devices such as these are part of our everyday lives, but in 1943, these capabilities existed largely in the realm of science fiction.

Doodle Dandy's overarching themes—of democracy, of citizenship, and of society's responsibility to its children—had formed a continuous, deeply embedded thread throughout the life of Junior Programs, and a sampling of newspaper headlines provides clear evidence that with *Doodle Dandy of the U.S.A.,* the Junior Programs Players made good on their mission. "Children Roar Approval of 'Doodle Dandy'" (*Greensboro Daily News*, NC, n.d.); "Doodle Dandy, U.S.A. is Funny and Wise" (unknown source, n.d.); "Highest Praise Ever Given a Play for Children!" (unknown source, n.d.); "Doodle Dandy is Delightful" (*New York Post Weekly Picture Magazine* Oct 24, 1942); "A Rollicking Play with Music" (*Jefferson City Post Tribune*, MO, n.d.); and "'Doodle Dandy' Delightfully Staged" (*Schenectady Union Star,* Schenectady, NY, Feb 3, 1943).

According to the *New York Times* (Oct 19, 1942), "The little play-with-music is simply told by Saul Lancourt and was acted without pretension or any effort to be cute . . . Mr. Lancourt has staged the affair with a disciplined hand, so that, although there is much motion, none is wasted. The interpretive dances by Ted Shawn were a childish delight." Lauded as a "Play Building Good Citizenship" by the *Tennessean* in Nashville (Nov 8, 1942), "Doodle Dandy of the USA . . . is a story of the gallant fight for freedom *by children* [emphasis added] of a typical American community . . . The US Office of War Information has pointed out the importance of developing a resolute morale by the teaching of good citizenship, and Doodle Dandy, written and produced by Saul Lancourt is a perfect vehicle for this purpose." The Trenton, New Jersey, *Times* (April 2, 1943) also highlighted an important underlying theme of the play: "In adventurous fashion, employing all the color, fun and mystery of the theatre, he [Lancourt] has told *how children can democratically join together and oust a would-be dictator from their town*" [emphasis added].

The story of *Doodle Dandy* begins "on a cloud somewhere in space" in the "shining office of Freedom, Incorporated. The office clock—really Father Time with a circle of numbers on his belly, his scythe as the pendulum, and his arms as the clock hands—chimes the hour, "It's nine o'clock, Freedom Incorporated Time, it's nine o'clock, Freedom Incorporated Time."[186] Thomas Jefferson, Benjamin Franklin, and Anne Hutchison arrive, put their timecards into the clock to record their arrival, and express their concern that the head of the Complaints Department, Doodle Dandy, is once again late. Father Time suggests they fire Doodle Dandy and hire someone reliable. A knock on the door indicates the arrival of an applicant for the job. Ben Franklin suggests a tour of the office, especially the "Hearograph" and "Seeograph" departments. They focus both machines on Springville, a town being taken over by a small-time dictator. The new job applicant can hear a Springville woman talking: "Yes, I know this is Election Day, but I absolutely haven't the time to go down and vote. It really won't make any difference" (9). Her voice is soon replaced by a man's voice: "I'm much too busy to go to the meetings . . . Yes, I know he's done some things we none of us approve, but I really haven't time to waste at Council meetings" (10).

Jefferson and Franklin bemoan the lack of involvement on the part of the citizens of Springville, and the growing threats from Humphrey Dumphrey, the small-time dictator trying to take over the town. They explain to the applicant that they had spent their lives protecting the rights and freedoms of the country, and that they were continuing to do that through Freedom, Incorporated. When they sensed something going wrong, they would send Doodle Dandy down to help, "but only when the people are ready to help themselves" (14). To their great consternation, they have been unable to help Springville because Springville is not ready to be helped. Having completed the tour, they decide to hire the applicant in Doodle Dandy's place, and they ask him to sing the Liberty Song as part of his orientation.

"Come, join hand in hand, brave Americans all,

And rouse your bold hearts at fair liberty's call" (15).

The applicant begins to dance to the joyful tune, and slowly sheds his outer clothes, revealing blue tights spangled with stars and a red and white shirt, revealing that he is none other than Doodle Dandy. He begins to sing:

> I'm faster than light . . .
> And freer than air . . .
> I'm all Americans past,

III. THE PRODUCTIONS: PART I—THE JUNIOR PROGRAMS PLAYERS

All Americans present,
All Americans future,
All Americans free(17)!

Suddenly, the bells and lights of the "Hearograph" and "Seeograph" start to go off. Trouble in Springville! They can hear a conversation between Dumphrey and Ben Budd, the editor of the Springville newspaper: "I'm running this town, Mr. Budd—and everyone here will do as I say . . . The Mayor and the Council have turned the government over to me." Budd replies, "But the people elected them not you" (19)! Dumphrey counters with, "I'm going to run this town my way, and anyone who doesn't like my way had better get out . . . You can't stop me, Budd. You and that newspaper of yours!" (20). Budd concedes that he, on his own, may not be able to stop Dumphrey, "But when we get together, you won't have a chance" (20).

Franklin and Jefferson decide it's time to send Doodle to Springville. As Doodle leaves, he sings:

Junior Programs *Doodle Dandy of the U.S.A.*
Doodle Dandy (Sam Steen) and his Lucky Star (Barbara Gaye)
(Doodle Dandy of the U.S.A., 23)

> Since life is for Freedom,
> And Freedom's our life,
> Americans free
> Are America's future (22)!

Scene 2 opens with a luminous blue light and the appearance of Doodle's Lucky Star. She is dressed in the classic tulle skirt of a ballerina, and when Doodle leaps onto the stage, they dance together, from cloud to cloud until they finally arrive on earth. The Star departs, and Doodle dances up and down the aisles of the auditorium before seeing an encounter between one of Dumphrey's henchmen, Rush, and Mike, the newspaper delivery boy. Rush has just overturned Mike's wagon of newspapers. Doodle, invisible to them, puts the newspapers back in the wagon.

Rush and Mike look around, trying to figure out how the papers got put back in the wagon. An escalating conversation ensues as Mike tries to leave to deliver his papers, but Rush insists that a visit to Dumphrey's office is in order.

In Scene 3, Dumphrey is sitting at his desk finishing a radio speech. "I, Humphrey Dumphrey, will lead you out of the darkness of democracy . . . to those who cling to the outworn ideas of democracy, let me give warning . . . I . . . will brook no interference. . . I will speak to you daily at this time to give you my orders" (33). Rush appears and struggles with Mike, pushing him into the office. Mike protests, and Dumphrey sends Rush to get Mr. Budd, the editor of the newspaper. Rush takes out his gun; Doodle, still invisible, trips him and picks up the gun. Rush, unable to find his gun, can't figure out what's going on. We see Dumphrey throw his gun to Rush, but Doodle catches it mid-air. Finally, Rush just leaves to find Mr. Budd. Dumphrey and Mike argue about why Mike no longer needs to deliver newspapers, with Dumphrey telling Mike that "Elections are a thing of the past" (41) because people just don't know what they want; they have to be told what's good for them, and Dumphrey will be the one to tell them what to do. He goes on to warn Mike that his teacher, Miss Drake had better "keep her nose in her books" (42) if she knows what's good for her, and Mike says, "That's funny . . . that's just what she says you shouldn't do . . . She says you ought to lift your head up and see the world around you" (42). Dumphrey disagrees. "All you need to know is enough to do the job given you. More knowledge than that will get you into trouble . . . I know what's best for Springville" (42). Rush returns without Mr. Budd, and the scene ends with

Dumphrey and Mike leaving to find Budd, while Doodle engages Rush in a series of mischief-making encounters: Rush closes the curtains; Doodle (still invisible) opens them; Doodle takes a picture off the wall and Rush, seeing the picture floating toward him, screams in terror and runs from the office.

In Scene 4, Doodle sings and dances as he makes his way to the newspaper office.

> Doodle Dandy's back in town,
> He's a fighting man who won't go down,
> Nobody kicks our freedoms aroun'
> While Doodle Dandy's handy...
> There's his vote,
> There's his voice,
> There's his chance
> To make a choice ...
> There's his dance,
> There's his hope
> Of an equal chance ...
> Be a Doodle Dandy just like me,
> Help protect our liberty,
> A happy man is a man who's free (45).

Scene 5 takes us to the newspaper office where Budd, Miss Drake, and the pressman, Henry, are waiting for a response to Budd's editorial warning people about Dumphrey. Budd exclaims, "What do you have to do to Springville? Put chains on everyone before they realize they're on the way to slavery?" (54). Dumphrey and Mike burst in, and Budd learns that Dumphrey has prevented any of the newspapers from being delivered. An altercation ensues, and Dumphrey warns Budd that if he doesn't do Dumphrey's bidding, there won't be a newspaper to be delivered, and if that happens, Budd will be responsible for making it impossible for Mike to earn the money he needs to go to college. Mike protests that he wouldn't want to deliver a paper that wasn't telling the truth about what was going on, and that if he wasn't going to be able to think for himself, there was no point in his going to college. Dumphrey, exasperated, slaps Mike across the face, knocking him down. The act ends with threats all around, Dumphrey leaves, and Doodle tries to inspire Budd,

Henry, Mike, and Miss Drake, encouraging them to sing along:

> Freedom's a sun that never goes down,
> Don't let the black clouds gather! . . .
> Freedom's a child straight and strong,
> Playin' in the sun the whole day long, . . .
> Black clouds agatherin'
> Blow, wind, sweep 'em away! . . .
> Freedom's the air, without it you're dead, . . .
> If we let the black clouds gather (64).

Act II finds Budd and Doodle asleep in the newspaper office, and in a corner, we see part of the Freedom, Inc. office. Ben Franklin and Father Time are trying to communicate with Doodle, who abruptly wakes up, marveling at a dream he was having in which he, Doodle, was alive again. He had joined Mike and the others, who, working together were able to run Dumphrey out of town, thereby saving Springville from the loss of its liberty and freedom. Franklin acknowledges the importance of dreams. "Then dream, Doodle—dream hard. Make your dream come true. You can do it Doodle. Anyone can—if he dreams hard enough . . . Men's dreams have always brought the best changes" (71–72).

Doodle begins to dance his dream and slowly, he becomes human. After a moment of darkness, we see him with a pair of plain pants over his blue star-studded tights. Budd wakes up and confirms that Doodle in now visible. Miss Drake and Michael arrive, and they hatch the idea of inviting Dumphrey and all the townspeople to come to a show at the high school auditorium. Scene 1 ends with everyone figuring out what needs to be included to make the people of Springville see how dangerous Dumphrey is. Mike muses, "Well, we want them to know that Mr. Dumphrey isn't going to let them do the things they want to do . . . If you take away one liberty, you end up by taking away all of them, and that isn't the way America was built." Miss Drake responds, "that's our theme! America was built by a free people who worked together. Everybody built America. . . Our songs and dances will tell the story" (88–89).

Scene 2 opens with a radio announcement about a free gala celebration in honor of Mr. Dumphrey, and a show about what he plans to do for Springville. Members of the cast walk up and down the aisles of the auditorium with signs about the show.

III. THE PRODUCTIONS: PART I—THE JUNIOR PROGRAMS PLAYERS 129

**Junior Programs *Doodle Dandy
of the U.S.A.,* Doodle Dandy (Sam Steen)
at the High School Play**
(Doodle Dandy of the U.S.A., 89)

In Scene 3, Budd welcomes the whole town to the show, "Spring In Springville – 1803," and he reminds the audience that that was "around the time Thomas Jefferson was President" (92). The show opened with Ted Shawn's pantomime ballet about how Springville was built. They use the metaphor of a barn raising to illustrate the need for everyone to be involved:

> Their strength together they did brace,
> With one great heave it was in place. . .
> Now that's the way to get things done,
> You need the help of everyone (94).

Budd then stepped forward and reminded the audience that that was the same way the American government was built. "If it took all the people to build a barn, it certainly took all the people to run the government" (95). The second part of the show, another Ted Shawn ballet pantomime, told the story of how many people were involved in making a loaf of bread. The set showed a series of vignettes—a store and storekeeper, a baker and his oven, a miller and his mill, and a miner and his mine. A little girl and her mother sing with the other actors joining in a lively chorus as they dance from vignette to vignette:

> My mother called to me, And this is what she said,
> Go down to the store, and buy a loaf of bread . . .
> Chorus after each verse: I danced down so happily, so very very snappily,
> My mother sent me out to buy a loaf of bread.
> The storekeeper listened, and this is what he said,
> Let's go to the baker, and get the loaf of bread . . .
> We talked to the baker and this is what he said,
> The miller has the flour, for to bake the bread . . .
> We went to the miller,
> In his mill so neat,
> Go down to the farmer,
> For to get the wheat . . .
> We came to the farmer,
> A-milking of his cow,
> He sent us to the blacksmith,
> For to get a plough . . .
> We came to the smithy,
> Hammering at his anvil.
> He made us a plough,
> With a wooden handle . . .
> The farmer ploughed the field,
> The wheat it grew so high,
> He took it to the miller,
> When it was nice and dry . . .
> The miller got the mason,
> To build a dam so sound,
> To give the water power,
> To turn the mill wheel round . . .

> The miller ground the wheat,
> Until it was so fine,
> He put it in a sack,
> And sewed it up with twine . . .
> While the baker made the dough,
> We went to get the coal,
> The miner dug it out,
> Of a dark and spooky hole . . .
> The dough was kneaded well,
> The coal was glowing red,
> The baker put in the dough,
> And soon it came out bread . . .
> The storekeeper wrapped it,
> And gave it straight to me,
> I took it home to mother,
> As proud as proud could be . . . (96–102)

Once again, Budd steps forward and reminds the audience that a loaf of bread is not made by one person, and that great leaders—like Jefferson and Franklin and Lincoln—were great because they were the "voice of the people." A "plant" in the audience yells out, "What's that got to do with Springfield?" (102). Budd steps aside and the curtain opens on Mike costumed as Mr. Dumphrey, and the chorus sings:

> In Springville City there does dwell
> A certain man, you know him well. . .
> He walked the city far and wide,
> I am your master, thus he cried . . .
> Give up your freedoms, he did yell,
> Put on these chains, they'll fit you well (103–4).

Dumphrey tries to stop the show, but he is trapped. Mike innocently asks whether Dumphrey hadn't, in fact, tried to do all the things the chorus had enumerated? Budd turns to the audience, which has now become the 'people of Springville' and asks: "Do you think we ought to go on building our country with *everybody's* brains, *everybody's* work, and with *everybody* having a say in it? . . . Do you think that I ought to be allowed to write the truth . . . that Miss Drake . . . ought to go on teaching boys and girls to *think*? . . . Then what do we do with Mr. Dumphrey?" And how can we make sure "there are no more Mr. Dumphreys, ever" (106).

Collectively, at the audience's vocal urging, they throw Dumphrey out.

When the "show within the show" is over, they discover that Doodle is no longer there. They search everywhere, calling him to come back. Finally, from off stage, they hear Doodle's voice: "I'm with you all the time. I'm inside of you! You're all Doodle Dandies. If you're a real American, you can be a Doodle Dandy" (107).

And all across the country, the children responded with glee.

> [Doodle Dandy] had the youngsters shouting for democracy with as much vigor as they yell for a hit at a ball game . . . the boys and girls, their minds geared to flying squadrons and rough riding cowboys, looked a little askance at a celestial young man named Doodle Dandy who made sprightly leaps across the stage. But when the young man in the person of Sam Steen flitted thorough the audience and assured the boys and girls that Doodle was 'all Americans past and present' they were won over . . . the youngsters chortled with delight at Doodle's mischievous antics. Fisticuffs, excitement, humor and slapstick combined to keep the young ones on edge . . . there was a sympathetic guffaw when it was discovered that Doodle was as poorly versed in spelling as he was well versed in the tenets of freedom loving Americans . . . And to the adults who attended the show's first appearance in Milwaukee, there was something real and American in the unpredictable young Doodle who loved a good time but who prized freedom even more (*Milwaukee Journal*, WI, n.d.).

An Omaha, Nebraska, review by Jake Rachman (Feb 19, 1943) reinforces this image, saying, "Sam Steen [the actor playing Doodle] is the spark plug of the production. He is a clever dancer, a pantomimist, an actor, a comic, an acrobat and he uses all of his varied accomplishments to give the kids a good time. He even dances through the aisles to such roars of approbation as Tech auditorium has never heard."

Dance Magazine (Feb 1943) highlights several of the key issues of interest to Junior Programs: the preservation of democracy, a sense of collective agency on the part of the community, and a thoroughly engaging story:

III. THE PRODUCTIONS: PART I—THE JUNIOR PROGRAMS PLAYERS

> At last some one has produced a show that really sells democracy to the youngest generation . . . [and] [i]t's as much fun as the show, to see the kids drink in the high-stepping drollery. . . and hear them shriek with laughter . . .[T]he story sets out to sell the kids on Democracy and by George (Washington), it succeeds. It also manages to keep them hilariously amused all the while it is doing it . . . The folks in the play finally decide to win their bulldozed citizenry back to democracy by giving a local entertainment that will explain the necessity of democracy and how to make it work . . . The real audience becomes the audience of local citizenry and is treated to one of the most charming programs, which dances out in the simplest, most basic and entertaining manner the whys and wherefores of democracy . . . Take the whole family . . . because we all need it. But the most remarkable thing of all is that we don't realize we are being given a sermon because it is such a knock-down, carry-you-home good play, with catchy music and excellent dancing all thrown in for good measure . . . [and] be sure all the children you can find go . . . It's an excellent dance program, and the most entertaining and convincing presentation of democracy we've seen yet.

Even the one "mixed" review agrees that the "story and the moral thereof fitted down to the last moment of today's problems."

> Monday night, in Albert Taylor hall a new and most modern play was put on by a group of young professional players . . . It was the first of its kind that the town has seen, in which interpretive dancing joined with modern, rather inharmonic music. Almost tuneless songs were sung. The gay story was entirely symbolical and somewhat fantastic, and yet the story and the moral thereof fitted down to the last moment of today's problems. It has been engaging the controversial discussion of the thousand Emporians who saw it . . . One opinion contends that it was pretty terrible: the other that it was bright, beautiful, a harbinger of the new American drama . . . But this affiant desires to say that he enjoyed it and would like to

see more of its kind. Whereupon, we stand ready to receive the slings and arrows of outraged opposition. Let 'em come! We'll catch 'em with our teeth and spit 'em back! (*Emporia Gazette,* Emporia, KS, Feb 1943).

That the production was seen as extremely timely was made clear in review after review. Louis Kroenberger of PM (n.d.) tells us, "Doodle Dandy shows children what democracy and freedom really mean. It does so with a minimum of preaching and a maximum of entertainment and succeeds, I should think, rather well . . . [and it is] enlivened with capers, touched with fantasy, and not too long on speechmaking or flag waving." Walter Kiernan, a prominent International News Service columnist and radio host (unknown source, NY, Oct 13, 194?) titled his article "Big War Show for Children Starts Tour. Doodle Dandy of the U.S.A. Explains Conflict to Young Minds." "*The kids have a stake in this war* . . . [They] cannot escape its influences or consequences and *at last someone has gotten around to explaining it to them in words they can understand.* [emphasis added.] Doodle Dandy is starting out on tour this week and when its season's run ends in June, 180,000 youngsters from coast to coast will probably have a more graphic idea than their parents have of what this nation is fighting for . . . Doodle Dandy will play 120 cities under the auspices of civic organizations and is described by Dorothy L. McFadden . . . as the 'most significant work' the organization has undertaken." The National Federation of Music Clubs (n.d.) agreed. "Now in its seventh season, Junior Programs has played 1,950 performances to young audiences totaling over four million. It has become an American institution—its staff, its sponsors and its local committees believe it to be an important part of national defense." And an important part of the national defense was helping the younger generation get a head start on understanding how to defend America's democracy.

Much of the success of the play can be attributed to the fact that Mr. Lancourt is never condescending to his youthful audience, and he has written the play in a way that makes it clear that *the children themselves have agency in the preservation of Democracy.* [emphasis added.] He does everything possible to actually engage the youthful audience in the unfolding of the story. At various points, Doodle, the evil Mayor, and several other characters dance up one aisle and down another; at several other points, Doodle asks the audience a direct question and waits for an answer; still later Ben Budd, the newspaper editor asks the audience a series of questions culminating with, 'Then what do we do with Mr. Dumphrey?' And the audience invariably shouted an answer. At one point, '. . . when Doodle explained that everyone lived in his own Springville, one small person added, 'And Brooklyn.' (John Beaufort, *Christian Science Monitor,* n.d.).

While these audience engagement devices may seem rather ordinary today, they were highly unusual at the time, as was the message embedded in the play—*that the children, themselves, were part of the national defense.* According to the magazine *PM* (Dec 28, 1942), a liberal daily afternoon newspaper published in New York City during the 1940s, the performance, a "sort of juvenile and less direful 'It Can't Happen Here' . . . attempts to show children what democracy and freedom really mean with a minimum of preaching and a maximum of entertainment, and it succeeds rather well." And, according to the *New York News* (Dec 16, 1942.), the play was "an affirmation of life in contradistinction to its negation which is the philosophy behind the Hitler Youth and the Mussolini Youth with their military drills of 4-year-olds, and other perversions of the human spirit."

Although the play never mentions the war, many reviewers were quick to make the connection. The *Times Union* (Jacksonville, FL, Nov 8, 1942) described Humphrey Dumphrey as "a villain who had the ideas of the Hitler boys of Europe and Asia, doing business as the Axis . . . The said Humphrey Dumphrey seemed in a foul way about to throttle the town, muzzle the newspaper and the radio, and to provide a new order in education . . . By Act II, Scene 3, in the high school auditorium, "they provided a rail like vehicle for [Dumphrey's] hurried exit into oblivion. It worked, and it turned out to be a good lesson in unity and citizenship. It was lively entertainment with a purpose."

The *Ledger Enquirer* of Columbus, Georgia (Nov 8, 1942) made similar connections:

[Doodle Dandy] proceeds to help a fearless newspaper editor and a freedom loving teacher conquer a would-be dictator. Mike, the newspaper delivery boy . . . joins the editor and the teacher in presenting a play to the people of Springville. [It is] a story in symbolic dancing and songs showing the abomination of dictators in our way of life. The play was designed to make the people think for themselves and accordingly, it made our audience of little people think and answer the questions as they were thrown from the stage . . . Doodle Dandy was a lovable character from the minute he appeared. His dancing was a suggestion of mischief which placed him in each child's heart immediately . . . The tunes were lively and patriotic and made you want to sing with the characters. We were privileged at this time to have such a play brought to Columbus as it presented the principle for which we are fighting. It is necessary now for children to understand the war and the things we are trying to preserve. There is no better way to present this to them than by such a play as Doodle Dandy.

The choice of examples from American daily life, (a barn-raising dance, and a bread-making dance and song), also illustrated how important it was for everyone, including the young people, to join together to oust the would-be dictator:

During the course of demonstrating how union of effort is the best builder not only for barns and food products but for stable conditions of community existence, there were two exhilarating group dances. That of the [barn-raising] pioneers in . . . slouch hats and buckskin trousers [and the women in] sunbonnets and full skirts" all dancing "to variations by Elie Siegmeister on the theme of an old Kentucky mountain air. His music for the "bread" ballet was original and other numbers by this specialist in folk tunes brilliantly illustrated the progress of the spirit of Doodle Dandy through the life of the nation . . . One of the charming sections of the pageant was the 'bread' ballet. The lovely voice of a woman recited: 'My father [sic] sent me to buy a loaf of bread,' while in pantomime the company followed back from the grocery to the raising of the wheat, the grinding and the baking with coal [that] miners had brought from the bowels of

> the earth. As many must work together to accomplish a loaf of bread, so many must speak to create a government ("Democracy is Theme for Ballet", unknown source, New Bedford, MA, n.d.).

The *Daily Worker* (Dec 30, 1942), in its weekly article discussing "What's on in the Theater" tells us that "'Fascists and Tories won't like 'Doodle Dandy of the U.S.A.' But you and your kids will." And a *New York Times* review (Dec 30, 1942) summed it up: "[I]t is acted with professional taste and beautifully staged. There are few better ways of spending an afternoon . . . Let's hope that the theatre is packed with youth all week."

Given their raison d'être, if there had to be a final production for Junior Programs, there could not have been one as fitting as *Doodle Dandy*. The play's focus on democracy—on the need to explain it to the next generation of citizens in a way they could understand, and to dramatize the constant vigilance needed to maintain it in a compelling way—embodied not only the social, political, educational, and artistic mission of Junior Programs, but also integrated the many things Junior Programs had learned about how to successfully make theater for young audiences. First and foremost, the script focused on subject matter of importance. It treated children with respect, *explicitly depicting them as active agents in democracy's survival.* The production was both entertaining *and* educational, and met the quality standards Junior Programs had set for themselves. The production was artistically innovative in its use of projections, and in the way it integrated each element of the authentically American music, song, and dance as a means of pushing the dramatic plot forward. There were no interludes; there was nothing superfluous. It was all designed to stimulate the young audiences' imagination; to make them think. And *Doodle Dandy* managed to do all this in a way that highlighted and embodied the aspirations embedded in the American Dream. Rather than pointing out the nation's failures, the production used an elegantly simple set of powerful story-telling metaphors—the barn raising and bread making—to convey a core truth: that by acting collaboratively as a community, it was possible to make the American Dream a reality.

Taken together, all five plays commissioned by the Junior Programs Players made it clear that the performing arts could offer their audiences far more than entertainment, and that it could do so in an exciting but unpretentious and natural way. They were able to make complex concepts and ideas such as democracy, community, and the richness of the different cultures, races, and ethnicities accessible, and they did so with an age-appropriate integrity such that "easy-to-understand" never became "simplistic or patronizing." Similarly, their commitment to authenticity, incomplete as it was by today's standards, brought those racial and cultural differences to life in a way that made them appealing and desirable rather than strange and unsettling. In a sense, they embodied Oskar Eustis' view of the theater as a place for the exploration of alternative ideas in a way that created both empathy and a sense of community.

Few would argue with the fact that far more is still needed to achieve the level of "narrative reparations," and unity of purpose required to sustain a vibrant democracy, but the road map the Junior Programs Players created provides guidance for the work that remains. However, the Players were just one of the three Junior Programs companies. The following chapter explores the artistry, innovations, and accomplishments of the Junior Programs Opera, and the Junior Programs Ballet.

IV. THE PRODUCTIONS: PART II—THE JUNIOR PROGRAMS OPERA & JUNIOR PROGRAMS BALLET COMPANIES

The Junior Programs Opera Company

Often considered the most esoteric and elite of all the performing arts, opera is wrapped in grandeur and tradition, with larger-than-life stories, characters, and settings—and a reputation for putting many of its audience members to sleep. The very idea of an opera company devoted exclusively to productions for children—how was that even possible?

In "Opera Provides Optimum Benefits for Children," the authors suggest that not only is opera for children possible, but they posit that "children live out their daily lives quite naturally on an operatic scale." Growing up is, in a sense, an operatic experience. It is filled with passionate emotions, mythic quests and waves of epic struggle, magical discoveries, and youthful voices shrieking with joy or sobbing with pain as they try to make sense of what it means to be human—all of which are part and parcel of the operatic form.[187] McFadden would likely have agreed. Her early, somewhat serendipitous connection with the National Music League's (NML) production of *Hansel and Gretel* made the question of an opera company for children real. But *Opera News* had its doubts: "Can opera be given to children of six?"[188] For McFadden, engaging the audience of tomorrow during their earliest years in the best of American culture was the whole point of Junior Programs, and she was all about providing parents with high quality alternatives to what she saw as the unwholesome, tawdry fare on offer. "Children's taste," she believed, "is good and right until our adult world perverts it."[189] "We, the American audience have the power of choice . . . [Because we are paying for it, o]ur entertainment material is exactly what we . . . make it."[190]

Lancourt's answer to the *Opera News* question about six-year-olds was a resounding "Yes!"

Musical America tells us, "His almost revolutionary approach to . . . reshaping traditional forms in opera, ballet, and theatre, and injecting into them a new vitality, is a most important factor in the rapid growth of Junior Programs' audiences." Discussing his experience adapting Junior Programs' second opera production, *The Bumble Bee Prince,* Lancourt shared his approach.

> We have to start shaping a production like this with a complete realization of the obstacles all opera productions must carry for presentation to the American public . . . We must assume that people go to the opera with the preconceived notion that it is going to be dull. That is just what we believe opera shouldn't be. It should be full of life, action, color, movement! It must always keep the audience's attention, command its interest. The reason people sleep through operas is for lack of action, excitement, and life. Operatic companies aren't even rehearsed for anything but the music . . . [but] Junior Programs operas require a marriage of music with the arts of dancing, pantomime, of singing and acting. In 'The Bumble Bee Prince,' for example, there was a problem of what to do with an opera containing some of the finest music ever composed set to a narrative in which there were several lazy passages. We found a lot of placid beauty. But that wasn't enough, so we simply had to make changes. Now, we haven't disturbed the musical line. We've kept all its beauty but filled it with action by taking the emotion which music carries and translating it into rhythmic movement. During the lazy passages of singing and narrating, we've made other people on the stage do things to heighten the effect of what is being told in the songs and narrative.[191]

From the outset, Lancourt, who had been stage manager and then director for the NML production of *Hansel and Gretel,* had a clear vision of how to make opera appeal to their youthful audience. An undated Junior Programs press release, "Junior Programs Develops New Stage Techniques for Young Audiences," provides a glimpse into his iconoclastic working methods:

> Like most successful innovators, Lancourt has an impatient and uncompromising attitude to the failures of the past. The old drama, opera and ballet died on the road, he says, because it didn't deserve to live, trying to get away with outmoded forms, hand-me-down props, and third-rate performers or worse. It is no wonder that those flopped miserably in an effort to compete with motion pictures which used the most expensive artists, scenery and production and sold them to the public at rock-bottom prices . . . Only recently when better performers and productions have taken to touring has the road begun again to show signs of life' and fortunately for Lancourt, 'there is no lack of the finest American artists for the stage . . . We choose them carefully for Junior Programs. We have also spared no efforts to devise scenery, props, lighting, and equipment for touring productions that will reproduce on practically any auditorium stage in the country the same modern impressions that have till now been possible only in the best New York theatres . . .' Lancourt helped to achieve these results by what he calls an adjustment of the stage to the tempo of the twentieth century. His approach is one of a fearless attack on dogma and iron-bound tradition. He stepped up opera to make it as fast in movement, action and suspense as the sprightliest of musical comedies, preserving intact all the melodic beauty and emotional impact of the musical score.

One example of these "adjustments" was the elimination of repetitive arias; another was ending the tradition that all stage business stops during the singing of an aria. According to the Galveston, Texas, *Tribune* (Jan 19, 1940), "the singers in Hansel and Gretel have been trained to commit no such errors. That they are helping to raise the standards of musical appreciation in America goes without saying. The resulting interest of thousands of children, most of whom had never seen an opera before in their lives, is sure proof of this."

Lancourt's success in reimagining how opera should be staged was made somewhat easier given the stability of the Junior Programs opera singers. American-born and trained, most of them continued in the roles they had played in the NML's production of *Hansel and Gretel* when it was transferred to Junior Programs, and they remained with the company for the whole of its existence.[192] Several were former members of the American Opera Company, a troupe formed in the late 1920s at the Eastman School of Music in Rochester, New York. Lancourt's preference for American Opera Company singers was no accident. A main purpose of Eastman had been to reintroduce the art of acting into operatic performances; and Lancourt, determined to eliminate the pompous gestures of traditional opera, made sure that Junior Programs' productions and rehearsals focused not only on the music, but on acting, action, lively movement, and humor as well.[193] This Eastman training, with its emphasis on clear enunciation and pantomime, was an important key to Junior Programs' operatic successes: "When a singer was doing a solo number on one part of the stage, the other members of the cast performed various stage business at the other side in order to keep the action moving."[194]

Lancourt introduced four additional innovations which supported his view of how to make opera both accessible and compelling to a youthful audience. Taken together, they became identifiable hallmarks of the Junior Programs Opera's success. The first was a *focus on the essential musical core*, the impetus behind their decision to use a piano accompaniment rather than a full orchestra. While it was also true that—from a practical point of view—it would have been financially impossible to tour both an opera company and a ballet company each with full orchestras, Cecile Sherman, who sang the roles of Gretel in *Hansel and Gretel* and the Bad Sister and the Swan Princess in *The Bumble Bee Prince,* explained the decision: "We find that the addition of an orchestra only serves to heighten the children's bewilderment. They have enough to grasp as it is. And . . . the volume of the orchestra militates against the singer's enunciation."[195]

The second innovation was Lancourt's creative *use of a Narrator.* In the tradition of a Greek chorus, this "invented character" appeared, either in front of the curtain before each act or seated at the side and told "in simple poetry what was to happen during the forthcoming act."[196] Fitting the narrator's words to the music, Lancourt fashioned lively scripts for the narrators such that the *New York Sun* (Dec 28, 1937),

IV. THE PRODUCTIONS: PART II—THE OPERA & BALLET COMPANIES   143

speaking about a performance of the *Bumble Bee Prince*, noted, "Perhaps the most intelligent idea . . . was the narrator who prefaced each scene with a summary of the action and encouraged the listeners to answer her cleverly planted questions. This task was excellently managed by Lanni Carvell." This "new addition" to the opera cast was an immediate success, and quickly became part of all Junior Programs' opera and ballet performances. By making the opera's story understandable to even a very young child, they were able to make their productions easily accessible to those unfamiliar with the operatic art form. Lancourt also used the role of narrator for the Victor recording of *The Bumble Bee Prince*. Absent bright and colorful sets, visual action, and appealing costumes, he recognized the need for some device that would capture and hold the young listeners attention as they enjoyed the recordings.[197]

The third innovation—more common today but unusual at the time—was the company's decision that all the operas would be *sung in English*. The well-known Metropolitan Opera baritone, Lawrence Tibbett, was especially pleased by this decision. "I wish to reaffirm my belief in the purpose and aims of Junior Programs . . . I firmly believe that America will know no opera of its own until the beauty of our own language in song is realized, as it is in all Junior Programs operas . . . the coming generation will have no . . . love for the great operas of the past until they have an opportunity to hear them well performed in their own tongue."[198] However, singing in English did not automatically guarantee comprehension, but two reviews attest to the quality of training Lancourt required of their singers. From the Floral Park, NY, *Gateway* (Jan 12, 1939), we learn "that a striking feature of their performance was its clarity. English operas are not necessarily intelligible to their listeners, but this one was. No lines were blurred or obscured, which made it possible for the youthful audiences to derive a maximum of pleasure from the spectacle." And praise for Alma Milstead, one of the leading Junior Programs' singers, noted, "Her enunciation is a joy . . . she sings with style [and] has a gift of being able to immerse herself entirely in the music . . . [and] one senses instantly her sincerity, innate musicianship and fine sense of proportion" (Salem, OR, *Journal*, March 1, 1941).

The fourth innovation was Junior Programs' focus on its *educational partnerships*. As we will see in Chapter V, CCSUs for each opera were sent to all participating schools prior to the arrival of the performance. As a result, "by the time [the children] come to the actual performance, they know all the arias and the entire story."[199] Tibbett also pointed out another unique opportunity for learning that Junior Programs offered: the company filled the gap between conservatory training and the Metropolitan Opera House by providing young American singers with the opportunity to learn the repertoire and gain the on-stage experience needed to move forward in their careers.[200]

As with the Junior Programs Players and their pioneering focus on a series of what might be called cross-cultural, cross-racial "narrative reparations," Lancourt's bold and innovative approach to reimagining opera was successful in both making the operatic canon more accessible to a youthful audience, and in capturing and holding the attention of the next generation. The company produced three fully staged operas: *Hansel and Gretel,* *The Bumble Bee Prince,* and *Jack and the Beanstalk.* The following section examines each of the three operas, providing a synopsis of the story, brief comments about the composer, why the opera was chosen, key features of the production, and an overview of how the children responded to the experience.

IV. THE PRODUCTIONS: PART II—THE OPERA & BALLET COMPANIES

THE OPERAS

Hansel and Gretel [201]

"Gingerbread House In "Hansel" Needs Police Protection, It Seems — The Children, You See, Love to Sample It"

(Indianapolis, Indiana *Times*, Feb 7, 1939)

Junior Programs Opera Company's *Hansel and Gretel*
Gingerbread House and Witch's Oven
Hansel (Marion Selee) and Gretel (Cecile Sherman)
(Lancourt's personal papers)

By acquiring the widely acclaimed NML Opera Company's production of Engelbert Humperdinck's masterpiece *Hansel and Gretel*, Junior Programs was able to honor their *Credo*'s commitment to make the best of classical music and singing accessible to the children of America, no matter where they lived, and to "hit the ground running." That they succeeded is evident in multiple reviews of their performances. The Meridian, Connecticut, *Record* (n.d.) noted the "rapturous cheering that was heard . . . and the young audience was so entranced by the story that the fact that the entire opera was sung hindered not in the least their enjoyment of it . . ." The Kingston, New York, *Daily Freeman* (n.d.) went on to say, "Owing to the fact that it was impossible to accommodate all who wished to hear the opera . . . which was given twice this afternoon, it has been decided to repeat the opera Saturday morning at 9 o'clock in the Kingston High School auditorium. So large was the attendance this afternoon at both performances that it was necessary to call on the police to assist in handling traffic." In Fort Wayne, Indiana, the *Journal Gazette* (n.d.) opined: "If 'Hansel and Gretel' is any indication what the children of this country like, we need not concern ourselves with the prospects of the cultural life of the next generation . . . The sprightliness of Humperdinck's music was played to the hilt by the youthful but thoroughly capable cast. With evident enjoyment in what they were doing, the characters capered about the stage with a spontaneity that captured the large audience from the very beginning."

Humperdinck had written *Hansel and Gretel* at the request of his sister, Frau Adelheid Wette, as an unpretentious "little singspiel" to entertain her children. Using several well-known German folk songs as his theme, Humperdinck's enthusiasm grew, and in 1893, the singspiel became a full-fledged, three-act opera—a simple children's story with elaborate, complex music now recognized throughout the world as a masterpiece.[202] The Mamaroneck, New York, *Times* (Feb 8, 1940) review sets the stage, describing the Village of Illsenburg near a wild and rocky woodland deep in the Hartz Mountains of Germany. It was here that German children would travel to see a large rock known as the Witch's Kitchen and to listen to the popular tale of the wicked witch who turned children into gingerbread.

According to the RCA Victor libretto, Act 1 took place in the rustic, tumbledown cottage in the woods of Peter, the broom maker.[203] As the curtain parts, the audience saw Hansel making a broom, while Gretel was knitting stockings. Their parents had gone to town to sell their wares, leaving the children to work on their own. But they soon tired of working and lamented their plight. Hansel sang: "What's to be done? Who'll give me milk and sugar, for bread I have none?" Gretel, perched on a high stool, mending a long white stocking, replied:

> Brother, come and dance with me,
> Both my hands I offer thee,
> Right foot first, left foot then,
> Round about and back again.

They dance breathlessly until their mother unexpectedly returns. Angry at their idleness, she chases Hansel, waving a stick and accidentally knocks over the jug of milk. "Wait, wait until your father comes home," she sings, and then sends them off to the woods to gather strawberries so they would have something to eat. Soon, their father arrives home, carrying a large basket of food he was able to purchase because he had sold all his brooms at the village fair. Noticing the children's absence, he asks where they were, and when he hears they had gone into the woods, he sings of the Witch who:

> . . . stalks around,
> With a crinching, crunching, munching sound,
> And children plump and tender to eat,
> She lures with magic gingerbread sweet. . .
> In the oven red hot she pops all the lot;
> She shuts the door down until they're done brown

Both mother and father rush out to look for the children, but Hansel and Gretel are now deep in the forest, eating as many strawberries as they are putting into their basket. Gretel soon tires, and "As night spreads her mantle over the forest, the shadows grow longer and longer . . . the children throw themselves on the . . . grass [and] . . . the Sand Man come to put them to sleep.

> I shut the children's peepers, sh!
> And guard the little sleepers, sh!
> For dearly do I love them, sh!
> And gladly watch above them, sh!

When the children awake the next morning, they see a little house made of cakes and candy. The roof is chocolate, the chimney a peppermint stick, and the walls are made of gingerbread. As Hansel and Gretel eagerly break off pieces of the house to eat, they hear a voice from within.

"Nibble, nibble, mousekin, who's nibbling at my housekin?" Suddenly, the Witch emerges and grabs Hansel when he and Gretel try to run away, but the Witch raises her stick and sings:

> Hocus pocus, witch's charm,
> Move not, as you fear my arm!
> Back or forward do not try,
> Fixed you are by the evil eye!

The stick begins to glow, and Hansel, captivated by the light, is locked in a little cage by the Witch, who then throws log after log into the oven until a roaring fire glows. The Witch, standing on tiptoe at the oven door, fails to see Hansel escape from his cage, and "he and Gretel push her with all their might and topple her right into the oven . . . flames in the oven leap higher and higher, the crackling grows louder and louder until the whole thing becomes red hot and explodes with a terrific crash . . . [and] Hansel and Gretel are surrounded by a group of little children whom the wicked Witch had turned into gingerbread." The final moments find the Witch herself turned into gingerbread and dragged from the ruins of the oven, while the father sings:

> Such is Heaven's punishment,
> Evil works will have an end.
> When past bearing is our grief,
> God, the Lord will send us sure relief.

The reviews from every corner of the country attest to the success of the Junior Programs' approach to opera designed for a youthful audience. The headline of the Youngstown, Ohio, *Daily Vindicator* (Nov 18, 1936) reads, "Crowds Greet Fairy Opera Everywhere—Ticket Sell-out in Eastern Cities." The Danbury, Connecticut, *News-Times* (n.d.) called the performance "a gorgeous entertainment . . . an unmitigated delight . . . clarified by the exceptionally fine diction of the singers. To say that the children were interested throughout would be putting it mildly. They were spell-bound. [It was] a well-nigh perfect performance . . . the singers were of the

Junior Programs Announcement Flyer for *Pinocchio* **and** *Hansel and Gretel*
(Lancourt's personal papers)

highest professional and artistic caliber . . . the vigorous, spontaneous acting . . . the simple but imaginative stage settings . . . the tuneful gaiety of the music . . . [all combined to] put the entertainment across with such unmistakable success."

According to the Mamaroneck, New York, *Times* (Feb 8, 1940), "Cecile Sherman as Gretel, a diminutive, vivacious blond, acted and sang with such sprightly grace we are convinced we are seeing a young girl ready to play. With her clear bell-like soprano which blends so beautifully with that of the lovely contralto, Miss Marion Selee, who plays that mischievous and lively boy, Hansel, we are entranced as we watch these two irresistible youngsters dance merrily around the room, upsetting a cup of milk, which for them is supper."[204] Another review in the Larchmont, New York, *Times* (Feb. 15, 1940) tells us, "The sprightliness of the music and the spontaneity of the action brought an element of charming gaiety to the whole production. Cecile Sherman who sang the role of Gretel carried out the happy spirit of the opera with her rare sense of comedy and the high caliber of her soprano voice. Marion Selee, mezzo soprano, played the part of Hansel and blended her voice tellingly with Gretel's during the duet 'Prayer Song.' [O]ne is intrigued with the imaginative touch of Kenneth MacClelland's scenic genius: for we experience that feeling that we are in a foreign country."

Musical America (Feb 10, 1940) testifies to the unusual degree of "audience engagement," describing how, as Sherman knelt, hands folded in prayer during her duet with Selee, "a small boy rose from his seat and joined her in singing 'The Prayer Song,' completely oblivious of his surroundings. The hushed audience had lost itself so completely in the performance it seemed altogether natural for one of them to give full expression to his emotions." The reviewer goes on to say, "This is no isolated instance . . . [there was] a proclivity on the part of children to immerse themselves wholly in a world of inspiring make-believe . . . Directions will be shouted to the sympathetic characters . . . on how to escape pursuing villains [and s]houts and cheers will greet virtue's triumph."

An unidentified reviewer, in describing how engaged the children were, commented that the production was so real that "when the witch screeched in her high, thin voice, 'Gretel, where are you?' a little child in the front row cried excitedly, 'There—in the house!'" During a matinee in Wilmington, North Carolina, "a horrified yell rose from one corner of the audience as the old witch made her entrance" (Charlotte, NC, *Observer*, Dec 1939). In Williamsport, Pennsylvania (Jan 27, 1939), there was "unbridled relief . . . on the tiny faces in the audience when hero and heroine surprised their captor by pushing her into her own oven." And from the Morgantown, West Virginia, *Dominion News* (Nov 12, 1936), we hear: "If the musical dialogue between Hansel and Gretel dragged in a few incidents, it was not the fault of Marion Selee and Cecile Sherman who played these respective parts, but of Mr. Humperdinck himself, for whom I felt a bit sorry; for could the composer have known what beautiful music the voices of these two girls made of his difficult score, surely he would have written many more duet passages for them to sing . . . [and] many singers of note claim that, next to Wagnerian opera, the role of the Witch . . . is one of the most difficult scores to sing." This reviewer went on to say, "the scenes for the opera . . . were delightful and realistic; the Gingerbread House did actually look good enough to eat." But the Indianapolis, Indiana, *Times* (Feb 7, 1939) questioned the latter assumption: "The gingerbread house . . . undergoes considerable wear and tear . . . It actually looks as if it were made of gingerbread, studded with orange, lime, lemon and licorice gumdrops . . . The children in the audience never fail to come up on stage after the performance to touch and feel and handle it . . . Those carried away by an excess of experimentation have learned that it doesn't taste nearly as good as it looks."

A letter of praise to McFadden from Alice Fay Garland, president of the Haverhill Central Council Parent-Teacher Association of Haverhill, MA, sums up the production's impact rather poignantly: "We find that practically all those who attended the series last year are asking for tickets this year. Is this not the best praise a child can give? . . . One little boy, whose clothing looked as though he came from the poorer group looked up at me during the last performance and with his eyes sparkling said, 'It was worth the 50 cents wasn't it?'" (Dec 16, 1936). Finally, according to journalist and music educator, Charles Plotkin (unknown source, n.d.), "[Junior Programs has been] successful in inspiring a genuine appreciation and understanding of the arts of opera, ballet and concert music in young people . . . Junior Programs manages to attain these ends by employing several distinctive production techniques. Explaining these, Mr. Lancourt, who directs most of the organization's offerings, declares that liveliness, humor, and action are counted among the essentials in every Junior Programs production."

With this early and unqualified success, there was an understandable concern on the part of both McFadden and Lancourt as to whether the company would be able to replicate such a success with their next production.

The Bumble Bee Prince[205]

"'Bumble Bee Prince' Enjoyed by 3500 — Rimsky-Korsakoff Opera Well Received"

(*Worcester Daily Telegram*, n.d.)

**Junior Programs Opera Book Cover for *The Bumble Bee Prince*
Illustration by Sheilah Beckett**
(*Saul Lancourt, Garden City Publishing Co., Inc., New York, 1940.
Author's personal collection*)

Understandably, the importance of Junior Programs' choice of a second opera loomed large. From the time of their founding, both McFadden and Lancourt had been scouring the world for appropriate stories that would delight their young audiences and help introduce the youth of America to the best in the performing arts. During a personal trip to Europe, McFadden happened to hear of a performance at the Moscow Children's Theatre of Nikolai Rimsky-Korsakov's opera, *Tale of the Tsar Saltan*, based on a poem by Alexander Pushkin. McFadden attended a performance and immediately realized its potential for Junior Programs. As it turned out, 1937 marked the hundredth anniversary of the death of Pushkin, Russia's greatest poet. With the exception of Shakespeare, no other writer's poetry has inspired as many songs, symphonies, and operas as Pushkin, and opera companies all over the world were celebrating this centenary. While Rimsky-Korsakov was Russia's most beloved composer, and the *Tale of the Tsar Saltan*, written as an entertainment for the tsar's children, was a favorite in Moscow, the opera had never been performed in the United States. The idea of a premiere would likely have been appealing.

Much of Rimsky-Korsakov's music was based on Russian folk melodies. Only "The Flight of the Bumble Bee," composed for this opera, had become a concert classic in the Western musical canon. It seemed fitting that for the 1937–38 season, Junior Programs offered Rimsky-Korsakov's opera as a follow-up to *Hansel and Gretel*. Upon McFadden's return to the United States, they were able to find a score for the opera, but the libretto was in German. In her unpublished autobiography, McFadden recalls translating the text into English herself.[206] She then engaged Marion Farquhar, a well-known translator and lyricist, to work with Lancourt and the internationally acclaimed Russian Julliard Music School piano coach and musical arranger, Gregory Ashman to adapt and shorten the opera for a young American audience from its original two-and-a-half hours to an hour-and-three-quarters (Salem, OR, *Statesman*, Apr 3, 1940). To be sung in English, the adapted version was renamed *The Bumble Bee Prince* (*New York Herald Tribune*, Dec 28, 1937). In her autobiography, McFadden also shares an amusing incident in which Lancourt, home sick for a few days "tried desperately to keep in touch with the men constructing the scenery by phone . . . [but] when it was time to load the truck for the opening performance [of the tour] in Schenectady, the things they had built wouldn't all go in! . . . [So,] Saul and I [had to take] the train [to Schenectady] with some leftover props . . . [and] travelers in Grand

Central station were much amused to see me carrying a life-sized giraffe head and neck onto the train—our beloved Joop mascot!"[207]

The Bumble Bee Prince opened in New York City with special "Christmas Matinees for Young People" on Monday, December 27, 1937, at the St. James Theatre. In attendance were the offspring of such notables in the music world as Jasha Heifetz, Irving Berlin, and Walter Damrosch (New Bedford, MA, *Standard Times,* Apr 12, 1940). As the curtain rose, the young audience found themselves in Russia, in the peasant cottage of the Bad Sister and the family nurse, Babaricha, as they lazily watched the Good Sister, Militrissa, do all the housework. As she cleans, Militrissa sings her wish to be the Tsar's wife and present him with a handsome son. Overhearing her song, the Tsar makes her his bride and orders the Bad Sister and Babaricha to work in the palace kitchens. Consumed by jealousy, they plot revenge. In Scene 2, in a chamber of the palace, having sent news of the birth of a son to the Tsar who was away at war, Tsarina Militrissa sings her baby to sleep. The Bad Sister and Babaricha steal the letter to the Tsar and replace it with one in which it says that the Tsarina has given birth to a monster. Horrified, the Tsar orders Militrissa and her infant to be cast into the sea. The servants obey, and Militrissa and her baby are pushed into a barrel and cast into the sea.

Act II takes place sixteen years later, on the shore of a magical island held under the spell of the Hawk-Magician. The barrel had floated ashore on this barren island, and we see the young Prince, Guidon, almost grown to manhood. One day, out hunting, he sees a hawk attacking a swan, and he shoots the hawk. The Magician's spell is broken, and the lovely Swan Princess thanks Guidon for freeing her. Like a mirage, released from the evil Magician's spell, a beautiful minareted city suddenly appears on the horizon, and its people welcome Guidon as their new ruler. Nevertheless, learning that two mariners will be setting sail for the land of the Tsar, the Prince longs to go with them to find out why he and his mother had been banished so many years ago. Overhearing Guidon's wish to see his father without revealing himself, the Swan Princess turns Guidon into a bumble bee, and he flies off to find the Tsar.

Act III returns to the Tsar's palace, where the two sailors tell the Tsar about the magical island and the sudden appearance of the beautiful minareted city. The Tsar expresses his desire to go see the magical city but is dissuaded by the Bad Sister and

Babaricha. The Prince, in his guise as a bumble bee, becomes angry and stings the two women, causing all the courtiers to run to and fro trying, without success, to capture the bee. Buzzing behind the Tsar, the disguised Guidon pushes his father toward the ship about to return to the enchanted island.

In the final act, the Prince returns to the island where the Swan Princess restores him to human form, whereupon they declare their love for each other. Soon, the Tsar arrives and is welcomed by Guidon, who asks if the Tsar has a wife and children. The Tsar admits that in a fit of temper and to his eternal regret, he had banished them. Guidon assures the Tsar that sorrow does not last forever, whereupon the Tsar asks about and is shown a magical hen who lays a golden egg. Astonished by such a miracle, and still lamenting the loss of his wife, he asks for another miracle—that his wife be restored to him. In the nature of magical islands, the Tsarina is reunited with her husband and introduces him to their son. Overjoyed, the Tsar embraces them. The wicked nurse and evil sister try to slink off unnoticed, but a watchful guard deposits them at the Tsar's feet. Enraged, the Tsar orders them to be hung, but the Tsarina begs for mercy. The opera ends with the Prince and his Swan Princess, the Tsar and Tsarina, and all the court rejoicing and dancing, and "For all we know they may be dancing yet."[208]

The reviews of *The Bumble Bee Prince* speak to the success of Lancourt's iconoclastic approach. The Wilmington, North Carolina, *Star* (Nov 23, 1939) comments, "Although liveliness, humor and action are not usually associated with opera, the Junior Programs Opera Company counts them among the essentials . . . A record of hundreds of operatic performances without a single yawn in the audience is the result of Junior Programs singular production technique . . . [and] the response of thousands of children attests to the success of the methods employed [by Junior Programs]." The Nashville *Tennessean* (Jan 5, 1941) was in full agreement: "Mr. Lancourt . . . has made opera not only understandable but also enjoyable to millions of children." And, according to the Indianapolis *Star* (Mar 14, 1940), "[Lancourt] has made the production full of life, action, color and movement, and combines the arts of dancing and pantomime with singing and acting."

A similar sentiment was expressed by Marion Selee, who sang the role of the Wicked Nurse, Babaricha. She concluded that "children are unconsciously more critical than adults of musical performances. If the diction can't be understood or the action isn't clear, they become distracted. Children demand truth and verisimilitude . . . the singers must look the parts they portray. When these demands are met, then the children will enjoy an opera as well as . . . a movie" (Cincinnati, OH, *Times Star*, Mar 19, 1938). The Hollywood, California, *Citizen News* (Mar 25, 1940) made a similar comment, noting that the opera was "ingeniously adapted by Saul Lancourt and Marion Farquar . . . The cast sang well, uniformly showing good voices and making a significant impression with the fact that they really acted, dispensing with the pompous gestures of traditional opera, [and] Tom Williams fine enunciation made every word audible." While clarity of the narrative was an important key to holding the interest of their young audiences, the Manitowoc, Wisconsin, *Herald Times* (May 17, 1940) also commented on the acting: "As for the acting itself, it was unusual in its burlesque and fairy tale manner. It made even the older members of the audience want to hiss the Bad Sister and Babaricha, the wicked nurse."

In Green Bay, Wisconsin, the *Press Gazette*'s John Torinus (n.d.) writes of:

> An intensely interesting experiment in opera, opera reduced to its pure essentials without destroying any of its beauty or power, and presented for a children's audience . . . can be definitely declared . . . a success . . . The opera was intended as a mental shock . . . Its purpose was to knock from their minds the popular and current abuse of even the name of opera as something effete, artificial and high-brow. The aim was to show children that opera is merely a play which is sung, and that all one needs is the universal human trait of love of music to enjoy it. . . [Although] whispering was apt to break out in the quieter scenes . . . Miss Cecile Sherman, a member of the company, had an interesting comment . . . "We can tell . . . when they are whispering from mere boredom or when they are whispering about the opera and about us, and most of the time they are talking about us. That we do not mind at all."

Subsequent reviews support these assertions. Quotes ranged from the New York *Journal American* (1937) with, "They shrieked; they giggled; they ohed and ahed" to the *Brooklyn Eagle* (Dec 31, 1937) that was moved to write, "a capacity audience of youngsters was enthralled with the colorful fantastic setting, the gay costumes, and the melodious tunes to which this English version of Alexander Pushkin's fairy-tale was set . . . the story was explained with charming intimacy by informal prologues before each act . . . and the enthusiastic applause left no doubt as to the success of the performance." In Columbus, Georgia, Maxine Garrard of the *Enquirer* (Feb 10, 1939) tells us that the highpoint of the opera occurred when the Swan Princess turns the young Tzarevich into a bumble bee: the audience "screamed and stood up in their seats" and as the bumble bee "dashes madly around the court stinging the people as they try to elude him" excitement reigned supreme.

Special mention was also made by the Jamestown, New York, *Evening Journal* (Mar 6, 1940) of the big red and brown hen, "who before your eyes laid a golden egg from which sprung a bouquet of roses," and of the huge eagle that flew low over the waters until it was stopped in flight by the Tzarevich's arrow. Both the Salem, Oregon, *Statesman* and the Yakama, Washington, *Republic* shared an aside concerning a bit of backstage anxiety, noting that during the rehearsal, when the Tzar sings, "'*Pretty hen, little hen, lay me an egg!*' no one was really sure if the hen would perform, and there was a tremendous sigh of relief heard all over the stage when the hen laid the egg, right on cue" (*Statesman,* Apr 3, 1940). It was a feat that "caused many oohs and aahs from the front row to the last row of the balcony" (*Republic*, Apr 13, 1940).

National magazines such as *Time, Newsweek, Musical America,* and *The New Yorker* also found the production praiseworthy. According to *Musical America* (n.d.): "A charming adaptation of Rimsky-Korsakoff's 'Tale of the Tsar Sultan' was presented . . . before an excited and appreciative audience of children . . . [It was] clearly and deftly presented. Cecile Sherman as the Bad Sister and Marion Selee as Babaricha, the Wicked Nurse, were expert in pantomime and sang the opening duet and the later passages with excellent diction. Alma Milstead as the Good Sister made an appealing picture and was acceptable vocally . . . Esther Lundell played skillful accompaniments, although an orchestra would naturally be more effective. Credit was owing to others, also, for the bright, tasteful costumes and the simplicity to which the entire production was wisely held." From the West Coast, in the *Los Angeles Times* Isabel Morse Jones (n.d.) echoes the description of the young audience as "rapt listeners . . . enchanted, first with the gorgeous curtains and sets, and then with the well-sung music." She, too, found the piano accompaniment to be "a bit thin," but goes on to say, "The dancing Bumble Bee had excellent ballet technique, but was not credited in the cast list, [and] Kenneth MacClelland is probably not Russian, but he has a Russian flair for setting a fairy tale . . . He made the picture-book music alive with his color and line."

Time magazine (Nov 25, 1940) added, "Last week a Manhattan audience screamed and yowled with delight at this tale . . . The audience: 1,600 school children, aged 5-15 (700 more were turned away). Admission: 25cents." Reviewers from across the country agreed. Helen A. F. Penniman of the Baltimore *News Post* (n.d.) began her review with "The 'Standing-room Only' sign was brought out to welcome the company . . . From the topmost row of the gallery to the very front of the orchestra, every seat at the Lyric was filled with an interested audience." But *Reader's Digest* (Jan 1939) recounts a bittersweet consequence of Junior Programs' popularity. "In another city, after every seat for Bumble Bee Prince was filled, several hundred children were lined up in the street clamoring to see 'the opera.' When they learned that there was no more room, they all began to cry. The entire block was filled with sobbing children; the police had to be called out to act as comforters."

The Illinois *Post Tribune*'s Edna Kay Gibson (May 21, 1940) also described the audience:

> If one can visualize over 1,200 children, laughing and talking at the same time, shouting greetings to their friends, and a few engaging in a friendly exchange of fisticuffs, then like a miracle see them transformed into a spell-bound audience that literally hung on to every word and action that took place . . . one may know the success of "The Bumble Bee Prince". . . the kiddies seemed to enjoy the fantastic story even more than their elders for they had been taught in their school work the story of the opera and how to enjoy it and they had come prepared to understand each move of the artists as they appeared in their respective roles. It was everything one could desire in juvenile entertainment. The story was particularly appealing, the costumes were vivid with color, and there was plenty of action . . . and who, either young or old, wouldn't thrill to a dancing bumble bee or a magic hen that laid golden eggs. And what young heart wouldn't

beat just a little faster when the floating swan princess turned into a beautiful girl that married the handsome prince . . . [and] the cast enjoyed playing before their young audience, their enthusiasm being nothing short of contagious . . . It was indeed hard to imagine an opera without an orchestra but the exceptional work done by Jacques Radunsky [sic], pianist, throughout the program was more than adequate for the occasion and he provided a whole orchestra within himself.

Elizabeth Copeland, of the *Richmond News Leader* (Jan 18, 1941) echoes Ms. Penniman: The exquisite production which was a treat for the eye and ear . . . [and] [m]usically . . . contains some of the composer's most exciting and fanciful music . . . is perfectly complimented by the equally fanciful and spirited libretto . . . And throughout the work is found, both musically and dramatically, all the color, sly humor and gaiety which is part of Russia's contribution to the world's art." In "'Bumble Bee Prince' Delights Audience of Young and Old," George Harris (unknown source, n.d.) writes, "The beautiful and woefully unfamiliar music of the 'Bumble Bee Prince' was a true delight in itself—indeed there was a real thrill in hearing such a work for the first time . . . The staging and costumes were as beautiful as those of any operatic production ever given in Richmond . . . [and] although there was only piano accompaniment, which was brilliantly played by Jacques Radimski [sic], the music and its full meaning were there. And with the lighter instrumental background, voices that were some of them of delicate rather than a powerful beauty had full scope. Instead of a program we had a full account of each scene by a narrator, done vigorously and distinctly by Howard Laramy, who also proved his vocal qualities in the part of a messenger."

Tyra Lundberg Fuller of the *Worcester Daily Telegram* (n.d.) was somewhat less enchanted: "Although the entire opera is tuneful and appealing, it contains few outstanding numbers." She went on to express two reasons for her disappointment: first, that only a total of 3,500 attended the two performances; and second, since Worcester Memorial Hall has 3,500 seats, and it was a "well-known fact" that when the hall was only half-filled, the quality of the sound was not as robust as it could be, she found that the lower than "sold out" turnout had a negative effect on the quality of the sound. The Worcester *Telegraph* (n.d.), however, felt that "The pianist did a splendid piece of work in playing the entire instrumental part of 'Tzar Saltan,'" and went on to comment about the "delightfully Arabian-Nightish plot," the excellence of the voices, and the "striking baroque scenery and colorful costumes." *The New Yorker* (Jan 8, 1938), too, did not seem to mind the piano accompaniment and noted, "It seems that both Junior Programs and its auditors have a promising operatic future."

The Manitowoc, Wisconsin, *Herald Times* (n.d.) similarly praised the production. "There was no playing down to a children's audience, which was one thing this critic appreciated, being of the opinion that children do not like to be played down to. The scenery, as designed by McClelland [*sic*] had as much to do with the success of the production as the actors themselves. Colorful, with a bright fancifulness that carried completely through the story it was appropriate to the last degree . . . The opera [also] gave school children the chance to perform with professionals as they served as the chorus background creating some-thing of local interest to the whole scene . . . [and] the addition of the Lincoln [High School] orchestra under the direction of Rufin Boyd which played between acts was an added bit of diversification and held the children's attention well." The reviewer for the Olean, New York, *Herald* (March 2, 1940) also noted that the "six principles [were] augmented by six Olean vocalists who comprised the assisting chorus."

These two references to Junior Programs' use of a local chorus identifies yet another Junior Programs innovation: their core belief in the concept of "community engagement." While the benefits of such engagement were to be found primarily in its organizational structure (see Chapter VI), by creating an opportunity, in appropriate situations, for the involvement of local singers, we can begin to understand how thoroughly their core values permeated their entire approach to their work. A thoughtfully worded invitation included in the materials they sent to their network of local sponsoring organizations highlights this point. Titled "A Suggestion to Local Choruses," it proposes that:

> A local group of from four to twelve male or female singers . . . appear in simple Russian peasant costumes for short choruses. A number of towns have already cooperated in this way with great success. There is no remuneration for these singers . . . but they

seem to have thoroughly enjoyed their appearance with the Junior Programs Opera. The idea has local publicity value, and it adds to the excitement of the children in the audience to see their relatives and friends. From a musical standpoint, the additional chorus volume was much appreciated. The choruses are very short and simple. Copies of the music may be obtained from our office at 10 cents each. Costumes of simple full skirted dresses and bandannas for the women, smocks with sashes, plain trousers and high red or black boots for the men, can easily be borrowed from friends. Detailed costume and other suggestions will be sent with the chorus parts . . . [and t]he success of the idea will depend entirely on the careful selection of really good voices and singers that are accustomed to taking direction and will be earnest in their preliminary rehearsals.[209]

With *The Bumble Bee Prince*, Junior Programs' creation and use of the role of narrator also provided another opportunity for community involvement. When there was local talent of high quality available, the company was eager to engage them to play the part of the narrator. In a news clipping from the Baltimore *Morning Sun* (Dec 12, 1937), we learn that "Mrs. Hazel Bornschein, of this city, will appear in costume before each act to explain the story and background of the opera." The Fairmont, West Virginia, *Times* (Mar 22, 1938) reports that Mrs. Edward J. Hunter appeared before each act to tell the story of what was about to happen. "Strikingly attired in a Russian peasant dress with high patent leather boots, a full red skirt and red kerchief, Mrs. Hunter presented the action clearly and with charm. She left her audience eager for the next act." In Cincinnati, Mrs. Thornton Jewett, director of the Mariemont Children's Theater, donned the costume of a Russian peasant in the role of narrator, and in Floral Park, New York, Miss Virginia Maurer, a physical education teacher and former actress, volunteered—at Junior Programs' request—as narrator (*Gateway*, Jan 12, 1939). In Rockville Center, New York, Lorena Robbins Nutzhorn, a locally known voice coach, stepped into the narrator's role (*Owl*, Jan 13, 1939), and in Columbus, Georgia, the narrator was Mrs. Maurice Loidans (*Columbus Enquirer*, Feb 10, 1939).

A New Jersey *Times* review (Jan 21, 1938) summed up the Junior Programs approach to opera for children, commenting: "The response to *The Bumble Bee Prince* was more than gratifying to Mr. Lancourt whose ambition was to instill a love and appreciation of opera in American children, practically from the time they emerge from the cradle. All over the country thousands of children have learned to love opera the way he gives it to them, and they think it's great fun."

Jack and the Beanstalk[210]

"Jack Climbs That Beanstalk — Really — Children Giggle, Gasp, Clap At Opera Interpretation Of Fairytale"

(unknown source, n.d.)

On November 5, 1940, Franklin Delano Roosevelt was reelected for a tradition-breaking third term. It had been a hotly contested election between Roosevelt and Wendell Wilke, and the mood in the country was tense. Roosevelt had pulled the country out of the depths of the Great Depression and, sensitive to the strong isolationist trend, he promised to keep the country out of the European war. Once the election was over, one can easily imagine a collective sigh of relief and a readiness, even a longing, for something light and amusing, some novelty, perhaps with a little edge to it, but full of color and magic. If one's antennae were also finely tuned to the gathering storm clouds and the rumbles of thunder from Europe, one could pick up increasingly audible whispers of the need to pivot from a largely Eurocentric cultural canon to one that acknowledged, elevated, admired, and centered distinctly American cultural accomplishments as well. The theater had Eugene O'Neill and Clifford Odets, and dance had Doris Humphrey and Martha Graham. Opera, however, remained dominated by European composers. George Gershwin's *Porgy and Bess* (1938) is often considered the first real American opera, but Junior Programs' choice of Louis Gruenberg's *Jack and the Beanstalk* (1931) gave an American composer the opportunity to influence the development of the next generation of opera lovers.

The *Morning Mercury* (New Bedford, MA, Nov 8, 1940) said, "A happier choice for post-election frazzled minds than 'Jack and the Beanstalk' could not have come to us here for this Junior Programs opera . . . is splendid dramatic fare—enthralling for the children and holding interest in its every moment for the wise grownups

IV. THE PRODUCTIONS: PART II—THE OPERA & BALLET COMPANIES   163

who attended ... There is a dramatic breadth in the entire production. The music by Louis Gruenberg is brilliantly descriptive; John Erskine's text has clarity, charm and the literary touch to be expected of this transcriber of classic tales." According to the Baltimore, Maryland, *Morning Sun* (Feb 21, 1940), the opera, represented "a definite departure from the European tradition ... We have made an effort to encourage native singers, educated and trained for their musical careers in American music schools. There is no lack of talent either in writing or performance in our own land." These sentiments are echoed in the Pittsburgh, Pennsylvania, *Liberty Ledger* (Mar 1, 1940) which comments that the opera was written by an American composer and librettist and sung by a cast of American singers, all critically acclaimed by New York critics. Erskine's libretto is characterized as "distinguished by its analogies to real life and especially American in its character. Gaily satirical, the tale is handled ... in a spirit of pure comedy, quite different from what most people have come to expect in an opera."

Opera News (Dec 16, 1940) echoes the *Liberty Ledger*'s assessment of the importance humor and dramatic action have as a means of keeping children engaged. "Junior Programs' operas are selected not only for their musical beauty, but also for their dramatic stories and humor, with the result that the children exclaim at the end ... 'Gee that was swell.' Operas for the very young, must, of course, be produced with a special technique. Junior Programs' production director, Saul Lancourt, insists on lively action, with elimination of endless arias, [and] occasional spoken interludes whenever feasible ... 'Jack and the Beanstalk'... lent itself especially well to this method." According to the *New York Herald Tribune* (Feb 4, 1940), the opera, originally written in 1931 and performed by students at Julliard, was adapted by Gruenberg and Erskine especially for Junior Programs. It had its first public performance in its revised form at the Brooklyn Academy of Music in early February 1940.

Louis Gruenberg (1884–1964) was a Russian-born American pianist and composer. He wrote a number of operas, including *The Emperor Jones,* based on the play by Eugene O'Neill, which premiered at the Metropolitan Opera in 1933. In 1939, he moved to Los Angeles and composed the scores for several Oscar-nominated films, receiving several nominations for best score.[211] Olin Downes, music critic of the *New York Times* (Nov 21, 1931) said of Gruenberg's music, "Gruenberg's brilliant and dexterous orchestration [is evident, and] ... he is master of the orchestral and harmonic . . . and occasionally there are excellent musical jokes, such as the reference to the music of the giants . . . in Wagner's 'Ring.'. . . [I]t is lively and tuneful . . . [and] Mr. Gruenberg's scoring is full of color." Another review (unknown source, n.d.) describes the score for *Jack and the Beanstalk* as "spicy," with "some full-bodied tunes and a clever harmonic structure reflecting Ravel, Richard Strauss and others, including even Cole Porter."

John Erskine (1879–1951) was a well-known American writer, educator, and musician. He had taught at Amherst College and Columbia University, where he was instrumental in creating the General Honors Course which, in turn, inspired the Great Books movement. He published one hundred books, novels, pieces of criticism, and essays, as well as opera lyrics. Several of his novels were made into films.[212] Erskine said he had three theories about opera librettos: "that a libretto should be entertaining and a comedy . . . that a libretto should be based on a plot already familiar to the audience . . . [and that a] libretto should be the barest outline, an unadorned structure, and the words should be chosen not for their own sake but to support the music. If a libretto were self-sufficient poetry, to add music would be an impertinence" (unknown source, Nov 25, 1940). Downes of the *New York Times* emphatically did not agree with these guidelines. Nevertheless, he says, "Mr. Erskine has treated his theme wittily and in a highly characteristic manner" (Nov 21, 1931). The Pittsburg, PA *Liberty Ledger* (March 1, 1940) agreed. "Gaily satirical, the tale is handled by the librettist in a spirit of pure comedy, quite different from what most people have seen."

The story of *Jack and the Beanstalk* was known to almost every American adult and to most American children, "but it acquired new charm in the operatic presentation with gay verses by John Erskine set to lilting music by Louis Gruenberg" (Astoria, OR, *Evening Astorian-Budget*, n.d.). In addition to its music, what also set the Junior Programs adaptation apart was its production details. According to the Junior Programs synopsis, in Act 1, Scene 1, the audience finds Jack and his mother destitute. Their clothes are ragged, and they have no money or food. Jack's father has been killed by a Giant who has stolen his lands and treasures: a bag of gold that is always full, a hen that lays golden eggs, and a harp that can play any tune one might wish to hear. The only possession they have left is an old cow. Though Jack loves the cow dearly, he decides it must be sold to buy food for his mother and himself.

But Downes, in the *New York Times* (Nov 21, 1931), reminds us that this is an Erskinean cow, a philosopher cow. "This cow is sagacious and reproachful. This cow stares people in the face and utters misanthropic truths. Jack tried to lure her . . . At the fair there would be singing, but the cow doesn't like music. There would be puppets and acting, but the cow doesn't care for drama. Mention of the butcher was anything but tempting . . . The Cow comments, 'Eliminate the butcher and the rest will take care of itself.'" The Trenton, New Jersey, *Times* (May 5, 1941) concurs. It describes the ribby cow as "too old for milk, [but] she is highly articulate and musically expressive. When Jack . . . [has] to sell her, she immediately sets up a harmonious howl. A lesser cow might have ambled off placidly, [but] the Erskine cow . . . has spirit. When Jack tries to interest her in the excitement of the market place, she glowers and protests in *basso-profundo* baritone, a most remarkable protest. She balks all the way, scolds Jack soundly for forgetting the days when he had used her for a charger or for plowing when it would always spoil the butter. And when Jack makes his trade, it is the cow who is smart enough to insist on being sold for a handful of beans which an old witch claimed would return the treasures of Jack's departed father."

Junior Programs Opera *Jack and the Beanstalk*
Jack (Alma Milstead) and his Cow (Tom Williams and Ford Ogden) on the Way to Market
(JP Scrapbooks)

Scene 2 takes place at the county fair where a butcher and a tanner both want to buy the cow. But Jack had agreed not to do that. Suddenly, a little old woman appears and offers to buy the cow—on one condition. Jack thinks she looks too poor to pay a decent price, but when she offers to return his father's treasures and give him an enchanted princess as his bride, he agrees. He holds out his hand for the treasures, but all he gets from her is a handful of beans. When he starts to eat them, the old woman shrieks, "Plant them tonight and be a Prince tomorrow." Scene 3 finds Jack back home. He tries to pretend he has bargained well, but his mother berates him for his folly and horrified, throws the beans to the ground. Immediately, the beanstalk begins to sprout and grows on stage until it disappears from view. Jack is astonished, his faith in the old woman is restored, and he eagerly starts to climb the beanstalk, crying, "I will be a Prince tomorrow."[213]

Act II, Scene 1 put the audience on the road to the Giant's castle. Waiting in front of the castle is the beautiful Princess. As soon as she sees Jack, she disguises

Junior Programs Opera *Jack and the Beanstalk*
The Road to the Giant's Castle
Jack (Alma Milstead), the Princess (Cecile Sherman), and the Giant (Howard Laramy)
(Lancourt's personal papers)

herself as the Old Woman. She warns him that the Giant will try to kill him, but that it is his duty to enter the castle and retrieve his father's treasures. According to Downes (*New York Times*, Nov 21, 1931), by successive tricks, Jack outwits the Giant, and one by one the treasures are recovered.

After each of Jack's exploits, the Old Woman/Princess encourages him to the next riskier quest. Act II, Scene 2 finds the nearsighted Giant eating dinner in his kitchen. Having satisfied his hunger, he falls asleep. Jack creeps in and tickles the Giant's neck with a knife. When the Giant turns to scratch his neck, letting go of the bag of gold, Jack snatches it and runs. Awakened, the Giant runs after him.

In Act II, Scene 3, we see the Old Woman waiting by the roadside. Jack gives her the bag of gold. She hides it, then hides Jack in a potato sack. The Giant grabs the sack and takes it back to the castle. In Scene 4, we see the Giant again asleep in his kitchen. Jack cautiously creeps out of the sack and throwing it over the Giant's head, grabs the hen that lays the golden eggs, runs back to the Old Woman and gives her the hen. One final time, he returns to the castle kitchen and manages to convince the Giant not to kill him, saying that he will tell him where he has hidden the other two treasures, if only he may hear the magic harp play its music. The clearly not-to-bright Giant agrees. With a bit of cunning, Jack commands the harp to play a lullaby. Again, the Giant falls asleep. Jack grabs the harp and runs. In Scene 5, we watch as Jack and the Old Woman, with his father's three treasures, scramble down the beanstalk, but the Giant, awakened again, pursues them.

In the final Act, we see Jack's mother in front of her cottage, grieving for her lost son. Suddenly, Jack, having climbed down the beanstalk, appears, pursued by the Giant. Too heavy for the beanstalk, the Giant falls, and the air goes out of him in sight of the audience. The Old Woman, suddenly transformed into the beautiful Princess appears, and the opera concludes with Jack, his Mother, the Princess, the Cow, and their rejoicing neighbors all hailing Jack's victory. A wedding is arranged, and all live happily ever after, including the Cow, now garlanded with flowers.

While there is enduring appeal to this old fable, the real success of Junior Programs' *Jack and the Beanstalk* was a good example of the old adage, "The devil is in the details." The beanstalk actually grew, sprouting from the stage "to great heights before the gaze of the audience, and children watched open-mouthed as Jack started his long climb to meet the giant" (Midland, MI, *Midland Daily News*, n.d.). And there was the "obedient Hen, an ingenious creature who flapped her wings, cocked her head, and without much ado, at the command of the giant, promptly laid an egg on the stage table—not once, but twice" (unknown source, n.d.).

Another review tells us that the children "giggled rapturously . . . at the awkward cow whose knees wobbled at the thought of the butcher" ("Jack Climbs That Beanstalk—Really," unknown source, n.d.). And a review titled "Opera for Children" (unknown source, n.d.) opines that "Mr. Erskine and Mr. Gruenberg have contrived at least one character that deserves the immortality of Ferdinand and Dopey. This is a somewhat cynical Cow, with more than a little of Pooh-Bah in her makeup. Tom Williams, as the forequarters, gave a rollicking, sly interpretation of the part, in the antics of which he was aided by Ford Ogden as the hindquarters." The Astoria, Oregon, *Evening Astorian-Budget* (n.d.) declared, "A cow and a giant stole the show . . . And quite rightly, too, for it isn't every day that one sees a blue-eyed cow (with devastatingly long eyelashes and snapping nostrils) that utters sage words in a rapidly changing voice and dances amusing jigs."

An undated article, "Sardonic Old Cow Plays Role in Opera," explains that this is a wise and sardonic old Cow who makes "cynical comments on the weakness of the human mind, the silliness of romance and the tragedy of age . . . And it is the cow who gives voice to a few leavening sentiments of disillusion at the wedding ceremonies when Jack wins his princess . . . With the wisdom of age, she [the Cow] counsels moderation in all things and deliberation rather than haste in the perennial chase for the pot of gold at the end of the rainbow, which is probably empty anyhow, for, as she sings with her double voice:

> Everything comes of waiting,
> The grass in the meadow
> Never grows faster
> For wishing; and more than haste
> It's meditation that makes milk.

Another unidentified source exclaimed, "What a giant! The gorgeous, striding fellow assumed by the genial Mr. Laramy. With his lift of 14 inches weighing 20 pounds, the near-sighted miser stood 7 1/2 feet in his boots. And a sweet contented soul he was found to be, prating of the quiet of his home 'standing by my own fireside.'" "Opera for Children" (no source, n.d.) calls him "A distinctive vocal and dramatic characterization . . .as the tooth-brushing Giant, an artful combination of jitterbug and Charles Laughton's Henry VII [*sic*]." However, another review from an unknown source tells us of two little girls with "long curls and mere ruffles for skirts." When the giant first appeared, the "little brunette hid behind her braver friend, crying "I won't look at that bad man."

MacClelland's whimsical sets were repeatedly praised. The *Evening Astorian-Budget* (Astoria, OR, n.d.) says, "Particularly enchanting was the giant's home with props in gargantuan proportions to fit their owner. Among them were a lopsided alarm clock, a huge chair and table and three bins labelled 'Herrings,' 'Cookies,' and 'Animal Crackers.'" The Midland, Michigan, *Midland Daily News* (n.d.) tells us, "A seven and a half foot giant caused excitement among the audience of over a thousand adults and school children . . . when he swung his big club around in a fearful manner, but he turned out to be the kind of giant who remembers that his mother has told him to brush his teeth every day. He remembered too, and brushed them right in front of everybody with a toothbrush as long as your arm." Downes, of the *New York Times* (Nov 21, 1931) commented, "In all this there is much amusing business and by-play, much indirect ridicule of the solemnities and pomposities of opera and the grand passion. Jack remains a young 100 percent American, who does not in the least grow up . . . The virtue of the lines is their twists and puns and shrewd witticisms, and . . . liveliness of Mr. Gruenberg's score." A review of the production by Junior Programs from Mt. Lebanon, Pennsylvania (n.d.), paraphrases Downes's earlier assessment of the opera "as clever, abounding in witty lines, and music that is rich in melodic material, in delineation and in sprightliness. It is so good in its field that there may be some who will rank it with the best things Mr. Gruenberg has composed."

There was also praise by the *Morning Mercury* (New Bedford, MA, Nov 8, 1940) for a local boy, Albert Gifford of Fairhaven, who filled the role of Jester, an often-used narrative innovation of Lancourt's to ensure that an opera or ballet's story would be easily understood by even the youngest child. "In this connection it may be stated that our sincere congratulations go to Albert Gifford of Fairhaven who seems to have found his niche in this type of company. Mr. Gifford is carrying an interpolated role that of a jester, but one unquestionably contributive to the understanding of the plot

... It has been well seen to that important turns in the story are presented in two ways that a young audience may readily understand ... The local tenor capered and sang before the curtain, his strong voice easily penetrating a babel of child shoutings [before the curtain rose] ... Like all the cast, Mr. Gifford pleased by his good diction. His tenor was also that heard from the Giant's singing harp."

In Baltimore (unknown source, n.d.), at the Lyric Theater, both the singing and the acting were deemed praiseworthy. "When Albert Gifford as the Jester stepped before the curtain to sing a prologue in clear, ringing tones, he set the merry whirl of the opera going with a spirit and superior vocalism that were characteristic of the entire cast. Marion Selee as the Mother sang with cello-rich quality and Cecile Sherman revealed a full fresh voice ... Convincing, too, was Alma Milstead ... although her voice had less power and freedom of production ... [and a] distinctive vocal and dramatic characterization was that of Howard Laramy as the tooth-brushing Giant." Another review (unknown source, n.d.) characterized Sherman's delivery as an "easily soaring, pure, brilliant yet richly furnished tone. Her acting has grace, spirit and comic fire at demand, enabling her to slip in and out from Princess to old dame with equal verity." The *Hawk-Eye Gazette* (Burlington, IA, n.d.) pronounced Sherman the "embodiment of childhood's fairy princesses," while Alma Milstead as Jack "was a favorite of the cast, playing her part with a grace and nimbleness, and singing ... in a clear soprano voice." It's interesting to note that, for both Sherman and Milstead, this was a return to the roles they played in the original 1931 Julliard production. The *Morning Mercury* (New Bedford, MA, Nov 8, 1940) praised Kenneth MacClelland's sets, with a lush growing beanstalk "broadly and dramatically" imagined, and "behind every impersonation of the characters is felt the capable hand in direction of Saul Lancourt."

The reception of the opera in Burlington, Iowa, was typical. As the *Hawk Eye Gazette* (n.d.) relates, the production was sponsored by the Federation of Women's Clubs. The audience of 1,700 people packed the auditorium, with standing room only for many adults. "From the topmost row of the gallery to the very first row of the auditorium, every seat held a charmed listener" who gave their fascinated and rapt attention to the entertainment. "Although in most instances a teacher or principal sat with his or her group ... discipline was not necessary, and the teachers soon were lost in the beauty of the production and the artistry of the presentations ... The wit of John Erskine . . . was not lost in the singing, for each artist enunciated with such clarity that every word was understood . . . the children applauded loudly. Their pleasure was obvious as they squirmed in their seats with excitement and delight, and leaned forward to watch, enthralled." We hear, too, from the *Chico Enterprise* (Chico, CA, n.d.) "It was to be expected that when John Erskine undertook to write his first opera libretto there would be some upsetting of applecarts in operatic tradition. The gifted and versatile author, musician and composer . . . is a non-conformist of the first water, and when he wrote the libretto for the American opera "Jack and the Beanstalk" he cheerfully threw all the hallowed rules of the game out of the window," describing it as a "fairy opera for the child-like."

And from the Western city of Monroe (unknown source, n.d.):

> Yesterday afternoon a fairytale came true. And if audience reaction is a gauge of the success . . . of 'Jack and the Beanstalk,' the P.T.A. sponsored opera may be set down as a triumph . . . The scenery, too, was delightfully conceived—Jack's mother's tumbledown shack with its crooked chimney and unpatched thatching, the ramshackle stall from which the cow contributed her humorous tidbits to the opening scene, the interior of the giant's kitchen with everything built to scale to his size . . . And helping to make the 'ohs' and 'ahs' more enthusiastic were the deftly styled costumes. The princess tallied with every description of what a storybook princess should be, from the tiny sparkling crown in her golden curls to the flowing high-waisted gown of blue chiffon. Even Jack and his mother shed their rags in the final scene to emerge resplendent in satin and silk and golden slippers.

The many laudatory reviews of the Junior Programs Opera production of *Jack and the Beanstalk* make it clear that the company's decision to include an American opera in its repertoire sent an important musical message—that an American opera was in no way out of place in company with *Hansel and Gretel* and *The Bumble Bee Prince*—two of the European canon's best. It also laid to rest much of the skepticism concerning children and opera. According to the Manchester, New Hampshire, *Leader* (Feb 8, 1938), "Saul Lancourt . . . aspires to instill a love and appreciation of opera in American children." The *Brooklyn Eagle* (Dec 26, 1937), in promoting *The Bumble Bee Prince* at the Academy of Music, agreed. "Mr. Lancourt's confidence in opera's brighter future is based on the very good reason that he has succeeded eminently in his work."

One further Lancourt innovation is worthy of mention before moving on to an examination of the Junior Programs Ballet. In her 1939–40 annual report to the Junior Programs Board, McFadden mentions the successful publication of several books and phonograph record albums. The Whitman Publishing Company planned to issue the "story books" of *The Bumble Bee Prince* and *Robin Hood,* and RCA Victor planned to follow up its recording of *The Bumble Bee Prince* with a recording of *Hansel and Gretel.*

> In planning the recorded adaptation of 'The Bumble Bee Prince,' along with liveliness, humor and action, all hallmarks of the Junior Programs approach to opera for young people, 'The Bumble Bee Prince' as recorded by the Junior Programs Opera Company introduces a novel technique in operatic recording by integrating versified narration with the singing and music to clarify the development of the story. Mr. Lancourt put these theories into practice . . . For a recording of an opera, he realized some method would have to be devised to hold young listeners' attention throughout, in the absence of colorful stage settings, costumes and visible action. The solution he contrived is in the classic tradition of the Greek chorus embodied in the voice of a narrator, who introduces the opera, its characters and settings, and comments throughout on the progress of the plot. Mr. Lancourt wrote verses fitted to descriptive music in the score, which intriguingly achieve their purpose of making opera easily intelligible even to the very young.[214]

The Newport News, Virginia, *Herald* (Dec 9, 1940) also tells of "Two books based on Junior Programs productions, 'The Bumble Bee Prince' and 'Robin Hood,' released only this year are now on thousands of children's library shelves, and phonograph recordings have been made by one of the largest firms in the field of Junior Programs operas, 'Hansel and Gretel' and 'The Bumble Bee Prince' and of the ballet 'Robin Hood.' Both books and recording adaptations were prepared and written by Saul Lancourt, the Junior Programs production director." These books and records were widely reviewed and advertised in numerous publications.[215] From the various ads and mentions of the recordings and books, both appear to have been coveted gifts at holiday time—but their real value was making both the music and the stories accessible to thousands of children 365 days of the year.

Connecting With The Audience

Several characteristics account for Junior Programs Opera's success in introducing opera to its youthful audience. Their first production, *Hansel and Gretel*, inherited from the NML, was a known success. But that of *The Bumble Bee Prince* and *Jack and the Beanstalk* were not a given. That they were so successful suggests that "*Only the best is good enough for children*" was more than a motto. From the newspaper and journal reviews, we know that their productions appeared to spare no expense in terms of the lavish and imaginative sets, costumes, and props. But we also know that behind the visual appeal, there was a solid theatrical, musical and socio-political foundation. By pairing a distinctly American composer with operas from two of the most outstanding European composers, and by selecting the best-trained American singers, their work embodied the values articulated in their *Credo*. Their choice of operas also reflected their ability to walk the fine line between artistic integrity and a sensitivity to national and international events: with *The Bumble Bee Prince*, their US premier of the opera connected them to the worldwide celebration of the hundredth anniversary of Pushkin's death; and with *Jack and the Beanstalk*, their choice reflected the nation's need for something light and amusing after the trauma of the Great Depression and a tense and fraught election.

Their success was also a tribute to Lancourt's commitment to challenge generations of what he regarded as outdated and pompous operatic tradition. First, he ensured accessibility with his decision to have all the operas sung in English, to use only a piano accompaniment, and through his innovative and creative use of a narrator. Second, his elimination of repetitive arias enabled them to adapt each opera in terms of length and a lively pace of storytelling. And of equal importance, with his action-oriented staging, and his insistence that acting and pantomime be seamlessly integrated into each production, he made opera exciting and engaging for his young audience. As a result, the Junior Programs template proved to be a reliable recipe for repeated success. Lawrence Tibbett's assessment is succinct and to the point: "As I see it, Junior Programs, Inc., is performing the function of bringing opera . . . to the youth of the country in admirable fashion."[216] And Pierre Key, well-known music editor and critic, and founder of the *Musical Digest*, was heartened by signs that "we'll have become an opera-giving and opera-going nation," and one of the "signs" he mentioned was "the Junior Programs Opera company designed to appeal chiefly to children . . . The singers are excellent and experienced . . .[with] better voices and better in sheer vocal art than our D'Oyley Carte friends from London."[217]

The Junior Programs Ballet Company

The 1920s, 1930s, and 1940s were a period of ferment in the American dance world. European and Russian classical ballet were being challenged by dancers such as Isadora Duncan, Ruth St. Denis, Ted Shawn's Denishawn Dancers, Martha Graham, and Doris Humphrey. For these dancers and several of their contemporaries, dance was not about classical technique or impersonating swans or firebirds. According to Humphrey, who was part of a turning away from European traditions, "There is only one thing to dance about: the meaning of ones' personal experience." She went on to say, "My dance comes from the people who had to subdue a continent, to make a thousand paths through forest and plain, to conquer mountains and eventually to raise up towns of steel and glass."[218] The Denishawn Company talked about "musical visualizations," and Martha Graham and Hanya Holm were interested in how the human body expressed emotion. These were critical moments in the development of American dance forms. In a sense, these larger creative explorations had cracked open the status quo of classical European ballet, making it easier for the Junior Programs Ballet to creatively address their key challenge: how to create dances that would not only introduce children to the art form, but make them want more?

According to McFadden, to do this, she and Lancourt engaged Edwin Strawbridge, an internationally well-known dancer-choreographer.[219] Strawbridge had recently led a large company of forty dancers with the New York Philharmonic at Lewisohn Stadium and had performed at the coronation of Japan's new Emperor, Hirohito.[220] But Strawbridge also had a deep belief in the importance of dance for children. In keeping with Dewey's educational philosophy of engaging the whole child, Strawbridge possessed a unique understanding of what dance could offer to every child, and he believed the fundamentals of dance should be taught to all children in the same way that every child is taught to read. "Correct body posture brings a healthy development to body, nerves, muscles and mind . . . When a child dances, his spirit lifts his body into joyous movement. This creates deep breathing . . . [and] gives an even beat to the heart. Truly inspirational movement brings relaxation to body and mind, and a relaxed body and mind can be taught almost anything . . . Observing the child, one finds that his body is relaxed and free while absorbed in a task which interests him thus enabling him to learn with little effort, while he is tense and fidgety when trying to learn something that does not interest him. Why not, therefore, first teach the child relaxation, so that he can more easily learn."[221] According to Strawbridge, in addition to the benefits of learning to dance, watching good dancing also promoted a child's imagination. "A child watching the dancer becomes one with him and is filled with the same buoyancy and lightness. His imaginative faculty is quickened and he lives in the fantasy portrayed for him . . . Since the ballet tells its story through constant action and movement, it holds the attention of the child . . . and thus the intent of the story."[222]

Strawbridge's view of dance as an integral and critical part of the generic process of learning offered a perfect fit for Junior Programs' overarching belief in the performing arts as a pedagogical medium able to greatly enhance a child's desire to learn about a broad range of subjects. Strawbridge believed that dance's ability to hold a child's attention enabled whatever moral message a story contained to make a deeper and lasting impression:

> In "Pinocchio" the child is made aware of the unhappiness brought to himself and others by being disobedient and running away from responsibilities . . . In 'The Princess and the Swineherd', one sees the results that come from being selfish and vain . . . Children love stories that point a moral if this is done lightly, joyously, and harmoniously. For this reason, and also because of their natural delight in seeing beautiful motion and colors, they have welcomed our Junior Programs type of ballet stories. We dancers . . . can feel our young audiences dancing and . . . feeling every bit of our play with us. It is a thrill never to be forgotten,—an audience that cannot be equaled.[223]

Strawbridge also believed that "the way we hold our bodies, which is to say the way we dance through life, tells the world how we expect to be treated." In "Pantomimes Help to Express Your Mood" (Binghamton, NY, *Sun*, Feb 18, 1941), Letty Lynn elaborates on the way Strawbridge connected dancing with living. "We are all dancing every moment of our lives . . . [and] dance, as an art form interpreting feeling and thought through physical movement, should be understood by everyone as a practical aid in his everyday life." What he was saying, in essence, was that through dance, one becomes aware of the intimate and important connection between one's body and one's sense of emotional wellbeing—a connection that can affect every aspect of one's life. He even created what he called a "dictionary of pantomime" in which he set forth the physical manifestations of different emotional states which he used as a guide for expressing emotions through dance, and which he believed also described the ways people expressed their emotions in life.[224]

Strawbridge's technical abilities were broadly admired. According to John Martin, dance critic at the *New York Times* (n.d.), Strawbridge had "lightness and elevation, strength and clarity, and above all a distinct quality of beauty in his movements." Julian Bowes of *The Billboard* (n.d.), a theater magazine, noted that "Not since Nijinsky has there been such a Dancer . . . In the vanguard, Strawbridge advances. Whether interpreting abstract ideas or characterizing some eccentric or grotesque figure with a flash of humor, he executes his sketches with a vigor and volatility that leave an indelible impression on the mind's eye." The *Boston Globe* (n.d.) described Strawbridge as "the impersonation of joy. No one watching can doubt it." The *New York Herald* (n.d.) said, "Mr. Strawbridge has a distinct feeling for composition and possesses the faculty of appearing to float a moment longer in his leaps than is compatible with the laws of gravity." From the Parkersburg, West Virginia, *Sentinel* (Feb 2, 1937) we hear, "Edwin Strawbridge, with an amazing technique at his command has astonished audiences and dance critics with his lightness, elevation, strength and indescribable grace of movement . . . His delightful sense of humor and of the fun of story telling through dance make him the ideal impersonator of Pinocchio."

Strawbridge's combination of a philosophy of dance as a means of enabling children to learn more easily, his belief in dance as a way to express a characters' emotions, his outstanding classical technique, and the joy and humor he brought to the four ballets he choreographed for the Junior Programs Ballet—*Pinocchio, The*

Princess and the Swineherd, The Adventures of Puck, and *Robin Hood*—make it clear that the Junior Programs/Strawbridge partnership was a highly productive and successful relationship. From the outset, with the needs of their young audience foremost in their minds, Lancourt and Strawbridge reimagined how best to introduce the art form to children. Together, they developed what they called a *dance-play* or *narrative ballet*—a form that married story, dance, pantomime, *and* narration. As with opera, the introduction of a narrator into each of the dance productions ensured that even the youngest child would be able to fully enter the world created on stage; and several of the narrators were so skillful in altering their voices to suit each character that it often seemed as if the dancers themselves were speaking.

As with their opera productions, each of the ballets transported the children into a world of fantasy—with sets, costumes, and special effects that left them wide-eyed and attentive, and likely unaware that they were also learning how stories could be told through physical movement. The following section explores each of the ballets, with a synopsis of the story, a description of the production, and the impact it had on the young audiences.

THE BALLETS

Pinocchio[225]

"Entertainment in 'Pinocchio' Entirely New"
(New Haven, Connecticut, *Journal-Courier*, April 22, 1937)

Junior Programs Ballet Announcement Flyer for *Pinocchio*
(*Lancourt's personal papers*)

Like *Jack and the Beanstalk*, *Pinocchio* was an extremely popular fairy tale known to just about everyone regardless of age, and the Junior Programs Ballet was not the only company offering a production of the classic tale. During roughly the same timeframe, the FTP staged multiple productions of *Pinocchio* in a traditional, straightforward dramatic format. According to Hallie Flanagan, the FTP production was "funny, beautiful and gay . . . [and] achieved the rare distinction of being childlike without being childish."[226] Directed by Yasha Frank, the FTP production received a full spread in *Life* magazine and was selected as the first children's play to be broadcast on television. When the FTP was forced to close by the House Un-American Activities Committee in 1939, as a fitting tribute, Frank rewrote the ending of the play. Instead of Pinocchio becoming a real boy, he turned back into a puppet. In the final scene of the final performance, the stagehands dismantled the set—in full view of the audience—and placed the puppet, Pinocchio, in a casket emblazoned with the legend "BORN DECEMBER 23, 1938; KILLED BY AN ACT OF CONGRESS, JUNE 30, 1939."[227]

Fortunately, a similar fate did not befall the Junior Programs production choreographed by Strawbridge for the 1936–37 season. The New Haven, Connecticut, *Journal-Courier* (April 22, 1937) headline announced, "Entertainment in 'Pinocchio' Entirely New." The article went on to say, "There have been plays, operas, ballets and other attractions, but never before in this country, has there been produced for children a narrative ballet. Interest in the performance, which will be given under the auspices of the Connecticut Child Welfare Association and the Journal-Courier, with the assistance of the League of Women Voters, is already keen with workers at the . . . Association . . . besieged for reservations."

Pinocchio had been developed into a narrative dance-play script by Dorothy Coit, cofounder of the New York City King-Coit Children's Theater and School.[228] She had adapted it from the original Italian bedtime story by Carlo Collodi, and it was Lancourt's intention that the dialogue would be expertly rendered by a narrator who would introduce each of the characters and interpret their actions like a wandering storyteller of old. Strawbridge quickly saw the creative possibilities in adapting the immortal children's classic into a narrative dance that Junior Programs would send out on tour after *Hansel and Gretel*. Under Lancourt's overall direction, and with a musical score by Mable Wood Hill, the finished production was first seen at the Bayes

Theater in New York during the 1936-37 holiday season.[229]

Program material for the production in Lancourt's personal papers describes the music as full of "descriptive charm and subtlety of expression" which brought out "all the humor and pathos of his [Pinocchio's] adventures." It advised the children to "Listen for the sounds of sawing wood [and] hammering," as Geppetto fashions the mischievous puppet. And when the Cat and the Fox lie to Pinocchio so as to steal his gold pieces, the children are alerted to "a tremendous groan in the music, and everyone listening knows that what is being said is not the truth." The program also goes on to describe the dancing: "When . . . Strawbridge dances . . . his arms and legs and body move with the same jerky motions . . . [as marionettes,] their arms and legs and body set in motion by unseen hands pulling strings."[230]

The performance opened with Pinocchio coming to life in the workshop of the old woodcarver Geppetto and playfully pulling the carver's wig off and putting it on his own wooden head. Pinocchio tells Geppetto he wants to go to school, but Geppetto does not have the money—until it occurs to him that he can sell his coat. Scene II gives the audience first a remorseful Pinocchio, who has sold his school ABC card for a penny to go see a comedy, and then a happy Pinocchio recalling that the proprietor of the comedy had given him three gold pieces. As he watches the three gold pieces come alive and dance, a cunning Fox and Cat appear, ready to cheat him of his gold. They persuade him to come with them, pretending they will help him get more gold. Scene III takes place in a dark forest. The Cat and Fox catch Pinocchio and, mocking and taunting him, hang him from a tree. They dance off, leaving Pinocchio alone and frightened. Enter the beautiful Fairy with the Blue Hair in a chariot drawn by two White Mice. The mice untie Pinocchio and spirit him off to the fairy's castle.

Act II begins with Pinocchio attended to by two eminent doctors, the wise Dr. Owl of the "elevator eyebrows" and Dr. Crow with his pince-nez glasses. They prescribe some medicine, but Pinocchio is afraid to take it. The Blue-Haired Fairy persuades him it is safe, and he is immediately restored to health. He promises to return to Geppetto and love him and go to school. In Scene II, Pinocchio is on his way home when he encounters a boy named Lamp Wick who is on his way to "The Country of Playthings," a land where everyone plays and never has to go to school. Pinocchio joins Lamp Wick and his Donkey, and Scene III finds them in the land of play. When night falls, the children are driven from the playground by the Donkey Driver, and in Scene IV, we find Pinocchio and Lamp Wick wearing dunce caps to hide the Donkey ears each has grown as they ran from the playground chased by the Donkey Driver. In the final scene, they stumble across a big white tombstone emblazoned with "Here Lies the Fairy with the Blue Hair, Dead with Grief for Having Been Abandoned by Her Little Brother Pinocchio." In an agony of remorse, Pinocchio falls to the ground, whereupon the Fairy with the Blue Hair, who is not really dead, calls out to him. She has been resurrected due to the sincerity of his grief. His joy is evident as she explains that there is always hope if your heart is good, and she grants him three wishes. His first two are to get rid of the donkey ears he and Lamp Wick have grown; and his final wish is to be reunited with Geppetto. Geppetto appears in a new coat and having learned his lesson, Pinocchio is turned into a real boy by the Fairy with the Blue Hair.[231]

Strawbridge danced Pinocchio as "a gay and mirth-provoking puppet" to great acclaim. A news clipping from New Bedford, MA (unknown source, n.d.) describes Strawbridge; "Dressed in scarlet breeches and pointed cap, with a billowing blouse of green polka-dots, he embodied the essence of Pinocchio." According to the New York *World Telegram* (n.d.) "the children rejoiced and sorrowed with him in all his exploits." The Parkersburg, West Virginia, *Sentinel* (Feb 2, 1937) noted, "His delightful sense of humor and the fun of story-telling through dance make him the ideal impersonator of Pinocchio." In Morgantown, West Virginia, the *Dominion News* (March 15, 1937) thought Strawbridge "superb . . . [and he] never lost the character and quality of the little wooden marionette. Throughout the ballet, [Strawbridge] was delicately abstract, yet realistic enough to carry even a sophisticated adult into fairyland."

Sharing chief dancing honors, depending on the year of the tour, were Lisa Parnova, Frances Rands, and Virginia Miller, as the Fairy with Blue Hair. According to the Huntington, West Virginia, *Herald-Dispatch* (March 9, 1937), "Lisa Parnova, like one of the Ballet Russe ballerinas left behind, pirouetted on the toes of her pink satin slippers and tossed her blue cellophane hair as the beautiful 'Blue Fairy.'" Ms. Parnova had been the prima ballerina of the Cologne Ballet before joining Strawbridge's Junior Programs Ballet. From the New York City *Bronx Home News* (April 17, 1938), we learn that Frances Rands, age nineteen and formerly a member of the Fokine Ballet Company, became the premiere danseuse for the Junior Programs Ballet, dancing the role of the Fairy with Blue Hair. Another news clipping (unknown source, n.d.) comments, "She was as airy as Mr. Strawbridge was droll, and both were in high favor with the Juveniles." A New Bedford, MA, news clipping (unknown source, n.d.) characterized Virginia Miller as "exquisitely dainty . . . Her first entrance in Scene 3 . . . might well have been every child's dream of fairyland materialized. Dressed in a huge ballet skirt of faint blue, a silvery shade matched by her long curling hair, and carrying a star-pointed wand, she toe-danced onto the stage driving two harnessed, velvet-eared white mice. After rescuing the puppet . . . she was well on her way to winning every small heart in the audience, and those of the parents, too."

Three different actresses performed the role of narrator over the course of the production: Lanni Carvell, Julia Vaughan, and Martha Picken. Carvell, a well-known actress, originated the part, and "changed her voice with lightening-speed for each of the characters—a rough-voiced shout for the Donkeyman, and hee-haws for the Donkey" (unknown source, n.d.). The reviewer for the New Haven, Connecticut, *Journal-Courier* (April 22, 1937) was clear: "To Miss Julia Vaughn must go the lion's share of the credit for the phenomenal success of this novel entertainment. Dressed in the timeless costume of the troubadour, and sitting close to her audience, she speaks the lines of all the protagonists . . . suiting her tone of voice to each character." In later productions, Martha Picken, dressed in pageboy garb, addressed the audience in New Bedford, Massachusetts, as "Your Majesties of the Province of New Bedford" and explained her role as that of storyteller. Seated at one side of the stage, often in the shadows, she proceeded to "give robust vocality to the dance-pantomime. As Pinocchio, her voice became squeaky, for Gepetto, deep throated, while her Fox and Cat had a screechy quality" (unknown source, n.d.).

An early accolade from a Utica Junior League telegram states, "Pinocchio Tremendous Success Packed House of Three Thousand Thrilled Production Unbelievably Good" (Nov 26, 1936). The Rockford *Morning Star* (Feb 26, 1937) told a similar story. "It's not a simple thing to keep an audience of some 2,700 people, most of whom are very young and very wriggly almost breathlessly attentive for a matter of an hour and a half. . ." The Fairmont, West Virginia, *Times,* (Feb 13, 1937) concurred. The production was "so ideally suited to an audience of children . . . [that they] paid the production the highest tribute possible, that of spellbound silence." In New Bedford, "row after row of pigtails and Eton collars squealed with delight yesterday afternoon as Junior Programs, Inc. presented 'Pinocchio,' a narrative ballet in two acts, in the auditorium of the New Bedford High School. So small were many of the spectators that it almost seemed as if the Girl's League of the school, which sponsored the event, could have arranged half-seat admissions for a generous majority of the audience" (unknown source, n.d.).

Of special interest were the extraordinary masks and costumes worn by each of the animal characters. The masks for the Cat, the Fox, Dr. Crow, Dr. Owl, and the two White Mice were fashioned by the artist Bill Baird. The Parkersburg, West Virginia, *Sentinel* (Mar 12, 1937) describes the two White Mice "dressed in white velvet coats and knee breeches, edged in white fur. Mice masks covered their heads, and their hands and shoulders drooped timidly as they tip toed back and forth across the stage during the performance." The Lowell, Massachusetts, *Leader* (April 5, 1937) noted that "combining modeling, color work, and processing, mask making releases . . . the creative imaginative skill which many children possess but are rarely inspired to use."[232]

Clearly, the Junior Programs Ballet was on to something. In her autobiography, McFadden recounts an incident at one of the dress rehearsals to which they had invited several groups of children from various orphanages and settlement houses as guests. "After enjoying the PINOCCHIO ballet, [they] simply stayed in their seats at the end, and asked if they couldn't see the 'second show'—as they did in a movie theatre!" This assessment was reinforced by the Parkersburg, West Virginia, *Sentinel* (Feb 2, 1937) which gives us a glimpse into how Junior Programs performances were valued by the communities in which they performed. Included in the *Sentinel* review, we find the comment, "All the children in Parkersburg attended, including refugee children staying at Old St. Joseph's Hospital during and since the flood." "The flood" had devastated Parkersburg and the surrounding areas from Memphis to Cincinnati on January 25, 1937, just a week before the *Sentinel* review. The water, cresting at almost sixty feet, left thirty-seven dead, hundreds missing, and 450,000 people displaced. The threats of typhoid, diphtheria, and dysentery were real, and streets, stores, and buildings were inundated, underwater, or pushed off their foundations while workers sought to move whatever they could to higher ground. But the Junior Programs performance of *Pinocchio* was not cancelled! An extraordinary tribute to the company, and to the extraordinary value the community placed on what the

Junior Programs Ballet had to offer. Parkersburg took the old theatrical adage "the show must go on!" seriously.

The Princess and the Swineherd[233]

Following the enormous success of *Pinocchio*, for the 1937–38 season the Junior Programs Ballet added *The Princess and the Swineherd* to its repertoire. Based on a story by Hans Christian Andersen, *The Princess and the Swineherd* was a morality tale about the hazards of pride and self-importance. Unfortunately, none of the Junior Programs' materials contained more than snippets of information about the production. How this story came to be selected is unclear, but McFadden notes in her autobiography that she wrote the initial script for the narrative dance-play.[234] From several newspaper articles (*New York Times*, Sep 24, 1939; Virginia *TMS Dispatch*, Feb 25, 1940; Cincinnati *Enquirer,* Jan 27, 1938), we learn that Strawbridge choreographed *The Princess and the Swineherd* dance-play to music from the most melodic compositions by Scandinavian composers Grieg and Sibelius, as well as Schumann, Pierne, Brahms, Beethoven, and Ole Olsen. The musical score was compiled by Moritz Von Bomhard, director of the Princeton University Symphony Orchestra.

One hand-lettered poster for the first production (n.d.) promotes it as a cheerful and amusing entertainment:

You Liked "Pinocchio"

Then You <u>Must</u> See

THE PRINCESS and the SWINEHERD . . . . . .

from the story by Hans Christian Andersen

A line drawing of a smiling pig dancing was followed by:

More adventures of mischievous, lovable story-book characters
brought to vibrant life by

JUNIOR PROGRAMS own BALLET COMPANY

A new and unique form of entertainment combining music,
dance and drama into an amusing and spectacular production
for young and old.

Another marketing program booklet announces: "The sorcerer makes a Magic Pot that plays tunes and tells what everyone in the kingdom is having for dinner! The two Merry Piglets, Arabella and Susabella learn to dance. Beautiful, colorful costumes and settings, tuneful music make this one of our most charming dance-plays. Versatile-voiced narrator interprets the story."[235]

The story, based on Andersen's fairy tale of a very proud princess and her downfall, was adapted for Junior Programs by Princess Constance Pignatelli di Montecalvo, a playwright who was also one of Junior Programs Board members.[236] The opening scene finds the prince of a small kingdom interested in finding a wife. To woo the daughter of the emperor, he sends her a rose from a bush growing on his father's grave. One sniff of its sweet fragrance would banish all sorrows. He also sent a nightingale that could sing any melody one desired. Each gift was in a silver case, but when the Princess opened the gift with the rose, she was disappointed that it was not an artificial one. When she opened the case with the nightingale all her ladies praised its singing, but the Princess was again displeased. Why was it not like the mechanical bird in the late Empress's music box? She refused to receive the Prince.

The Prince was not discouraged. Disguising himself as a commoner, he applied to the Emperor for a job. The only one available was as Swineherd. The Prince accepted. He worked all day taking care of the pigs. But at night, he crafted a beautiful little pot with bells around the rim that played a little song when its water boiled. When one put a finger into the rising steam, one could smell all the food being prepared in every hearth in the town. One day, when the Princess and her ladies were passing by, she recognized the tune and sent one of her ladies to buy the pot. The price was "ten kisses from the Princess." Shocked, the Princess tried, unsuccessfully, to bargain. But she wanted the pot so she commanded her ladies to spread out their dresses so no one could see her, and she paid the ten kisses.

Meanwhile, the Prince was busy making a Magic Rattle that could play all the dances known since the world began. Again, the Princess heard the music, but this time, the price was a hundred kisses. Against her will, she agreed. Again, her ladies spread out their dresses, and the Prince received the hundred kisses. Curious as to why there was a crowd of ladies around the pigsty, the Emperor went to investigate. When he saw his daughter kissing the Swineherd, he became angry and banished both of them. Full of regret, the Princess wished she had accepted the Prince. Disappearing behind a tree, the Prince threw off his rags and emerged in his princely garments. The Princess bowed, but he spurned her, saying that she had rejected his honest gifts, but had been willing to kiss a swineherd to acquire a few toys. "You have no one to blame but yourself." With that, he returned to his kingdom and married another Princess.[237]

The first performance of *The Princess and the Swineherd* took place at the Brooklyn Academy of Music, the afternoon of January 14, 1939 (*Brooklyn Eagle*). The various materials and newspaper reviews in the Junior Programs Scrapbooks document performances of *The Princess and the Swineherd* in at least twenty cities across the country (see Appendix I). Although McFadden acknowledged that the production was not as popular as *Pinocchio*, a review from Portland, Oregon, reported, "Although we expected a good performance we had no conception of the beauty and perfection of the production. Every member of the cast is outstanding and the stage crew an excellent one—everything moved on the dot—our auditorium was packed—ages from 80 to 2 1/2, all of them fascinated. What more is there to say but thank you—thank you—all we want now is more Junior Programs."[238] And from Oakland, California, we're told, "The children just loved it—and sat spellbound which we consider the test. We have rarely had any performance which went over as well as *The Princess and the Swineherd*. We have had telephone calls and letters since, telling us of our audience's enthusiasm. This production is certainly a great credit to Junior Programs!!"[239]

The Adventures of Puck[240]

"Shakespeare Brings Pleasure to Topeka Audience Friday"

(Topeka, Kansas *Journal*, March 22, 1941)

For lovers of the Western theatrical canon, there can be no more fundamental a question than that of how to introduce children to "The Bard." Junior Programs' answer turned out to be another innovative and winsome production. In keeping with the company's iconoclastic approach, rather than do yet another traditional dramatic version of Shakespeare's *A Midsummer Night's Dream* cut down to child-sized bites, Lancourt and Strawbridge decided to accept the artistic challenge of turning a portion of Shakespeare's most delightful comedy into a dance-play. Renamed *The Adventures of Puck*, and using Felix Mendelssohn's *A Midsummer Night's Dream* score, it took them eighteen months to match the Bard's words with Mendelssohn's music. Both men agreed that "dovetailing" the words with the score was one of the most difficult things they had ever done, but the audience response—both the children and the adults—indicated that the "production pains had not been suffered in vain" (Musical America, Feb 10, 1940). And according to the Topeka Kansas *Journal* (March 22, 1941), their focus on the quarrel between Titania and Oberon made a "marvelous contrast to the droll, rustic comedy" of Bottom and his fellow actors in *Pyramus and Thisbe*, Shakespeare's "play within a play."

Mendelssohn's Overture, Op. 21, was originally written as an independent concert piece when he was seventeen years old. Sixteen years later, it was incorporated into his Op. 61 as its overture. The music is noteworthy for its many instrumental effects, including the sound of "scampering fairy feet," and the braying and "hee-hawing" of the strings signifying Bottom when he turns into an ass.[241] From an undated Junior Programs' marketing piece, we learn that "Mr. Strawbridge set himself to the task of fitting the Shakespearean verses to Mendelssohn's musical phrases, and the resulting synchronization of dancing, music and dialogue, as spoken by narrator, Martha Picken, may be counted among the most difficult accomplishments in modern ballet production."[242]

Dance Magazine (Feb 1941) describes Strawbridge's "ever popular 'Adventures of Puck'" as a ballet adaptation:

> Mr. Strawbridge's offerings are not all-out ballet. Rather they are 'dance-plays' which feature folk dances combined with ballet and modern forms . . . While impish Puck, queenly Titania, frolicsome Bottom and the rest of Shakespeare's moonstruck characters go through dance-pantomime, a versatile-voiced narrator speaks all their parts during the course of the play. Dancing, naturally, plays a major role in the presentation . . . The combination of ballet, pantomime and narration makes for a presentation easily 'digested' by children. They are charmed not only by the story action, but particularly by the entertaining dancing of Strawbridge, [and] his partner Virginia Miller . . . It is heartening to see how enthusiastically Strawbridge's

ballet-plays are received by young people to whom ballet is something foreign. Rarely does attendance run below 2,000 at each performance. Recently in Tuscaloosa the group played to 12,000 children.[243]

In *Adventures of Puck,* we see a paring down to essentials. The Topeka, Kansas, *Journal* (March 22, 1941) notes that by omitting the subplots, *A Midsummer Night's Dream* was cut to three acts, putting the focus of the ballet on the quarrel of Oberon and Titania "which made a marvelous contrast to the droll, rustic comedy of [Bottom and his cohorts] . . . As Puck, Edwin Strawbridge gave an amazing performance of the impudent, heartless elf who caused much of the trouble in the play. Virginia Miller was beautiful and graceful as Titania, [and] one of the most amazing performances of the show was that of Martha Picken, the narrator, who read all the parts of the comedy ranging from the roaring lion to the lullaby sung by the fairy queen."

According to several Junior Programs press materials, the production was filled with a profusion of color and variety. The costumes, by Henry Ormond and Christine Thompson, were significantly different from those in the traditional dramatic productions of Shakespeare's comedy. In this ballet production, Titania and Oberon's "courtiers" are costumed as woodland creatures, beetles, katydids, and butterflies, rather than as elves and fairies with gauzy wings. The butterflies, "resplendent in iridescent hues of the rainbow, with long flowing wings" flutter around Titania, while the "beetles and other insects are in Oberon's train. Designed for an effect of individuality, rather than a chorus group, every costume differs from the next, descriptive of the character portrayed in color as well as form. Mustardseed, for example, is in mustard yellow, Peas Blossom is the natural [purple] color of the flower, and Cobweb in a neutral gray." Bottom the Weaver and his rustic band are, as Shakespeare himself describes them, "all hempen homespun." Titania's costume, "a triumph of luminous splendor," adheres to "folk legend describing her attendants gathering for their mistress' robe, delicate spider webs sprinkled with shining morning dew." Her mist-like garment is dotted with a profusion of light-reflecting gems, and her moon-silvered hair is crowned with a tiara of stars and dewdrops. Oberon, however, following the tradition set forth by the poet Dryden, is clothed in romantic military garb, complete with a plumed helmet, and a cuirass of blue-colored fish scales. Puck's outfit, on the other hand, is that of a satyr "with tousled hair of black and green, and he has pointed ears. His simple costume is in keeping with the character of legend, who hated the clothes of mortals, and covered himself carelessly with bark, moss, and leaves of the forest."[244]

The scenic design made full use of great differentiations of color, with Titania's bower in a woodsy dell replete with "blue moonlight effects against a background of graceful trees, surrounding a rippling brook where the sweet thyme grows." For the rehearsal of their comic play, Bottom and his buffoonish friends meet where "[d]ark trees [are] silhouetted against a night sky, with tawny colors heighten[ing] the rusticity of the clownish characters."[245] Even this brief description of the costumes and scenic design, the embodiment of any child's fantasy made manifest, again indicates that the Junior Programs Ballet took its commitment to quality seriously. As Lancourt had promised, their touring productions were equal to those on the Broadway stages.

The marketing materials tell us Mendelssohn's music is "one of the daintiest bits of musical humor ever composed." Op. 61 is considered one of his greatest works, "a youthful musical genius to match the wit of Shakespeare's verses." Popular for over a hundred years, his music "breathes its witchery and spell in every measure. Highly descriptive, it transports auditors effortlessly to the forest dell of Oberon and Titania. A scherzo of sprightly music fashions the dancing of the wood sprites. There is the unmistakable scamper of mischievous Puck, the foolish antics of Bottom and his buffoon companions, all developed with a delightful musical fancy. As interpreted by Solomon Rokoff, concert-master, and Leo Polski, pianist . . . [the] music provides a charming setting in sound for the action of the dancers. The production, conceived by the eminent American dancer, Edwin Strawbridge, who enacts the role of Puck, is the very first to adapt in ballet form Shakespeare's original verses to the entire Mendelssohn suite in a continuous flowing rendition."[246]

The ballet unfolded in three acts—Titania's Bower, In the Forest, and Titania's Bower. As the Overture began, the scene was set in a moonlit wood, "where moving phantoms of light and shadow flit through the eerie realm of the unconscious as spirits and fairies." The dancers dance a story, the narrators say the words; every gesture of their hands, each step and movement of their arms and bodies has something to do with the story."[247] We are introduced to the antics of Puck, the quarrel of Oberon and Titania, and the comic blunderings of Bottom and his fellow craftsmen as they attempt to dramatize the play-within-the-play of Pyramus and Thisbe. A musical scherzo has Oberon instructing Puck to search for "a little Western flower, milk white now purple with loves wounds." Soon, the music segues into a Nocturne, and we see Oberon squeezing drops from the flower on Titania's eyelids. "Titania, the Fairy Queen, is a lovely stately dancer, proud and haughty in all her movements, for she is ruler of all the fairies. Oberon also dances with dignity and quiet grace. The fairies, in the shape of moths and butterflies and beetles, flutter and twist and turn very lightly as they flit through the forest . . . The main character is Puck, a mischievous elf, so all his movements are quick and darting, like sunlight on rippling water . . . he jumps from place to place . . . The humans in the story [are] very crude and heavy by contrast, with clumsy motions of their arms and legs and many foolish bumps and tumbles."[248] The ballet concludes with Mendelssohn's famous Wedding March as the dancers pantomime the triple wedding of Theseus and Hippolyta, Lysander and Hermia, and Demetrius and Helena.

According to the *Fairmont Times* (WV, n.d.), "Strawbridge, as Puck, lent an appealing nimbleness and grace to the character of the wood sprite. Easy to watch at all times, his imaginative fire dance at the opening of the third act stood out as an exciting creation." And Junior Programs marketing material adds that "Strawbridge stands alone among premier dancers in his genius for delighting adults with his art while he convulses the children in merriment." It also notes that "Educators will welcome this ballet as a focal event in the study of Shakespeare."[249] The reviewer also found that "the dancing, the score, the pantomime and the narration were blended almost perfectly throughout . . . [and there were] jolly, slapstick delineation of the antics of Bottom and his fellow yokels." In Saginaw, Michigan, *The News* (n.d.) tells us "The adults in the audience enjoyed the play as much as did the children." From Gary, Indiana (unknown source, n.d.), we hear that "audience response was delightful and heartening to adults who have faith in the cultivation of taste and the development of appreciations—but who may sometimes have that faith sorely tested."

Given the descriptions of the performance, it seems safe to say that this Junior Programs production was not one which sorely tested parental faith in their effort to cultivate taste and appreciation in their children. Rather, with the sets and costumes a feast for the eyes of every child in attendance, and with the Strawbridge choreography and dancing, Mendelssohn music, and Shakespearean language almost perfectly blended throughout, *The Adventures of Puck* could not help but leave all who attended wanting more.

Robin Hood[250]

"'Robin Hood' Ballet Cheered by Capacity Audience of Children"
(Ashville, N.C., Citizen Times, Dec 15, 1940)

The final Strawbridge dance-play, *Robin Hood*, was also one of Junior Programs' most lavish and well-received productions. Based on the popular English legend, an early review from the Baltimore *Sun* (Dec 28, 1940) notes that Lancourt and Margaret Carlisle, responsible for the musical arrangements, "went back to original sources for this version of the legend of Sherwood Forest." Carlisle had spent the previous eight years in England at London's British Museum and the libraries of Oxford researching ancient ballads, folk songs, and madrigals. Based on her research, the melodic motifs of the *Robin Hood* score were transcribed from a unique and rich mix of musical sources: there were two hitherto unknown ancient English hunting songs; a hymn from the era of Thomas a Becket, 'My Mind to Me a Kingdom Is'; a parchment manuscript of a thirteenth-century troubadour's song by del la Halle which provided the central theme; street cries of medieval London that infused the Tinker's Song; and the Yuletide music of the earliest English Christmas carols accompanied the dances. (Baltimore *Sun*, 1940; Evansville, Indiana, *Courier*, Jan 26, 1941).

According to a Bridgeport, Connecticut, review (unknown source, Sep 28, 1940), Lancourt's research took him deep into a study of twelfth- and thirteenth-century English lore, searching through myriad ballads about Robin Hood to identify a version best suited to a children's ballet. As even a cursory review of historic sources concerning the origin of the Robin Hood legends demonstrate, there are numerous versions from which to choose. Some early ballads characterize him as a combative thief who truly lived "outside the law." Others question whether he was of royal birth or of yeoman stock.

> But now it appears that Robin Hood was never an outlaw, for all his reputation. Original researches in sources 700 years old disclose the fact that the renowned 'outlaw' was a champion of the highest law of the land—that of the King . . . It was from ancient verses written in the hoary Anglo-Saxon of the period of Chaucer . . . that

> Lancourt came across . . . a little known account of the man who was known as Robin Hood. He was the foster son of the noble Earl of Huntingdon who, when he was about to come into his Earldom was driven into exile by . . . the Sheriff of Nottingham. Far from openly resisting the looting Sheriff who was feared and hated by everyone for his depredations against the poor, Robin Hood determined to yield his estates and retire to the woods until such time as he could seek justice from the King himself (Providence, RI, *Journal*, Jan 26, 1941).

"Most popular of all English ballad heroes, Robin Hood was "the ideal champion of the commons, a valorous and merry forester living the free and joyous life of the woodlands." Such was the description accorded him by no less an authority than George Lyman Kittredge of Harvard.[251] And, according to the Providence, Rhode Island, *Journal* (Jan 26, 1941), this Lincoln-green-clad habitant of Sherwood Forest was endowed with heroic virtues of no small measure, being "manly yet merciful, proud yet courteous, openhanded and ready-witted, a protector of women and religion."

It should be no surprise that, given their youthful audience, the version Lancourt chose for the Robin Hood ballet depicts him as a young man of deep moral principles. "From this point on, it was only a step to the adaptation of the script itself to ballet form . . . [and] to Lancourt's great surprise, a request came from the Garden City Publishing Company for a manuscript of the story for a juvenile book. Without at all meaning to do so, Lancourt thus became in one fell swoop producer and script writer of a ballet and author of a book—all because he 'discovered' Robin Hood wasn't an outlaw" (Bridgeport, CT, unknown source, Sep 28, 1940).

Additional research into thirteenth-century forms of merrymaking also identified various pre-Christian rituals, such as bringing in the Yule Log and the tradition of feasting on a gilded peacock stuffed with savory treats. According to the New Orleans *Times-Picayune* (Dec 1, 1940):

> Long before the English Christmas ceremony of the boar's head . . . it was traditional in the castles of British noblemen to carry in the gilded peacock, chief delicacy of the yuletide festive board. Hardly a castle in England at the time of the Crusades was without its strutting peacocks . . . When Christmas came in England it was the custom a

thousand years ago to kill and roast the largest peacock in the castle, stuff it with all kinds of sweets, and then cover it with a coat of purest gold. The lady of the castle most distinguished by birth and beauty won the honor of leading a processional which carried it into the feast. That was the ceremony of the gilded peacock, and it will be again brought to life in one of the scenes of the Junior Program's ballet, 'Robin Hood.'

Another happy custom of that vanished era . . . was that of having the lord of the castle step down from his authority . . . his court jester taking his place as the master of misrule. Under such a ridiculous reign everything was made topsy-turvy, with the ladies behaving like knights and vice-versa, the brave pretending to be timid and the gentle ferocious . . . These gayeties usually took place at Christmas time, and since this will be represented in the 'Robin Hood' ballet, much of the real flavor of the long-forgotten yuletide of Old England will be represented on the stage.

According to the Child Study Association, Act I began on Christmas Eve, 1250, at Gamwell House in Nottinghamshire. It is the birthday of Robert, foster son of the Earl of Huntingdon, the day he is to come into possession of the land and titles of the Earl. His childhood friend, Lady Marian Fitzwalter, now one of the Queen's ladies-in-waiting, has come from London to celebrate. As the feasting begins, the great Yule Log is carried in to the fireplace and lit, and Marian leads the presentation of the gilded peacock on a silver platter. At the height of the revelry, a peasant rushes in and throws himself at Robert's feet, begging for protection. He confesses that to prevent his family from starving, he has shot one of the king's deer and is now being chased by the sheriff. When the sheriff arrives, he demands that Robert hand over the culprit. To save the poor man, Robert claims it was he who shot the deer. Bearing a grudge against Robert, the sheriff demands that Robert give up his title and leave his estates that very night. Robert's guests protest and want to fight the sheriff, but Robert persuades them that the only way to best the sheriff is to appeal to the king for justice. Lady Marian promises to appeal to Queen Eleanor.

Act II finds Robert in Sherwood Forest where he takes the name of Robin Hood. Many men, having heard of his good deeds to the poor join him, forming a merry band. They spend their days hunting and taking their surplus food to the poor in the surrounding villages. From time to time, if a traveler encountered Robin, fought fairly, and proved to be skillful, he would be invited to join the merry band. In this way, Little John, the Tinker, and Dick of Banbury became members of Robin's merry band.

Junior Programs Ballet *Robin Hood*
Robin (Edwin Strawbridge) and His Merry Band of Archers
(JP Scrapbooks)

One day, Robin, Friar Tuck, and Little John discover a royal page lying on the ground. He and another page had been looking for Robin to take him to the Queen but were attacked by the Sheriff of Nottingham. Both were sentenced to hang. One

IV. THE PRODUCTIONS: PART II—THE OPERA & BALLET COMPANIES 195

of the pages had bribed a guard and escaped. Robin and his men set out to rescue the remaining page, and in doing so, even managed to capture the sheriff. But in the confusion of discovering that one of the pages was Lady Marian, the sheriff managed to escape. Robin's men hurry off to pursue the sheriff, while Robin and Marian go off to meet the Queen.

Act III finds them at the Queen's court on the day of a big festival. All the knights and yeomen will engage in feats of combat to prove their skills with lance and bow. A richly caparisoned hobby horse combat opened the festival and introduced a jovial note into the scene, followed by a demonstration of Robin's skill with bow and arrow. Of course, Robin outshoots all the others.

In the final round, Gilbert of the White Hand hits the bull's eye, but Robin's arrow shatters Gilbert's, and Robin is declared the winner. The Queen presents him to the King, who, after listening to Lady Marion's account of Robin's encounter with the Sheriff of Nottingham rewards Robin by restoring his lands and title.[252]

A brief reference (unknown source, n.d.) to an organization using *Robin Hood* as a fund-raiser—Young America Wants to Help, an organization affiliated with the British War Relief Society— offers a possible hint as to what may have influenced Junior Programs to choose the story of Robin Hood as the subject for their fourth ballet: empathy with the plight of the United Kingdom was growing, and they may have viewed *Robin Hood* as a gesture of support and an acknowledgement of the many historical connections that existed between the two countries. Whatever the reason, the fall and winter of 1940 found the company performing to large crowds of children in Wheaton, Illinois; New Orleans, Louisiana; Asheville, North Carolina; Baltimore, Maryland; and St. Petersburg, Florida. *The Independent* (St. Petersburg, FL, Nov 1940) showered praise on the production:

> No previous Junior Programs productions, which have been seen by 3,000,000 youngsters throughout the country, ever displayed such a profusion of trappings in the way of scenery, costumes, lighting and effects. 'Robin Hood' will bring to life in three scenes the simple grandeur of the interior of the Earl of Huntingdon's castle, the exhilarating delight of sights and sounds in . . . Sherwood Forest, the awesome majesty of the Court of King John and Queen Eleanor, and the brilliant color and spectacle of a knightly tournament . . . Performers will change their costumes no less than four times for

each artist, and in the stylized backgrounds there will be on view every artful appurtenance to convey the true feeling of a never-to-be-forgotten era of England's romantic past . . . Covering the whole space of the backdrop in the first scene, for example, will be an authentic reproduction of one of the largest and most priceless tapestries in the fabulous collection of the New York Metropolitan Museum of Art. A hunting scene of merry England woven by hands dead these seven hundred years furnished the central motif for a scene of rustic festivity in the castle of a British hunting lord. The second act . . . a riotous blending of greens, yellows, and reds, captures the essence of the original ballad's lyrical painting of Sherwood Forest. Here all the jolly company of yeomen, archers and followers, Friar Tuck, Little John, the Tinker, and Robin Hood will cavort, practicing merry pranks on one another and leading the soldiers of the wicked Sheriff of Nottingham a comic chase. The Lincoln-green hooded costumes of Robin Hood's followers are a result of the painstaking researches into authentic sources. For the third and final act, the magnificent splendor of a Thirteenth Century English court will be revealed just as it appeared in olden times. Rough masonry and huge stone columns predominate in the background, a fitting setting for the thrones of the King and Queen, while off to the side and in the distance may be seen the Field of Honor, bedecked with innumerable gaily-colored pennants fluttering from the tents of the jousters.

The *Times-Picayune* (New Orleans, Dec 8, 1940) called *Robin Hood* "scintillating." The review, by Margaret Elaine Scott, begins with the following:

> Now Heaven bless thy grace this day,
> Say all in sweet Sherwood,
> For thou didst give the prize away
> To merry Robin Hood.

What boy or girl will ever forget these lines which were written on the scroll attached to the arrow which Robin Hood shot through the sheriff's window to tell him the prize-winner of the shooting

IV. THE PRODUCTIONS: PART II—THE OPERA & BALLET COMPANIES

match at Nottingham had been none other but the very outlaw he was seeking? And who will ever forget Robin Hood?

The headline for the *Citizen Times* (Ashville, NC, Dec 15, 1940) read "'Robin Hood' Ballet Cheered By Capacity Audience of Children." The review goes on to say, "Delighted cheers and screams of laughter greeted the presentation of 'Robin Hood.'" A Macon, Georgia, review (unknown source, n.d.) tells us: "Two thousand happy children swayed at will by the enchanting voice of Martha Picken, applauded the brave deeds of admirable Robin Hood . . . No one of the numerous members of the Junior Programs Ballet . . . including the famous Edwin Strawbridge, uttered a word. But the expressive dancing, along with the flawless narration made a big hit with the youthful audience . . . No report had been made by the [Macon Junior] League last night on the financial outcome of the venture, but the delighted shouts of the youthful audience should go far to pay the group for the effort if admissions were insufficient to do that."

The Wellsburg, West Virginia, *Daily Herald* (n.d.) tells of 2,000 people attending the performance in an auditorium that had only 1,500 seats. To accommodate the overflow, "improvised seating was arranged in the aisles while the standing room in the rear was entirely crowded." And the *Lake Forester* (Lake Forest, IL, Sep 26, 1940) took particular note of the music:

> Played on a recorder, rendering in mellow tones, the regular twelve note eight tone scale, and a portable reed organ simulated the ancient lute . . . the music they played, harking back to a period when wandering troubadours traversed the highways of England earning their bread by entertaining people at markets or in a nobleman's court, as fortune dictated, serves better than anything else to revivify the true spirit of Britain. Delicately rhythmic for the dance measures, vigorously lusty for martial arts, tender and melodious for the romantic mood, the music of ancients reduces emotions to their basic essentials. The ornate embellishments of an advanced and more complicated art are lacking; and yet the effect is often more telling on the musically untrained ear. Among the musical highlights . . . [are] an entire concert of medieval melodies . . . a unique 13th century

tune by del la Halle . . . two hitherto unknown old English hunting songs . . . [and] a tune based on street cries of medieval London.

And a LaGrange, Illinois, review titled "Robin Hood is Beautifully Given" (unknown source, n.d.), we hear:

> Children of LaGrange and Western Springs [Illinois]—at least about 1500 of them . . . had a thrilling time . . . Tiny youngsters of the first and second grades as well as their elders—the eighth graders—sat with rapt attention, their eyes on the captivating stage, where for nearly two hours the story of 'Robin Hood' was so beautifully unfolded. The bedlam—and it is just that when 1500 children are awaiting the rise of a curtain—ceased immediately when the tall and attractive Miss Picken—in her Sherwood Forest costume, spoke—From the first instant the children were interested in what she had to say to them—and she had the personable ability of holding that attention to the final line of the play. . . It was not only the audience that enjoyed the play—for the actors had a grand time too . . . Lighting effects and acoustics—and a very well-behaved audience . . . added a lot to the success . . . Joop the [G]iraffe, talked to the children between the scenes. There was a dancing bear and a horse or two scampering around the stage via human legs—all bringing cheers from the audience. Music also has its charms and when Clarence Dissinger asked the 1500 children to sing, he found a ready response and their young voices raised enthusiastically in rounds and old favorites. There was an especially thunderous approval for 'Playmates'—and proof that there were 1500 loyal little citizens when they sang 'God Bless America.'

Kudos for Miss Picken abounded. According to a review from Hartford, Connecticut (unknown source, n.d.): "The choreography of the entire production was convincing, and the dancing was excellent. But without doubt, the choicest wreath of laurels must go to Martha Picken, the Narrator. For this was an audible as well as a visible ballet, and the narrative was augmented by the speech of the characters. Miss Picken took every part and so well did she fit her voice to the actions of the dancers that it was some time before people realized that the dancers were not speaking." And from St. Petersburg, Florida (unknown source, n.d.), we hear:

> Any person or group of people so entertaining that a large audience of school children is kept perfectly quiet must be good ... Interest of the children was held by the color and movement of the dancers, the unusual quality of suspense rare in this particular type of production, and by the excellent work of the narrator, Martha Picken, whose voice was the only one heard throughout the ballet. So convincing was she in speaking for the 20 characters that the children forgot that these characters were not speaking for themselves ... Setting played an important part in the success of the ballet. They furnished an authentic atmosphere of Old England with rich tapestries, gorgeous brocades and velvets and polished old woods ... a marvelous eye for color and each scene was a living picture. Sherwood forest made every child in the audience a potential Robin Hood or Maid Marian.

The Kenosha, Wisconsin, *Evening News* (n.d.) joined in: "A thorough understanding of child psychology was evident in the presentation, which was first shown when the narrator, Martha Picken, came out on the stage near the whirling hour glass which showed reversal of time to Christmas eve, 1250 A.D., and took her audience back with her to the 13th century." As for the dancing, "it left nothing to be desired ... [and e]specially fine acting was done by Charles Tate who was the comic jester and also Friar Tuck." Mary Tigner's newspaper review, "Robin Hood Ballet Pleases Large Audience" (Columbus, GA, n.d.) noted that:

> The production showed the influence of the Ballet Russe in method and staging. The story was told by a reader while the company, through dance and pantomime, portrays the theme in quick Russian tempo ... The scenery was most effective ... The dusky mystery of Sherwood forest [*sic*] in green, with silvery highlights ... the merry men in Lincoln green and Jolly Friar Tuck in brown, was a picture to long remember ... Flashing through the whole performance was the exquisite grace of Edwin Strawbridge ... The court Jester in his festive motley was [also] a great favorite ... [and] the ballet was given to a

capacity audience. All little Columbus, with Dad and Mother in tow was there in its swankiest bib and tucker, patent leather pumps, bubbling with enthusiasm. One small curly-head clutched her little companion and said, 'Oh, how can we wait until it begins!' . . . This production is a very good introduction to the ballet for those who are not familiar with it.

Junior Programs Ballet *Robin Hood***Robin (Edwin Strawbridge) at the Queen's Court Tournament**
(Lancourt's personal papers)

Other notable dances included the "All Hail, Robert!" during the celebrations at Gamwell House in Act I and the Morris dancing in Act III. Little John, in Act II, "was expert of limb and made several leaps over one of the men as graceful as a trout in a stream" (unknown source, n.d.). Other reviews focused on the "grace, intricate and ofttimes acrobatic dancing of the talented cast . . . [all of whom] wove a picture that will linger forever in the memories of children and adults" (Wheaton, IL, *Journal*, Oct 28, 1940). "There were squeals of excitement during the sword fight between

Robin and the three soldiers of the royal court, and the antics of the Court Jester as he danced caused glee and peals of laughter among the very young" (unknown source, n.d.). "The evening audience which was one half adults was just as enthusiastic . . . They listened with model attentiveness and applauded rapturously whenever there was an opportunity" (unknown source, n.d.).

As the dashing Robin, Strawbridge surpassed his previous successes, combining modern dance, ballet, and rustic folk dances of old England into what was clearly an exuberant and engaging introduction to the dance for millions of children. With the Peacock Processional, the bringing in of the Christmas Yule log,[253] fighting with a quarter staff, the royal archery tournament, the centuries-old madrigals, and a cast of characters ranging from knights, court ladies, and jesters, to yeomen, tinkers and peasants, *Robin Hood* also vividly brought to life a piece of the history of one of America's major allies.

Connecting With The Audience

The ballet company's innovative new genre of the narrative dance-play—with its finely tuned mix of dancing, music, mime and narration, and visually engaging sets and costumes—once again turned out to be a formula for success in introducing the art form to millions of children in a way that left them with a desire for more. And while there were no overall social or political criteria guiding the commissioning of the four Junior Programs Ballets, their choice of *Robin Hood* suggests that going forward, even their dance-plays could help to create a sense of connection and empathy for other countries and cultures. The various reviews also attest to the consistently high quality of each of the productions, enabling Junior Programs to offer a nationwide audience of youngsters a colorful and lavish visual world second to none. Indeed, their unique blending of authenticity and fantasy—from the detailed copy of a medieval tapestry in the Cloisters of the Metropolitan Museum of Art in *Robin Hood* to the mood lighting and shimmering iridescent hues of the woodland creatures' costumes in *The Adventures of Puck*—created a world on stage that could not fail to ignite the imagination of their youthful audience.

In many ways, the Junior Programs Ballet was more than just a troupe of accomplished dancers. As with the opera company, the ballet company ensured that its dancers were also skilled mimes, able to stamp each role with an individuality which created a series of memorable characters: Pinocchio, the Fairy with the Blue Hair, Mr. Owl, Puck, Titania, Bottom, Robin Hood, Friar Tuck, Maid Marion, and the evil Sheriff to name the most obvious. And judging from the reviews, the narrator, too, became a compelling character in her own right. The company's dancers also were able to draw children in with feats of athletic and acrobatic prowess, introducing them to a world of grace, physical accomplishment, and ensemble movement, as well as connect with their audience in creating a world that fully engaged the whole child, visually, emotionally, and imaginatively. The company's joy and energy were consistently contagious, and their audience rewarded them by growing and returning, year after year. The Mt. Clemens, MI, *Monitor's* (March 4, 1941) comment that the Junior Programs Ballet Company had "the longest and most extensive tours of any professional [dance] troupes in the country" confirms their popularity, and a similar comment in numerous other reviews[254] suggests that Junior Programs played an important role in making dance more accessible to the nation's children. Both John Martin (*New York Times,* June 23, 1940) and Walter Terry agreed that the Junior Programs Ballet was "helping to build the intelligent, adult dance audiences of tomorrow by acquainting children with the excitement of ballet" (*New York Times,* Jan 4, 1942).

Their multiple artistic, sociopolitical, economic, and cultural accomplishments clearly entitle Junior Programs to a secure place in the history of TYA. However, their work included two additional and equally important innovations. First, their belief that the performing arts could be used to make a broad range of pedagogical subject matter come alive in ever richer and more stimulating ways. Second, their unique national network of local sponsoring organizations, without which their national tours would not have been possible. Chapter V explores the ways in which Junior Programs used their productions to achieve their educational aspirations, and Chapter VI examines the organizational and administrative arrangements that connected them to the communities in which they performed, as well as making their extensive schedule of national tours possible.

V. THE EDUCATIONAL INNOVATIONS

The Junior Programs Approach to Education

Junior Programs was never afraid to break with tradition, but in the 1930s and '40s, in the realm of professional children's theater as an educational intervention, there was not much tradition to break. The settlement house movement had found educational value in engaging the children themselves in the experience of staging amateur theatricals. We also know that as part of Clare Tree Major's *Threshold Players'* productions based on classic children's literature, she developed supplemental materials for the New York Association of Teachers. But the breadth and scale of Junior Programs' correlated curriculum study units (CCSUs) was something fresh and new, and it soon became an integral part of their company profile.

Five factors appear to have influenced their commitment to develop a comprehensive range of CCSUs to support their *Credo*. First was the paradigm shift in the way society viewed children—from the child as potential labor to childhood as a protected period necessary for the healthy physical, emotional, and intellectual development of the future citizens of a democracy. A second paradigm shift was occurring in the educational arena. The new approach, consistent with Dewey's principles, no longer viewed the child as a tabula rasa to be filled with a preexisting package of information. Instead, it sought to engage the whole child in a set of experiential, aesthetic, and communal interactions enabling them to grapple with the ever-present challenges of democracy. Third was the participation of parent councils, teachers, and students McFadden had witnessed during her study of children's theater in Europe. Fourth were the goals and values articulated in Junior Programs' *Credo,* making clear the need to find effective ways of bringing people of diverse racial and ethnic backgrounds together. And fifth was the untapped potential they saw in the performing arts as a catalyst for making the standard K-12 curricula come more fully alive, thereby making both individual and collaborative learning more vivid, stimulating, integrated, and exciting.

William Vickery, editorial secretary of the Service Bureau for Intercultural Education had identified two objectives for the kind of intercultural education embodied in Junior Programs' *Credo*. The first focused on the need for children belonging to the dominant white society to develop a respect and affinity for children of the many minority groups. To achieve this, he believed it would be necessary to correct the "false impressions" and "misinformation" he viewed as the cause of much of the racial and ethnic othering, replacing it with learning about the many strengths and contributions of other cultures. The second objective was to help children from the multiple minority groups to feel a sense of belonging. This entailed learning about and recognizing the positive contributions their forebearers had made to the nation's development, while feeling a sense of pride in those contributions. Vickery applauded Junior Programs for deliberately selecting productions which represented the different races and nationalities in the best possible light—and he was gratified by the way he saw teachers using the interest aroused by the Junior Programs performances to "motivate a study of ethnic groups in their own community." In one community, he saw *Pinocchio* become an opportunity for teachers to explore issues related to the othering of Italian immigrants. He saw how *The Bumble Bee Prince* inspired a local exhibit of Russian art objects, providing still another opportunity for teachers to bring diverse groups together. And he acknowledged *The Adventures of Marco Polo* as yet another way for students to learn about the many important achievements of the Chinese civilization.[255]

Today, most theaters for young audiences engage in a variety of educational programming, and many children's theaters have dedicated staff to develop and present those programs, both at the theaters themselves, and in selected school classrooms. Almost by definition, learning about the performing arts is collaborative and experiential, and there is an increasing focus on engaging with socially responsible material, a recognition of the unique impact theater can have in the larger community.[256] There is also the American Alliance for Theatre and Education (AATE), the national organization whose vision includes having a robust theater arts curriculum in every school, and there is Theatre for Young Audiences-USA (TYA-USA), as well as the International Association of Theatre and Performing Arts for Young People (AASITEJ). Each of these organizations engage in numerous educational activities related to children's theater. However, Junior Programs' view

V. THE EDUCATIONAL INNOVATIONS

of the pedagogical opportunities presented by the performing arts differed from today's approach in an important way. As the AATE vision indicates, most of the current pedagogical efforts are focused on a curriculum related to the performing arts themselves. This is also the case for most performing arts educators typically employed by a performing arts company or university. If the former, they may take an educational program they have developed into the schools to supplement what front-line classroom teachers are themselves unable to offer their students. This includes the development of skills in acting, or playwriting, or they may work with students on an in-school production of a specific play. They may also develop an overview and information about a production at their theater or facilitate a post-show student discussion of the performance. At the university level, the focus of the performing arts faculty is primarily on developing the skills of the next generation of actors, playwrights, directors, set designers, lighting designers, and arts educators.

As indicated earlier, the Junior Programs' view of the educational potential of the performing arts was broader. They viewed the artistic, social, political, economic, *and* educational perspectives as integral to their work. These five perspectives were woven together, creating an energizing synergy. From the outset, McFadden believed that the more their young audiences understood the social, political, economic, and artistic issues related to a performance, the more enjoyable, meaningful, and memorable the performance would be. They viewed the actual subject matter of their productions as both an artistic and an educational springboard—one that would offer front-line teachers in the many traditional academic disciplines a set of professionally developed pedagogical materials that would enhance their own ability to engage their students in a deeper, more integrated understanding of a production's subject matter. Thus, in addition to learning more about the various performing arts, Junior Programs' correlated curriculum study units (CCSUs) enabled K-12 front-line teachers to deepen their student's exploration of the history, social issues, economics, and political implications of a production's story. CCSUs for science, social studies, literature, creative writing, the visual arts, home economics, shop, and physical education, as well as for music, dance, and drama were all part of their pedagogical package.

A CCSU for an art class might have students painting posters to advertise an upcoming performance or making masks such as those seen in *Pinocchio* to create an exhibit for the school's entryway. A CCSU for shop might include instructions on how to build a model stage set or to create special props, while *The Adventures of Marco Polo* utilized a blueprint for building a miniature version of a Chinese junk. Home economics might include a pattern for a costume, or a recipe from a particular ethnic culture, or for *Run, Peddler, Run,* instructions for making candles. A science class could explore the Chinese invention of the printing press, or the discoveries of coal, gun powder, and asbestos, while a social studies class could learn about the many ethnic cultures that were a part of Chinese society. CCSUs for *The Emperor's Treasure Chest* included information on Brazilian history, geography, economic development, and politics. The physical education unit for *The Reward of the Sun God* included instructions for playing the Hopi corncob game, and for *Robin Hood* there were instructions for teaching archery, and for history or social studies, resources focused on the English feudal system. In "Mansfield [Ohio], the entire school system . . . set aside six weeks in which every department created a program taking full advantage of the Junior Programs performances . . . Departments of English . . . stimulated the writing of original compositions and poems . . . and similar adaptations of . . . materials [were] employed . . . by departments of social studies, history, [and] geography."[257] Collectively, the Junior Programs educational materials, coupled with the productions themselves, became a visible and visceral way to integrate the many separate strands of the educational experience into an organic whole.

Educational Partnerships

This expanded view of the performing arts as an educational catalyst was made possible because, from its inception, Junior Programs had formed key partnerships with leading educators, many of whom represented the most prestigious and progressive educational institutions in the country. For example, the Horace Mann School, an experimental and developmental unit of Columbia University's Teachers College, was founded on the belief that "every person, regardless of their background, should receive a public education based on the principles and practices of a free society."[258] Horace Mann (1796–1859) himself believed in women's suffrage and that slavery should be abolished; and Columbia's Teachers College reflected the views of leading scholars, social reformers, practitioners, and philanthropists, all of whom were dedicated to addressing the problems created by industrialization, immigration, deep economic divisions, and the challenges posed by race relations, public health, education, and crime. By linking educational practice with theory and research, they viewed themselves as an ongoing source of identifying solutions to these problems.[259] Partners such as these—either members of the Junior Programs Educational Guidance Committee[260] or subject-matter experts commissioned by the committee—were able to take a production script, identify key concepts and facts, and develop age-appropriate CCSUs for a broad range of subjects. This provided a pedagogical framework that enabled teachers to use the CCSU in their own classrooms. Just as importantly, these CCSUs enabled them to work together *across* academic disciplines to knit individual units into a synergistic whole. Unlike traditional school curricula, life—and by extension the role of citizen—is not divided into a neat series of discrete subjects and departments. Accordingly, one of the important insights derived from Junior Programs' experience is a recognition of the ability of the productions themselves to integrate a range of compartmentalized subject matter into a more coherent, integrated, and memorable experience.

This approach also enabled Junior Programs to develop relationships with local schools and teachers across the nation. These partnerships were strengthened by the company's local "sponsoring organizations" and marketing model (see Chapter VI). A key feature of this model was the early engagement of school superintendents and principals with the local Junior Programs' sponsoring organizations, a move that ensured that key school leaders were involved in the choice and scheduling of upcoming productions. This early inclusion made it easy for the local schools to see Junior Programs as a valuable pedagogical resource, providing front-line teachers with modules to enrich their classroom teaching. The practice of sending the CCSUs two to three months before the production arrived gave teachers the time needed to integrate these supplemental materials into their regular lesson plans. It also ensured that most of Junior Programs' young audience would arrive at the performance with a broad familiarity of both the artistic elements of the production (e.g., the life of the composer, the style of music or dance, the artistry of sets and costumes, etc.), and the performance's historical context. Where relevant, students would also acquire a working knowledge of the social, economic, and political themes pertinent to the production. These CCSUs were viewed by both Junior Programs and the local schools as an important benefit of each production. They were just as integral to Junior Programs' mission of passing on the nation's cultural and political heritage to the next generation as were the productions themselves.

A headline in the *New York Times* (Nov 20, 1938) gives an overview of one of Junior Programs' partnerships with local school systems: "Junior Programs Presentations Linked to Class Work of 500,000 Pupils." The article paints a positive picture of their innovative approach. "Our experience in the correlation of grade and high school curriculum and activities programs with opera, ballet, drama and concert entertainment designed for young people has been most encouraging," Mrs. McFadden reported. "Under the guidance of the educators and other specialists on our advisory council, we have prepared materials for classroom use both in advance and following presentation of our programs." Echoing this assessment, music educator and journalist Charles Plotkin wrote that the educational materials developed by Junior Programs were "a stimulation of a cultural awareness in children and young people . . . in cities [such] as Utica and Binghamton, New York, and Gary, Indiana . . . [where] music supervisors have directed student orchestra, band, and choral renditions . . . [and] the students prepare an entire production of their own, not only playing, singing and dancing the various roles, and supplying the musical accompaniment, but also designing and making the costumes and scenic effects. When the professional production is presented, they have an opportunity to compare it with their own, and by talking with the performers to acquaint themselves at first hand with the way things should be done" ("School Audiences Applaud," unknown source, n.d.).

Junior Programs also shared the belief of Dr. Hugh B. Woods, director of the Curriculum Lab at the University of Oregon, and a leading member of the Educational Guidance Committee:

> Professional programs have increased educational value for children of all levels. He emphasizes, however, that it is necessary to help children prepare for these programs if full understanding and appreciation is to result . . . Each unit is based on extensive research and several experienced teachers have contributed to each of the units. Ellen McClellan Wilshire, a critic teacher of the University of Oregon High School, has directed much of the research work and has compiled the many suggestions regarding activities and sources of materials that have been contributed by those who have worked on the units. Each unit contains a general overview, suggested

approaches or methods of introducing the unit, an extensive list of suggested research activities, evaluation materials, and bibliographies. Suggestions for coordinating the work of the art, language arts, social studies, music, home economics, physical education, and other departments is included in each. Each pamphlet is adapted to all grade levels.[261]

In keeping with the high standards and quality of Junior Programs' artistic work, their educational work appears to have been similarly impressive. A Junior Programs' marketing brochure (1940–41), shared some of the reasons teachers valued the company's work: From teachers in Rocky Mount, North Carolina, we hear, "These programs have increased music response. . . [that] would have required a year or two to achieve otherwise." Jane Stewart, Music Supervisor of Elementary Schools in Mt. Lebanon, Pennsylvania, reiterated the successful connection between the educational materials and the performance, explaining how "the children . . . have been prepared for each of the . . . productions . . . We have found that it motivates the interest and creates a better understanding . . . Children, just like grown-ups, are delighted to see or hear something with which they are familiar and that is another reason we appreciate the material [Junior Programs has] sent us."[262] *Cue Magazine* (n.d.) also pointed to the significance of children being introduced to opera. "Proper exposure is all important for music appreciation, and here is where Junior Programs, Inc. has carved itself a much needed niche in operatic circles . . . It teaches children how to walk in firm, musical steps before having to hit a Wagnerian stride," and it likens an unprepared exposure to opera to a child "who has surreptitiously smoked a cigar at the ripe age of five . . . [They are] generally not tempted to repeat the experience, however fine the cigar." Students in Fairmont, West Virginia also responded enthusiastically, as relayed by the *Times* (Mar 22, 1938): "Thanks to the efforts of the schools' music supervisors, and the cooperation of the Women's Club storytelling group, the young audience was familiar with various aspects of opera technique and with the story of the opera, and when Mrs. William Welton, chairwoman of the Children's Theater Bureau of the League, asked if the audience would like Junior Programs to offer another series of plays the following year, every hand went up."

Parental Education

Early in the process of implementing their mission, Junior Programs also realized it was not only the children who needed to be educated. Parents, too, needed to broaden and refine their understanding of what quality entertainment for children looked like, and of how that fit into the broader educational pantheon. That the arts needed to be entertaining to capture and hold a child's attention was not in dispute. However, according to Junior Programs, parents also needed to become more demanding. On March 12, 1938, in collaboration with the Parents League, the Radio Committee of the Child Study Association of America, the National Recreation Association, and the Lincoln School of Teachers College, Columbia University, Junior Programs sponsored a conference on the "Audiences of Tomorrow." One of the issues addressed was parental involvement, and the *New York Times* (March 1938) noted that the conference urged that cultural training for parents was needed: "They [the parents] need to be taught how to appreciate the Arts more than the children do."

McFadden was especially articulate on this subject. In an article for the *Journal of the American Association of University Women*, she urged parents to reach beyond the negative approach of only protesting entertainment they deem harmful to children. Instead, she suggested "a really intelligent approach"—one she defined as a simple study of what types of cultural entertainments were available in a community, how much it cost to attend them, how many children attended, and of what ages. Such a study would provide a baseline and identify gaps; and the early engagement of local schools and colleges could help to implement that study. It should also identify the other community organizations and institutions most likely to be interested in improving the local cultural choices available for children. She goes on to describe how to share such a study with the local community, highlighting the usefulness of having a knowledgeable non-local leader as facilitator to manage the discussion objectively.[263] In another article, in keeping with Dewey's focus on the whole child, she is clear that it is a parental responsibility to ensure that there are "wholesome, creative, and morally and mentally valuable" out-of-school activities available for every child, if for no other reason than "Our entertainment material is exactly what we, who pay for tickets, make it."[264]

Others also addressed the issue of parental responsibility. Covering a lecture to the Chatsworth Avenue School PTA meeting by I. D. Taubeneck, a popular and progressive teacher at New York City's Bronxville School, titled "Parents Urged to Help Children Think," the New York *Larchmont Times* (Oct 12, 1939) tells us that "Parents should be the first to realize their duty in making children aware of the contemporary world." Taubeneck went on to say, "too much emphasis in education is placed on 'remembering' instead of 'thinking.' To help children think would help unlock the potentialities that lie within him [*sic*], thus enabling him [*sic*] in time to help solve the economic problems which seem too formidable for the present generation . . . Only through this medium can democracy be preserved . . . for turning to guns was an admission of defeat, an admission of too many unsolved problems." The Casper, Wyoming, *Times* (1938) also had a few critical words concerning parents. "Parents are often poor critics of children's entertainment. You'd be surprised at the amount of second-rate entertainment that is passed off on children because their parents don't know any better. Children like all sorts of things, they like variety and familiarity, so Junior Programs sends informative material well in advance so they can know something about the play before they see it. Schools like this material too. An advance notice of an Indian play was the signal for all kinds of Indian projects in one group of history classes. It all has to be in the guise of 'fun.'"

An Overview of the Correlated Curriculum Study Units (CCSUs)

Regrettably, the Junior Programs CCSUs and related materials in the Junior Programs Scrapbooks are frustratingly incomplete, as are the materials in both McFadden's autobiography and Lancourt's personal papers. Further inquiries made to the library at the University of Oregon, where several of the CCSUs were developed, were initially unsuccessful in locating any complete examples of Junior Programs' curricular materials. However, persistence was finally rewarded when a single draft copy of the CCSU for *The Emperor's Treasure Chest* was located at the University of Illinois Library. Incomplete though the CCSUs may be, what is available offers an important and intriguing picture of the depth and breadth of Junior Programs' work in this arena.[265] The CCSUs, often some fifty pages in length, appear to fall into two categories. Those for the operas and ballets focused primarily on expanding students' knowledge about national musical styles and periods, information about the composer, and a fuller understanding of the cultures from which the stories were derived. Those for the Junior Programs Players productions focused on a broader range of subject matter. If we look at this latter group of CCSUs through the lens of creating "reparative narratives" for marginalized groups, we can see that they provided the front-line teachers with an array of opportunities and resources to help reframe the negative narratives Hollywood continued to apply to communities of color, and immigrant and Indigenous cultures. To this end, these CCSUs offered a range of resources and materials that applied the core principles of democracy to an enhanced and more accurate understanding of Native American, South American, and Chinese cultures, enabling the teachers to emphasize the ways in which the diverse cultures enriched and complemented the American culture. Incomplete as they are, the CCSUs for the Players' productions appear to have been designed to encourage students to develop new, more positive ways of understanding and engaging with a broad range of differences—historically, socially, politically, economically, and culturally. And, in keeping with the Caspar, Wyoming, *Times* assertion that the activities recommended in many of the CCSUs needed to be "fun," the activities suggested were just that—creative, interactive, and out of the ordinary.

According to the information available, each CCSU contained three detailed plans—for primary, intermediate, and high school grades. Each included grade-appropriate reading lists, sheet music, phonograph records, directions for dances and games, biographies of composers, and national maps, as well as materials exploring the culture's history, social mores, economics, politics, geography, and literature. For example, the bibliographies for *The Reward of the Sun God* recommended resources such as *The Indian How Book*, the contents of which corrected many of the "false impressions" and "misinformation" embedded in Hollywood films. This alternative material replaced those negative impressions with a more accurate picture of a culture based on courage, integrity, honor, and generosity.[266] Another recommended book, *Ancient Life in the American Southwest*, chronicled the rebirth of Pueblo pottery as a significant folk art in San Ildefonso, New Mexico.[267]

The CCSUs for *The Adventures of Marco Polo* focused on the historical aspects of Polo's travels and introduced contemporary East-West relations in a way that helped students view Pacific American relations in a new light.[268] For more advanced students, there were materials related to problems of race relations, guiding students through an exploration of civilizations other than their own. "As the pattern of world unity emerges it becomes increasingly important to know more of older civilizations which, though westernized in some aspects, yet retain in large part the manners, customs and attitudes of past centuries... The study of Marco Polo can help students to understand the long slow struggle by which man has advanced and can help to give them a desire to perpetuate the gains achieved with such infinite pains throughout the centuries." And, always, the goal was to develop "individuals more capable of effective living in our democratic social order."[269] Similarly, the CCSU for *The Emperor's Treasure Chest,* posed a series of pointed questions aimed at increasing students' understanding of race relations in Brazil, its economic and political importance in the impending world conflict, and with the United Kingdom as our ally, the CCSU for the ballet, *Robin Hood* contained a section on English history and culture.

Numerous local reviews of Junior Programs productions lauded their educational materials. In Washington, Pennsylvania, school music departments, orchestras, bands, and choruses learned about the composers, listened to phonograph records, and could obtain the actual sheet music, which enabled students to sing the arias and play pieces of the music, and "follow with attuned ears every bar of music" (*Reporter*, Jan 17, 1940). The Montgomery, Alabama, *Advertiser* (Nov 18, 1941) begins its review of *The Adventures of Marco Polo* with an acknowledgement of the historical excellence of the accompanying CCSU, calling it, "one of the most comprehensive study units on the known world of the 13th century." The review goes on to praise it for enabling "teachers of every grade ... to stimulate interest ... and formulate a wealth of projects in music, social studies, painting, stagecraft and other arts."

CCSUs for social studies classes were rich and varied, seeking, in the broadest possible way, to give children of every age an inside view of daily life in different historical periods and in vastly different cultures and countries. For *The Reward of the Sun God,* students could enter the world of Native American spiritual beliefs and learn about their ancient myths and rituals, Indigenous family life, medicine men, and laws. For *Run, Peddler, Run,* there was material on many aspects of early American colonial life. Units on Brazil for *The Emperor's Treasure Chest* challenged social studies classes not only to compare the racial, political, economic, and educational virtues and assets of Brazil with those of the United States, but also to directly address the different ways the two countries chose to manage racial issues and classifications. A study unit for *Robin Hood* provided material about medieval life. It examined stories and customs that included not only examples of songs and poems about the lords of the manors and traveling minstrels, but about serfdom and the monarchical laws that governed virtually every aspect of medieval daily life. For *The Adventures of Marco Polo*, there were materials on Persia and India, a racial melting pot antedating America by thousands of years. There was information on thirteenth-century social thought; education in China; and the religious and racial tolerance prevalent in China under the leadership of Kublai Khan. Suggested projects included activities such as interviewing travelers, nationals, and other authorities on foreign countries; making scrapbooks with pictures and articles on architecture and painting; and creating exhibits, posters, radio skits, ads, and articles for the school newspaper publicizing the upcoming production. These CCSUs were also promoted by William Vickery, editorial secretary of the Service Bureau for Intercultural Education.[270]

Students could learn about famous Indigenous leaders such as Hiawatha, Tecumseh, and Crazy Horse through resources developed for *The Reward of the Sun God*. *The Emperor's Treasure Chest* CCSU included material on the colonial conquest of Brazil, as well as the country's natural resources, geography, and economics. CCSUs for the older students also introduced them to current political issues: What were the aims and agreements of the Pan American Union? Were European markets necessary to Brazil's balance of trade? There were also materials supporting a comparison of the "negro slave problem" in Brazil and the US, and one section made mention of a June 1939 article in *Fortune*, which told about "the civil rights, liberties, and human respect" accorded to "the Negro and mulatto" in Brazil, "the likes of which they have never been given in the United States."[271]

A history class for *Robin Hood* could study feudal times in England, and there were extensive bibliographies on American colonial history for *Run, Peddler, Run*. The early history of American democracy, a study of the Bill of Rights and a focus on leaders such as Benjamin Franklin and Thomas Jefferson were featured for *Doodle Dandy of the U.S.A.* Those for *The Adventures of Marco Polo* included maps of Asia, information about the Polo family, and materials focused on Venice. Additionally, students could learn about the Polo's meeting with Kublai Khan, Chinese leaders up to and including Chang Kai-shek, as well as the similarities and differences between the political and economic systems of Venice and China from the thirteenth century up to 1942.

During physical education classes for *Robin Hood*, students could try their hand at archery or tumbling. For *The Reward of the Sun God*, there were instructions for playing Indigenous games. A shop class might make a replica of an Elizabethan theater for *The Adventures of Puck*, or a model of a thirteenth-century Venetian ship for *The Adventures of Marco Polo*. Home economics classes could bake a gingerbread house in conjunction with a production of *Hansel and Gretel*. Students might sew costumes based on designs from *The Adventures of Puck*, make soap or candles according to a colonial recipe for *Run, Peddler, Run*, or even fashion a Hopi headdress for *The Reward of the Sun God*.

Art classes designed posters, and students could try their hand at block printing, bookmaking, mapmaking, carving, flower arranging, tie-dying, painting, mural-making, and sketching to illustrate life in countries depicted in each production. Suggested activities included a visit to an importer of oriental/Persian carpets or a field trip to a local museum. As the Fairmont, West Virginia, *Times* (Jan 30, 1942) noted, the "life and times of Marco Polo is being used as a motif in art classes [and] children are also being given an opportunity to create the type of ship Marco Polo sailed in [as well as] a list of books dealing with Marco Polo's adventures." CCSUs on how to choreograph dances and on instructions for folk dances from early America, as well as from Brazil or Venice were available for dance departments. Music classes were offered a broad range of materials—sheet music, phonograph records, and extensive bibliographies about the composers and the type of music in each production. There was *Early American Songs and Dances,* as well as phonograph records of early American dances for *Run, Peddler, Run.* There were ancient songs and English ballads, or the score for playing the Tinker's Song on the recorder for *Robin Hood* as well as song sheets of old American ballads for *Doodle Dandy.* There were also bibliographies on the life and works of Mendelssohn; and study units also included knowledge about musical instruments from appropriate historical periods, as well as from countries such as Brazil or China.

Drama departments were provided correlated study units on how to create radio programs or research guides leading to the dramatization of episodes in the life of Marco Polo. Or a CCSU might help a class create a play illustrating life in various countries. There were simple narrative versions of Shakespeare's *A Midsummer Night's Dream*, as well as notes and sources on the life and times of Shakespeare and the theater of his day. Literature classes might read novels about China, such as Pearl S. Buck's *The Good Earth* (1931) for *The Adventures of Marco Polo*; and *The Reward of the Sun God* suggested *Flint and Feather* (1912) by Canadian poet Pauline Johnson, as well as *The Land of Little Rain* (1903), a collection of short stories, essays, and poems by Mary Hunter Austin; and for *Run, Peddler, Run*, there was *Bound Girl of Cobble Hill* (1938) by Lois Lenski.

Junior Programs was also unique in the importance they placed on bringing all the many academic disciplines together into an interdependent whole. There were sections in each CCSU entitled "Culminating Activities," that included guidance on how to integrate the work from multiple disciplines into schoolwide programs. Departments were encouraged to collaborate, using readings, musical scores, and choreography notes to plan and produce an operetta with music, dances, costumes, and stage sets involving multiple school departments. There were suggestions for assembly programs, dramatizations, pantomimes, skits, and glee club presentations of songs, music, and dances. Older students engaged in discussions and debates dealing with aspects of daily life in non-Western cultures, as well as an examination of contemporary relationships among the countries they studied.

There was literally something for everyone as the CCSUs attempted to provide the richest context for each production. And these educational units explicitly encouraged teachers to think of additional experiences for their classes, emphasizing that "in every instance the children themselves should be given the opportunity to suggest things that they want to do."[272]

From prominent Metropolitan Opera star Lawrence Tibbett, we also learn that Junior Programs' developmental focus was not limited to K-12 students. Tibbett believed the training and experience gained by Junior Programs' professional roster of young singers, dancers, and actors was invaluable. From his perspective, Junior Programs filled the gap between conservatory training and the Metropolitan Opera House. "There are no small local opera companies where young singers can learn the repertoire and gain the experience they need so badly . . . the development of a strong traveling company is the answer to this problem and the ultimate solution lies, I feel, in the hands of Junior Programs." He went on to say that "I am encouraged to believe that Junior Programs, Inc., is well on its way to becoming a force of growing influence in the molding of America's future musical and cultural tradition" (*Opera News*, Dec 16, 1940).

V. THE EDUCATIONAL INNOVATIONS

Using the medium of live theater to actively engage their young audience in deepening their learning about a broad range of artistic, social, political, and economic issues was threaded through the Junior Programs mission. The breadth and depth of Junior Programs' fusing of performance and pedagogy—particularly the belief that the CCSUs should precede as well as follow the performance—was a major innovation. Its organized approach, involving a broad range of educational and child development professionals and specialists, and its national scale of distribution, broke new ground. Unique, too, was the systemic nature of their approach. It is one thing to develop a CCSU for a music or theater class. However, using the potential of the performing arts as an educational catalyst to develop a CCSU with material for virtually every school department, *and* suggesting ways that multiple departments could collaborate on a culminating project speaks to a level of pedagogical sophistication that has seldom been duplicated.

Today, in what too often feels like a rear-guard effort to compensate for the elimination of most of the creative arts from school curricula and budgets, we find a theater's teaching artists often visiting the public schools as a guest or temporary add-on to the formal curriculum, and often only for the higher grades. However, Junior Programs' CCSUs were created to be direct resources for the day-to-day teaching staff at all grade levels of the public-school systems. That the Educational Guidance Committee continued to produce these study units until the end of Junior Programs' existence speaks to their perceived usefulness by the teachers themselves, and it is not hard to imagine the sense of loss those teachers must have felt when similar study units were no longer forthcoming. Despite their being incomplete, it is worth taking a closer look at what still exists for several of the CCSUs in order to appreciate both Junior Programs' vision, and what they actually did.

The Junior Programs Players Correlated Curriculum Study Units (CCSUs)

The materials available from the CCSUs for the five plays are confirmation that the Educational Guidance Committee considered the Players' productions a pedagogical opportunity to support teachers and students in a wide-ranging exploration of important current and historical social, political, economic, and cultural issues. The "entry points" for these journeys might be the need for an increased understanding of a given culture (e.g., Hopi, Brazilian, or Chinese), or for gaining a deeper understanding of an important issue (e.g., democracy, colonial history, or enslavement in Brazil). However, once "in," the CCSUs cast a wider net that included a creative range of projects focused not only on the performing arts, but on history, social studies, economics, political science, crafts, literature, and games—all to be woven together in what the Guidance Committee called Culminating Activities.

The Reward of the Sun God

Regrettably, only the extensive bibliography for this CCSU was included in the Junior Programs Scrapbooks. Nevertheless, there is much that may be inferred from the Educational Guidance Committee's choice of books in terms of the kinds of learning experience the CCSUs sought to provide; and from both the newspaper accounts, and the content of the books themselves, there is evidence that the committee's goal was to offer an antidote to the negative stereotypes so many Americans had of Native Americans.

"Children like all sorts of things, they like variety and familiarity so Junior Programs sends informative material well in advance so they can know something about the play before they see it. Schools like this material too. An advance notice of an Indian play was the signal for all kinds of Indian projects in one group of history classes" (Caspar, Wyoming *Times*, 1938). In Connecticut, "children in schools in Manchester, East Hartford, South Windsor and Thompsonville [were] singing Indian songs, playing Indian games and modeling Indian utensils in clay and making Indian headdresses and learning Indian words in preparation for the play, "The Reward of the Sun God". One of the games the children have been learning is the Corn Cob game" (unknown source, Mar 11, 1940).

Lancourt's personal papers include directions for playing the Hopi corncob game:

> To try this racing game in your gymnasium or out of doors, you must have as many dry corn-cobs as players. If you can't find corn-cobs, try a stick the same length or a long pine cone. Tie one end of a strip of rag about 10 inches long to the stem of the cob and tie a knot at the other end. Each strip of rag needs to be of a different color so each player can identify their own corn-cob. Each player takes

off their shoes and socks, and sits at the starting line and places the knotted end of the rag between their big toes and second toe, with the end of the rag up toward the foot. Then each player lies down on their back. When the signal is given, each player swings his right leg up in the air, tossing the cob as far as they can behind their heads. Each player then gets up as quickly as possible, runs to his corn-cob, lies down, puts the rag between his toes, and tosses it again, repeating this until the cob is tossed over the finish line. The one who reaches the finish line first, wins. Alternative ways to play include who can make their first toss go the farthest, or hit the highest spot on a wall, and perhaps you will think up new variations. Do write and tell us whether you enjoyed the game.[273]

Additional games were identified in a resource list from the National Recreation Association, which included Bulletins #3805, *Indian Games*. The CCSU also included a Camp Fire Girls publication, *Following Indian Trails*, and *The Book of Indian Crafts and Indian Lore* (1928) by J. H. Salomon focused on the practical and symbolic use of drums, and shields, as well as patterns for making tipis, clothes, bows, arrows, and wigwams, and recreating ritual events.[274]

In aggregate, the bibliography attests to the curriculum's focus on introducing students to a multifaceted positive perspective of Native American culture. In *The Indian How Book* (1927) by Arthur C. Parker, a prolific writer and Native American of Seneca, Iroquois, and Anglican heritage, he included seventy-four sections on Native American ways of life. These materials explored how Native Americans courted, married, treated women, how they went to school, bathed, smelled, cut their hair, painted their faces, gave their greetings, cracked jokes, danced, sang, played games, dressed, made hats and moccasins, embroidered, found food, cooked, ate, made gardens, hunted buffalo, what medicines they used, how they took oaths, held secret lodges, worked their spells, overcame witches, talked to and tamed animals, venerated the eagle, and used the calumet [peace pipe].[275]

Edgar Lee Hewett, whose *Ancient Life in the American Southwest* was instrumental in gaining passage of the Antiquities Act of 1906 was also included. This act was an important step in efforts to have Indigenous lands and cultures designated as national monuments. Hewett contributed to the creation of Bandelier National

Monument and the Chaco Culture National Historic Park, as well as the rebirth of Native American pottery as a significant folk art. Indeed, the San Ildefonso Center for Native American Pottery exists due to his efforts.[276] Ernest Thompson Seton's *The Gospel of the Red Man* is still listed on Amazon as "one of the best books on Native Americans ever written," and includes information from Native American sources of the time about Indigenous creation stories, mythology, spiritual beliefs, family life, ancient teachings, and stories about different Indigenous prophets, including Hiawatha, Tecumseh, Crazy Horse, Sitting Bull, Wabasha, Geronimo, and Wovoka. Written shortly after the Great Depression, a *New York Times* review of the book (July 12, 1936) lamented Seton's view that the white man's way had failed but acknowledged that "the stories told here of the white man's conquest are terrible and shameful enough to give us . . . some very bad moments." [277]

Under the Turquoise Skies, by Will H. Robinson (1928) chronicles the story of the ancient cliff-dwellers of the American Southwest. *Flint and Feather* by Canadian writer Pauline Johnson was a volume of poetry with enduring appeal. *The Soul of the Indian* by Dr. Charles Eastman, of Santee Dakota, English, and French ancestry advocated for living in harmony with nature and for Indigenous freedom and self-determination. A member of FDR's Committee of 100 Reform Panel, he contributed to the New Deal's commitment to developing models of tribal self-government. He was the first Native American awarded a degree in Western medicine and the first to write an Indigenous history from the Native American point of view. Author of nine books on Native American life, and an international speaker on Sioux ethnohistory and Native American affairs, he worked for the Bureau of Indian Affairs as a physician on the Pine Ridge Reservation.[278]

The Land of Little Rain by Mary Hunter Austin consisted of short stories based on her years of observing the flora, fauna, and people of the Owens Valley, California, desert. Considered a "seminal work of environmental writing," three themes connect the stories: the supremacy and divinity of nature; the negative consequences of the disconnect between humans and nature; and the positive consequences of the harmony between humans and nature.[279] Austin's unsentimental voice, marginalized by the male-dominated nature movement at the time, made *The Land of Little Rain* itself a critique of the patriarchal conventions of nature writing. Author of thirty-three books on life in the American West, Austin was also an activist for women's

V. THE EDUCATIONAL INNOVATIONS

rights.[280] Frank Bird Linderman's *Indian Why Stories* (1915) chronicled imaginative explanations by members of the Blackfeet, Chippewa, and Cree tribes of a wide range of Indigenous myths and legends.[281] Linderman was an activist and ally for the rights of Montana's Native American tribes, and was adopted into the Blackfeet, Cree, and Crow tribes. As a member of the Montana state legislature and later Assistant Secretary for the State of Montana, he became a staunch advocate for the creation of the Rocky Boy Indian Reservation for several homeless Chippewa and Cree tribes.[282]

While these resources presented an overwhelmingly positive view of Indigenous cultures, the inclusion of *The American Indian* by Clark Wissler (1917) indicates that the CCSU did not shy away from the controversial aspects of racial discrimination. Wissler was a well-known figure in the field of cultural anthropology. However, he was also actively engaged in the eugenics movement, the aim of which was to purify the American population by eliminating people with so-called undesirable hereditary qualities. He was a "proponent of a hierarchic racial theory that saw Africans on the lowest and Nordics on the highest rungs of a racial ladder." This "theory" was part of "scientific racism," the now discredited pseudoscientific belief that empirical evidence existed to support or justify the racial superiority of whites.[283] The inclusion of Wissler suggests that the Educational Guidance Committee may have viewed Wissler's beliefs as an important facet in any discussion related to the social dynamics of othering, and that they were not afraid to provide resources that would stimulate frontline teachers to explore the complex issues of race, discrimination, and democracy with their students.

Given the themes of the bibliographic selections, it is not hard to imagine what the more complete CCSU might have included, and limited though it may be, this overview provides a sense of how Junior Programs productions and educational components were designed to work in tandem to create more positive narratives of Indigenous communities.

Run, Peddler, Run

The activities and research involved in the creation of *Run, Peddler, Run* was a serendipitous example of the kind of education the CCSUs were designed to stimulate and support. As described in Chapter III, Katherine Center searched long and hard to unearth the materials and resources she needed to help her students gain a rich and engaging understanding of what it was like to live in colonial America—a time when the very foundations of American democracy were being formed. Center wanted resources that would enable her students to *experience* what that life was like, including the ways it differed from, and the ways in which it was the same as their own lives. By providing teachers with the materials and resources they needed, the CCSUs were designed to shortcut that time-consuming process, making a teacher's extensive upfront investment of personal time unnecessary.

It seems likely that the core of the *Run, Peddler, Run* CCSU included the resources Center described in Chapter III. She had added several dozen additional texts that focused on true stories of children in various periods of early America, and for history and social studies, there were stories of the daily life of early American colonists, most prominently Lenski's *Bound Girl of Cobble Hill*. The book was a realistic account of the life of a young, indentured servant, told in a way that helped students understand the hardships of indentured servitude. Lenski did not gloss over the social and economic injustices. Her goal was to present the suffering experienced by the socially and economically marginalized bound girl in a way that engendered empathy and emphasized the need for students to see her as a flesh-and-blood human being with feelings, hopes, and dreams not unlike their own.[284] *Old Time Schools and School Books* by Clifton Johnson (1904) offered a picture of colonial schools and introduced young readers to the issues related to gender inequities in education. Given the home economics activities Center's students experienced, it seems likely that there would have been several home economics activities enabling students to experiment with the many "made from scratch" household objects of the colonial era. It was experiences such as those that had left Center's fourth graders with great sympathy for Lenski's bound girl in the tavern.[285]

There were also resources for social studies classes, including a series by Alice Morse Earle on *Home Life, Child Life, Stage Coach and Taverns, and Customs and Fashions in Colonial Days*. There were books like *Hawkers and Walkers in Early America* by Richardson Wright as well as a Yale pamphlet, *Roads and Road Making in Colonial Connecticut*, that discussed the laws requiring men to work on maintaining the public highways or pay a fine. *A History of Travel in America* by Seymour Dunbar, with excerpts from diaries and journals, and *We The People* by Leo Huberman, filled with vivid and colorful stories that would "provoke good discussions" were also on the annotated list. And *The Arts and Crafts of New England* by George Dow (1927), with its reprints of advertisements from Boston newspapers about "Runaway Servants" (185) or "Servants Arrived from Ireland to be Auctioned Off" (280) would have been of particular interest to social studies teachers.[286]

Building on what Center had already collected, members of the Educational Guidance Committee[287] added a set of supplementary readings and other materials organized into grade-appropriate and subject-matter specific curricula. The readings included *Brewer's Dictionary of Phrase and Fable,* a witty journey through culture, legend, and language of the American colonial period that included excerpts from old newspapers and historical political alliances; Hubbard and Babbitt's *Anthology of Poetry for Young Children,* in particular "The Peddlers Caravan" (259); St. Nicholas' *The Tin Man*; Elizabeth Coatsworth's *The Peddler's Cart;* and the *Illustrated Magazine for Young Children.*[288] For a drama class, *Historical Plays of Colonial Days* by Longmans Green (1912), with plays the children themselves could perform was included. Music teachers could make a selection from *Early American Songs and Dances,* compiled by Julia Cummings Sutton, or "Jolly Old Roger" a song from *A Garland of Green Mountain Songs* edited by Helen Flanders that was used in the production of *Run, Peddler, Run*. There was also *Green Sleeves,* with the Elizabethan Restoration music used by Shakespeare, complete with instructions for learning the actual dance. And to round out the music curriculum, the study unit included phonograph records of quadrilles (Chillicothe-*Virginny Shore, O Susanna, Arkansas Traveler,* and *Captain Jinks)* as well as extremely popular traditional tunes such as Durang's *Hornpipe, Soldier's Joy,* and *Lady of the Lake.*[289]

Taken together, the *Run, Peddler, Run* CCSU provided a lively, vivid, and interestingly nuanced account of the colonial period, making the time, place, subject matter, and characters come alive in a colorful and vivid way—one that would appeal to and hold the interest of children of all ages.

The Emperor's Treasure Chest

As noted in Chapter III, *The Emperor's Treasure Chest* was a unique collaboration between Junior Programs, the Columbia Broadcasting System, the Brazilian Consulate, and the Pan American Union. Together, they translated FDR's Good Neighbor Policy into something alive, relevant, and meaningful for thousands of school children. Their shared objective was to give the children of the United States an understanding of and insights into the South American way of life, and to do so in a way that emphasized the connections and the differences with life in North America. In a sense, the numerous educators involved in this whole undertaking validated Junior Program's basic premise—that the performing arts was a vibrant and compelling educational catalyst. Dr. Wood, director of the Curriculum Lab of the University of Oregon, and member of the company's Educational Guidance Committee shared his belief "that the learning impulses of the pupils are greatly stimulated through seeing professional stage productions of drama, ballet, and opera."[290]

The *New York Times* (n.d.) also underscored the value of the CCSUs created for *The Emperor's Treasure Chest*, observing that "An educational committee, led by the University of Oregon, has prepared integrated units of study endorsed by the Pan American Union and Brazilian consulate." The article goes on to describe a cross-section of sixteen school systems that would be participating in the special program based on the "lore and life of Brazil." The school systems represented both urban and rural schools,[291] and each school had committed four to six weeks to projects linking material across the full range of school departments. Their intention was to explore everything about the country—including making models of a typical church, a fazenda (an estate or farm) and typical housing. The students would also learn to sing Brazilian songs; dance the rhythmic steps of a carnival dance; make festival costumes; and discuss and debate both historic and contemporary Latin American social, economic, and political issues. Special assemblies would highlight original student written dramas, and once they had attended a performance of the play, students would spend another four weeks analyzing and discussing what they had learned from the whole experience.[292]

Dr. Wood was clearly excited about the project and in the unit's foreword, he describes the opportunity and necessity of learning more about our Latin American neighbors:

> At no other time in American life has the study of our Latin American neighbors been so important . . . This unit recognizes and takes its purpose from two factors in the social situation today: first, as never before, we need to understand the <u>culture</u> of other peoples, their art, music, folklore, festivals, philosophy, customs, mores and

V. THE EDUCATIONAL INNOVATIONS

> ways of living, as well as their economy, government and political life . . . Second, as never before, for the safety of civilization in the Western Hemisphere we must try to understand Latin America better and above all we must try to help her understand American people as they really are—not as represented by our economic interests there. We must try to break down on the part of Americans the concept of Uncle Sam as benevolent advisor to an exploitable colony. The peoples of Latin America must be met on an equal footing and in mutual respect, and the 'democratic way of life' must dominate our economic and political relationships . . . To achieve these purposes, we must redirect our teaching in the classroom.[293]

As the CCSU on Brazil is the only complete unit I have been able to find, I have included significant portions as an example of the scope and extent of the Educational Guidance Committee's work. The title page refers to this unit as the third in a series for Junior Programs, but unfortunately, it does not identify the productions addressed in the two previous units.

The Preface of this CCSU points out that while the play itself is not specifically didactic, it contains multiple situations which link elements of the play to the CCSU's content. For example, mention of Jose's desire to become a trader on the Amazon offered an opportunity for a discussion of transportation and industrial issues in Brazil. The setting of the play—in Pera and Rio de Janeiro—offers the contrast of life in a Brazilian market town and in a major modern city, while the treasure, buried by the deposed Emperor, Dom Pedro, provides an opening to explore the history and government of Brazil. The table of content for the CCSU lists an Introduction, Approach Activities, Research Activities, Culminating Activities, and an Evaluation, and acknowledges the active involvement of the Pan American Union, the Brazilian Pavilion of the New York World's Fair, the Brazilian Information Bureau, the National Federation of Music Clubs, New York's Riverside Museum and the Museum of Modern Art, and the University of Oregon High School (unnumbered page).

Designed to pique the curiosity of students, the Introduction opens with "Brazil--there is a name to conjure with. It echoes with power and mystery; it suggests the great jungles and the reaches of mighty rivers . . . The word Brazil comes from "brasa" which is Portuguese for "live coal" . . . [and] It teems with possibilities. Who can guess its potential wealth, and since power is based on wealth, it's potential power? What role will it play in the future drama of the world? Is Brazil herself aware of her strategic position in these changing times? . . . What are Brazil's problems, racial, political, economic, educational, religious and physical? What do all these elements contribute toward her national and international character?" The Introduction goes on to sketch out Brazil's early history as a colony of Portugal when in 1500, Pedro Álvares Cabral "found himself in the harbor of Porto Seguro. In the name of the King of Portugal, he claimed possession of the land." Preoccupied with the defense of its Far Eastern discoveries, King Joao III of Portugal delegated the government of these South American lands to a group of powerful nobles who were "an active inconvenience to the state at the time." It was considered a clever plan in which huge feudal land grants saw these great lords undertaking the settlement and development of this new country at their own expense. "The great task of colonizing this vast country" was carried out by these Portuguese nobles who conquered the interior, "subduing Indian tribes, creating plantations, [and] cutting roads" (1–4).

The Introduction goes on to discuss the influx of a broad range of other European and Asian immigrants in addition to the Portuguese, most of whom tended to settle in the major cities. In 1822, Brazil declared itself an independent "republic of the United States of Brazil," governed first by a son, and then a grandson of Portuguese King Joao VI. Dom Pedro II (1831 to 1889) was "exceedingly liberal, [and] fostered representative government, encouraged immigration and freedom of the press." Nevertheless, in a bloodless coup, the divisions between various of the Brazilian states and other sections of the country became more pronounced. State and federal laws were "often at cross purposes," with states only enforcing the federal laws when it was in their own interest to do so. At this point, the Introduction suggests that "An analogy might well be drawn here to a similar situation existing in our own United States just prior to the Civil War" (4). However, unlike the United States, in 1937, Getulio Vargas ended the democratic form of government, "dissolved the houses of assembly, and became the "benevolent despot" of Brazil . . . However, it has been stated that should the question of Getulio Vargas' manner of government be put to a vote, it would probably be endorsed by the common people" (5).

At this remove, we cannot know whether such an assertion was true or not, but the Introduction goes on to proposes an interesting series of questions for both

V. THE EDUCATIONAL INNOVATIONS

teachers and students; some quite provocative, but all aimed at drawing students into deeper explorations.

> What is the position of the United States in relation to Brazil? What raw materials does this country depend upon which are imported from Brazil? How would this country be affected if those imports were restricted or cut off completely? What manufactured products does Brazil import from the United States and from other countries? Since she has a wealth of water power and raw materials, what has prevented her from becoming self-sufficient? Will she not become so in the near future? How will this relationship to Brazil be affected should a European power attempt domination of Brazil? What are the aims and agreements of the Pan American Union? How binding are they? Are they based on sound economic policy as well as wishful political thinking? Are not the markets of Europe necessary to Brazil's balance of trade? In the past, a large part of Brazilian trade has been with England. How does the present world situation affect that? . . . As the world becomes aware of it will Brazil become the center of economic warfare? (5).

The Introduction finishes with "Brazil is to South American what the United States has been to North America--the land of opportunity. Each country has offered expanding western horizons and has felt the push of westward migration. Each country has great wealth of natural resources . . . Each country has been a melting pot for Europeans, Indians and Negroes . . .These two countries with many parallels in their development, facing may of the same problems, should profit from a greater mutual knowledge and cooperation" (6).

The Introduction is followed by a series of Approach Activities, the purpose of which is to "arouse interest, to motivate students to further study, and to help them get an overview of the whole area." It proposes the use of "What is Your I.Q. on Brazil?" a hundred-question quiz developed by the Brazilian Information Bureau. This would be used to kick off a series of class discussions in which students could share what they already knew about Brazil, what more they thought they wanted to know, and why. From these discussions, they could then create a set of objectives for their work.

The Approach Activities then offer an extensive bibliography of "browsing activities" that include "free lance perusal" of a broad range of materials including articles from *National Geographic, Life, Science News Letter,* and *Travel,* as well as novels, histories, maps, films, music and radio broadcasts that would introduce students to "Brazil in general, early Portuguese explorers, Indians of Brazil, early machines used . . . modes of transportation . . . airports . . . harbors, forests, rivers, cities, different national and racial types, steps in making rubber, steps in growing coffee . . . natural resources . . . early and modern customs [and] different flora and fauna" (11). The use of maps was highly recommended: "The student who has once discovered the "magic carpet" fascination of map study is well on the way toward developing a hobby . . . not only for the present school days, but for all his future life as well. A variety of maps should be displayed, since each will serve a distinctive purpose" (11).

The bibliography of maps and films of Brazil included a large "art" map (38 by 50 inches) with cut-outs representing typical features of the land designed to be colored and mounted. Another map showed the country's natural resources and industries, while still another showed other parts of the world where coffee was produced, as well as the stages by which it was prepared for final consumption. The films—for Elementary and Junior High grades—explored the great cities of Brazil, the country's wealth, and current US political and economic relationships with Brazil. Also included were films of trips up the Amazon, with a focus on depictions of native peoples, wildlife, the immense drainage basins and jungle products such as Brazil nuts, and wild rubber. These films also showed the cities of Manaos, Santarem, Belem, and Para (the latter the setting for *Emperor's Treasure Chest*). Students would also be able to explore the Amazonian lowlands (Sao Salvado, Sao Paulo, Santos, and Rio de Janeiro), and see the principal agricultural and industrial products of Eastern Brazil (coffee, cocoa, cassava, sugar, tobacco, pineapples, silk, and shoes). This would help them answer the question, "How did the physical aspects of the country affect the culture, and the social and economic status of the people?"[294]

A five-page bibliography provides a broad range of resources in support of these activities and the questions they raised. Titles ranged from *Man Hunting in the Jungle,* the *Brazilian Fairy Book, Magic Tooth and Other Tales, Tales of the Pampas, Jungle Paths and Inca Ruins, Adrift on the Amazon, Indian Air,* and *The Parrot Dealer* to *Brazil: A Study of Economic Types, Brazil Today and Tomorrow, Brazil, Your Golden Opportunity,* and *The People and Politics of Latin America.*[295]

V. THE EDUCATIONAL INNOVATIONS

As the American School of the Air was a partner in developing the CCSU, a brief description of radio programs from the Columbia Broadcasting System's Teacher's Manual, 1940-41 was included. The manual had been prepared by their Department of Education, and it provided data about the increased use of radio broadcasts in the classroom. It also noted that "Far from supplanting teachers, the broadcasts are designed to supplement and vitalize their work, by bringing into their classrooms the living world in the form of important national and world events and of fine dramatic and musical talent. They are planned to broaden student's horizons and inspire them to increased reading and greater interest in their work." The unit provided the weekly schedule of programs: Monday - Americans at Work focused on where our commodities come from; Tuesday - Wellsprings of Music; Wednesday - New Horizons in geography, history and natural sciences; Thursday - Tales from Far and Near focused on literature; Friday - This Living World explored current events and current problems (14–16).

Speaking directly to teachers, the designers prefaced the extensive list of research activities with an interesting caveat: the CCSU offered a robust list of activities in the hope that "the teacher and student in every grade will find something of value for each . . . [and] It is not expected that any one group will attempt to encompass all of the activities. The student should have his curiosity stirred and satisfied, but not surfeited." They also hoped that "The elementary and intermediate grade school teachers [would] use selective judgment in choosing those things which will appeal to the tastes of students in their age groups" (16).

The Research Activities listed in the CCSU suggest activities related to social studies topics, the language arts, interviews, and readings from an extensive bibliography. This section proposed creating scrapbooks, and researching artwork, costumes, food, health issues, and music, including Brazilian composers and folk music. For geography and social studies classes, materials offered a Magic Carpet Series entitled *Touring Brazil*. This series was recommended for geography classes grades four through nine, and social studies classes grades ten through twelve. Included in the resource lists were several travel agencies students might contact as part of planning a variety of hypothetical trips to different parts of Brazil. There was material for junior and senior high school students interested in studying political and economic relationships, especially the "economic war being waged for the trade and good will of Brazil and South America between Europe and the United States." The unit included several key articles such as "Hitler's Plan for South America," "What South America Thinks of Us," *The People and Politics of Latin America* and *Brazil: A Study of Economic Types*[296] (18–19, 24–25).

The Pan American Union in Washington, DC also contributed a large selection of additional materials exploring Brazil's problems—racial, political, economic, educational, religious, and physical. These materials posed questions about the country's virtues and assets, noting that "the search for the answers should seize the imagination of any thinking student" (16).

Again, speaking directly to teachers, the unit recommended that "The teachers of elementary and intermediate grades may wish . . . to emphasize the physical aspects of the country; the natural wealth of field, forest, and mine; or the racial components of the people and their cultures which would include art, music, dance, literature, and drama. Another interesting project would be the examination of some of the great cities of Brazil such as Rio de Janeiro with its romantic harbor . . . São Paulo . . . the heart of the coffee state . . . or Petropolis . . . known as the city of flowers." There was also Recife, "a city built on islands." Secondary teachers, however, would "probably wish to put the emphasis upon social, political, and economic inferences of Brazil's wealth" (17).

Under the heading Language Arts, the unit offers examples of original work that would interest the more advanced students. Among the possibilities are "dramatization of such material as historical incidents of Brazil, any aspect of Brazilian life, life on a fazenda (plantation), or court life at the time of Dom Pedro. It also included a pageant of Pan America in which are represented all national and racial groups of North, Central, and South America as well as the islands of the Caribbean; a study of Indian life in Brazil or life in the Amazon jungles using parts of *Green Mansions*, by W. H. Hudson, or incidents from any other book of fiction or travel about Brazil. There was also guidance for the writing of plays about life on a coffee plantation; and puppet shows, dramatizing some of the stories from South America" (19). Additional activities included Letter Writing to various organizations to obtain specific information, with a note that the Junior Red Cross would be willing to arrange for a group of students (but not individuals) to write to a group of Brazilian students. The unit also highlighted the value of interviewing travelers or even members of *The*

Emperor's Treasure Chest cast, and perhaps inviting one of the travelers to "come into the class room for a group interview by the entire class." The creation of Scrapbooks was also encouraged, as well as subject matter for letter writing. Interviews and scrapbooks included "modern Brazil, feudal Brazil, great cities of Brazil . . . Brazilian theatre and drama, Brazilian "festas" and carnivals, other amusements such as native Indian and negro dances, languages of Brazil, Brazilian art, and many other topics of the student's own choosing" (21).

Art Departments were encouraged to get involved, with students drawing or building models of a "Brazilian church, fazenda and house" or creating "papier mache or plaster of paris" contour maps of the various regions and cities. Making linoleum block prints of coffee blossoms, or stencil designs of Brazilian flora and fauna were additional possibilities. Paintings and drawings of cartoons and posters using characters in the play as subjects, and watercolor sketches of Brazilian costumes, landscapes, and people were also proposed. And for the elementary and intermediate grades, the construction of a "sand table" in which "could be built a relief map, model town, plantation, and Brazilian garden" (27).

Home Economics students could supply the costumes for members of the cast of original student dramatizations about Brazil. They could also dress dolls and puppets in costumes which would characterize different national and racial strains of Brazil. Or a class could make a "study of Brazilian food products and their markets. These foods would include coffee, naté, (a type of tea), medicinal herbs, and numerous other useful plants and tropical fruits." A "study [of] the variety of diet and the nutritional diseases resulting from an unbalanced diet" was also suggested; and a Culminating Activity for this focus might be a Brazilian dinner or banquet" (27). Listed under the heading of Health, but more likely appropriate for a science class was a study of Brazil's public health problems, including the water supply, and a study of the "unique "Snake Farm" at Butantan in São Paulo (27).[297] "Under this department, studies could be made of the status of science in Brazil as evidenced by residence of scientific men, number and importance of inventions and discoveries, and their bearing on social and industrial development of the country" (32).

The Music Department was an important focus for the CCSU, and it included a three-page bibliography of musical sources, prepared with the help of Dr. William Berrien (28-30). There was also a Supplemental "Brazilian Songs Suggested" compiled by Ellen McClellan Wilshire, Agnes Fay, and the Junior Programs Music Advisory Committee.[298] The unit also included an article from the *New York Times* (Feb 11, 1940) by Margaret I. Steward on Brazilian folk music. Steward writes that Brazilian musicians such as Villa-Lobos, Mignono, and Guarnieri were starting to "command worldwide attention." According to her, three sources influenced their music: the native Indian element, the Portuguese melodic element and the African rhythmic element." Together, they have created "an original and ethnical expression. With its quantities of forms, exuberant and characteristic rhythms and melodic quality, it is as varied, complex and beautiful as Brazil itself." She goes on to note that, "Music was an important part of the rites and ceremonies of the Brazilian aborigines," that "the influence of the Gregorian Chant, taught by the Jesuit priests, is still noticeable in the old folk music," and "the coming to Brazil of the African Negro had . . . [a] far reaching influence on Brazilian music." She provides numerous examples of how these several influences were absorbed, concluding that they all provided "an inexhaustible source of inspiration for modern Brazilian composers" (30–32).

It was examples such as this that supported and encouraged Junior Programs' belief in the value of non-European cultures, and the bibliography of musical resources contained both written and recorded selections to enable glee clubs and school orchestras to play some of this music. Examples included a musical travelogue through Latin America, featuring the national anthems of the Latin American Republics, with piano arrangements and words in the original languages of each country (available for $1.00) as well as printed English translations (available for .25). There were also recordings by Victor of *Songs from the Interior of Sao Paulo*, and *Choro*, an urban musical form as well as Brazilian recordings of *Afro-Brazilian Voodoo Songs*, with information on where such recordings could be obtained (28–29). The musical scores and words for two of the songs from *The Emperor's Treasure Chest* were also included, as well as the score for a Brazilian tune called *The Sailing Boat*, with the suggestion that students compose appropriate words for it (34).

Culminating Activities for the CCSU were designed to provide students the opportunity to "review and summarize their experiences" in a way that embodied the concepts and attitudes embedded in the unit. These activities would also provide the basis for "evaluating the success of the unit." An assembly program, exhibits, a quiz program, a carnival, and an operetta were recommended activities. The assembly program might consist of original dramatizations of Brazilian history and culture. The glee clubs could perform Brazilian songs, and the orchestra could play Brazilian music. The physical education classes could demonstrate popular Brazilian folk dances and social dances, and parents and the public could be invited to attend. As part of the "marketing campaign," various exhibits could be mounted in classrooms or other public places prior to the arrival of the Junior Programs production. These exhibits might include student art work; scrapbooks; construction projects of a model fazenda; and dolls dressed as Brazilian Indians. The Culminating Activities also encouraged the possibility of "borrowing actual Brazilian art from local citizens and arrange them in a display" (35).

A quiz, similar to the Brazilian IQ Quiz was another possibility, and could include a set of questions based on the work students had done. By documenting the knowledge the students had before and after their engagement in the various Approach, Research and Culminating Activities, the quiz could be a useful part of the Evaluation Activities (35–36). Two additional activities were recommended: the organization of a Brazilian themed Carnival, with students wearing appropriate costumes and performing Brazilian dances and folk music: and the preparation of an operetta. The CCSU acknowledged that this would require "a high degree of cooperation from all teachers," but encouraged the school to consider it because it served to integrate all that had been learned "across all subject matter lines." The script could be written in "the language arts class, necessary research to assure authenticity of costumes, events, etc., [could be] carried out in social studies, music arranged in music classes (use available music with adaptations), production directed by the dramatics teacher, costumes made in household arts, scenery made in art and industrial arts classes, and publicity handled by the commercial classes." And if there was a Brazilian consulate nearby, the CCSU hoped an invitation would be extended to them (36).

The final section of the CCSU contained the Evaluation Activities. There were two parts to the evaluation. First, the teachers' evaluation of how well the activities had increased the knowledge and development of their students—with advice to focus on concepts and "the ability to apply logical reasoning to the solution of some of the problems relative to Brazil and our relations with her," rather than on factual details (38). Second, there was the distribution of a questionnaire to the teachers who had participated. The questionnaire was preceded by a personal note from Dr. Wood indicating that the CCSU was an experiment—an answer to the "insistent demand for specific suggestions on how to prepare boys and girls" for both the "Junior Programs productions and for unit materials on South America," and he hoped the teachers would participate "in the improvement of these materials" (unnumbered page).

The questionnaire consisted of the following questions.

1. In general, did you find these materials helpful?
2. At what grade levels were they most helpful?
3. In what ways were they not suitable for other grade levels?
4. Which parts were least used and therefore might be left out in the revised form?
5. Which suggestions proved impractical, and therefore should be omitted or revised?
6. Was this true for all grade levels or certain ones?

On a separate sheet of paper will you kindly:

1. Itemize by page and line number, all grammatical and typographical errors.
2. List any inconsistencies or inaccuracies in the philosophy underlying the unit or the suggestions made for its development. (Indicate page.)
3. List any additional good references similar to those on pages 6-7, 9-10, 12, etc.
4. List and describe other activities in which your pupils engaged, or write us a complete description (diary or 10g would be helpful) of how you introduced and developed the unit. (Indicate grade level.)
5. List the evaluation activities that you used and send copies of any tests or other instruments used in the evaluation of the children's experiences.
6. Give us any other suggestions or comments that will be constructive in revising this unit.
7. Did you use the Junior Programs play, "The Emperor's Treasure Chest?" (unnumbered addenda).

It is, of course, a major disappointment that none of the actual evaluations of the Brazilian CCSU appear in any of the archives. According to the University of Oregon library, a search of Dr. Wood's archives did not contain any Junior Programs materials. However, the fact that, according to various press reports, the CCSUs continued to be developed and distributed for the subsequent productions of *Robin Hood, The Adventures of Marco Polo, Doodle Dandy of the U.S.A.,* and *The Adventures of Puck*, suggests that whatever evaluations Dr. Wood received from the unit on Brazil, or any of the previous units were positive enough to continue the experiment.

The Adventures of Marco Polo

As the nation moved closer to war, the production of *Marco Polo* became Junior Programs' contribution to the increasingly urgent need for America's youth to understand the history and culture of a country deemed a potential ally. As with *The Emperor's Treasure Chest*, the Players viewed *Marco Polo* as an opportunity to create an exciting new and more accurate narrative about the Chinese peoples. Professor Wood, this time in conjunction with Alva Graham, a school principal in Portland, Oregon, was responsible for the development of the *Marco Polo* CCSU. Unfortunately, only the Table of Contents and outlines for the Suggested Plans for the Primary and Intermediate Grades were included in the Junior Programs Scrapbooks and Lancourt's personal papers. Still, they provide an overall picture that matches the assessment of the Montgomery, Alabama, *Advertiser* (Nov 18, 1940) which declared Wood's *Marco Polo* curriculum "one of the most comprehensive study units on the known world of the 13th century." It enabled teachers of every grade "to stimulate interest in the ordinary studies of the classroom and formulate a wealth of projects in music, social studies, painting, stagecraft and other art." Using Marco Polo's journey from Italy to China, Wood and Graham not only explored the social, economic, and political history and customs of China, but included material on the cultures of Italy, Persia (now Iran), and India as well. The CCSU overview suggests that:

> Today, as never before, we need to augment our knowledge of peoples and countries in Europe and Asia. An understanding of contemporary life should rest on a knowledge of earlier ages, especially the early Renaissance when trade and discovery inaugurated the movements, which we now call scientific and technological,

culminating in modern industrial civilization . . . This unit . . . can contribute much to the student's . . . understanding of social forces operative today . . . [and] it can bring home . . . an appreciation of the cultures of other peoples, their art, music, and folklore . . . As the pattern of world unity emerges it becomes increasingly important to know more of older civilizations which, though westernized in some aspects, yet retain in large part the manners, customs and attitudes of past centuries. The study of Marco Polo can help students to understand the long slow struggle by which man has advanced and can help to give them a desire to perpetuate the gains achieved with such infinite pains throughout the centuries . . . [and it can help develop] individuals more capable of effective living in our democratic social order.[299]

William Vickery, editorial secretary of the Service Bureau for Intercultural Education also viewed the CCSU as an opportunity to explore the commercial interdependence of the Eastern and Western hemispheres, as exemplified by the early international trader and businessman, Marco Polo, and his family. Vickery also sought to emphasize the importance and relevance of the "fine spirit of religious and racial tolerance . . . prevalent in China under the leadership of . . . Kublai Khan."[300]

The Table of Contents for the CCSU begins with the above Overview, then Purpose and Objectives, and a section on Marco Polo and His Times, which includes a Biographical Sketch of the Polos; sections on Venice and Italy, home of the Polos; material on Persia (Iran), Land of Mystery; Marco Polo and India; and finally, units on China, Yesterday and Today. This is followed by sections on Research and Expressional Activities, Culminating Activities, Evaluation Activities, a Bibliography with a section especially adapted for children, and another section for teachers and older students, followed by an Appendix with a Plan for Primary Grades, another for Intermediate Grades, and then High School Grades. The supporting material includes Marco's initial journey, his return to Venice, the second journey of four years, culminating in his meeting Kublai Khan and his seventeen-year stay in China, followed by his return to Venice. There are sections on Venice, its history, art, commerce, and the church; on Persia, focused on its people, housing, food, clothing, and social life; on Marco Polo in India—considered one of the earliest cultural "melting pots"—its wars, village life, superstitions, and trade; and finally, China—with material on its philosophy, religions, customs, court life, and inventions. There is also a discussion of Marco's limited view of China, a comparison of him with Columbus, and the inclusion of contemporary material about Chang Kai-shek, former President of the Republic of China,[301] as well as the difficult relationship between China and Japan.

There were three primary objectives of the Plan for the Primary Grades: the appreciation and enjoyment of the Marco Polo story; its use as a means of providing motivation and stimulation for musical, artistic, constructive, and expressional activities; and to further the socialization of young children by motivating them to further reading, as well as oral and written expression. To realize these objectives, the CCSU proposed the use of pictures from magazines such as *National Geographic* and *Asia*. They also recommended the use of slides showing the countries and peoples visited by Marco Polo; records of music from the countries he visited; and, to provide a sense of immediacy, stories and discussions by children and adults who had visited or lived in Italy, Persia, India, or China. Research Activities included listening to records and music and viewing pictures of the countries visited, art and construction activities such as painting, murals, drawing or carving to illustrate life in countries dealt with in the story, or the planning of an imaginary trip to China. Culminating Activities identified various types of exhibits, performing songs and dances from one of the countries, or dramatizing parts of the story.[302]

Intermediate Grade objectives focused on three things: using the enjoyment of the music, dance, art, and literature of far-off countries as a way to understand the customs of other people; increasing the understanding of the interdependence of all peoples, and the similarities and differences of the problems they faced; and stimulating the development of the students' skills in artistic, expressional, and constructional activities. Suggested Approaches included those identified for the lower grades, as well as viewing films and illustrated talks by travelers and nationals of Asian countries; the use of music, songs, and radio programs focused on Italy and the Near and Far East; and extensive bibliographic recommendations, including novels such as Pearl S. Buck's *The Good Earth*. Research Activities included a wide range of possibilities. A group of students could dramatize episodes in the life of Marco Polo or illustrate life in the various countries through which he travelled. They could focus research on Venice, Persia, India, or China, on a study of Venetian church morality plays, or an investigation of transportation and communication in the thirteenth century. Other possibilities included food and housing in early medieval times; thirteenth century farming practices, or various scientific inventions. A student could also plan an imaginary trip to the countries visited by the Polos. Development of radio skits, art posters, tie dying, ads and articles written for the school newspaper, and costume making were also options. An ambitious possibility was the planning and producing of an operetta with music, dances, costumes, and stage sets done by students from various school departments. Also included was the creation of scrap books and articles, models of local houses and furniture or a Chinese junk, and the study of social thought and education in the thirteenth century as compared with today. Suggested Culminating Activities were a broad range of exhibits and assembly programs by the glee club, and presentation of the operetta or other skits. This unit also advised teachers to look for opportunities to connect students with more intensive studies in any area of their personal interest.[303]

The Plan for High School Grades included most of the above objectives and materials with a further exploration of maps of Asia. The Research Activities contained art and construction activities involving modeling, block printing, book making, costume making, map making, painting, oriental flower arranging, murals, drawing, and building. It also suggested the creation of scrapbooks of pictures and articles on architecture and painting that illustrated life in countries drawn from the story. Additionally, this unit compared Marco Polo with Columbus; and explored the difficult relationship between China and Japan, as drawn from then current events and history. It suggested museum visits, and a study of early Chinese inventions in the areas of agriculture, chemistry, printing, science, and health, as well as art, poetry, and literature. Culminating Activities included multiple possibilities. They could organize exhibits of models, paintings, or posters. There were assembly programs that might include dramatizations, pantomimes, and skits, or a glee club presentation of songs and music. Or they could organize discussions and debates dealing with various aspects of Western and Eastern life, political and economic systems, or the similarities and differences between thirteenth century Venice and China.

Evaluation Activities for the three Plans ranged from assessing the contributions students made to the various activities; student development of aesthetic appreciation of the Chinese culture; and their ability to engage in cooperative work. Students could

V. THE EDUCATIONAL INNOVATIONS

also be evaluated for their growth in the ability to plan and organize work, and the effectiveness of their participation in discussions and debates regarding Western and Eastern life. For the more advanced students, evaluation was also based on whether the CCSU led to a more intensive examination of any aspect of the curriculum or a more thorough exploration of contemporary relationships among the countries involved.[304]

There were two additional supplementary resources available, one an explanation of the dances choreographed by Ruth St. Denis, in which she described how "Eastern dances emphasize movement and rhythm of the head, torso and arms, and the body from the hips up—in contrast to western dances which emphasize motions of the hips and legs," and she explains that in the symbolic Sword Dance . . . the "horrid grimaces made by the dancer as he whirls the sword about his head, thrusts and parries, are . . . to frighten his enemies and the evil spirits.[305]

A second resource, likely based on a Junior Programs press release, appeared in the Jackson, Tennessee, *Sun* (n.d.) and offered a wonderful primer on the *Marco Polo* musical score. Titled "Oriental Music Is Adapted for 'Marco Polo,' Strange Rhythms And Melodies Woven into Score for Play," the piece speaks to the authenticity of the production:

> Melodies based on the plain songs and Troubadour songs of medieval Europe, Asiatic and Tartar music preserved in its original style whenever possible, [and] authentic Mongolian airs, all in the pentatonic scale, and centuries-old folk music of Armenia, Persia, Siberia and Tibet will be heard and seen by an audience of young people . . . on November 5 . . . Many of the qualities of Oriental music are intriguingly achieved with a wealth of melodic beauty by the composer, Margaret Carlisle. In the interpretation, the singers obtain a mystic plaintiveness characteristic of the East, with a pure sweetness that is almost childlike and impersonal in tone. The musical instruments used in China at the time of Kublai Khan's rule are recreations for the 'Marco Polo' music, either actually in great gongs, cymbals and rhythmic blocks, or with effects obtained on the Solovox, simulating reed pipes, bamboo flutes and bowed zithers . . . Miss Carlisle explains that in providing a musical setting for Venice, where

> the first act of 'Marco Polo' is laid, three troubadour songs became the song of the gondolier and the dances that are actual dance songs of the period—[the] Estampite [*sic*], Piedi and Volta round dances. The descriptive narrative of the Journey of Marco Polo is furnished by Miss Carlisle with a musical background of folk music of most of the European and Asiatic countries through which he traveled . . . At the court of Kublai Khan the music is of course of Mongolian origin . . . The ancient Mongolian and Chinese music were usually sung with instrumental accompaniment in unison, varied by cross rhythms whose patterns are far more intricate than those of European music . . . Studying as a modern composer under the eminent Joseph Schillinger, whose teaching influenced the late George Gershwin when he wrote 'Porgy and Bess,' Miss Carlisle comments on the unusual affinity between modern music and that played and sung in medieval tunes.

A pre-performance article from Mt. Pleasant, Michigan tells us they were looking forward to both the *Marco Polo* CCSUs and the production. "How the modern professional stage injects beautiful music, dancing and drama into the learning of children who study the history and geography of ancient China will be revealed here when the new Junior Programs' production . . . is presented at the college auditorium . . . under the sponsorship of the Child Study Club" (*Isabella County Times-News*, Oct 28, 1940s). After reviewing the outline of the *Marco Polo* CCSUs content, it seems safe to say that the Mt. Pleasant audience of young people would not be disappointed.

Doodle Dandy of the U.S.A.

As the country continued to move closer to war, the US Office of Education articulated one of its over-arching goals: "The aim is to keep so clear the fundamental issues of the war that understanding will kindle and keep alight a flaming devotion to the cause of democratic freedom."[306] In a one-line description of the story, the same press release underscores Junior Programs commitment to the same goal: it is a "story of the gallant fight for freedom *by* the children of a typical American community [emphasis added]." This emphasis on the agency of the nation's youth was echoed by Gladys Swarthout, Metropolitan Opera mezzo-soprano and chair of the

V. THE EDUCATIONAL INNOVATIONS

Junior Programs National Sponsoring Committee: "[There is] the equally important consideration that the children to whom Junior Programs is bringing the best in entertainment, are going to be the ones in whose hands will lie the reconstruction of a shattered world. They must be trained for that responsibility in every way and the Arts must not be neglected in that training, for our future is in their hands."[307] Dr. George N. Shuster, president of Hunter College, also noted in a preface to the published version of *Doodle Dandy of the U.S.A.* that "the play is also a fine educational experience. What could be more important than honest efforts to convey to young people the spirit of America? Our country's history is not all sweetness and light. Its citizens have struggled constantly for good government, for freedom of speech and of the press, and for high civic ideals . . . [but] Our democracy is always in danger . . . Doodle Dandy makes all this very clear."[308]

It would have been hard to find a better example of using the performing arts as an educational catalyst in service of teaching democratic citizenship than *Doodle Dandy*. Therefore, it was extremely disappointing to have been unable to locate any of the formal CCSU materials —especially in light of the description contained in the Elmira, New York, *Advertiser* (Jan 25, 1943).

> 'Doodle Dandy of the USA,' Junior Programs' exciting new musical play . . . has struck a bull's eye for timeliness and inspiring subjects, according to educators. . .[and] it succeeds in giving the youngsters a rousing good time while pointing the way to the basic concepts of American democracy . . . Members of Junior Programs' educational guidance committee have come forward with many original and helpful suggestions for school correlation to tie in with the performance, so that it may become a vital part of the new curriculum with its important emphasis on the study of our democratic ideals. With their help, junior programs [*sic*] has prepared special educational material, based on 'Doodle Dandy' and its theme of the four freedoms, and including biographies and reading lists of Benjamin Franklin and Thomas Jefferson who figure in the play, song sheets of old American ballads and patriotic tunes, and a wealth of school projects, ranging from a study of the Bill of Rights to an appreciation of press and radio today . . . [The play] does not sacrifice one bit of theatrical excitement in carry through its educational work.

Fortunately, similar to *The Reward of the Sun God,* the bibliography entitled "Books for Elementary Grades on Thomas Jefferson,"[309] offers some interesting insights into how closely the pedagogical, developmental, and democratic values of the books' authors matched those of Junior Programs, especially regarding how best to engage their youthful audience. Several of the books recommended by Muriel Schumacher of the Albany Public Schools illustrates this congruence. For example, dipping into Wilbur F. Gordy's 1901 *American Leaders and Heroes*, the congruence of author's pedagogical approach with that of Junior Programs mission seems remarkable. Gordy writes:

> In teaching history . . . [c]hildren of that age [ten to twelve] like action. They crave the dramatic, the picturesque, the concrete, the personal. When they read about . . . [Thomas Jefferson], they do far more than admire their hero. By a mysterious, sympathetic process they so identify themselves with him as to feel that what they see in him is possible for them . . . In this process of passing from deeds to the hearts and heads of the doers the image-forming power plays a leading part. Therefore a special effort should be made to train the sensuous imagination by furnishing picturesque and dramatic incidents, and then so skilfully [*sic*] presenting them that the children may get living pictures. This I have endeavored to do . . . by making prominent the personal traits of the heroes and leaders, as they are seen . . . in the environment of their every-day home and social life . . . . With the purpose of quickening the imagination, questions 'To the Pupil' are introduced at intervals throughout the book . . . It is hoped, therefore, that this little volume will furnish the young mind some conception of what our history is, and at the same time stimulate an abiding interest in historical and biographical reading.[310]

The bibliography also includes two books from the *Democracy Readers*, a series of seven books—two for the first grade, and one each for the next five grades. *Pioneering in Democracy* by Edna Morgan, book number V in the series (79–85), presents attractively formatted sketches of Jefferson's life. *The Growth of Democracy*, by Edna McGuire and Don Rogers, book number VII (42–55), focuses on Jefferson and the Declaration of Independence. A description of the *Democracy Readers* says, "our children must be made aware of their priceless heritage, if, *as adults, they are to pay more than lip service to democratic principles* [emphasis added]. The various authors of the series focus on twelve characteristics of democracy and stress the individual virtues of "cooperativeness in all situations, work before play, respect for the rights of others, helpfulness, fair play, kindness, the practice of hospitality, and eagerness for education."[311]

First Steps in the History of our Country, by William A. Mowry and Arthur May Mowry (16–85), also resonates with Junior Programs' approach. In the Preface, the authors describe the importance of history, but assert that it should not be a "history for more mature pupils, boiled down to the size of a small book for smaller boys and girls." They propose a tailored approach based on a focus in which "events presuppose *actors* who bring about the events. It is the action . . . that makes history . . . interesting . . . [and] history must be written in an "entertaining and engaging manner" so as to "cultivate a taste for further reading and study." While the authors include a set of questions at the end of each chapter, they urge teachers to formulate their own questions, and they also strongly advise that *different answers on the part of the students is to be encouraged* [emphasis added] as "independence of thought and expression is of deep importance." It was somewhat amusing to note that they also recommended that dates found in the text "should not be memorized" (7–8).[312]

Good Stories for Great Birthdays (304–13) by Frances Jenkins Olcott, offers a set of brief vignettes about Thomas Jefferson: "The Boy Owner of Shadwell Farm" and "A Christmas Guest" sketch Jefferson's boyhood on a remote Virginia farm, and his friendship with Patrick Henry. Without any comment, the sketches mention his ownership of slaves and goes on to address his writing of the Declaration of Independence in "The Author of the Declaration," and "Proclaim Liberty." Finally, in "Only a Reprieve," the vignette calls him an Abolitionist, quoting his comment, "This abomination must have an end," and noting that he had included a "clause condemning the slave-trade, as an "assemblage of horrors" in his draft of the Declaration. The clause was removed from the Declaration by the Convention, and the vignette ends with the following: "From the time of Jefferson until the Civil War, slavery to be or not to be, was the burning question. Men and women, especially those belonging to the Society of Friends, devoted their lives to the abolition of slavery . . . [and] this momentous question," [Jefferson] wrote, "like a fire-bell in the night, awakened and filled me with terror. I considered it at once as the knell of the Union. It is hushed, indeed, for the moment. But this is a *reprieve* only—not a final sentence." And again, he said, "I tremble for my Country, when I reflect that God is just; that His justice cannot sleep for ever [*sic*]." The book continues: "Nearly a hundred years of slavery passed after the framing of the Declaration, then on North and South fell the terrible retributive punishment of the Civil War."[313] Today, with good reason, calling Jefferson an abolitionist would be laughable, but in the early 1940s, with the fate of democracy at issue, Junior Programs did not have the benefit of "critical race theory's" more accurate assessment of many of our national heroes.

Several additional books are listed as more suitable to being read aloud by the teacher. Schumacher notes that *Champions of Democracy* by Joseph Cottler (25–46) emphasizes political ideas, and is written in an interesting way, but she cautions that it has some difficult vocabulary. Schumacher describes *Boyhood Adventures of Our Presidents,* by Frances Cavanah, as "very readable stories suitable for very good 5th and 6th grade readers," or she adds, it could be read aloud to a group by the teacher. Schumacher also comments that Gene Lisitsky's *Thomas Jefferson* is by far the most interesting book, but too difficult for most intermediate readers. However, it would lend itself to having the teacher read it aloud to a class. From the Junior Programs perspective, such an approach, with the usual follow-up questions and discussion would likely be seen as an excellent way to build community among a group of students.

The final book in the recommended bibliography, *Codfish Musket,* is a fictional story of a teenage boy caught up in the dream of establishing a transcontinental trade route to the Northwest as a more economically viable means of conducting trade with China. According to a *New York Times* book review (Dec 20, 1936), the book's author, Agnes Danforth Hewes, believed that commerce was not simply about exports and imports or debits and credits. Rather it was "the lifeblood of history and the inspiration and result of great adventure." As a fictional secretary to President Jefferson during the time of a thriving China trade, young Dan Bolt, the fictional hero, was enthralled by the vision of a "greater America." Sometime after Lewis and Clark set out on their great expedition, Dan was entrusted with reaching them with the message of the Louisiana Purchase, a message that would prevent the threatened

V. THE EDUCATIONAL INNOVATIONS 245

secession of the West. The book review depicts his travels: "By saddle horse, stage coach, Conestoga wagon, by pack train and flat boat, across the Alleghanies, down the Ohio, through the forests, Dan followed the trail of Westward pushing America . . . It is a colorful panorama of this phase of American history . . . of settled old Boston, the raw new Washington, and the crude brawling life of the frontier."[314] And again, in the context of Junior Programs' core beliefs, the action-oriented novel offers an appealing picture of youthful agency.

The resonance of this list with Junior Programs' core beliefs is unmistakable. Both agree that the performing arts and education should be lively, action oriented, and aspirational—and all within the student's realm of experience. Both agree that the approach must appeal to the head *and* the heart, and that neither should talk down to their young audience. Absent the actual CCSU, the bibliography does provide at least some general sense of what the unit might have been like.

Lancourt's papers also contained the "Notes on the Music of "Doodle Dandy of the U.S.A." These notes describe the music as "an original, specially composed score for piano (with Solovox[315]) and voices and provides a framework within which teachers can begin to explore the play's music with their class. It contains action and background music, ballet and pantomime music, songs and choral music as part of, and incidental to the action. Several folk songs dating back to early America are woven into the score, and the spirit of the whole is based on the feeling of American freedom songs. Various styles, from the simplest nursery rhyme to the most dissonant modern harmony are used, according to the demands of the dramatic situations." Three excerpts provide examples of the relationship of the music to the dramatic action.

> [We hear,] DOODLE'S DISCOVERY. [W]hile the company sings the second verse of the Liberty Song, the pretended Montmorency [Doodle in disguise] discards his clothing to the strains of impish background music—and, as the music gets more and more impudent—almost drowning out the singing—[it] is discovered [that Montmorency is] Doodle Dandy. [In] I'M FASTER THAN LIGHT, Doodle explains his own meaning to America in rhythmically spoken lines, interrupted by racy trills, scale passages and background music, supporting his pantomimic movements. [In] I'M ALL AMERICAN

FREE, Scene 1 closes with a restatement of Doodle's credo which now grows into a song of happiness and faith in America, [s]ung by the whole company as the lights fade.

[In Scene 2,] the shifting clouds surrounding 'Freedom, Inc.' are portrayed by a soft lyrical theme (Solovox flute). As Doodle's Lucky Star appears, and starts to dance, the poetic theme becomes more lively and breaks out into an outburst on Doodle's appearance. Rhythmical, comic and descriptive dance music accompany Doodle's dance with the Star while descending to earth . . . [and a]s Doodle reaches the earth, a theme already heard in the Overture emerges—'Doodle's Happy Tune'. It grows bright and strong as Doodle goes into the audience in search of Springville. It describes his walking, dancing step. [Scene 4's] DOODLE DANDY'S BACK IN TOWN [is] a lively, playful tune that shows us Doodle as the protector of all our freedoms. Brief strains of 'Yankee Doodle' are heard, showing the relationship between the Doodle of today and of 1776.

[In Act II, Scene 2] The ballet-pantomime, 'Spring in Springville,' is in the form of a Theme and Variations, the theme being that earliest of native American folk songs, 'Springfield Mountain.' The variations accompany the pantomime and dance movements and describe the various stages of the settlement of Springville and the house-raising. There is a 'Dance of Rejoicing' in free folk-dance rhythms and a jubilant 'Roof-raising Dance' - in both of which the melody of 'Springfield Mountain' goes through numerous transformations. Besides the two dances, there are eleven variations. A LOAF OF BREAD dance pantomime is similar in structure to the preceding except that the opening melody is an original one and there are twelve variations. The various trades and occupations presented are also characterized musically: i.e. - the farmer has a short country-fiddler's dance; the smith a heavy clog-dance refrain; the miner's music is 'dark and spooky', etc. The whole dance ends in a general finale of rejoicing.[316]

V. THE EDUCATIONAL INNOVATIONS

That the production itself had significant educational value is attested to in an undated publicity release from the Dramatists Play Service, Inc. which notes that the play had been "highly recommended by the Associate Superintendent of Junior High Schools of New York, by several principals in New York and elsewhere, by music supervisors . . . throughout the country, by representatives of the Federal Children's Bureau, by the office of War Information in Washington and by many other individuals, newspapers and associations."[317]

We also learn that "For the first time in New York, a play will move directly from Broadway to New York's public schools." Eleven performances of a "Real Broadway Play" were scheduled in elementary and junior high schools in Manhattan, Brooklyn and the Bronx, with tickets set at 25cents apiece—the deficit from school performances to be covered by Junior Programs, Inc. (Ticket prices at the Belasco Theater for capacity audiences ranged from a high of $3.30 to a more affordable $.85.). These performances of *Doodle Dandy* were "presented by an arrangement with the Board of Education of New York and . . . approved by the entire Board of Superintendents."[318] As part of this project, Junior Programs developed a *Doodle Dandy* Contest inviting the students who attended the play to write additional verses to the *Doodle Dandy* theme song. The prize was a $25 War Bond. The verses had to have the same rhythm as the original verses, and need to focus on democracy, one of the four freedoms or any other patriotic idea. As with the teacher evaluations, it was extremely disappointing that none of the archives contained any of the entries.

While only 8,000 of New York City's one million school children, from 22 of the city's public schools would be able to see "Doodle Dandy," both school officials and Junior Programs were hopeful this experiment would lead to bringing professional theater to all school children in the near future (*Daily Worker*, n.d.). When approving the program, Assistant Superintendent John. J. Loftus said, "Besides being a good story, 'Doodle Dandy' is an excellent object lesson in democratic co-operation which any child can understand and appreciate." Unfortunately, this experiment in bringing professional theater directly into the schools was cut short by the US entry into WWII. Nevertheless, despite Junior Programs' untimely demise, the perspectives articulated in the various newspaper sources and other documents makes it clear that their Educational Guidance Committee clearly understood the needs of the two audiences they were attempting to reach—local frontline teachers and their students.

The Junior Programs Opera Correlated Curriculum Study Units (CCSUs)

The focus of the CCSUs for the Junior Programs Players was quite broad, encompassing social, political, economic, and cultural issues as well as the performing arts. The study units for the operas, however, focused primarily on the music and musical forms, the composers, and the myths and fairy tales on which the operas were based. We know there were grade appropriate CCSUs for the operas as they were referred to in many of the newspaper reviews, as well as in Junior Programs' marketing materials, but unfortunately, the actual materials in the Junior Programs Scrapbooks and Lancourt's and McFadden's personal papers was sparse. There was no information at all for *Jack and the Beanstalk*, a smattering of resources related to *Hansel and Gretel*, with little more for *The Bumble Bee Prince*. Even the bibliographies were not very helpful as proxies for what the CCSUs might have contained. Several were "borrowed" from the *Metropolitan Opera Guild*, and focused more generically on composers, music history related to a particular period or style, and the stories on which the operas were base.

Hansel and Gretel

Hansel and Gretel was Junior Programs' first opera production, inherited from the NML. Therefore, the scarcity of educational materials may be due to fact that the Educational Guidance Committee had not yet developed its more robust template. Be that as it may, we do know from some of the newspaper reviews that the music-focused resources were a valued Junior Programs' innovation. One reviewer singled out the *Hansel and Gretel* CCSU for particular praise: "One unique feature of their [Junior Programs'] work is to send correlative material to be used in the schools prior to each program. The children of Radnor and Rosemont Schools have done some beautiful projects" (unknown source, n.d.). And from Washington, Pennsylvania, another review tells us the "audience of children ranging from 5 to 15 years of age, followed with attuned ears every bar of music because they had been singing the arias and choruses and studying the story in their school classrooms for several weeks preceding the performance" (*Reporter*, Jan 17, 1940).

Several untitled pages related to *Hansel and Gretel* in Lancourt's personal papers tell us there was a biography of Humperdinck written especially for children, as well as a description of the story adapted from *The American History and Encyclopedia of Music,* Vol. 2, edited by W.L. Hubbard. There was also a brief supplementary reading list compiled by members of the Junior Programs Educational Guidance Committee. It included multiple versions of *Grimms' Fairy Tales,* all featuring extensive and exquisite illustrations—just the sort that would appeal to a child's imagination.[319] The *Complete Book of the Great Musicians* by Percy Alfred Scholes, Vol. 2 (43–57) was one such resource. Scholes's pedagogical style seems to be in keeping with Junior Programs' approach to engaging a young audience: he used stories from a composer's childhood, coupled with a representative piece of music to draw the children in—step by step—to develop their listening skills, sometimes using "games of the author's invention." As the children were ready to learn more, a chapter seemed to appear magically, explaining the next step. In essence, the author was inviting the children to "join the musical community," and learn "how the paths of the different musicians intertwine, and how supportive they are of each other."[320]

The Bumble Bee Prince

A *Baltimore Post Review* (n.d.) made special mention of the valuable resources provided by the Junior Programs Educational Guidance Committee, and the CCSU for *The Bumble Bee Prince* included generic materials curated by the *Metropolitan Opera Guild* with "Notes for the Study of Opera." This included sections on Grand Opera, Lyric Opera, and Ballet in Opera. There was also a "Supplementary Reading List" of Russian fairy tales listed by appropriate grade levels (e.g., *Picture Tales from the Russian,* Valery Garrick, 1920—grades 1-2-3; *Russian Grandmother's Wonder Tales,* L.S. Houghton, —grades 4-6; and *Russian Fairy Tales,* Nesbit Bain). In addition, there was background information on Russia, and stories about Russian children (e.g., *When I was a Boy in Russia,* V.K. Debogorli-Mokievich, 1916—grades 1-3; *Made in Russia,* W.C. White, 1932—grades 6-8; and *Adventures of Misha,* Sergei Rozanoff, 1938—grades 2-3).

There was also information for teachers on the life and work of Alexander Pushkin, one of Russia's most famous literary talents, and the source for the original opera, *Tales of the Tzar Saltan,* from which *The Bumble Bee Prince* was adapted. According to these materials, Pushkin was educated at the Tsar's School, an institution reserved for the thirty most brilliant boys in Russia, where he excelled at writing poetry. He traveled throughout Russia and consorted with nobles and peasants alike; he lived at court and in villages; and his writing reflected his broad and eclectic tastes. His life ended when he was killed in a duel at age thirty-seven. His popularity—akin to the Western reverence for Shakespeare—lived on, and there are numerous musical works based on his stories and poems (e.g., *Coq d'Or* by Rimsky-Korsakov, *Boris Godunov* by Mussorgsky, and, of course, Rimsky-Korsakov's *Tale of the Tzar Saltan.*). One "Teacher's Page" from these materials describes both the small Russian village in which Rimsky-Korsakov grew up and the folk songs he heard that told of the life and beliefs of the Russian people—including the legend of a prince transformed into a bumble bee. The material describes the processions and dances, the gorgeous, brilliantly colored clothing, and how much Rimsky-Korsakov loved village pageantry. As a young man, he became an officer on a ship that sailed around the world, and he never forgot a night when they sailed through an ocean aglow with particles of light and flying fish. According to this "Teachers' Page," all these and his many other experiences are reflected in his music; and it seems clear that his colorful life would have great appeal to children of all ages.[321]

A "Russian Music" list, compiled by Julia Cummings Sutton, author of "Children's Masterwork Hour," included a list of phonograph records of the opera—especially the recording of *The Bumble Bee Prince* by the Junior Programs Opera Company (Victor B-527-28-29-30; 4 double-face records, $1.40). There was also a list of recordings of other Rimsky-Korsakov music, and the sheet music for "The Flight of the Bumble Bee." This included moderate to difficult pieces for clarinet solo with piano, cornet solo with piano, flute solo with piano, alto saxophone with piano and xylophone solo with piano. There were also phonograph records of other Russian composers.[322]

Given the popularity of the Junior Programs operas, and the references to the CCSUs in various news reports, we can only speculate as to whether there was ever a unit for *Jack and the Beanstalk,* or whether it has simply been "lost." As to why the units for *Hansel and Gretel* and *The Bumble Bee Prince* are so meager, it seems possible that, at least for *The Bumble Bee Prince,* the materials currently available are simply incomplete.

The Junior Programs Ballet Correlated Curriculum Study Units (CCSUs)

In terms of the CCSUs for the Junior Programs Ballet, the availability of materials was only marginally better. None of the collections included CCSUs for two of the Junior Programs Ballets' dance-plays, *Pinocchio* and *The Princess and the Swineherd*. However, although the records are frustratingly incomplete, there were CCSUs for *The Adventures of Puck* and *Robin Hood*.

The Adventures of Puck

The Table of Contents for *The Adventures of Puck* indicates that it was a fully fleshed-out CCSU, although few of the actual pieces were in the various collections. There was an Introduction, a section on Objectives, the Approach, a Synopsis of "*A Midsummer Night's Dream,*" a Synopsis of *"The Adventures of Puck,"* a section on the Life of William Shakespeare, the Life of Felix Mendelssohn, Research Activities, Culminating Activities, and a set of After the Ballet: Evaluating Activities. A section entitled "Leads to Other Units," a Bibliography on Shakespeare and His Times, and an Appendix completed the unit. It was developed by Ellen McClellan Wilshire and Dr. Wood of the University of Oregon, with input from teachers and librarians from Pierre, South Dakota, Eugene Oregon, and New York City, as well as representatives from the Office of Education in Washington, DC.[323]

The Approach section included the use of pictures from various sources, and information on Mendelssohn's music. The synopsis links each part of the story to its related piece of music. For example, "Oberon instructs Puck to search for a little Western flower, milk white now purple with love's wounds (Scherzo); Oberon squeezes the flower on Titania's eyelids (Nocturne); triple wedding of Theseus, Hippolyta, Lysander, Hermia, Demetrius and Helena (Wedding March). For the younger grades, the materials describe how the dancers "dance" a story. "The narrators say the words, but every gesture of our hands, each step and movement of our arms and bodies has something to do with the story . . . The main character is Puck, a mischievous elf, so all his movements are quick and darting, like sunlight on rippling water . . . he jumps from place to place . . . [whereas] Titania, the Fairy Queen is a lovely stately dancer, proud and haughty in all her movements . . . [and] Oberon [the King of the Fairies] dances with dignity and quite grace. The fairies, in the shape of moths and butterflies and beetles, flutter and twist and turn very lightly as they flit through the forest . . . The humans in the story seem very crude and heavy by contrast, with clumsy motions of their arms and legs and many foolish bumps and tumbles."

The CCSU included a brief account of the "little that is known about the life of Shakespeare, augmented by some descriptions of life in London during the sixteenth century." There was also a summary of the life of Felix Mendelssohn, who was "born in Hamburg in 1809." A short description of the French occupation of Hamburg followed, along with his family's flight to Berlin and then Paris, where he began his musical studies. The materials also included a description of Mendelssohn's friendship with Goethe and material on the symphonies Mendelssohn composed from age twelve through seventeen, including *A Midsummer Night's Dream*.

The CCSU then summarized the type of music Mendelssohn wrote and offered a set of Research Activities, suggesting that the language arts teachers take the lead, in cooperation with the other school departments. These activities included dramatizations, oral and written reports, letters, and the creation of scrapbooks. There were also sections for the shop and home economics teachers (e.g., the construction of an Elizabethan theater or Anne Hathaway's cottage, or patterns for the making of costumes). There were dances to be taught and practiced in physical education classes, and songs and ballads for the music classes to play and sing. Culminating Activities included a costume party, an assembly program, and, of course, attendance at the Junior Programs performance. In addition, there were Evaluation Activities for after the performance including an Appreciation Check List and the writing of "Impressions." There were Bibliographies as well as three appendices: detailed Primary, Intermediate and High School Unit Plans. Unfortunately, none of the grade-specific plans were among the CCSU materials.

There was, however, an unusual piece among the Junior Programs press materials for *The Adventures of Puck* entitled "WHEN SHAKESPEARE WAS CENSORRED BY THE PURITANS." It chronicles an incident occurring on a Sunday in 1631 in a small English town. Shocked by the performance of a group of traveling players of Shakespeare's comedy *A Midsummer Night's Dream,* a group of Puritans of the same sect that established the American Boston colony with its Blue Laws, persuaded Archbishop Laud to punish the troupe by issuing an official decree:

Likewise wee doe order, that Mr. Wilson, because hee was a speciall plotter and contriver of this business and did in such a brutishe manner acte the same with an asse's head, and therefore hee shall, upon Tuesday next, from six of the clocke in the morning till six of the clocke at night, sitt in the Porter's Lodge at my Lord Bishopps House, with his feete in the stocks, and attyred with his asse head, and a bottle of hay sette before him and this subscription on his breaste:

> 'Good people I have played the beaste,
> And brought ill things to passe;
> I was a man, but thus have made
> Myselfe a silly asse.'

How this piece was used in the classroom is unknown, but fortunately, nothing similar seems to have happened to Charles Tate, who danced the role of Bottom in *The Adventures of Puck*.

Robin Hood

A more robust, though still incomplete CCSU for *Robin Hood* full of suggestions for music study, balladry, choral speech, and other classroom activities was found in the Junior Programs Scrapbooks, and taking a page from the Junior Programs' social, political, and economic mission, it also included materials and suggestions related to daily life in feudal England—with stories, songs, and poems about the lords of the manor *and* the serfs, as well as traveling minstrels, archery, tumbling, and old Yuletide customs.[324]

Ellen McClennan Wilshire of University High School, Oregon, developed the CCSU which contained an Overview and Introduction that explores the history of the Robin Hood legend and its many different sources—from Fulk Fitzwarin, a nobleman who had displeased the King to the Junior Programs choice of Robert, the foster son of the Earl of Huntington. There were introductory materials on the feudal system and the oppression of the Church, the social organization of the manor and the manor house, and the social system of mutual obligations between the nobility and their peasants. Additionally, there was a discussion of social class (aristocrats, serfs, and clergy), and resources covering the Norman Conquest and the Crusades. There was also material on the traditions of hunting and falconry, as well as Christmas traditions in multiple European countries. The important implicit message in the CCSU was that dance, and the story of Robin Hood, was not something separate and apart from the various elements of everyday life; that in essence, they were related to all the other social, political, and economic concerns. Dance was a language, and if you learned to understand it, it could tell you, eloquently, about a time and place and a social order.

The CCSU could be easily adapted to every grade level and included the suggestion that "teachers of the different subjects should develop the units together." There was a section on Developing Appreciation with the objective of stimulating creative expression, and again the possibility that subject matter boundaries be ignored so that multiple disciplines could be involved in the planning and meeting of objectives. There was a Synopsis of the Story, and a set of Research Activities focused on several themes for Social Science classes—including the advantages and disadvantages of the feudal system, the Church and what led to the Protestant Revolution, as well as issues related to oppression and social betterment. The CCSU also discussed the agricultural system, and for Literature, the reading of some of Chaucer's Canterbury Tales. A bibliography on medieval life also supported these units.[325]

The CCSU also suggested oral and written reports on a variety of subjects. It recommended choral speaking and the poems and stories of King Arthur. Various exhibits and art projects included a study of clothing, and the making of costumes. And it juxtaposed an examination of social customs, including the manners and etiquette of the royal court, with an examination of health conditions, and sports—including archery, tumbling and hunting. A page listing "Ancient Sports" included a book entitled—*The Sports and Pastimes of the People of England* by Joseph Strut. In it, the material described how to hold a whistling match, with the winner defined as the one who could "whistle the longest without laughing." The book also included a yawning match, a jingling match, a version of Blind Man's Bluff, sack running, smock races (for girls), and a wheelbarrow race.[326] The inclusion of games and celebrations in several of the Junior Programs CCSUs was an insightful way to capture the attention and engagement of their youthful audience. It provided an easy opening into cultural difference—be it the exploration of the history of "The Blazing Yule," or a discussion in a history or social studies class of the origins and early observance of Yuletide in France, Serbia, and Yugoslavia.[327] And it was likely no accident that the proposed

V. THE EDUCATIONAL INNOVATIONS

Culminating Activities included a mock medieval tournament, as well as a medieval banquet.[328]

The *Robin Hood CCSU* also provided detailed information for the music department about several relevant recordings to support the teaching not only of musical history and appreciation but of how the social and cultural organization of a society is expressed through music—that music is a language that is both culturally specific *and* universal.

The recordings and scores for Act I included:

1. Now is the time of Christymas—15th century carol. Bax arrangement for ballet; Carlisle arrangement for records
2. A March based on the 13th century fragmentary tune "Robin Loves Me" by de la Halle

    This tune is used throughout the ballet for Robin's theme (recorded)

3. Misrule Dances—consisting of:
    a. Moll Sims—ancient dance tune (recorded)
    b. Over the Hills and Far Away—Marlborough Wars song, used later by Gay in *Beggar's Opera* with different words
    c. Pastoral Dance (Harpsichord Airs)
4. Welcoming Guests Dance— Gavotte from Harpsichord Dances (recorded)
5. Yule Log Song (recorded)—words by Robert Herrick [1591-1674]
    a. Bear Dance—Dance of the Elephant—Saint-Saens
    b. Bull Fighter Dance— (Bolero treatment of Robin Loves Me)
6. Peacock Carol —(recorded) words—old Carol
7. Dance following—Respighi arrangement of ancient ballet dances
8. Reprise of Gavotte for departing of guests
9. Robin Loves Me Theme in major then minor, under dialogue ending in Recorder solo (Record 3)

The list for Act II included:

1. Hunting Ballet
    a. The Hunt is Up

b. A Hunting We Will Go (arrangement of two old hunting songs, recorded)

2. The "vows" from a hymn by William Byrde (recorded) [Pslams, Sonnets & Songs, 1588]

3. My Mind to Me a Kingdom Is [Edward Dyer, 1543-1607 or Edward de Vere, 17th Earl of Oxford 1550-1604]

4. Tinkers Song—collection of Old English Songs by Lane Wilson (recorded)

5. Pages Hanging—Robin Loves Me theme

6. Finale—Three Dances from German—Minuet, Jig and Morris Dance from "Merrie England" Suite

The list for Act III included:

"Here we must digress from the authentic tunes to suit the ballet form and story, but we have kept the flavor."

1. Opening Dance—arrangement of aria from Le Roi et le Fermier (17th Century) (recorded) - by Monsigny

2. Here's a Health Unto His Majesty (England Minstrelsy)—one line recorded (6)

3. Hobby Horse Dance—Shepard's Fennel Dance—by Balfour-Gardiner

4. Morris Dance—Henry VIII Dances by Sir Edward German

5. Torch Dance—Henry VIII Dances by Sir Edward German

6. Finale—Reprise of Christymas Dance (Recorded—6)[329]

The unit for music teachers also included a "Suggestion for Children's Participation in the Junior Programs Robin Hood Ballet":

> The children of your school orchestra who are playing either the recorder or other wind instruments will undoubtedly be specially interested to know that one of the Junior Programs musicians, Mr. Sol Rokoff, is playing the recorder on the stage at certain points in the ballet . . . We would like to suggest that children might enjoy playing on the recorder the 'Peacock Carol' from our mimeographed sheets; or 'The Tinker's Song' from the same sheets if transposed to the key

of D. '<u>The Hunt is Up</u>', another of the tunes used in the ballet will be found in almost any schoolbook of songs, and could be played by the school orchestra. If desired, the children could play either the above music or any other recorder music during the intermission of the actual ballet performance . . . We hope the attached leaflet will be of help.[330]

While incomplete, the *Robin Hood* CCSU suggests that the Educational Guidance Committee saw dance and music not only as major forms of the performing arts, but as a normal and integral part of any civil society. As such, the art forms were not only manifestations of the social and cultural dynamics of their time and place but were capable of influencing the nature of their time and place. This sense of interdependence seems to carry through to the unit's final recommendation—that the teachers use the *Robin Hood* CCSU not only to spark ideas for additional experiences for their classes, but that "In every instance *the children themselves should be given the opportunity to suggest things that they want to do*" [emphasis added]. We can see in suggestions such as this yet another example of how deeply and completely Junior Programs' respect for their young audiences was threaded through everything they did.

Junior Programs' Synthesis of Education and the Performing Arts

Incomplete as the CCSUs are, what is available provides an impressive and inspiring picture of both the range and depth of the Junior Programs educational materials. The CCSUs are also evidence of the company's commitment to significantly extend the role and impact of the performing arts in the education and development of the next generation. In this, they were unique in several ways. First, their commitment to "*Only the best is good enough for children*" was evident in the caliber and composition of the members of their Educational Guidance Committee—all leaders in their respective fields of childhood education and child development, as well as in their related organizations.

Second, the reviews and comments found in the various news media acknowledge the work of the Educational Guidance Committee as providers of a significant and valued resource offered directly to classroom teachers. Unlike many of today's theater-based teaching artists whose work and presence in the classroom supplements the work of front-line teachers, the Junior Programs CCSUs were designed as direct, grade-specific resources for the broad range of front-line teachers. In a sense, the Junior Programs' CCSUs not only deepened the education of millions of children, but also educated many hundreds of teachers who came to view the performing arts as a desirable and important part of an overall curriculum. An article in an unidentified Montgomery, Alabama, newspaper (Nov 24, 1940) tells us, "The pupils took eagerly to a huge variety of studies related to the performances . . . These included classical music, geography and history as well as songs and dances of South America, England at the time of the Crusades, Scandinavian folk lore, colonial America, [and] Russian folk lore. Carefully devised under the supervision of the educational committee, the material is integrated with commonly practiced teaching of English languages, social studies, arts and drama."

Third, the Junior Programs educational focus was holistic and systemic, with material in the CCSU for almost every school department within a collaborative Culminating Activities framework. In conjunction with the performances themselves, these activities served to knit the various pieces together into a unifying whole. The various CCSUs were designed to enabled front-line teachers to collaborate across school departments, strengthening the sense of community at both the teacher and student levels. In this way, the Junior Programs' model embodied and expressed not only Dewey's new educational principle of *engaging the whole child*, but also his belief in the *experience of community* as a key part of the educational and developmental process in a democratic society.

Fourth, was the national scope of both their performance and educational efforts. As part of their national educational presence, Junior Programs participated regularly in a wide range of professional educational gatherings. In March 1938, they convened a national conference bringing together people involved in motion pictures, theater, radio, music, and education at Columbia University to consider the problems of the "Audiences of Tomorrow" (*Motion Picture Herald*, Mar 12, 1938). The conference was part of a much larger desire among many of the participants to create a national movement focused on and advocating for more cultural education in the schools and in the community. One immediate goal of this meeting was an effort to persuade motion picture theater owners to regularly present special matinees of traveling cultural stage shows for children as part of their community-based contribution to a national movement for the cultural enlightenment and education of young people. There was some discussion as to the possibility of some profit for individual theaters, but it was acknowledged that such profit would likely be nominal. The chief benefit would be the goodwill the theaters would generate from the various women's clubs, parent-teacher organizations, and school systems. Another example of their participation in national educational forums was an advertisement in the *New York Times* (n.d.) for "A Free Course Devoted to The Child in Wartime," with McFadden speaking on The Child and His [*sic*] Amusements.[331] And according to McFadden, herself, she spent a significant portion of her time "on the road" delivering countless talks—at PTA conventions, AAUW sessions, sponsoring organization meetings, and a wide variety of other educational and community settings.

Junior Programs own publicity materials also affirmed the growing popularity of their CCSU materials and teacher's manuals as an integral part of their high-quality productions. When they announced the development of a "new and exciting version of Robin Hood," or "A new play from South America . . . in cooperation with the Columbia Broadcasting System," there was not only an uptick in requests for future performances from cities and towns they had already visited, but a growing number of cities and towns were willing to contract for their productions while the productions were still in the process of development. Given the array of positive responses to the various CCSUs, it is not hard to imagine that the demise of Junior Programs was experienced as a loss by both teachers and pupils. The question now is, "How can today's performing arts leaders and organizations take advantage of the Junior Programs approach in the context of today's needs and circumstances?" (See Chapter VII.)

VI. THE ORGANIZATIONAL INNOVATIONS

Vision, mission, and artistic and educational excellence may inspire and motivate. But Junior Programs was a new enterprise of three distinct companies in three separate art forms. Each had a yearly schedule of extensive national tours. To manage such an organization requires a structure and infrastructure that is stable *and* nimble, proactive *and* responsive, *and* able to coordinate and communicate effectively between hundreds of moving parts. To complicate this challenge, Junior Programs existed at a time when the primary means of long-distance communication was the US Postal Service, and when manual typewriters were the primary means of producing letters and documents. There were no copy machines: copies were made with carbon paper, one or two at a time, or on a mimeograph machine. Telephone technology was still new. The first transcontinental phone call occurred in 1915, and area codes were not assigned until 1947. Someone at the Junior Programs headquarters in New York City could not simply pick up the phone and dial a number to reach someone in California.

Nevertheless, McFadden and Lancourt managed to craft an organizational infrastructure well suited to their needs. While much of the documentation of the company's day-to-day activities no longer exists, it has been possible to piece together an impressive picture of a coordinated, highly participatory organizational design. The artistic, production, and seasonal scheduling activities were centralized in New York, and the on-the-ground touring and delivery activities were delegated to a broadly decentralized national network of local Sponsoring Committees composed of civic organizations and local leaders. All told, as of 1940, there were well over three thousand people across the country volunteering their time to make sure the Junior Programs tours were a success. (*Musical America*, Feb 10, 1940, 275).

VI. THE ORGANIZATIONAL INNOVATIONS

This chapter focuses on two important aspects of Junior Programs' organizational model: first, the formation and operation of the local Sponsoring Committees, and the way that infrastructure anchored Junior Programs in the nation's communities; and second, Lancourt's production process, responsible for ensuring that every production embodied the company motto, *"Only the best is good enough for children."* Together, these laid the foundation for an organizational infrastructure with the ability to support each company's rapidly growing touring schedule. This organizational design gave new meaning to the concept of access. It not only enabled them to deliver their innovative, high-quality, socially relevant performances and CCSUs to four million children. It enabled them to reach children and communities well beyond the urban centers, and to engage them in a unique experiment, one whose goal was nothing less than the successful preparation of young audiences for their role in sustaining and enriching America's democratic culture.

Local Sponsoring Committees

In 1936, Junior Programs' first New York office at 221 West 57th Street was headquarters for McFadden and Lancourt.[332] Also based in New York were secretary, Mary Hatton, and art director, Walter Roach. Lancourt also brought in Charles Plotkin, a music educator and journalist who successfully handled publicity. Early staffing also included six field secretaries, each responsible for whatever needed to be done in their respective regions: Hope J. Clark covered Long Island, Remington Korper focused on Eastern Pennsylvania and the South, Doris Lamb had the Middle West, Marjorie Manning, New England, Anne Merritt, Southern New York and Alice Windsor, New Jersey.[333] Their work consisted of organizing, problem solving, troubleshooting, and providing logistical and marketing support to the local Sponsoring Committees in their respective geographies. Other names pop up in various archival materials, but there was little additional information about individual staff members or about how the staff evolved as Junior Programs grew.

A preponderance of local newspaper reviews and national articles discuss the importance of these local Sponsoring Committees. Without their extensive and tireless work, Junior Programs' tours and performances would not have been possible. Success required the involvement of dozens of local civic organizations, from the Kiwanis, Rotary, and College Clubs to the parent-teacher associations (PTAs) and

Chambers of Commerce. However, the backbone of many Sponsoring Committees was the local chapters of the Association of the Junior Leagues of America (AJLA). Motivated by a sense of social responsibility, debutantes Mary Harriman and Nathalie Henderson founded the Junior League for the Promotion of the Settlement Movement in 1901. They believed women had an important role to play in improving their local communities through education, volunteerism, and charity. While an understanding of the dynamics and politics of social and structural reform have changed dramatically since the Junior League's founding more than a century ago, it was not only an important volunteer institution, it was also a significant social force at that time.

By the second decade of the twentieth century, the Junior League's work had shifted away from the Settlement Movement. In the 1910s and '20s, it embraced local health, welfare, cultural and recreational work, juvenile justice, and arts programs, and especially children's theater. Child health and welfare campaigns were also added to the menu of activities its members were encouraged to support in one way or another.[334] Today, after multiple waves of feminism, it is sometimes difficult to imagine a time when most married women were still referred to in print by their husband's name: Mrs. George So-and-so. Nevertheless, however they were described, it's clear that the women of the Junior League not only put in enormous amounts of volunteer time, but in doing so, developed a truly exceptional set of organizing skills. They regarded their various projects as their civic duty and responsibility. Literally thousands of organizations and causes—including Junior Programs—reaped the benefit and could not have succeeded without them.

An active clubwoman herself, McFadden was a great believer in the importance of community involvement. As she wrote, "It is not a question of the population or wealth of a town, but only of a determined and expressed desire on the part of individuals and organizations of a community made effective through real action which have brought good drama, music and other forms of fine arts to communities which really want them."[335] Together with the help of the field secretaries, cities and towns across the country, with populations ranging from under five thousand to more than hundreds of thousands, formed local Junior Programs Sponsoring Committees. Local civic groups organized to sponsor either individual productions from one of Junior Programs' three companies or, more often, a "season" of two or

VI. THE ORGANIZATIONAL INNOVATIONS

three productions, one from each company. News outlets large and small described the process by which sponsoring groups contracted with Junior Programs to become part of their touring schedule.[336] The *CBS Student Guide* (Oct 1940) reported that "arrangements are worked out with local committees of sponsors composed of school authorities, women's clubs, parent-teacher associations and other civic groups through the central office of Junior Programs in New York. During the past school year, the Junior Programs Players had an audience of nearly a million children in cities and towns throughout the United States and Canada."

The *Junior Magazine* of the National Federation of Music Clubs (n.d.) ran an article titled, "How to Bring 'Doodle Dandy' to Your Community," explaining that "any interested group of individuals can form a committee to bring Junior Programs to their community. Write to Junior Programs, Inc. . . . for dates, fee, and general information concerning Doodle Dandy and other Junior [Programs'] musical productions." *Vogue* (Aug 1, 1940) told its readers to "write a letter to Junior Programs, Inc. at 37 W. 57th St., and they will give you all the information–how to plan a performance for the children in your community, and how to figure the costs for it. On the day of the performance, Junior Programs, Inc. arrives, complete with actors, scenery, lighting effects and costumes. With remarkably little effort on your part, and at a cost to themselves of seldom more than 25cents you will give the children a chance to prove to you that they don't have to be taught to enjoy good music or ballet or opera or suitable plays."

A picture of one of the more robust of the local organizations, described in the Seattle *Times* (Apr 24, 1940) illustrates how the model played out on the ground. "The women who are trying to take the gangsters and the horrors and the horseplay out of the entertainment for juveniles and who march under the banner of Junior Programs, Inc. truly were amazed at the swift growth of their organization, the local branch being one year old, the national four . . . Mrs. Darwin Meisnest, one of the founders of the Seattle Junior Programs Inc . . . was reelected head of this group for the next year. New board members were named . . . [and] serious business . . . included reports of officers and committee chairmen." One of the reports shared the group's history from a day the previous spring "when it was decided by a group of eleven charter members" to officially incorporate as Junior Programs, Inc. of Seattle. "There was a Treasurer's Report, a report from the Executive Field Secretary on the spread of the organization's work," a scrapbook from the organization's Historian, a Membership report, a Publicity report, a Theater Committee report, and a Program report. And least it become all work and no play, there was a skit, much of it written in sprightly rhyme, by Mrs. John P. Patten, Mrs. Gerald de Garmo, and Mrs. Webster Augustine, which was both 'historical and hysterical.' And their organization gave credit where credit was due. They acknowledged that Junior Programs, Inc. of Seattle could not have done it "without support from the City of Seattle and the clubs and organizations all over the city—Campfire Girls, Girl Scout Councils, Jr. League, AAUW, music and drama departments of the University, the Seattle Public Schools, the teachers and principals, and the PTA of the Seattle Public Schools." The Annual Meeting concluded with a presentation of a Joop the Giraffe pin set with brilliants by the board to Mrs. Meisnest. "Thus the adult 'Joops' march on, carrying the banner of better entertainment for children, and the junior 'Joops' . . . stretch their necks to see what's around the corner for next year's amusements . . . I feel the grownup 'Joopers' like these Junior Programs productions just as much as do the children. For we grownups never quite outgrow our love for fairy tales." The Seattle *Post Intelligencer* (Apr 24, 1940) also ran an article about the meeting. "It was with that shaky laugh of adventurers whose efforts have been finally successful that members of the board . . . reviewed their first year. They laughed when they thought of their first tentative budget of $500—actually they spent $2,665.27 for 5 productions and have $717 to start the new year. And the new year will bring . . . the opera *Jack and the Beanstalk*, a ballet, *The Princess and the Swineherd*, a play, *Run, Peddler, Run* . . . [and] Junior Programs will be expanded the coming year to serve ten Washington cities instead of the four of its first year, and still more Oregon towns will have the program."337

Engagement of local sponsoring groups took many forms. There was, of course, the local financing of the programs. The Syracuse, New York, *Journal* (Mar 24, 1938) describes various clubs donating blocks of seats for underprivileged children for *The Bumble Bee Prince*, with tickets distributed to the school principals. From Winston-Salem, North Carolina, (Feb 19, 1939), we hear that the Junior League gave away 600 to 1,000 tickets, with blocks of tickets going to each city school. They also provided transportation for the young audience members, with two Junior Leaguers on each bus. Ticket prices were kept very low, with no profits, so that as many children as possible might attend. In Roanoke, Virginia (*Times*, Feb 19, 1939), the Junior League provided tickets for *The Bumble Bee Prince* for the children of the Baptist, Lutheran, and Catholic orphanages as well as musical instruction and storytelling. According to the Los Angeles *Examiner* (Mar 17, 1940), other sponsoring groups such as the Panharmonics, the junior group of the Women's Committee for the Los Angeles Philharmonic Orchestra, were busy getting ready for *The Bumble Bee Prince* at the Pantages Theater by making stuffed giraffes at the home of their chairman, Bernadine Culver.[338]

In Hibbing, Minnesota, bringing *The Bumble Bee Prince* to town was clearly a collaborative effort. The school's music groups and classroom teachers worked to establish the background and appreciative understanding of the opera. Local children would entertain the audience between acts with appropriate folk dancing; children could "earn" their tickets through a crayoning contest with the cooperation of the Hibbing *Tribune*. There was an Auditorium Committee, and the Finance Committee recruited patrons and patronesses willing to pay for seats in a "reserved section" of the auditorium to underwrite ten-cent prices for children's tickets. There was a team of hostesses for each aisle to help with the taking off and putting on of coats and to answer questions, and ushers would seat deaf and crippled children and students of the sight-saving class.[339] Everyone worked to make the performance an "unforgettable entertainment in the lives of Hibbing children" (*Tribune*, Apr 19, 1940). The East St. Louis, Illinois *Journal* (Mar 23, 1938) in "Pupils Save for Children's Play" describes a voluntary "Savings System" formed by one hundred and fifty pupils: "Entirely voluntary, and at the request of the pupils themselves the spare penny and nickel savings have been given by the pupils to the room teachers to ensure the price of tickets to all three shows, the first two of which were 'Pinocchio' and 'The Reward of the Sun God.'"

In Lake Forest, Illinois (May 9, 1940), the head of the speech department of Lake Forest Public Schools, Miss Madeline Bowers, announced plans for Junior Programs to present a play, an opera, and a ballet during the next school year: *Robin Hood, Run, Peddler, Run*, and *Jack and the Beanstalk*. On June 7, 1940, the Duluth, Minnesota, *Herald* reported that, "Representatives of Junior Programs, Inc. a non-commercial non-profit organization promoting plays, ballets, concerts and operas for children were in Duluth yesterday to discuss with civic leaders the possibility of bringing such productions to Duluth . . . Field reps explained the aims of the organization .

. . [and b]eginning this fall, operas, plays and ballets will be presented to more than a million children in 40 states." Burlington, Iowa (unknown source, Oct 1940) saw an Adult Membership Campaign, letting everyone know that the best way to bring Junior Programs to Burlington was for all the organizations to work together, to step up and become a member. By selling four adult memberships, one could earn a free membership. By November 8, the campaign had been an unqualified success, with the North Hill School reporting 100% membership; and many of the women's clubs were purchasing Junior Programs tickets for underprivileged children.

In Indianapolis, the *Independent Times* (March 15, 1940) describes local mothers planning several theater parties prior to the arrival of *The Bumble Bee Prince*. In St. Petersburg, Florida (May 28, 1940), the Children's Theater Bureau committed to a season of *The Princess and the Swineherd*, a ballet with narrative; *The Bumble Bee Prince*, with a narrator between acts; and *Run Peddler Run*, a historical play set in the New England of 1730. In Jacksonville, Florida, Miss Alberta Brenner spoke to members of four business clubs, business and professional women's clubs, the Pilot Club, University Women of America, and home economics teachers, all of whom voted to underwrite Junior Programs coming to the city (March 14, 1940).

Getting the word out was key. The Greensboro, North Carolina, *News* (Feb 15, 1939) informed readers that, "If the children of Greensboro . . . don't know about the opera . . . it won't be because the Junior League hasn't made a big effort to tell all. Members of the League are making speeches almost daily before the schools and parent-teacher associations so that no Greensboro boy or girl will miss knowing that the fairy opera with music by one of the world's great composers is among the most beautiful and most entertaining music dramas that could be offered." In Albany, Oregon, reservations for a Junior Programs production could be made at Dawson's Drug Store without charge (*Democrat*, March 14, 1940). In Charlottesville, Virginia, a booth at Jarman's Book Store was set up for ticket purchases. In Peru, Illinois, a musicians' group launched a Junior Programs project, gaining the support of other area organizations, including groups in nearby Tonica, Spring Valley, Mendota, and Granville, with eight committees including the school chairman, the PTA, and teachers (*News Herald*, March 19, 1940). In Charlotte, North Carolina, the *Observer* lists the music department of the University of North Carolina and the Artists' Bureau of the State Federation of Music Clubs as active participants in local Junior

Programs activities (Dec 1939). In Worcester, Massachusetts, the Kindergarten Club sponsored a performance of *The Bumble Bee Prince*, with the proceeds to be used to send delegates to the forty-fifth annual convention of the Association for Childhood Education (*Post*, Feb 10, 1938).

Other cities and towns saw similar levels of local involvement: In Seattle, the Boy Scouts served as ushers (*Times*, Nov 22, 1939). Stagehands were recruited from area high schools, the ROTC helped at the doors, and the Girl's Civic League also provided ushers, while the school band played martial airs. New Castle, Pennsylvania, was home to another coloring contest for *The Bumble Bee Prince*, with the winner receiving two tickets to the opera (*News*, Feb 22, 1939). There was another *Robin Hood* coloring contest, with an autographed photo of Robin Hood (presumably Edwin Strawbridge) as the prize. One account noted, "Between the second and third acts, winners in a poster contest conducted among students in the schools were announced." For another production of *Robin Hood*, students were asked to make posters illustrating incidents in the story, and winners were announced between the second and third acts of the performance (unknown source, n.d.).

The State, South Carolina's progressive newspaper, reported on a Robin Hood archery contest: twenty-four arrows each at twenty, thirty, and forty yards, with the grand prize a silver loving cup from Hamilton Jewelers, and first prize an archery set (Dec 10, 1940).

The Hibbing, Minnesota, *Tribune* announced another feature that characterized many Junior Programs productions: local children would entertain the audience between acts with folk dancing (April 19, 1940). The involvement of local talent as an appealing extra was incorporated whenever Junior Programs felt that local performers would be of sufficient quality to complement rather than detract from the professionalism of a Junior Programs production. The Manitowoc, Wisconsin, *Herald Times* (n.d.) acknowledged the increase in local interest when local school children had the opportunity to perform with the Junior Programs professional singers as a background chorus for a performance of *The Bumble Bee Prince*. In Chapter III's discussion on *The Bumble Bee Prince*, the flyer "A Suggestion to Local Choruses" is described, as well as Junior Programs' practice of recruiting local narrators. Both were effective ways Junior Programs used to build and strengthen their relationships with local communities.

The Junior Programs Local Sponsoring Committees' Organization and Promotion Booklet

The *Junior Programs Committees' Organization and Promotion Booklet*, compiled from the lived experience of many of the initial Junior Programs Sponsoring Committees, provides a fascinating window into the kind of pragmatic, highly participatory, highly disciplined organization that enabled Sponsoring Committees to prepare successfully for the arrival of the Junior Programs productions. This set of guidelines, written by McFadden and distributed to every city and town to which the Junior Programs companies toured, gives both a detailed picture of how the model worked on the ground, and of how much it depended on broad-based, sustained, and active local community engagement. The Booklet itself is something of a masterpiece of organizational advice, and its level of specificity leaves no element needed for the overall success of a production unaddressed.

McFadden knew how important it was to tap into local organizational resources like the Junior League. She also had an innate sense for the kind of organizational infrastructure needed, and the kind of guidance and support that would have to be provided to a far-flung, highly decentralized set of local committees and activities. Not only is the Booklet an extraordinary piece of practical guidance, but in little more than sixteen pages it offers a "You Are There" picture of "A Day in the Life of a Local Sponsoring Committee," as well as a list of the many ingredients for successful community engagement. It was, in effect, Junior Programs' "secret sauce."

McFadden's introduction to the Booklet immediately sets a collaborative tone. Underscoring the importance of the effort, she positions the work of the local Junior Programs Sponsoring Committees as in the same league as the large, socially prominent membership drives for adult theater and concert events. She gives special credit to the substantive input from reports submitted by the Sponsoring Committees of Hartford, Connecticut; Binghamton, New York; Fairmont, West Virginia; Saginaw, Michigan; Utica, New York; Parkersburg, West Virginia; and West Orange, New Jersey. With her experienced understanding of those reading the booklet, she adds:

> We hope it will not frighten you! Not <u>all</u> these ideas were incorporated in <u>every</u> committee's plan. We know that each community presents its own problems, and that the number of children involved,

VI. THE ORGANIZATIONAL INNOVATIONS

financial status of the population, and many other factors call for various adjustments . . . But we have found that some committees seemed to function more smoothly than others, and many learned through experience lessons which were at times costly in money or good feelings. So here we have gathered some data which we hope will give you ideas and be of service to you. May we suggest that the committee read this booklet together, then discuss each section and decide what is applicable to its own community (1).

The Booklet includes a foreword, an overview of committee personnel, discussion of the *critical need to secure school cooperation*, and detailed coverage of a committee's responsibilities regarding budgeting, choosing programs, selling tickets, publicity and promotion, securing space, transportation, entertainment of the artists, and reporting. Highlights from each of these sections follow, and all quotes are from the Booklet.

Committee Personnel: Junior Programs productions are presented for the children of the entire community, and therefore, the committee itself should represent community cooperation for the welfare of all its children. "It is only by having at least two or three of the strongest organizations in town working together that the widespread publicity and goodwill which are so necessary, may be obtained" (2). McFadden identifies several possible groups—the Junior League, the American Association of University Women, the Child Study Group, the Children's Library, various civic and women's clubs, recreational departments, and PTA groups from public, private, and parochial schools. But McFadden is not naïve; she cautions committees not to "be scared by that bugaboo . . . but our groups won't work together . . . A little tact, and a fair division of labor and glory, will go a long way. Even if one group ends up by doing most of the work, the goodwill gained by having others help . . . make it all worthwhile" (2).

She goes on to caution them not to let a committee chair "do it all." They will wear out, and "then no one else will ever take over . . . because it looks too hard!" (2). Good executives get others to do much of the work. The committees that endure, year after year, "are those where many members are doing jobs they enjoy under leadership which keeps up enthusiasm" (2). She proposes that, in addition to the usual officers of chair, vice chair, treasurer, and secretary, committees include an auditorium chair, a transportation chair, a ticket chair, and a publicity chair. Further, and of critical import, "Every committee should have a school official as a special contact officer to interest and assist the schools in cooperating on the project"(2). The meaningful involvement of the schools was as important to Junior Programs as its theatrical, operatic, and dance productions. "*No matter what other group is left out of the committee, the school system should always be represented* [emphasis added]. The officials—superintendent and supervisors—will be of invaluable assistance if approached before programs are chosen" (3).

Show them, she says—photographs, circulars, and the Junior Programs service sheet—"Educators: Are You Using Junior Programs to Enrich Your Curriculum?" The service sheet contained enthusiastic encomiums from a range of school officials, and for twenty-five cents, a committee could obtain a copy of the Binghamton, New York report from Mrs. Stanley M. Metzger, 16 Edgewood Road, Binghamton, NY.

Tell them, McFadden continues, of the many prominent educators, such as Dr. Ina Craig Sartorius of New York's Horace Mann School, who support Junior Programs by lending their name because they believe in the work Junior Programs is doing.

Offer to send speakers to principals' meetings, teachers' meetings, and classrooms to explain the value of Junior Programs productions. If a committee has no qualified speakers, Junior Programs will help find some.

Emphasize the *active involvement of the children themselves* [emphasis added] both before and after the performances, and that audience participation is part of many of Junior Programs' productions. The materials provided by Junior Programs' Education Committee include examples of how one child can tell the story of the play to another, how older children can plan some form of presentation to younger children, or even how one class wrote a play about the fun of going to a Junior Programs' production and presented it at school assembly.

The Booklet suggests additional tips, titled MOST IMPORTANT OF ALL: Early in the spring, allow the schools to choose the programs that are most congruent with their curricula. Once they have done so, provide them with the appropriate Junior Programs educational materials, which include books, records, and a broad range of resources so that they can incorporate the very modest costs in their next year's budget. Another tip suggested that teachers should not be asked to sell tickets for the performances. Instead, teachers should concentrate on using the educational materials to engage the children in the excitement of learning about the key components of the play: the story, the history, the music, the cultures of other countries, the art of theater (e.g., costumes, sets, lighting, etc.), and the dances. Ask the principal to designate a time and a place where someone from the Junior Programs Committee can set up to sell tickets to the children. Finally, after the performance, "have a meeting or send a questionnaire (not too long or too often) or assist in showing an exhibit of the children's projects related to the show and get pupils' and teachers' comments on the program" (3). And a final tip: to ensure smoother functioning, make sure to select next year's committee before the end of the season. Ideally, part of the current committee will remain, new people and energy will be added, and the new chair will be someone from the current committee.

Program Choice: Variety, balance, and introduction to new experiences is a good rule of thumb when choosing programs. Like adults, children have different tastes and interests, and it is wise to check with other organizations to find out what they may have planned, and the dates of their entertainments. The Booklet also encourages a possible partnership with local amateur groups who may wish to present a short piece on the same program "if the production standards are kept high" (4). The committee should not shy away from the notion that so-called "highbrow" events, such as operas and ballets, can have great appeal to children. McFadden adds that to ensure a large audience, committees would do well to make sure that choices will appeal to boys, and that the committees are clear as to the age group they wish to attract. She also makes it clear that the final decision should be made by the group, not an individual (4).

Budgeting: The section on budgeting offers a simple formula: Multiply the number of seats by the price of a ticket to derive estimated income. Subtract estimated expenses from the estimated income from ticket sales. The resulting number is the amount a committee can spend on fees to the artists. If there are multiple ticket prices, the Booklet advises to either calculate an average or, to be safe, use the lowest ticket price. Many committees also use an array of higher-priced tickets (patron tickets, adult tickets, higher-priced tickets at the door, charity contributions from Kiwanis, Lions, and Rotary Clubs, and reserved seating sections) to cover the cost of empty seats and lower priced or free tickets for underprivileged children. The Booklet notes with some pride, "There are no empty seats in the best-run Junior Programs series! It all depends on the promotion campaign" (5).

Expenses to be covered were auditorium rental (usually, the cost of a janitor and heating when at a school), printing, union stagehands, postage, and stationary. McFadden notes that printing costs should cover fliers, tickets, car stickers (announcements pasted onto the rear car window similar to election campaign stickers) and printing local data on posters supplied by Junior Programs. Tips on minimizing costs detail the use of low-cost yellow copy paper for flyers, printed in school print shops or mimeographed, with local data printed by hand on posters, either by the committee or in student art classes. To minimize the cost of actual tickets, the Booklet suggests tickets be printed such that one ticket serves as admission to multiple events, much like a ten-ride train ticket gets punched for each ride, and even the cost of the actual ticket could be defrayed by running an advertisement on the reverse side.

Most committees found that a good publicity and promotion campaign eliminated the need for newspaper advertising; requirements for police and firemen were usually supplied at no cost; and most committees considered printed programs a needless expense. Ticket pricing suggestions covered single and series tickets, with prices ranging from ten to twenty or fifty cents for a single ticket, or season tickets of six shows for seventy-five cents, or three shows for one dollar. No detail was overlooked; ushers, chaperones, and press should be given free tickets.

Ticket Selling: Most effective are short, concentrated campaigns in which each school is allotted a specific number of tickets in proportion to its number of students. After a few days, unsold tickets may be reallocated to other schools, although the announcement that tickets will be reallocated often resulted in their speedy sale. Here, the Junior Programs *Credo* of making theater available to all children regardless of race, creed, or economic circumstances is actualized on the ground.[340] Students who can afford more than the price of the ticket are encouraged to bring extra money, with all the money going into a general fund "so that nobody knows who paid more and who paid less" (6). Some schools went so far as to set a price per room such that, unless everyone could go, no one could go. Free tickets were to be carefully distributed to those most in need, and guidance was provided by principals, social workers, and unemployment relief officers.

VI. THE ORGANIZATIONAL INNOVATIONS

An interesting psychological component was included in the campaigns. Based on experience in several cities in which many children had to be turned away because tickets had sold out quickly, the campaigns were advised to *always* let people know that in many other cities, "hundreds of children were turned away because they had waited too long to purchase their tickets." Even in towns where attendance at children's plays had been poor, when the committee *expected* Junior Programs tickets to sell and then *worked* to make that happen, ticket sales broke all previous records. In one city "neither the schools nor newspapers would cooperate . . . but 1100 tickets were sold by the committee by telephone! It can be done! There is something wrong if every ticket is not sold—so follow all the suggestions in this Booklet, and if tickets still don't sell, wire an S.O.S. for help to Junior Programs!" (7).

Promotion and Publicity: According to the Booklet, the committee's work was the key to ticket-selling success. "Unless the adults of the community are aware of the whole purpose and high standards of the project . . . the project may die at any time" (7). The Booklet cautions the committee not to be lulled by an initial success, because "as the novelty wears off . . . [and] Mother is too busy to . . . furnish transportation, or Dad wonders why on earth Johnny should go to a ballet . . . then attendance suddenly drops off . . . For real support and a project that will go on from year to year, a big community drive for the purposes of education as well as ticket selling [is needed], until every organization, postman, music lover, etc. in the community knows the broader, deeper what and why of the Junior Programs productions, as well as its artists, and the fact that it is part of a worldwide movement for children's theater. Laying this foundation will actually make future publicity campaigns go more smoothly" (7).

a. Specific activities suggested included the following:
    1. *Educate* every member of the committees so that they know everything about the programs, the artists, and the Junior Programs organization.
    2. *Plan* the publicity campaign well in advance (spring for the following year). Invite a press representative to a planning meeting to understand their needs as to timing and types of photos needed. Ask the local news to run at least one story in the spring with production details, a sure way to ensure that other community events will not conflict with the dates you have chosen, as "sometimes, only the early bird gets the worm" (8).

3. *Schedule* a panel discussion to which the whole community is invited. Include representatives from a range of clubs, educational institutions, and movie theater managers, on a subject such as "What Do We Get for our Amusement Money?" This will "awaken the whole community to the possibilities of more valuable entertainment for adults as well as children . . . A concrete plan, materials, and leader for such panels can be obtained from Junior Programs" (7).

4. *Engage* the education departments of Women's Clubs, Child Study Groups, and PTAs in discussing the problem of raising entertainment standards: e.g., parents' responsibilities in regard to taste; the Children's Theatre Movement at home and abroad; and how they spend family amusement money, etc.

5. *Ensure* that every story and event highlights the fact that "Junior Programs companies are <u>professional adults</u> of wide experience [and] . . . The rareness of professional stage presentations in any town in America today . . . makes such a presentation a big event and it should be played up as such" (8). In other words, Junior Programs is not just a series of amateur theatricals, films, and marionette shows. This "best practice" advice goes on to say that the focus on the professionalism of the company, rather than on the committee and its members, is what distinguishes the Junior Programs organizing committees from the typical benefit bridge party committees.

6. *Make* personal contacts with even the small organizations (e.g., private, and parochial schools), as well as key individuals and make sure they have "<u>one</u> mimeographed release describing your project" (8).

7. *Cooperate* with the other committees so a trip to a given school, for example, can serve multiple purposes.

The guidance goes on to detail the various methods of getting the word out about Junior Programs productions:

a. *Mimeographed sheets*: The schools will usually be willing to use their equipment, and often supply the labor, to copy the teaching materials supplied by Junior Programs, as well as copy letters to parents, etc.

b. *Fliers*: Colored paper, decorated with pictures (such as the silhouette of "audience heads" that is Junior Programs' trademark) should be sent home with every child and/or posted in every classroom. Flyers should include the name of the production, the place, short descriptions, where and when tickets can be purchased, as well as the names of sponsors and phone numbers of the ticket-selling committee members.

c. *Car stickers:* Make them brief and striking—"Junior Programs are coming to town!" (9).

d. *Bulletin boards:* Post flyers, posters, and photographs on as many bulletin boards as possible—in schools, parks, clubs, etc., and encourage high schools to contribute hand-painted posters.

e. *Newspapers:* Traditionally, the work of the Junior League and other social organizations were covered on the society page, or a page devoted to "organizational announcements." Junior Programs' goal was to get stories of upcoming productions on the front page, in news columns, or even in an editorial. A number of local organizing committees achieved this in multiple ways. They have highlighted the social and educational purpose of the productions as a community-wide project that included all children, not just a wealthy few, and have made tickets available for orphanages and children from poor families. They have provided articles written by local celebrities and educators; and built relationships with reporters, ensuring a steady stream of timely press materials and photos, complete with accurate information on dates and names. And they have underscored the many organizations in the community actively supporting the productions.

The Booklet encouraged the engagement of the editor of the children's page, if there was one, offering *The Crayoning Contest* as a special attraction that would increase circulation.

Junior Programs furnished special line drawings suitable for coloring for each of their productions, complete with instructions for where to submit them, what the prizes were, and the story of the play. The Booklet suggested multiple options, including handing the drawings in at schools, having the four best drawings displayed at the school. Then the drawings from all the schools could be brought together for the final selection of winners. The Booklet further noted that the best time to award the prize was at the performance, with the caveat that the winning artists had to be at the performance to win. Newspapers were often willing to sponsor additional contests, such as having children "draw" the story of the performance or for the best letter written after seeing the show—all with an eye to having the paper write a story about the contests.

Several examples of the contest drawings, one by well-known American illustrator Carroll Colby, were available in the Junior Programs Scrapbooks and in Lancourt's personal papers.

**Junior Programs Coloring Contest for *The Bumble Bee Prince*
Illustration by Carroll B. Colby**
(Lancourt's personal papers)

Each drawing was presented in a fairy-tale style, as an eye-catching depiction of a scene from the production, along with an accompanying press release announcing the contest winner. Linked to information about the contest and the actual production, the press release included the following:

> Wielding an imaginative set of crayons, young _____,
> the prize-winner, achieved an unusually fine effect in color with the
> winning drawing. The Carroll Colby outline [for *The Bumble Bee*

VI. THE ORGANIZATIONAL INNOVATIONS

Prince] is that of a merry company costumed in the stylized fashion of peoples who live in the Baltic Sea region against a background of traditional onion-shaped church domes. Calling for bold color not only brings out the gaiety of the scene but the mode of costumes and background the Colby outline inspired in the prize-winner artistic treatment considered altogether appropriate to the theme by the judges. With a dominant background of _____ (color), the winning colored drawing featured a profusion of _____ (list various colors used) and will receive as prize-winner an autographed photograph of Cecile Sherman, prima donna of the opera in her Magic Swan Princess costume. Presentation of the prize will be made at _____ by _____.[341]

The media strategy also included provision of a broad range of photographs supplied by Junior Programs, as well as local photos such as children buying tickets or reading a performance poster, a committee member reading the story of the play to her children, or children meeting one of the performers after the show. Junior Programs advised committees to submit their pictures to the media early, as rotogravure sections were usually planned well in advance.[342] The Booklet also suggested that, if special materials for such sections were needed, newspapers could let Junior Programs know and they would make sure to provide them early for the following year's production. The local stage manager was also prepared to cue local news photographers when to take the best pictures of the children watching the performance, typically at the climax of a scene as the curtain closed. School newspapers were especially encouraged to have their reporters cover the various events and write up interviews with various artists. An early contest in the Huntington, West Virginia, *Advertiser* (Dec 14, 1936) turned out to be such a successful way to engage young audiences prior to the arrival of the Junior Programs production that similar contests became a regular feature in almost all Junior Programs productions.

**Junior Programs Coloring Contest for *Robin Hood*
Illustration by Sheilah Beckett**
(Lancourt's personal papers)

f. *Store displays:* The Booklet noted that all kinds of stores were opportunities for performance-related exhibits of various kinds, as merchants loved anything that would cause people to stop and look at their windows or, even better, step inside. The Booklet advised committees to approach storeowners well in advance so that the window-dressers would have plenty of time to set up the displays. For bookstores, there were editions of *Pinocchio,* books on dance, books on Native Americans (e.g., John Louw Nelson's *Rhythm for Rain*), Russian fairy tales (Rimsky-Korsakov's *The Bumble Bee Prince*), and Grimms' fairy tales (*Hansel and Gretel*). Toy stores could display marionettes, dolls dressed in various costumes, and children's books. Clothing stores could exhibit figures wearing dirndls (*Hansel and Gretel*) or Russian costumes (*The Bumble Bee Prince*), while a Fairy with Blue Hair (*Pinocchio*) figure would attract attention. Gingerbread houses and cookies could be sold in candy stores and bakeries, as well as chocolate gold pieces illustrating the "dance of gold pieces" in the *Pinocchio* ballet. A department store in Little Rock, Arkansas, had a candy house on display to alert passersby of the upcoming performance of *Hansel and Gretel* at the East Side Junior High auditorium (*Gazette*, Nov 7, 1937). A poster of Dr. Owl giving Pinocchio his medicine might appear prominently in a drugstore window. Music stores could sell related records and sheet music, while art supply stores could display the winners of the various local poster contests. Department stores might feature collections of Russian or Native American art objects, gathered from local residents, as well as puppets made by local crafts groups or schools. And of course, all stores should be encouraged to put up posters.

g. *Other displays:* The Booklet left no stone unturned. Local museums and libraries were encouraged to use the production theme, composer, author, and history related to the story to create exhibits, drawing on their collections of art and books. Children's story hour at the local library was another opportunity to promote a soon-to-arrive production, and, for example, libraries could exhibit old and new editions of *Hansel and Gretel.*

h. *Special interest groups*: Organizations such as the Camp Fire Girls and Scout troops could be reminded that *The Reward of the Sun God* would be of particular interest to their members. Music teachers, musical societies, and musicians should not miss the opportunity to use the coming productions to explore Russian, German, Brazilian, and American music. Dance studios and teachers would want to study the ballet *Pinocchio* or *A Midsummer's Night's Dream*; German societies would delve into *Hansel and Gretel*; art classes would study the scenic and costume designs and perhaps even build mini-sets. Crafts groups would be fascinated by the masks in *Pinocchio* and try their hand at mask-making.

i. *Speaking campaigns:* For each major production, whenever it was logistically and financially possible, Junior Programs supplied a speaker for a full day. Their field staff and director were well aware of the impact an "outside person" could make on a local campaign. Almost nothing did more to sell tickets. In return, the committee was responsible for planning a well-organized series of short talks at various school assemblies, a radio interview or two, and a speech at a lunch, tea, or dinner. Local speakers were also important, and the committee needs to make sure that it could field a number of committee members or local celebrities. All these activities should be done with maximum efficiency, so as not to waste precious time.

j. *Social affairs:* The backbone of the best community outreach are the lunches, teas, dinners, and banquets sponsored by various members of the committee. Find as many reasons as possible to have them, suggests the Booklet, and make them engaging in every way possible, including having a compelling speaker, either external or local, and make sure that the events are covered in the local news outlets.

k. *Radio stations and movie theaters:* Engaging local radio stations was yet another opportunity to get the word out. Press releases provided by Junior Programs made useful announcements, and story scripts, parts of which could be read on a local children's hour or rented for a nominal amount from Junior Programs. The Booklet also offered a cautionary caveat: make sure the program is well-rehearsed and be sure to notify schools and other organizations of the broadcast. Other resources included national broadcasts such as the Metropolitan Opera's presentation of *Hansel and Gretel*. There was also a ten-question quiz for *Doodle Dandy* that could be either a radio promotion or a news release. The quiz included questions such as "What are the four freedoms? What was the popular song of the American Revolution? What did Mercury and Doodle Dandy have in common? How high up is a rain cloud?"[343] Movie theaters also offered the possibility of using a trailer a week before to announce the coming production.

l. *Other promotional ideas:* If a parade on any topic is occurring, decorate a float. "One town was having 'A Safety Parade' so the committee very cleverly decorated a float labelled 'Safe and Sane Entertainment for Children'" (12). Another town sponsored a bicycle-decorating contest using the theme of the

VI. THE ORGANIZATIONAL INNOVATIONS

upcoming production, with even the mayor and Chamber of Commerce participating. A promotion was part of an agreement with the New York City Board of Education to perform in a select number of the city's schools. For that project, Junior Programs developed a "Doodle Dandy" Contest designed to engage students in writing additional verses to the play's theme song. The new verses were required to have the same rhythm as the original songs and had to be focused on the theme of democracy and the Four Freedoms, with prizes ranging from a "Doodle Dandy" badge given to all contestants to a twenty-five-dollar war bond for the winner.[344]

The Booklet then shifts its focus to the auditorium, addressing issues of seat allotment, the stage, the artists, when the doors should open, ticket taking, windows, ventilation, ushers and hostesses, coats and wraps, candy, toilet and drink rules, intermissions, audience participation, announcements, dismissal, and closing. The level of specific detail is instructive—and astonishing!

Auditorium:

a. *Seat Allotment:* The younger children should be seated toward the front with adults in the back or at the ends of the aisles so that children do not have a problem seeing around them. "Seats for crippled children, sight saving classes and deaf children should be near a special side door . . . Some committees sell seats to the schools in blocks, then make seating plans and rotate the schools in different sections . . . for each performance. Once the charts have been made out, the auditorium chairman should meet with the school chaperones just before the performance to discuss behavior and seating problems; to acquaint chaperones with seating and assign definite entrances and exits for each school" (12).

b. *Stage:* The Junior Programs contract specifies in detail what is needed, and the auditorium committee is responsible for making sure that all items are available. For instance, the piano has been tuned and placed where it should be; there is proper lighting available over the piano and wherever something is to be read; and the projector, operator, and screen are where they should be. The contract goes on to specify that "BOY ASSISTANTS OR UNION STAGE HANDS SHOULD BE READY AT THE EXACT HOUR requested by Junior Programs, and if they fail to show up, it is important that the committee find substitutes. (The stage manager needs every minute of his two or three hours for setting up and should not have to scour a strange town for assistants—but this has happened!)" (12).

c. *Artists:* Someone needs to be in the auditorium to meet the artists when they arrive and make sure adequate accommodations are ready. "Artists <u>can</u> get along someway, and even be pleasant and efficient without mirrors, clean dressing rooms, clean toilet facilities, hooks and dress hangers, heated dressing rooms, tables and chairs for make-up and strong bulbs in the light fixtures—but oh—the joy and relief when these are supplied. Travelling two hundred miles a day and giving performances every day is exceedingly hard work, and every kindness is appreciated. Sometimes accidents on the road delay cars and trucks and the company has not eaten when it arrives. They will rarely speak of this, but blessed be the chairman who asks and brings in coffee and sandwiches while the cast is rushing into costume!" (13).

d. *Opening Doors:* Although some audience members arrive up to two hours before the curtain rises, the doors should not be open more than thirty minutes prior to when the performance begins. "Children amuse themselves better out of doors during such a long wait . . . If there is no large entrance hall" and the weather is bad, they may need to be admitted earlier. "But be sure to notify the stage manager . . . so that the front curtain may be closed, and none of the illusion spoiled. Someone playing the piano for songs while the children wait, helps pass the time" (13).

e. *Ticket Taking:* The Booklet included the usual detailed instructions: if there are multiple doors, have ticket takers at each door; if tickets are also being sold at the door, have that happen at a separate table; punching multiple use tickets is most efficient, or if children are wearing tags, they just pass through. The Booklet also suggested someone from the committee stand at a "strategic point" with a click counting device to "avoid letting in more than can be seated" because most "committees have obviated the need for actual printed door admission tickets." Also critical to keeping the lines moving are boxes for each kind of ticket to be sold and "plenty of small change on hand" (13).

f. *Auditorium Windows:* Windows had to be darkened. If there were no shades, blankets should be used.

VI. THE ORGANIZATIONAL INNOVATIONS 283

g. *Ventilation:* This needed to be addressed before the date of the performance, including whether windows and doors should be open to achieve adequate ventilation. This needed to be done before the performance so no light would seep into the auditorium during the performance.

h. *Ushers and Hostesses:* The advice offered in this section provided an intimate glimpse into Junior Programs' core values. The Booklet suggests one usher or hostess for every thirty children, the critical importance of the role, and the need for careful planning. Boy Scouts could be ushers, and there was a need to know where bathrooms and drinking fountains were located. Children should not lean over the front rail of the balcony, and other necessary rules needed to be enforced. It went on to say, "There is real danger in trying to enforce a military discipline, constantly pushing children down and shushing them. Scolding talks from the platform will not help either. Find a principal or teacher whom the children love and obey and ask for his or her help and suggestions. The training of well-behaved audiences has been considered important in many school systems, and the results show. But they were not accomplished by dictatorial methods" (14).

i. *Children's Wraps:* Many children are so excited about attending the performance that they often forget to take off their coats. Therefore, they should be instructed to take them off when they arrive (put mittens and caps in their pockets) and not put them on again until the performance is over. "Often the last minutes are the most beautiful of all to watch" and it is important not to disturb others before the curtain closes (14). Finally, don't forget to make an announcement as to the location of a lost and found.

j. *Candy*: There is no way to avoid this nuisance, but one means of solving this problem is to have the ushers walk row by row with a big open box into which the children can throw their candy wrappers and papers. "They make a game of tossing it from their seats to see if they can make a basket . . . paper bags are wadded up and thrown in, instead of being blown up and popped!" (14).

k. *Toilet and Drink Rules:* Here, the Booklet suggests that the subject should be discussed in the classroom before the date of the performance, emphasizing how unwieldy it would be to have thousands of children all needing to go at the same time. One solution was to make sure you "did it at home or in school before going to the show, and then wait[ing] until [you] got home" (14). Another approach was a rule of one trip per child.

l. *Audience Participation:* Here, again, Junior Programs values infuse the advice that children are permitted to talk back to the performers, whistle, etc. "Such audience activity is an excellent response, and the artists may be depended upon to keep it under control. What if the children do shout back something at the top of their lungs, when questioned? This hurts no one, and their curiosity will soon quiet them again and they will quiet each other, to know what happens next" (14).

m. *Intermissions:* The Booklet offers multiple ways to manage thousands of children during intermissions, the caveat being that whatever is done should be in keeping with the "atmosphere and spirit of the occasion" (15). Tap dancing or singing popular swing music, however, were deemed inappropriate between acts of Humperdinck's beautiful *Hansel and Gretel* music. More detailed ideas were included in the publicity material sent for each production, but possibilities included the high school band or orchestra performing a short piece in front of the curtain, or some "game songs where arms are used, and children clap or gesture . . . [or] calisthenics to music" (14).

n. *Announcements from the Platform:* The fewer and shorter the better was sage advice. "Children have no patience with official after official introducing each other . . . [it helps to] have the same person make the announcements informally, in a loud clear happy voice and they should be memorized not read" (15).

o. *Dismissal:* Adopting a row-by-row approach, often used at school assemblies, is one good way to empty a large auditorium in an orderly fashion, and planning some way to enable children with autograph books to go backstage is also important. Junior Program artists enjoy engagement with their youthful audiences, but it is important to make sure that the children are not "allowed to run about the stage, hindering the work of stagehands and perhaps damaging expensive properties and scenery" (15).

p. *Closing Time:* Communicating when the performance will be over is critical so that parents and caretakers know when to come and collect their charges. Here, the Booklet includes an interesting bit of advice: if adults arrive before the final curtain, "invite them to step into the back of the auditorium and see what the end of a performance is like . . . Often new committee workers or even patrons will be discovered in this way" (15). And finally, at least one committee member needs to remain at the auditorium until every child has been picked up. "It may seem strange, but some adults forget to call for children entirely, or wander in a half an hour late" (15).

Transportation: A range of options will be needed, especially for performances in large auditoriums. If a performance takes place in a school auditorium, it is often possible to use regular school buses. Sometime, public buses, trolleys, or subways may offer a special low rate. In places not served by public transport, it may be necessary to arrange for numbers of parents to drive groups of children to and from the theater. The Transportation Committee may also need to furnish appropriate transportation to ensure that "orphanages or groups of crippled children" (15) are able to attend, as well as arrange for the police or school patrol to manage the arrival and departure traffic.

Entertainment of the Artists: A post-show tea or supper is a wonderful way to both honor the artists and garner additional publicity from local newspapers. If time is short after a performance because the artists must leave for their next engagement, a small reception in the auditorium could be planned. The Booklet also reminds the various committees that events before the performance are not a good idea since artists seldom want to eat, drink, or talk before a show. However, "if sufficient notice is given, speeches or song recitals, etc. for an adult audience may be arranged for the same evening, at a very reasonable rate . . . [and] Suggestions about reasonable, comfortable hotels are always appreciated" (15).

Reports of the Year's Projects: Project reports are a helpful resource for next year's committees and should include an extensive array of detailed information. The booklet went on to detail what should be included, and how important it was in terms of capturing what the group had learned and applying it to the upcoming year's work.[345]

The Booklet concludes with the following words: "We hope that the length and detail of this booklet will not make you feel that a Junior Program campaign is heavy work" (16). No committee uses all the ideas included, "but a careful selection of those that seem most suitable to your situation" will ensure more efficiency and success. A final plea: "We trust you will let us know what has proved most valuable to you. Do send in any additions or changes that you would like to see made in future editions" of this Booklet (16).

The Production Process

Junior Programs at Work, an overview of the production process, described an eleven-step process the three companies followed for launching each production.[346] It began with the search for appropriate material, laid out the key production steps, and then went on to describe bookings, the scheduling of tours, and the distribution of the CCSUs. Much less detailed than the *Sponsoring Committees' Organization and Promotion Booklet,* it nevertheless provides a window into the process that enabled Junior Programs to consistently tour twelve successful high-quality productions. Each step had its challenges, but in the spirit of *Wei Ji* and guided by their *Credo,* they were able to turn most of them into opportunities, in part due to the collaborative culture they were able to develop.[347]

Step 1: Finding Appropriate Material

As discussed earlier, the dearth of suitable material for children's cultural development had become evident early on. This left McFadden and Lancourt with two choices: commission works on subjects or stories of particular interest or adapt preexisting works or popular fairy tales to their specific needs; they tapped into both approaches. Together, they reviewed hundreds of manuscripts and books in their search for material that could be developed into engaging and creative productions for children. Chapter III suggests that their choice of commissioned plays was influenced in part by subject matter that addressed social justice issues related to their mission, in part by external political opportunities, and in part by serendipity. We know the adaptation of Humperdinck's *Hansel and Gretel,* inherited from the National Music League, was a given, and we know that they worried about finding another opera to match *Hansel and Gretel's* success. When McFadden stumbled upon Rimsky-Korsakov's *The Tzar Saltan* during a European trip, that provided Junior Programs with the opportunity to introduce the American public to a world renowned but unfamiliar composer. According to McFadden, it was Lancourt's musical connections that brought Gruenberg's *Jack and the Beanstalk* to their attention. In many ways, it was made-to-order for their young audience.[348] It also offered the opportunity to add an American composer to their repertoire. The fact that several of the Junior Programs singers had been part of Gruenberg's original cast also would have been a plus. How or why the four dance-plays were selected remains a mystery. There were certainly any number of fairy tales and legends they might have chosen, but according to the many reviews, the choices they did make—*Pinocchio, The Princess and the Swineherd, The Adventures of Puck,* and *Robin Hood*—were well received. *Pinocchio* and *Robin Hood* turned out to be two of Junior Programs' most popular productions. It is also worth noting that their choice of operas and ballets reflect a mix of the well-known and the unfamiliar; and when the story was familiar, as with *Jack and the Beanstalk* or *Pinocchio,* they chose to present the story in an unfamiliar form—the former as an opera, the latter as a ballet.

However, there was another factor which contributed to the success of their choices, and that was the way their network of sponsoring organizations connected them to the communities in which they performed. McFadden traveled widely within the United States, giving talks about Junior Programs at educator's conferences, PTA conventions, and in all kinds of communities and local organizations.[349] She also travelled abroad, studying European and Russian theater for children—all of which kept her in touch with a broad range of community leaders across the country. Additionally, she was involved on a regular basis with numerous organizations which focused on the educational, social, and psychological needs of children. Finally, through her various organizational associations, she had a broad network of relationships with authors, musicians, and dancers. Lancourt, frequently out "on the road" working with one or another of the companies, was also in an ideal position to observe closely—in performance after performance—the reactions of their young audiences to the nuances of the company's innovative artistic and social choices. He, too, was part of an ongoing dialogue with members of the local communities, and several articles refer to these continuous conversations as input into their choice of material. This was especially true for the development of *Doodle Dandy*. In an article Lancourt wrote for the *New York Times,* he specifically refers to the confusion he encountered from audiences about the "big words about democracy and civilization," and "what all the shootin' was about."[350]

This focus on the community and its needs, and on Junior Programs' ability to meet those needs while at the same time fulfilling the requirements of their mission suggests an important shift in perspective. Traditionally, in the performing arts, it is the needs of the "art" that drives the decisions. However, as noted in Chapter III, McFadden and Lancourt's decisions were also influenced by contemporary social and political concerns. These included the evolving mood of the country as it emerged from the Depression, the inevitability of being drawn into the war, the very real threat to American democracy posed by fascism, and the continuous othering to which racial and ethnic minorities were subjected on a daily basis. Junior Programs' ability to strike a balance between the imperatives of the "art" and the needs of the "community" was an important factor contributing to their success.

Step 2, 3, and 4: Production

Once a storyline or script was selected, Lancourt, as artistic and production director, moved to the forefront. If it was an existing piece that needed to be adapted (e.g., the three operas), Lancourt would engage whatever additional expertise was needed. One example was Gregory Ashman, whom he engaged to help analyze, cut, adapt, and tailor *The Bumble Bee Prince*[351] based on the needs of their youthful audience. Typically, their challenge was to cut an hour or more from the original "without disturbing the musical line." If it was a new story, such as the case with the four ballets, Lancourt was responsible for commissioning and managing the script development, and, with Strawbridge, the creation of the musical score and the choreography. For the five plays, he and McFadden tapped their personal and professional networks of well-known writers, composers, and dancers. John Louw Nelson, author of *The Reward of the Sun God* and Charlotte Chorpenning, the director, were part of that network. Cecile Hulse Matschat, author of *The Emperor's Treasure Chest* was also part of that network, as were Margaret Carlisle and Ruth St. Denis for *Marco Polo,* and Elie Siegmeister and Ted Shawn for *Doodle Dandy*.

It is also clear from a comment in an undated Lancourt family letter that there were some initial selections that did not make it into full production. How often this occurred, or how formal a process it was is unknown. But in listing the operas, Lancourt mentioned one by a French composer, Daniel Auber, *Le Lac des Fees.* He went on to say that it "did not go into a full production" because "we did a few performances and found it wanting."

Lancourt also was responsible for hiring the directors, as well as selecting and supervising the set designers (often Kenneth MacClelland), and costume designers, who would then prepare the necessary drawings and sketches. The sets were built and painted in the Junior Programs workshop, although I found no information as to where it was located. There were a number of Lancourt family stories about the occasional last-minute call for "all-hands-on-deck"—including Lancourt's—to finish painting a set in time for a preview performance the following day. Repeatedly, the newspaper reviews from across the country agreed that the beauty and artistic creativity of the sets and costumes were second to none and integral to the popularity and success of every production. Judging from the way their audiences responded, and from comments captured in the reviews and articles about their work, the production teams Lancourt pulled together for the productions were able to develop a collaborative artistic and technical synergy. This enabled a level of stability in their production crews and performers which likely contributed to the success of their productions.

Another major accomplishment of the Junior Programs production design process, according to Lancourt, was the challenge of "devis[ing] scenery, props, lighting and equipment for touring productions that . . . [could be used] on practically any auditorium stage in the country. . . [in order to provide] the same modern impressions that have till now been possible only in the best New York theaters" (*The Independent*, St. Petersburg, FL, Nov 1940). In this, he made real the commitment to bring the best of children's entertainment to every part of the country, making sure that sets, costumes, wigs, and masks were designed and created with an eye toward authenticity, as well as portability. *Musical Digest* in East Stroudsburg, Pennsylvania (Nov 1937), mentions a tour of *The Bumble Bee Prince*, noting that having just completed a fall tour of the New England and Middle Atlantic states, "this completely equipped new portable opera production" will perform in New York during the Christmas season. Another review noted that, "the success of its production techniques . . . may be measured by the fact that the Junior Programs Opera and Ballet Companies . . . have the longest seasons and most extensive tours of any professional troupes in the country. The organization's more recently formed Players Company is now rated by dramatic critics as a factor of growing significance in modern theater."[352]

Step 5: Rehearsals

Having chosen the subject matter, commissioned the script, and put the wheels in motion for sets and costumes, it was Lancourt's responsibility, with the director, to hire the performers and begin rehearsals. Success typically depends on several factors:

first, the quality of the performers; second, the ability of the director to bring out the best in each performer by creating an atmosphere of collaboration and safety; third, crafting a coherent, unified interpretation of the material from its many moving parts; and fourth, having sufficient rehearsal time to pull it all together.

Many of the reviews reference the care with which Lancourt selected the various performers from among the finest young American artists of the time. In an article in the New York *Herald* (Nov 16, 1940), Pierre Key, when assessing the budding state of opera in the United States, acknowledged the importance of the Junior Programs Opera Company: "The singers are excellent and experienced . . . better voices and better in sheer vocal art than our D'Oyly Carte friends from London." And according to the New York City *Musical Digest* (Jan 1941), the level of excellence was in part due to the tenure of many of the company members. "Directed by Saul Lancourt, the company has suffered few changes in personnel from season to season. Along with Director Lancourt there have remained with it from the beginning Cecile Sherman, Alma Milstead and Marion Selee, sopranos, and Tom Williams and Howard Laramy, baritones. Kenneth MacClelland, scenic designer, and stage manager is in his fourth year." While not quite as stable as the opera company, there was a core list of actors for the Players productions, that included Barry Mahool, Viki Weldon, Roberta Barkley, Hana Karol, and Anthony James, each of whom performed in multiple productions. Similarly, the ballet company, consistently featured Edwin Strawbridge, as well as Sam Steen, Dale Lefler, Barbara Gaye, Virginia Miller, Charles Tate, Marguerite de Anguera, Cowden McCord, William Miller, William Cooper, Henry Omond, and Louis Venai in multiple productions. There was also the core group of narrators—Lanni Carvell, Martha Picken, and Julia Vaughan, all three of whom were significant contributors to the company's success.

The many reviews and interviews with Lancourt himself also acknowledge one of his most successful innovations—that the operas and ballets were rehearsed as much for the performers' acting abilities as for their musical and dancing skills. Conversely, at Lancourt's insistence, rehearsals for the Players were focused not just on the actor's acting abilities but on the rhythm, pacing, and "choreography" of the dramatic material as well.

Barry Mahool, one of the more experienced of the Players, mentions that *The Adventures of Marco Polo* had a four-week rehearsal period (Green Bay, WI, *Press*

Gazette, Oct 13, 1941). An adequate length of time for rehearsal is directly associated with the quality of the final production. It allows the actors to mine nuances of their characters, making them fully believable, three-dimensional beings, and it enables the director to ensure that all the individual parts are woven into a seamless and dynamic whole. In extended runs, periodic rehearsals are also critical for sustaining a high-quality performance. In the same family letter noted above, Lancourt mentioned that he went out to "catch a performance" on tour to make sure the pacing and tempo of the performers remained as originally rehearsed; and we learn from the New York *Morning Telegraph* (n.d.) that "Saul Lancourt . . . has gone to Annapolis, Md. to join the professional acting company of adult players and dancers and [will] remain with them until their arrival in New York. Lancourt is both the author and director of 'Marco Polo,' and he will conduct rehearsals of the company which has been playing a crowded schedule in 26 states since it began its season [before returning to New York]."[353]

Step 6: Previews

Junior Programs At Work acknowledges the importance of preview performances. Before being sent out on tour, every production scheduled a preview performance in New York for the Junior Programs Educational Guidance Committee and a live audience of children—the ultimate arbiters of a production's readiness for national consumption. These performances allowed the company to fine-tuning their performance and insured the level of "quality control" required by their motto—"*Only the best is good enough for children.*" Unfortunately, there was no information about, or examples of, the fine-tuning process.

Step 7: Bookings

The booking of the yearly season tours for all three companies unfolded concurrently with the development of each new production. These were arranged by the New York Booking Department which regularly corresponded with hundreds of local Sponsoring Committees in both the United States and Canada. During the first two years, in addition to organizing the tours for their own productions, headquarters also scheduled bookings for a broad range of individual offerings. These included Russian, Indian, and cowboy songs and dances; film adventures such as Clara Adams's zeppelin and seaplane flights, Norman McClintock's "Magic of Nature," or the Australian Troubadours—Joan and Betty Rayner, as well as marionette troupes, monologists, and musicians. True to its NML heritage, Junior Programs also organized a series of touring children's concerts as part of the already scheduled adult concert tours by several of the major symphony orchestras, namely the National, Rochester, Cincinnati, and Cleveland Orchestras. In a *New York Times* article, (June 25, 1939) Lancourt noted that this was part of Junior Programs' commitment to developing the musical "audience of tomorrow." To have a cultivated adult audience, children needed to be able to hear the best orchestras during their formative years.

However, as the company developed more of its own work, bookings focused primarily on organizing seasons of their own productions—typically, one opera, one ballet, and one play per season. McFadden refers to her early responsibility for the touring schedule as a "headache." Having committed to having all their "artists under Equity contracts, [and] guaranteeing them a minimum number of weeks of performances," in order to "break even," they had to "book enough performances (often two a day in the same auditorium)" in towns that were not too far apart. However, as they expanded the geography for the tours, it became more and more difficult to avoid extended gaps in the scheduling.[354] To some extent, this problem was addressed when Lancourt became involved. According to one report, he managed to reduce the 1937–38 deficit caused by the scheduling gaps from $23,000 to just under $13,000.[355]

Step 8: Field Secretaries

Effective field secretaries were essential to the success of Junior Programs. Field secretaries were assigned to a specific region of the country. They travelled from town to town to help organize the local sponsoring committees, make presentations to potential and collaborating organizations, speak directly with students, help select programs, help committees develop budgets, address organizational problems, help plan verbal and printed publicity, and, of course, serve as general troubleshooter whenever the need arose. A description from Highland Park, Michigan's *Highland Parker* (Jan 26, 1939) offers a window into a day in the life of a field secretary when it reported on Miss Margareta Lavender, who was associated with the Junior Programs Movement in the East.

> She visited all the Highland Park elementary schools to discuss the opera, *Hansel and Gretel*. She also helped organize public

VI. THE ORGANIZATIONAL INNOVATIONS

broadcasts and assembly meetings to generate additional interest. She connected with Toy M. Parsons, Director of Music in the schools at a meeting of music teachers to help plan for an extensive study of the opera, as well as having the children learn some of the songs—to be sung by the children during the intermission. Miss Lavender also helped engage Mr. Elmer S. Featherstone of the Instrumental Music Department as master of ceremonies to introduce the various songs to be presented during intermission. Other community groups engaged in preparation for the performance included the Police Dept. to direct traffic, with transportation for the students in school buses being organized courtesy of Russ Dawson Motor Sales and the Ford Motor company.

The Yakama, Washington, *Herald* (March 10, 1940) also reiterated the importance of the field staff, noting that from March 17 to March 20, a field executive from New York would be in Yakama to assist with contacts in the local schools and service clubs and help develop the various key committees (e.g., Transportation, Publicity, etc.) and a speaking campaign. An issue of the *Junior Programs Jottings*, a periodic newsletter sent to all local committees, contained a poem describing the life of a field secretary:

>Oh, the field secretary
>Leads a life very merry
>As she drives from town to town.
>She'll go for a week
>To Picayune Creek,
>While a chairman she tracks down.
>
>. . .
>
>The leader's found
>The rest gather round
>And the field secretary makes a speech.
>The group is fired
>Like Saints inspired,
>And vows every child to reach.
>
>. . .

> She tells all the young
> Of the coming fun
> And how little the tickets cost -
> She talks away -
> Twelve talks a day -
> Till her voice is almost lost . . .

What emerges from this and other descriptions of the sponsoring organizations is their work to include all segments of the community—from interested parents, educators, and college alumnae (e.g. PTAs, the AAUW and the College Clubs), local performing arts professionals (e.g. music teachers and ballet schools), local choruses and drama clubs to a wide range of local businesses (from drug stores and car dealerships to book and clothing stores), media and town or city services (e.g. school, transportation, and police departments) as well as the broad range of civic associations (from the Junior League to the Rotary, Kiwanis and other fraternal clubs). In a sense, coaching the sponsoring organizations in how to secure meaningful commitments from the whole community was the essence of the field secretary's job.

Step 9: Touring

Touring was part of Junior Programs' DNA. The company toured primarily by car, with specially built trucks carrying scenery, lighting, costumes, and other equipment. Tours varied in length, with some as long as twenty to thirty weeks. The schedule was grueling, often requiring a long drive immediately after one performance to arrive in the next town for a performance the following day. (The next section of this chapter provides a more in-depth look at the specifics of the Junior Programs tours.)

Step 10 and 11: Educational Materials

A major focus of Junior Programs, and one of its most innovative and critical components, was its Educational Guidance Committee. Composed of leading educators from across the country, this committee directed the preparation of a set of CCSUs for each production. Front-line teachers in school classrooms wherever a Junior Programs performance was to take place would use these materials, created by professional specialists from a wide range of academic disciplines and child development experts. The CCSU, often running fifty pages or more, went to every local sponsoring committee, along with complete instructions for their use. In turn, the sponsoring committee would distribute them to schools and front-line teachers for incorporation into the regular K-12 curriculum. Typically, the CCSUs were sent two or three months in advance to allow the school departments ample time to work on a unit related to the upcoming performance. The units provided ideas and resources for student projects not only for music, drama, and dance or physical education departments, but also for English, history, science, social studies, political science, home economics, and shop. One of the unique features of the CCSUs were their suggestions for collaborations among and between departments, and for assembly programs shared with the entire school. These various CCSUs were also designed in age-appropriate formats for the early grades, middle school, and high school levels.

In understanding how structures and processes reflect an organization's priorities, the fact that within this eleven-step process only the Production and Rehearsal steps focus internally speaks volumes. Seven of the eleven steps require some form of involvement and interaction with the community. This shift in focus—from a primarily internal, arts centered approach to one emphasizing a dual focus on the arts in relation to the social, political, educational and economic facets of a community—seems to have come naturally to McFadden and Lancourt, as well as many of the other company members. In fact, creating the organizational structures, infrastructures, and processes that anchored them in the community played a major role in their success. Their approach not only enabled them to *listen* repeatedly to an unusually broad range of inputs, but to observe, experiment, evaluate, and experiment again. It created an effective feedback loop to assess what did and didn't work—keeping and discarding accordingly. One of the biggest tests of the flexibility this afforded them—the lessons they learned about theater for young audiences and their growing knowledge about the needs of different communities—was evident when it became clear they could not continue to support three separate companies. Seemingly without missing a beat, they used their *Wei Ji* approach and were able to combine the three companies into one, touring two of their most impressive and successful productions—*The Adventures of Marco Polo,* and *Doodle Dandy of the U.S.A.*—for their 1941–42 and 1942–43 seasons.

On the Road with Junior Programs

Like the *commedia dell'arte* troupes of old, at the beginning of each school year the three Junior Programs companies would pile into their specially designed cars and trucks and set forth on a series of increasingly ambitious tours.[356] An Elkhart, Indiana, article gives us a small glimpse of life "on the road" for the performers. For a production of *The Adventures of Marco Polo*, the reporter describes the following: "Down in the orchestra pit a singer was rehearsing, squatting beside the piano. Nearby a dancer was limbering up, using the edge of the stage as an exercise bar. The stage was a mass of scenery in process of becoming 13th century Venice. From all sides, sounds of activity. In one room off stage, costumes were ready, and the eight male members of the cast were beginning to make up. Across the way the two feminine members were getting themselves ready for the opening scene . . . This was Elkhart High School auditorium at 2pm Tuesday, one hour and a quarter before curtain time for 'The Adventures of Marco Polo'" (unknown source, n.d.).

In another article, we hear from one of Junior Programs' leading actors:

> Cooperation is the essence of the company . . . each person in addition to his dramatic role, has other duties. One man, for example is responsible for placing the lights, another for seeing that the proper color shields are in the spotlights. Still another has charge of costumes, and someone else places properties. The myriad details which make for smooth performance are carried out by the cast with the aid of a stage crew of six high school boys who work under the direction of the stage manager . . . The present show opened Oct. 1 in New York and has been travelling since. The play went into rehearsal four weeks before opening. Playing seven shows a week, the company travels by truck and one large passenger car. The driver and one member of the cast take the scenery, costumes and property in the truck and the remainder of the cast ride in the car. 'Marco Polo' played Monday in South Bend, and today is in Mount Pleasant, Michigan . . . The Elkhart High School auditorium stage is adequate, but there are times when space is limited, and scenery must be adjusted. The company has an engagement next week in a town where the play will be given

in the school gymnasium, which has a 12-foot ceiling. There will be some figuring before the House of Polo, 16 feet high appears on the stage.[357]

Unfortunately, company records detailing the location, dates, and productions of Junior Programs tours are fragmented and incomplete. Thus, gaining a truly accurate picture of either year-by-year growth in bookings or piecing together a reliable semblance of their finances was not possible. Appendix I includes a partial reconstruction of locations, dates, and productions of Junior Programs' yearly tours, gleaned from the hundreds of articles and newspaper reviews. However, because articles often did not mention specific performance dates, or the reviews themselves are missing dates, this reconstruction is far from perfect or complete. Another caveat concerns the numbers quoted in the various articles. Some refer to miles toured, others to numbers of performances by one or another of the companies, while other reports aggregated the miles or performance numbers from two or three of the companies. Therefore, coupled with the lack of accurate dates, it was not possible to make an "apples to apples" comparison of the different sets of numbers. Nevertheless, the picture that emerges is one of impressive growth. Year after year, Junior Programs expanded its touring until it traveled the length and breadth of the United States. There were references to touring in Canada, but none of the available materials provided specific information as to when and where. Ultimately, as noted in numerous articles, the three companies appear to have had the most ambitious and comprehensive touring schedule of any professional company at that time.

The Fort Wayne, Indiana, *Journal Gazette* (Dec 13, 1937) characterized Junior Programs' growth as "meteoric": "The first year saw its opera, ballet and play companies touring 11 states. This year the children of more than 30 states will learn that Drama, Music, and Ballet as presented by Junior Programs are not dull and meaningless, but enjoyable and stimulative to thought as well as meaningful to life. The subject of commonplace entertainment and its effect upon young minds has long been a matter of deep concern to those entrusted with the training of tomorrow's men and women. It is to their aid and understanding that Junior Programs owes much of its growth." By December 20, 1937, *Time* magazine reported that over 500,000 children had attended Junior Programs performances, the most popular of which, somewhat surprisingly, were the ballets. During the following season, the tours focused primarily on their own productions of *Hansel and Gretel, The Bumble Bee Prince, Pinocchio, The Princess and the Swineherd,* and *The Reward of the Sun God,* although they still served as booking agent for the marionettes, monologists, films, and musicians. Another report noted that during the 1937–38 season, audiences at each performance of a tour reached the thousands: 6,000 in Macon, Georgia; 3,500 in Hartford, Connecticut; 3,700 in Worcester, Massachusetts; and 3,500 in Oklahoma (*Motion Picture Herald*, Mar 12, 1938). It is also worth remembering that Junior Programs was committed to an economically diverse audience. The Winston-Salem, North Carolina, *Journal and Sentinel* (Nov 2, 1941) comments that "many of the children have set out to earn their own tickets, season tickets being sixty-five cents, [and that] through the generosity of local citizens, every underprivileged child was given a ticket [to see *The Adventures of Marco Polo*]."

These extensive touring schedules were possible in large measure due to the popularity and success of their productions. There were headlines such as "Opera is attended by 5,000 children" (Detroit *Free Press*, March 13, 1938), reports that the "Demand for tix so great had to be moved to Paramount Playhouse" (Salem *Evening News*, Oct 21, 1939), or "'Hansel & Gretel' sold out, added evening performance for the general public and overflow of students" (Sarasota, Florida, unknown source, n.d.). In Gallipolis, Ohio (population 7,100), a ballet drew 1,500 children from all over the countryside (*Time*, Dec 20, 1937). The Montgomery, Alabama, *Advertiser* (n.d.) reports that, "an entire generation of American children is acquiring through the ballets of Junior Programs the appreciation of dancing as an interpretive art form that is already being reflected in growing public interest in the ballet."

The *New York Herald Tribune* (June 25, 1939) notes, "New Attractions Added; Touring Territory is Extended to Pacific." The article goes on to say that Junior Programs has "made arrangements to provide its full services for thirty-one states and Canada, while plans are being discussed for activities in six other states . . . The various companies' tours will take them as far as the Pacific Coast; requests for appearances in Hawaii and the Philippines had to be declined." *Reader's Digest* (Jan 1939) tells us: "Last year they drove 30,000 miles and filled 242 engagements. Junior Programmers have astonished me by the humor with which they recount their journeys through rain, mud, ice and dust storms in making their dates. Somehow the fact of playing to eager audiences of children gives these tours an aspect of adventure that makes hardship seem trivial. Performers get a thrill and a satisfaction that they never found in adult audiences . . . You must witness one of their shows to understand that thrill." Marion Selee, one of Junior Programs leading opera stars, added, "After an exhausting tour, we swear we will never try it again, but we always do. We can't resist such thoroughly satisfactory audiences."" The *Motion Picture Herald* (New York City, May 20, 1939) also offers an update. "The performers equipment and scenery travel in mobile units, playing in schools and municipal auditoriums and in film theaters in arrangements with the local exhibitor, who usually sets morning matinees . . . Performances totaled 323, an increase of 33 per cent over 1937-38, and number of different communities served 130, an increase of 16 per cent over 1937-38. A new opera and a new play will be added during 1939-40 to the organization's existing repertoire of two operas, three ballets and a play . . . [and] Saul Lancourt . . . scheduled 59 performances by the ballet company in 63 days out, and 49 performances by the opera company in 48 days out." These numbers clearly indicate a growing demand for Junior Programs' performances.

From the *Sheboygan Press* (Wisconsin, n.d.) we hear, "Junior Programs companies last year traveled 80,000 miles giving 558 performances to nearly a million children . . . and that the Ballet Company had engagements arranged for at least thirty weeks and perhaps more to be added." The Reading, Pennsylvania, *Eagle* (Oct 6, 194?) in a review of *Robin Hood* also notes that both the opera company and the ballet company "play nearly 30 solidly booked weeks from October to May." The *New York Times* (Nov 10, 1940) covered the opera company's thirty-week tour as it performed two productions—Rimsky-Korsakov's *The Bumble Bee Prince* and Louis Gruenberg's *Jack and the Beanstalk*. "To date, they have booked more than thirty engagements of the former, now in its third season and more than eighty of the Gruenberg work. They will play in the Eastern States during December, January and February, [and] . . . in the Southeast and deep South, going as far as St. Petersburg, Fla. and New Orleans." Similar coverage was published in the *New York Herald Tribune* (Nov 10, 1940): "It will be heard this month in southern New England, New York, Pennsylvania, Ohio, Kentucky, Michigan and neighboring states. Its route during the following six months takes it through the Southeast and Southwest to California, Oregon and Washington and thence eastward through Utah, Iowa, Minnesota, Wisconsin, Illinois, Pennsylvania and New Jersey." *Time* (Nov 25, 1940) reported, "last week, on the heels of the ballet troupe, the Junior Programs opera company went on a 30-week tour, its 10 members in automobiles, its scenery and costumes in a truck." Countless other articles and reviews describe the companies' grueling schedules. After a performance, sometimes a double bill of a matinee and evening performance, the performers would pile into their automobile, followed by a truck crammed with scenery, costumes, and lighting equipment. They would drive hundreds and hundreds of miles, arriving at the school auditorium, hall, motion picture theater, or municipal auditorium for their performance the following day (New Orleans *Times Picayune*, Dec 1, 1940; Tacoma, WA, unknown source, n.d.).

Lawrence Tibbett, a prominent American opera baritone wrote to McFadden to commend her for her work. "I am very happy to learn of the splendid progress made by your organization this year, with [y]our Opera Company booked for more than thirty solid weeks of engagements in the largest tour on record of any professional opera company in America . . . I am encouraged to believe that Junior Programs, Inc. is well on its way to becoming a self-supporting organization and a force of growing influence in the molding of America's future musical and cultural traditions. I congratulate you for your splendid success in this necessary and pioneering work."[358]

John Martin, of the *New York Times* (Jun 23, 1940), writes that the "annual report of Junior Programs, Inc . . . reveals a tremendous increase in the youthful public for dancing." He continues, saying that while the 1938-39 season "could boast only 59 performances, this last season succeeded in achieving 118 [and] . . . The record attendance at a single performance was for the ballet "Pinocchio" in . . . Tuscaloosa Ala., where 7,000 children were assembled." He also quotes McFadden, telling us that she "feels that though the programs have gone literally all over the country, they have still touched only a bare 2% of the age group to which they are directed."

The New York *Post* (n.d.) tells us that Junior Programs had toured through 22 states since October: "Actors, dancers, stage managers and musicians drive through floods, rainstorms, blizzards, sandstorms – and even sunshine – in a specially built automobile, while the two stagehands follow by truck with the 'works' – including a complete lighting system . . . They play an average of seven towns a week. Their favorite audience tale is about filling the Tuscaloosa, Ala. Auditorium, which holds 6,000 people, twice in one day – and the population of the town is 21,000." The New Orleans *Times Picayune* (Dec 1, 1940) notes that the Junior Programs' Ballet

Company was expecting to top its 1939 record of 118 performances—surpassing all other ballet company in the country. On January 12, 1941, Walter Terry of the *New York Herald Tribune* notes, "the ballet wing gave 150 one-night stands." *Dance Magazine* (Feb 1941) describes Edwin Strawbridge and his company of 8 supporting dancers, a ballet-mistress, stage manager, pianist and violinist as taking it all in stride. "Strawbridge plays nine shows a week, usually in as many cities . . . Often directly after an evening performance, the motor caravan will take to the highway, driving 300-400 miles through the night to make the next day's matinee in another town."

On June 22, 1941, we find the *New York Times* reporting that "The company recently gave its 1,750th performance since it incorporated in 1936 and has played to 3,500,000 children." Later in July 1941, we read of *The Adventures of Marco Polo* opening in New England on October first, after which:

> the production will play in the Eastern towns until October 11. On Columbus Day, the company will open a tour of the Midwest which will carry it through the states of Ohio, Indiana, Michigan, and Iowa. Part of November and the first two weeks in December will be spent fulfilling approximately 30 dates in the South. The company will then return for a gala Christmas season in New York City . . . January will see the beginning of the long trek to the West Coast with almost fifty engagements already booked between New York City and Los Angeles. March 15th to April 18th will be spent in the states of Oregon and Washington, Salt Lake City, and the surrounding territory will see 'Marco Polo' during the week of April 20th, with the company playing its way East through Montana, the Dakotas, Nebraska and the Midwest to arrive and close in Philadelphia on May 23rd (Elizabeth City, NC, unknown source, July 31, 1941).

According to a page marked "Summary Table" (circa 1943), from 1936 to 1943, Junior Programs gave 1,290 performances of its own productions in more than 250 cities and towns in 42 states and Canada, often returning to many municipalities multiple times a year. As their popularity increased, Junior Programs found themselves playing in as many as 220 cities and towns in a single year. In some years, the Junior Programs Ballet Company gave up to 156 performances; the opera company as many as 136; and the Players up to 104. McFadden was proud that, funded by private philanthropy, three million children had been able to see the best of opera, ballet, and drama at the average ticket price of ten to twenty-five cents, with free tickets for those who could not afford even so modest a price. To McFadden, their success thus far had proved three things: the real need for what they were doing; the intense receptivity of both their youthful audience and their parents; and that Junior Programs was able to provide productions to communities of every size and type, from rural villages to industrial centers and large cities. She also linked the company's success to the "voluntary efforts of parents, teachers, university women, and social and civic agencies" all of whom provided a proud commentary on "cultural development in a democracy." For her, this offered a solid refutation of the theory that there existed no alternative to the commercial sectors "lowest common denominator" form of entertainment.[359]

Of course, no tour ever existed without a few problems. The Winston, North Carolina, *Free Press* (Dec 7, 1939) described one missed connection that caused the cancellation of a show. "The company showed up . . . but was unprepared to put on the show. It developed that the company's schedule called for a night performance and the contract held by the Parent Teachers Council called for an afternoon performance. The disappointment of the audience was great. Little faces were tear streaked . . . Apparently the fault was at Junior Programs' HQ." The Winona, Minnesota, *Republican Herald* (Apr 25, 1940) describes another incident. "With three hours sleep after last night's performance at Burlington, Iowa, the Junior Programs company drove 300 miles this morning to arrive in Winona in time for an afternoon children's performance at the high school auditorium." No sooner had they climbed out of their vehicles, than they discovered the school authorities had no knowledge of the supposed performance. The snafu was traced to a letter of cancellation, regretful that they had been unable to raise sufficient money, that had somehow not been forwarded to the appropriate scheduler. Rolling with the punches, Kenneth MacClelland, set designer, and doubling, as he frequently did, as tour stage manager reportedly said, "Well, I guess we can sleep now." And on April 24, 1941, we hear from the Wheaton, Illinois, *Journal* of a cancellation of *Run, Peddler, Run* due to a scarlet fever epidemic in which the Wheaton Health Department banned all school functions. Again, taking it in stride, Junior Programs graciously agreed to release Wheaton from its contract.

Despite these little mishaps, the Burlington, Iowa, *Daily Hawk Eye Gazette* (Apr 6, 1940) sums it up nicely. "In their travels about the country, these modern maestersingers have captured the hearts of so many thousands of children, as well as their parents, as to have won a veritable 'Pied Piper' reputation." Schools, parents, civic groups, and most of all, the children, knew a good thing when they saw it!

Finances and Fundraising

Growth, as everyone knows, requires money. With Junior Programs' commitment to keeping ticket prices low, ticket sales would never come close to covering their costs. Regrettably, one of the biggest disappointments was the fact that none of the Junior Programs materials included sufficient or reliable financial information. There are various bits and pieces about company finances and fundraising, but nothing that would enable us to form a picture of how their fundraising efforts worked. McFadden bore the major burden of keeping the company afloat financially, but how she managed to do so for seven years remains something of a mystery. But keep it afloat she did! What follows are some of the bits and pieces.

Money raised from private donors was earmarked to cover their operating costs. One source indicated that during their first year, this was about $15,000.[360] Yet there was no explanation to be found of what was included in "operating costs" (South River, NJ, *Spokesman,* Jan 19, 1940). A December 10, 1937, *Time* profile of Junior Programs indicated "production costs" for the company of approximately $20,000 for the year. But were production costs in addition to operating costs, or were they overlapping, and if so, how did they overlap? Again, essential information is missing. The Williamsport, Pennsylvania, *Sun* (Jan 19, 1939) stated that maintenance of the New York office and other "overhead expenses" amounted to some $15,000 a year. However, what was and was not included in maintenance and overhead was not identified. Different sources also report different numbers in relation to a company deficit. One source puts the 1937 deficit at $16,000, noting that McFadden had been able to find three unnamed benefactors to "foot the bill."[361] However, another source states that in the 1938–39 annual report, McFadden showed a "decrease to $13,305 from the 1937-38 deficit of $23,772" (*Newsweek,* Jan 24, 1938).

We also learn that Junior Programs paid equity rates or better during 1939–40 to more than fifty adult professional performers, including opera singers, ballet dancers, players, musicians, lecturers, and puppeteers; and as a non-commercial company, they were exempt from paying taxes (Mt. Vernon, NY, *Arcus,* Jan 12, 1940). A news article asserts that each company received between $200 and $400 per performance. However, there is no mention of how or to whom the money was distributed (*Time,* Dec 10, 1937). While the Belleville, Illinois, *Daily News Democrat* (Jan 19, 1939) informs us that the cost to a community for a Junior Programs production was in the range of $200 to $300, the Albany, Oregon, *Democrat,* (Feb 29, 1940) sets the production cost at $350. Once again, there were no other details available. Clearly, "production cost" and "cost to a community" for a Junior Programs' production are not the same, but critical details as to how they relate to each other are lacking. Other articles inform us that the "cost" to use the various school auditoriums was often donated, but that is just one small "cost" when considered in terms of total cost. There was also no further information as to what else might be donated, or even what constituted an expense. Thus, it quickly became clear that it would be impossible to create any reliable picture of their financial or fundraising progress from such vague, disparate and sometime contradictory data.

What we do know is that for seven years, McFadden managed to keep Junior Programs funded through a combination of ticket sales, donated services, and private donations. We also know that she assembled several impressive boards, the membership of which represented many of the most prominent names in their respective fields. The Junior Programs letterheads reveal that the National Sponsoring Committee membership included what we might now term "heavy hitters" in a broad range of categories. There were stars from the theater and the musical world, university presidents, experts in child development, major philanthropists, scientists, museum directors, senior clergy, heads of hospitals and social justice organizations, as well as prominent social figures.[362] She also organized multiple advisory boards: The Music Advisory Board, the Radio Advisory Board, the Drama Advisory Board, and the Community Relations Advisory Board, each of which represented an impressive array of major organizations.[363] It would seem likely that all these names lent an important level of credibility to her actual fundraising efforts but were those efforts visits to individual or organizational donors, larger fundraising events, or some other activity is, regrettably, impossible to determine. It would be hard to imagine that this collection of well-connected, mostly well-heeled board members did not participate in some series of fundraising campaigns, but the who and the how—either as individual donors, or collectively as boards—remains a mystery.

The only documentation of actual fundraising events comes from the *New York Times*, *World Telegraph*, and *Brooklyn Eagle,* all of which mention that the National Sponsoring Committee of Junior Programs held a luncheon and fashion review at Coq Rouge on April 2, 1940, with debutantes as models. There is also an invitation to a luncheon given by the New York Sponsoring Committee in honor of Miss Katharine Cornell, Honorary Chairman of the National Sponsoring Committee. The event took place on the roof of the Hotel Pierre, on Wednesday, May 20, at 12:30 PM. Luncheon tickets were $2.50 ($53 in today's dollars), including tax and gratuity. There was also an invitation from the New York Sponsoring Committee requesting the "Pleasure of Your Company at Tea on the Stage of the Belasco Theatre . . . Immediately After the Matinee of 'Doodle Dandy of the U.S.A.' on Tuesday, December 29th at 4:30PM." Guests of honor included Miss Katharine Cornell, Mr. Saul Lancourt, Mr. Eugene Loring, Miss Flora Robson, Mr. Elie Siegmeister, Miss Gladys Swarthout, and Miss Peggy Wood. Tickets were fifty cents for adults ($10.50 in today's dollars) and thirty-five cents for children. A statement from Cornell, one of the "great ladies of the American stage," provides her perspective on the importance of supporting the Junior Programs companies:

> I believe that Junior Programs makes an important contribution to America's future cultural development. The theater cannot hope to survive on a high level unless we encourage the things for which Junior Programs stands—giving our own American children opportunities to see and hear the finest stage productions possible at low admissions within the reach of all . . . Junior Programs needs and deserves the support of all who wish to save and develop the world's cultural heritage. It is not enough that we should try to feed, house and clothe our own American children. There are other things vitally essential to them in a war-torn world. The spirit of democracy will not thrive in an atmosphere of only the physical and material. (unknown source, n.d.).

However, luncheons and other society events, no matter how glamourous, would never be enough to support the extensive touring of the three companies. And the Springfield, Massachusetts, *Republican* (July 14, 1940) comments that by the end of the 1939–40 season, Junior Programs had enlarged its scope, *nearly doubling its operations*. Ironically, this turned out to be both good news and bad news. Their goal was to keep on growing, but growth also meant an increase in expenses. These escalating operating costs could in no way be covered by their purposefully modest ticket prices, or, it turns out, by the fundraising McFadden had thus far done to keep the three companies "on the road."

We are alerted to their financial concerns in a one-page marketing piece, released to celebrate the company's 1,750th performance.

Not by Bread Alone

The spirit of democracy does not thrive in an atmosphere of only the physical and material. Children must have opportunities for cultural . . . appreciation of the arts, music and drama . . . [so they] become familiar with the beauty that has been created by the artists of every continent from time immemorial. The future of our country . . . now lies in the hands of our children.

Curtailment Necessary Unless—

For the season of 1941-42, Junior Programs will find it absolutely necessary to curtail its work unless its friends quickly respond by contributing a sum to any amount to make up a total of $31,205. Will you help make it possible for us to continue to fulfil the increasingly important cultural needs of the youth of the country? Your gift, added to others, will enable Junior Programs to celebrate its 1750 performance . . . secure in the knowledge that its vital work can continue . . . Please endorse our tremendous record of service and help keep our work going on a full scale by sending your gift TODAY. Fill in the coupon on the back of this page, detach and mail![364]

McFadden's autobiography also notes that in 1941, Junior Programs sought the help of a professional fundraiser—with no appreciable results. Indeed, she twice applied for a $15,000 Rockefeller Foundation grant but was turned down.[365] Why this seemingly sudden change of fortune? One factor may be found in external events. December 1941 was the date when the US entered WWII, and it soon became evident that many of Junior Programs' sponsoring organizations, as well as the company's other donors, were shifting their philanthropic focus to activities more directly related to the war.

McFadden and Lancourt began to see the handwriting on the wall. In addition to what appeared to be an inexorable shift in philanthropic priorities, their young male actors, singers, and dancers were beginning to be drafted. Then, in early 1942, the sale of new rubber tires became illegal; and toward the end of the year, as a means of preserving the existing automobile tires, gas was rationed, and a "Victory Speed" of thirty-five miles per hour was adopted.[366] It would be impossible to tour three separate companies. At first, they did what they had always done. Lancourt turned challenge into opportunity—successfully combining the drama, song, and dance of one merged company into *Marco Polo,* one of their most glorious productions. He did the same for *Doodle Dandy of the U.S.A.*, and each became one of Junior Programs' most successful productions. However, larger forces were at play, and by summer of 1943, touring even one company became unsustainable. What else they may have considered is unknowable, but what we do know is that despite their record of success after success, Junior Programs' touring productions came to an untimely end.

Funding the performing arts has always been difficult. The European model of government funding has its problems and has not been immune to drastic budget cuts; and the Federal Theatre Project's experience with government funding saw it become a victim of political censorship. Today's model of regional funding by wealthy donors and subscribers has also proved to be problematic, leaving the arts open to the constraints imposed by the personal tastes, preferences, and priorities of those individuals. Increasing access to the performing art for a broader and more diverse collection of people is a profoundly important goal. However, in the final analysis, when choices need to be made, people pay for the things they deem most essential to their lives. In this context, as McFadden noted in her remark about having reached only two percent of their target audience, Junior Programs was still in their "introductory phase." To most of their audience, the performing arts were new. Junior Programs was a most welcome and valued addition to their lives, but not yet deemed essential.

One way of framing the funding challenge is to pose the question, "How can we make the benefits of the performing arts compelling enough to be considered essential to a more diverse collection of people?" In devising an organizational structure that enabled Junior Programs to become a more integral part of the communities in which they performed, they were, in effect, exploring that question. Similarly, their efforts to position the performing arts as a vital part of the educational process, and as an indispensable component in educating the next generation of citizens in a democracy also addresses that question. However, that McFadden and Lancourt's "experiment" was cut short by the outbreak of WWII appears to have been unavoidable. One cannot always find the opportunity buried within a crisis, and there is no way of knowing how Junior Programs would have fared had they tried to resume production once the war ended. Nonetheless, their achievements from 1936 to 1943 were groundbreaking, and the information that *is* available establishes beyond any doubt their artistic, social, educational, and organizational accomplishments. That there was more they needed to learn and do is not surprising. The real question now is: What can *we* learn from their experiences, and how might those insights inform the challenges the nation and theaters for young audiences face today?

VII. THE JUNIOR PROGRAMS LEGACY

Taking Lewis Carroll's advice to "Start at the beginning and stop when you come to the end," this book stops at the untimely end of Junior Program's story in 1943. However, while 1943 may have been the end of the Junior Programs story, it is not the end of the story of theater for young audiences. In fact, the story of Junior Programs is, in many ways, the beginning of that much larger and longer story.

The Post–World War II Years

The postwar years saw a new and growing focus on children's theatre in the United States. In 1950, there was the Midcentury White House Conference on Children and Youth where, for the first time, children's theater was on the agenda.[367] The conference focused on the "primacy of spiritual values, *democratic practice* [emphasis added], and the dignity and worth of every individual." Six thousand delegates from virtually every discipline concerned with the welfare of children considered "*how to develop in children the mental, emotional and spiritual qualities essential to . . . responsible citizenship.*" [emphasis added][368] Further, "in order that the needs of minority groups might be fully considered, provision was made for representation by minority racial groups in numbers roughly proportioned to their contribution to the population of the nation."[369] There was also a national Children's Theater Conference in 1952 to promote the establishment of children's theater activities at the community level and advocate for increasing and maintaining higher standards. Many Junior League members were active participants, and it would not be surprising to discover that a number of the participants had been part of one or another of the Junior Programs sponsoring committees. One outcome of the conference was the Junior League's creation of a drama library, one that included not only scripts but "packages" of "sets, costumes and properties, and lighting equipment."[370] The 1960s saw another surge of interest in the arts and in children's theater. In 1964, both the International Association of Theatres for Children and Young People (ASSITEJ) and the National Council on the Arts were formed, and the National Endowment of the Arts was created the following year. Children's theater was included in both. The Elementary and Secondary Education Act, passed in 1965, established provisions that brought professional performing artists into schools for specific programs such as artists-in-residence or in-service training for teachers. The sixties also saw the formation of state arts councils in every state, all of which funded similar programs.[371]

During this same timeframe, colleges and universities were also establishing programs to better educate future teachers of the various dramatic arts, and there was even federal funding available from the US Department of Education for these efforts. These institutions of higher learning worked with local schools, creating productions for young audiences and workshops for teachers. A 1954 survey indicated that two hundred and twenty two colleges and universities had developed courses in drama and theater, and by the mid-1960s "centers for the study of child drama were developed at . . . California State University at Northridge . . . New York University . . . University of North Carolina . . . [and] the University of Oklahoma."[372] In 1965, the US Office of Education, through the Education Professions Development Act, funded ARTS IMPACT (Interdisciplinary Model Program in the Arts for Children and Teachers). This was a program designed to promote curriculum development and teacher training in the arts. Four organizations—the American Educational Theatre Association, the Music Educators National Conference, the National Arts Education Association, and the Dance Division of the American Association for Health, Physical Education and Recreation—were instrumental in launching the program. Its goal was to "achieve better balance between the arts and other instructional areas . . . to develop high quality visual arts, music, dance and drama educational programs . . . to conduct in-service programs . . . [and] workshops . . . to train teachers . . . and other school personnel in implementing the arts education programs." These groups also sought "to develop ways to infuse the arts into all aspects of the school curriculum as a means of . . . expanding the base for effective learning experiences in the total school program; [and] to enhance the quality of children's art experiences by drawing upon outstanding artists, performers, and educators from outside the school system."[373]

VII. THE JUNIOR PROGRAMS LEGACY

Today, there are one hundred and thirty-five established adult professional theaters for young audiences in cities across the nation[374], and several national organizations that address the various needs of those individual theaters. For example, Theatre for Young Audiences (TYA-USA) has a mission "to ensure that all young people have access to high quality theatre experiences." A chief concern is the "emergency of systemic racism," and an acknowledgement that they play "a vital role in shaping the [social] narrative through the stories we tell and those we don't tell to young people."[375] The Children's Theatre Foundation of America (CTFA) is a grant-making organization with a social and artistic mission to "reflect the diversity of race, gender, economic status and sexual orientation"—on stage, on staff and board, and in the audience. Additionally, it seeks to "dismantle racism in the stories we tell, the representation of people on stage, and in the discussions that occur before, during and after any performance.[376] The Arts Education Partnership (AEP) is a national network of more than two hundred organizations dedicated to increasing arts education and to communicating, collaborating, convening, and connecting "policymakers, stakeholders and leaders across the arts education field."[377] The YouthARTS Development Project is focused on at-risk youth, and the American Alliance for Theatre and Education (AATE) serves theater artists, in-service and pre-service teachers, professors, directors, scholars, and playwrights, sparking dialogue across disciplines. It is committed "to transforming young people and communities through the theatre arts." This includes the "voices, perspectives and experience of people who have been left out."[378] A final example is ASSITEJ, which is dedicated to the "artistic, cultural and educational rights of children and young people across the globe and advocates on behalf of all children regardless of nationality, cultural identity, ability, gender, sexual orientation, ethnicity, or religion."[379]

There can be little doubt that the landscape has changed since the days of Junior Programs. There has been a proliferation of regional and local theaters offering seasons of productions designed specifically for young audiences, and there are multiple national and international organizations whose missions focus on addressing the needs of both young audiences and the theaters that serve them. There has also been a significant awakening to the role the performing arts can and should play in dismantling systemic racism. And, as noted above, while insufficient to meet the needs, there has also been a tangible increase in financial resources.

The question now is "What can today's TYA community learn from the Junior Programs experience? Such an examination is relevant because, despite the passage of more than eighty years, and an increase in the number of companies and resources devoted to children's theater, the social, political, and economic challenges Junior Programs addressed in relation to the preservation of democracy and the development of the next generation of audiences are still among today's most pressing and urgent issues. It is in this context that Junior Programs' successes can provide a legacy of lessons, principles, and guidelines that theaters in general, and regional and national organizations focused on theater for young audiences, would do well to explore.

A Legacy of Learning

The legacy of Junior Programs is multifaceted. Their view of the performing arts and its role in society was expansive. Their commitment to democracy and its core values was clearly articulated. Their partnerships with educators and community leaders were part of their mission and organizational structure; and their belief in and respect for the importance of the nation's young people was an inspiration. For the purpose of assessing how their approach to TYA could help address current challenges, this chapter will focus on six interdependent categories: The Primacy of Audience Development; Reframing the Performing Arts – An Expanded Role for Theater In A Democracy; The Power of Partnerships I – The Role of the Performing Arts in Education; The Power of Partnerships II – The Role of the Performing Arts in the Community; The Role of the Performing Arts in Addressing Racism; and The Legacy of Artistic Innovations. However, in exploring these issues, it is important to note that the legacy of Junior Programs is not a recipe to be followed down the last half-cup of dramatic tension or teaspoon of rehearsals. Nor can we simply cut and paste specific programs or processes from then to now. McFadden's successful network of sponsoring organizations would be unworkable today as most women are now part of the daily workforce, and Lancourt's decision to have operas sung in English is no longer "innovative." Rather, we must identify and examine the underlying principles to see what they have to offer in the context of today's challenges.

The Primacy of Audience Development

In an article for the *National Parent-Teacher* magazine, McFadden described an early trip to Europe to see firsthand what different countries offered their children in

VII. THE JUNIOR PROGRAMS LEGACY

the way of cultural development.[380] She quickly realized that, for the performing arts to flourish in America, it would be necessary to develop an audience for those arts. Success would require *an intentional focus on the next generation*. Junior Programs was her answer to the need for that intentional effort.

The company's success in expanding their audience can be demonstrated in several ways. The continued growth of Junior Programs certainly was evidence of a growing audience of young people. Starting from a regional launch in the northeast, they spread to every part of the nation, including major cities and small towns, ultimately reaching four million children. The development of "seasons" was also evidence of growing demand; and at the end of each season, cities and towns often contracted for the next season's productions. John Martin, dance critic of the *New York Times*, credited the Junior Programs Ballet with the noticeable increase of an audience for dance. A letter from Metropolitan Opera star Lawrence Tibbett attested to the company's contribution to the development of an audience for opera in America, as well as for providing a "bridge" experience for American singers between training and performing at the Met.[381] And when *Doodle Dandy* previewed at Hunter College, the *New York Times* (Dec 30, 1942) hoped it would return to New York from its national tour for the holiday season because there was such a large audience of children who would flock to see it.

Fundamental to the achievement of such positive results was Junior Programs' honest and visible respect for the needs of their youthful audience. During McFadden's European trip, she saw firsthand the ways in which the various performing arts actively demonstrated their respect for their young audiences through the regular involvement of both teachers and children themselves. In Denmark, both were repeatedly and regularly involved in selecting and giving feedback on the plays they attended. Every play offered in Russia was tested and improved over the years as a result of feedback from both the children and their teachers.[382] Upon her return to New York, McFadden did not just copy what she had seen in Europe. Instead, she identified various local opportunities for evaluation and feedback from young audiences. This was accomplished in part through the New York production previews, a process specifically designed to ensure a production's readiness for touring by providing immediate feedback from a youthful audience as well as the Educational Guidance Committee and other key experts. In addition, the emphasis the company placed on significant community engagement also created a community feedback infrastructure. The *Junior Programs Committees' Organization and Promotion Booklet* developed by McFadden was itself based on extensive feedback garnered from a broad range of sponsoring committees. And by encouraging each local sponsoring committee to include local teachers and community cultural organizations early in the season's planning and selection processes, she indicated the respect she felt toward her community partners.

Respect for their young audiences, and a genuine interest in listening to and understanding their reactions and needs, seems to have been an innate part of both McFadden's and Lancourt's personalities. We hear repeatedly, from reviewers and other artistic leaders, that Lancourt "never underestimated" and "never talked down to" his audience. Respect for the children was also apparent in Lancourt's belief that, if the material was properly framed, young people were capable of understanding complex problems. *Doodle Dandy* was not a preachy staged version of a lecture on democracy: it was a vivid story of the struggle between democracy and fascism, told in a setting that was well within the realm of the young audience's experience. By depicting the young student characters as having a vital role to play in the fight against Springville's dictator, the production sent a powerful message to their youthful audience—that they had agency, and that they were already capable of donning the mantle of democratic citizenship. McFadden also made it clear that children from every part of the country sent enthusiastic letters sharing their reactions to the productions—and that she took this form of feedback seriously. Lancourt's 1943 *New York Times* article in which he explains how they arrived at the decision to develop *Doodle Dandy* as their next production is an example of the company taking all forms of feedback seriously. With four million children attending multiple productions over a seven-year period, there can be little doubt as to Junior Programs' success in the development of an audience for the performing arts. Yet they realized there was still a great deal more to be done regarding audience development as is evident in McFadden's remark that, thus far, they had only reach two percent of their potential audience.

In 2023, the need for an explicit focus on audience development is as urgent as it was in the 1930s—perhaps more so after the COVID-19 pandemic, especially given the visible aging of the traditional white adult audience for opera, drama, and dance. In an article in the *Los Angeles Times*, playwright Jeremy O. Harris "noted that the theater industry was in trouble long before COVID-19. He singled out the subscriber model as a system of support that failed years ago." He also pointed out that theaters' "obsession with funding expensive building projects was problematic . . . making companies increasingly dependent on the whims of wealthy, often out-of-touch board members." He went on to say, "There hasn't been enough innovation or inquiry around *how to inspire a new generation of people to go to these spaces, and to find community inside of a theater in their town* [emphasis added]."[383]

In Hamlet's words, "Ay, there's the rub!" How do we inspire the next generation to find a democratic community at the theater? If today's adult theaters are concerned about having a future audience—and they are—they might consider Junior Programs' default position: that a crisis should be turned into an opportunity. What might that look like today? Perhaps one way to develop the theater's next generation of audience would be to create a network of partnerships between regional theaters for adults and those for young audiences. Such a network could experiment and innovate in any number of ways. For instance, a network could share a broad range of resources; or they could create long-term relationships and partnerships between theater staffs, boards, artists, and their diverse local communities. Additionally, potential funders could be encouraged to rethink the prevailing belief that theater for young audiences is somehow the artistic and financial stepchild of the larger adult theater community. A second possibility is for TYA theaters to rethink and expand their approach to engaging with their communities (see The Power of Partnerships II below).

Reframing the Performing Arts – An Expanded Role for Children's Theaters in a Democracy

Junior Programs' conception of the performing arts as more than entertainment is one of their most valuable legacies. In considering the dissatisfactions that led McFadden to create Junior Programs, they had articulated a vision and mission that went well beyond the role of entertainment. They drew back the curtain on a complex of social, political, and economic concerns by providing stories that were lacking in the comic strips, radio programs, and Hollywood films being offered to the nation's youth. Guided by their *Credo,* they were able to find positive and appropriate ways to begin to deal with the multiple threats to democracy. As they saw it, it was not helpful to ignore the open, often scarcely veiled endemic racism, the need for a more multicultural, non-Western aesthetic, and the social and class difficulties of the nation's effort to absorb successive waves of diverse immigrant populations. In a sense, they laid the foundation for their legacy when they explicitly addressed these issues in their *Credo* and then in their productions.

It would have been out of character for them to settle for tinkering around the edges of "just entertainment" when McFadden's European trips had provided several alternative models. Ironically, it was *because* the performing arts were a medium able to engage children at the emotional, intellectual, cultural, and artistic levels during their formative years that the arts needed to play a more central role in preparing the next generation to be defenders of democracy. Childhood was a time when core values, attitudes, and life dreams were forming, and future choices were being made. To overlook the ability of the performing arts to give big abstract concepts—like democracy or racial diversity—an emotional, visual, and intellectual reality made no sense: it was too valuable an asset. By connecting the CCSUs to the stories on stage, the performing arts could open doors—enabling diverse cultures, histories, and a broad range of other subjects to come alive, transcending the page in exciting and appealing ways. Sitting together in an auditorium or gymnasium and engaging directly with a live performance also created a sense of being in community and in a collaboration of learners. Consciously and unconsciously, live performance is a "we're all in this together" experience, and it didn't take Junior Programs long to see the pedagogical potential of this dynamic. They were also clear that considering the performing arts as more than entertainment in no way diminished either the artistic value of their work or the enjoyment delivered by their productions. In ways appropriate to their youthful audience, they were simply acting in accordance with Oskar Eustis' definition of theater's purpose: to provide a stage for the examination of alternative ideas, and to do so in ways that created empathy and a sense of community. Their approach also offered what Dr. Tiffany Manuel refers to as an "on ramp" or "racial justice runway," with TYA productions extending invitations and opportunities to engage in age-appropriate conversations focused on exploring and reframing the dominant narratives related to race and class.[384]

With such possibilities, Junior Programs saw no reason to settle for a narrower role. This was bold thinking. They were, in the best sense, true believers in the performing arts as an *essential element in the fabric of a civilized democratic society*, and they appear to have been unafraid to challenge and disrupt the prevailing assumptions as to the

VII. THE JUNIOR PROGRAMS LEGACY

purpose of arts and culture in the nation's social, political, and economic order. They *knew* that the performing arts were not simply the "cherry on top." Democracy was not an abstract ideal for them; and the performing arts were, and needed to be, part of the everydayness of normal life. Further, they believed they had a responsibility, even a duty, to use the performing arts for this larger purpose. Acting on this mission was in society's best interest—as well as their own.

Current events, in particular the 2016 US presidential election, has provided a wake-up call, alerting the nation to an alarmingly dysfunctional polarization in the electorate, and signaling a rising wave of fascism, racism, and serious ruptures in the nation's democratic processes. Contemporary performing arts organizations could do worse than to examine Junior Programs' bold reframing of their role. The 2016 election generated a frantic scramble of participation, civic engagement and grass-roots electoral organizing. Fortunately, the work of countless community organizations and activists led to multiple defeats for the party of Trump in 2020 and in the 2022 midterms. However, that defeat will be short-lived if, as a nation, we do not take a serious look at the fundamental structures, infrastructures, policies, and programs that contributed to the current crisis. The threat of climate change—no longer in the future, but in the disaster-prone here and now—feels apocalyptic. Racism and antisemitism not only are tolerated but have been encouraged by the former administration. Immigration—the lifeblood of diversity—is once more a battleground. And the decrease in a commitment to democracy and democratic values among the nation's younger demographics, as reflected in the World Values Survey, is cause for alarm.[385] On January 6, 2021, the nation watched in horror as Trump supporters and white supremacists stormed the US Capitol. The collective gasp of anguished astonishment literally was heard around the world.

It is the urgency of our current context that suggests an expanded role for TYA-USA and its member theaters, and AATE, and its practitioners. How can the performing arts today contribute to teaching children about democracy and its requisite equity and inclusion—its value, and the importance of doing everything possible to preserve it? Junior Programs provided an example, and more than ever, we must find new and more effective ways to instill in our children a set of democratic values during their formative years. Who better than the theaters for young audiences to step into the mix? And lest we forget, *Junior Programs had no roadmap to follow.* Yet they stepped into the uncharted territory *con brio*, experimented, learned, persisted, and succeeded for seven years. One advantage we have today is the significant increase in the number of TYA companies that now exist in every part of the country. What could be achieved if, *collectively,* they brought their creative thinking and talents to bear—not only on what they think is possible, but on what they determine is really needed. *"Vision" is the ability to see what does not yet exist.* And reframing—what scholars of management call a "paradigm shift"—is what makes reimagining and real innovation possible. It enables the dialogue and the energy *to move beyond what is currently possible.* It cracks open the status quo so new possibilities can emerge, possibilities that literally do not currently exist. This is not a new experience for the performing arts. During the late 1950s and early 1960s, the performing arts purposefully and intentionally shifted paradigms—from the commercial Broadway theater model to a regional theater model. Now, some sixty plus years later, there is evidence that it is time for another shift, one that should emphasize the untapped potential and the necessity of the performing arts as vital for the more effective education of our children.

The Power of Partnerships I – The Role of the Performing Arts in Education

Junior Programs' expanded view of children's theater understood the performing arts as an untapped pedagogical resource—reaching well beyond education related primarily to the performing arts. Of course, they understood the importance of educating the next generation in the creativity and skills involved in playwriting, acting, directing, and stagecraft, but for Junior Programs, it was a "both/and" rather than an "either/or." This expanded understanding of their role in the educational arena led to their central partnerships with major educational institutions, the formation of their Educational Guidance Committee, and the extensive development of their CCSUs for each production. As a result, they were able to develop not only partnerships with leading educators and experts in various fields at both the national and regional levels, but with a sprawling network of local school systems and front-line teachers across the nation. It is clear from the numerous reviews and articles that these partnerships were a significant factor in the company's seven continuous years of success.

It is important to remember that these broader partnerships were not instead of a focus on learning about the performing arts. As is common in performing arts education today, Junior Programs' CCSUs engaged teachers of the performing arts and their students in collaborative learning about the various arts disciplines, with curriculum materials for each opera, ballet and play focused on developing an appreciation of the musical, operatic, dance, and dramatic forms. These CCSUs, and the productions they supported, taught millions of children that opera was not dull and boring. Rather, it could keep them at the edge of their seats. They showed millions of children that Pushkin and Shakespeare were not elite authors: they were first and foremost great storytellers. And dance was not simply people prancing around waving their arms: instead, it offered a magic carpet that could transport them to other times and places with fascinating stories and legends to share.

What was unique about the Junior Programs CCSUs was the inclusion of extensive material focused on the different cultures and societies in which each production was set. The CCSUs for *The Emperor's Treasure Chest, Reward of the Sun God, Marco Polo, Robin Hood, Run, Peddler, Run,* and *Doodle Dandy* are all good examples of the ways in which Junior Programs quite literally used the performing arts as a key to open the door to extensive learning opportunities across a broad range of pedagogical disciplines. Curriculum resources for these numerous academic disciplines provided existing teachers with an eclectic range of materials that enabled them to enrich their own pedagogy without a significant investment of their personal time to track down the appropriate resources. In addition to materials and resources that were subject matter specific, these CCSUs were also organized into age-appropriate groupings with practical advice and suggestions on how to integrate specific subject matter into a cross-disciplinary whole. The CCSUs included related research activities, dramatizations, suggestions for oral and written reports, and prompts for class discussions. There was help with Culminating Activities, such as assembly programs, debates, costume parties, or the staging of an operetta, as well as post-performance Evaluation Activities. The CCSUs also included extensive materials and bibliographies about the various customs, mores, history, geography, politics, economics, and literature of the various cultures featured in their productions. If Junior Programs had not defined its role as more than entertainment—*and* as more than education in the performing arts—millions of children might not have had the opportunity to understand and explore the many ways in which Indigenous peoples were not savages. In fact, in today's climate challenged world, the Indigenous relationship to the natural world and their sense of communal responsibility offers important lessons from which all cultures can learn. Students also would not have learned that in many ways, Brazilian culture was not so very different from their own: that Brazil had its own rich history, complex social, cultural, and economic systems, and an important role to play in the political world order. Indeed, they would not have learned that the Hollywood stereotype of marauding banditos and loose women could not possibly be referring to Brazil, or to any other nation! In addition, without a discussion of Brazil's brand of enslavement, millions of children may not have had the opportunity to learn that the American brand of enslavement was not inevitable. Furthermore, millions of children would likely not have been exposed to the rich histories of the ancient Southeast Asian cultures of Persia, India, and China, or to the twelfth-century Chinese scientists who are credited with inventing the magnetic compass, a device that made global navigation possible.

It was not that some of this subject matter was not already included in traditional K-12 school curricula. Rather, what was unique was the opportunity Junior Programs provided to teachers and students to engage with a richer, more extensive and integrated suite of well-organized, age-appropriate materials and activities, especially those designed to weave the many discrete academic disciplines together into an organic whole. In this way, Junior Programs productions gave children a far more vivid and experiential sense of the people and places depicted in the company's productions. The CCSUs also helped connect the big historic events (history) with the day-to-day—the food people ate, the clothing they wore (home economics), or the games children played (physical education). The materials also made it easier to see the relationships between the arts and the social customs that shaped their lives (social sciences), as well as how the way their government worked or the way the US related to other countries and cultures (political science) could affect their own lives. By framing and defining their core mission as inclusive of social, political, economic, and cultural pedagogy, Junior Programs was able not only to enrich a child's education but to make it more interesting and fun. With trips to a local Persian rug dealer before or after seeing *Marco Polo,* the boundary between school—where traditional learning took place—and life in the larger community was erased, thereby sending a message that learning could and should take place everywhere.

Given the current state of public education in the United States, it is more critical than ever to reach children during their early formative years. This is the time when

VII. THE JUNIOR PROGRAMS LEGACY

the foundation of their core values is being constructed, and during which modeling desired behaviors can have an enormous impact. If today's performing artists looked through *Wei Ji's* opportunity lens, it would be hard not to see the untapped potential inherent in the development of more substantive partnerships among and between the performing arts, child development experts, and subject-matter teachers in the nation's K-12 educational institutions.

That said, the current situation in education at all levels reflects a broad and deep malady afflicting American society. Judging by the widespread underfunding of schools and the increasing opposition to any form of "critical race theory," it is becoming harder and harder to pretend that we are taking our fundamental responsibility to the nation's children seriously. Given the wave of book bans and the growing list of subject matter teachers are forbidden to teach, it is hard to see how today's young people are being properly prepared to be "citizens of tomorrow." How will they be able to engage with the interdependent social, political, economic, scientific, and global forces at play effectively and thoughtfully? Will they be able to weave those forces into something congruent with America's founding notions of "we the people" and "liberty for all?" While concerns such as these were exacerbated by the Trump administration and its supporters, it is important to understand that these problems did not begin in 2016. For too many years, both Republican and Democratic administrations have paid insufficient attention to the development and maintenance of democracy itself, and to the education needed to support that form of government. Instead, a steady and intentional drip of cynicism has led to the widespread erosion of faith in the very concept of government. "Shrink it until it's small enough to drown in the bathtub" has been one pervasive Republican theme; the other, elitist, often Democratic, neoliberal wave of "meritocracy" has steadily pushed power upward to the point where ordinary citizens feel they no longer have a voice.

If there is any sector or system that should take the preparation of the next generation of citizens in a democracy seriously, it is our educational institutions. However, the wave of teachers' strikes during 2019 and 2020 has highlighted the devastating impact of the Trump administration's budget cuts on class sizes, on supplies and resources, and on the enormous challenge of truly educating children in core skills such as critical thinking, creativity, collaboration, and innovation—all essential skills for the practice and preservation of democracy.[386] Most schools no longer teach what used to be called "Civics" and, to the consternation of many, most curricula still focus on "teaching to the test"—for which critical thinking, questioning, exploring, and imagination are not vital requirements. And the arts, which teach *all* those skills and more, have become little more than an afterthought, an add-on, or elective—if they are offered at all! US schools are in desperate need of all kinds of partnerships. When engaging in advocacy, numbers count! The kinds of partnerships Junior Programs forged with school systems and teachers across the country could add significantly to the number of voices advocating for a substantive overhaul of the nation's educational institutions, especially those focused on K-12.

To provide today's "citizens of tomorrow" with the necessary values and skills requires more than becoming more knowledgeable about the arts. Junior Programs clearly demonstrated that their various productions could make almost every K-12 subject come alive, thereby inspiring children to dig deeper into learning. TYA practitioners are expert entertainers who know how to effectively hold children's attention, how to craft age-appropriate stories, and how to pique children's curiosity. Therefore, they can make learning even difficult subjects vibrant and exciting, a major reason broader partnerships make so much sense. Would not such a reimagining and reframing of a broader partnership between the performing arts and education be of immense value today? And who better than the arts and artists to imagine something into existence?

Nevertheless, it is easy to become overwhelmed by the weight of current events. How could any performing arts organization, especially at a time of extremely scarce funding for the arts, and after three years of barely surviving a pandemic, possibly be able to have an impact on a single school, let alone a whole school system? However, that may be the wrong question. Research in related fields indicates that times of turmoil or even chaos—when the status quo already has been disrupted and the future is unknown—may, in fact, be the time of maximum opportunity for trying something new and boldly ambitious.[387]

The Power of Partnerships II – The Role of the Performing Arts in the Community

Cutting across all facets of Junior Programs' work was their belief in the importance of actively engaging local communities. This belief not only influenced their organizational structure; they saw community involvement as a central characteristic necessary for the maintenance of democracy. They valued and respected the communities in which they performed, treating them as partners—no matter how far they were from the theatrical hub of New York City. McFadden's national network of local sponsoring committees proved to be a highly effective organizational structure for their work. As noted earlier, Junior Programs' partnerships with the local affiliates of the Junior Leagues was one of the strongest links in their community network. However, as discussed in Chapter VI, Junior Programs' engagement with the communities in which they performed went well beyond their association with the local Junior Leagues. The full range of civic and social organizations were tapped, from the Kiwanis Clubs to the Associations of University Women. Local businesses were involved, including drugstores, clothing stores, bookstores, music stores, and toy stores. They all became part of a public relations and marketing network, promoting the season of productions with play-related displays and tickets for sale. Junior Programs made every effort to help connect their sponsoring committees with local radio stations and newspapers with a range of press releases, contests, prizes, and photo opportunities. In addition to local public schools, there were social service agencies that worked with blind, disabled, and low-income children, as well as orphanages and hospitals. Professional associations of local music and dance teachers played their part, organizing a musical interlude during intermission or providing a local narrator for one of the company's operas or ballets. Police departments and transportation companies also participated on the day of performances. One outcome of this broad-based and sustained involvement was the willingness of community after community to contract for season after season of Junior Programs' productions. Empty seats at a Junior Programs' performance were a rarity. Communities clearly wanted what Junior Programs provided, and because of their partnerships, Junior Programs had their fingers on the pulse of what communities needed.

Today, we no longer have several generations of young and middle-aged women in every city and town able to commit enormous amounts of volunteer time to organizing civic and community activities. This makes it impossible to just replicate the community-based network of sponsoring organizations that enabled Junior Programs to sustain seven years of touring. However, the value of their legacy is not simply in copying what they did. It is in understanding the central importance of engaging the broader community as active participants. That is the important guiding principle in any successful effort to create a larger and more diverse audience base. How this principle of broader engagement could play out in different cities and towns today would no doubt vary, but the ability of TYA theaters to effectively reimagine a broader role for their community—and for themselves—will depend, in significant measure, on how successful a company is at more deeply understanding what we now call "community engagement."

Unfortunately, the term is currently applied with little precision. It can mean anything from assembling a local advisory committee for each production (and then letting it disband) to distributing free or discount tickets to local community organizations or schools. It can include forays into communities of color for specific productions or tapping local academic institutions for subject-matter experts to ensure an authentic production. Or it can be a longer-term strategy unfolding and evolving over a period of several years as new community-based partnerships emerge and new audiences are sustainably engaged. This lack of conceptual and practical precision in terminology is just one of many current problems. With so many live and virtual entertainment choices now available to both children and adults, and with the vast number of social media platforms at play, even getting a community's attention is more difficult than ever—especially since both the children and their parents are too-often over committed or chained to their screens. But again, least we forget, Junior Programs managed to succeed despite the competition they faced from the unstoppable success of the radio and motion picture industries.

One way to put Junior Programs' principle of community engagement into practice would be to define what is necessary in this arena with more precision. What is relevant in terms of their legacy is the clarity of their commitment to developing the next generation, and the inclusivity with which they communicated that message throughout the community. Today, we are fortunate that several bodies of knowledge exist about potential partnerships and the skillsets necessary to develop them effectively. Such information can be helpful in creating a contemporary version of meaningful and strategic engagement with the broader community. At its most basic, "A partnership is an arrangement where parties . . . agree to cooperate to advance their mutual interests."[388] It sounds straight forward, but it is full of nuance, especially when a partnership involves racial and economic differences. What are the real *mutual* interests? *Who* gets to define them? How do you build trust? Essential concepts here are listening and respect, concepts that were part of Junior Programs' everyday practice.

The fields of community organizing, and social justice are two disciplines that feature bodies of knowledge and skillsets that are valuable when considering community engagement. While there are literally dozens of models of community organizing (e.g. grassroots, social action, community building, coalition building, and social movements, among many others), there is a set of key characteristics most of the models hold in common. All include some form of direct participation and self-determination; they foster some level of democratic or participatory decision-making; they seek to build a local base to redistribute power and resources more equitably; and they work to develop local leadership. All these characteristics are in one way or another congruent with the values Junior Programs held. There is broad agreement that effective organizing in a community is not a quick fix or a "one-and-done." It requires a long-term strategy, and, like productive partnerships, success is based on mutual respect, inclusiveness, shared power, and *a willingness to listen more and talk less*. Success is contingent on identifying and acting on genuinely shared interests and concerns, identifying and engaging with local leaders, and pursuing a set of actions designed to build a sense of community empowerment.[389] Getting people to buy tickets is a by-product, an acknowledgement of value perceived, not the goal of the relationship. Successful community engagement is transformational, not transactional.

Specific efforts to apply community organizing models to the performing arts have been explored in "Queen of Green and Contessa of Community Outreach," by Seema Sueko, former deputy artistic director at Arena Stage. Her approach, which she calls Consensus Organizing, can be useful in surfacing mutual self-interest, cross-community collaborations, and audience development in diverse communities.[390] In May 2019, just prior to the pandemic, the New York Department of Cultural Affairs issued a request for proposals for "Community Organizing 101: Engagement Tactics for Cultural Organizations" for thirty New York City cultural organizations. They did so after hearing from the community that their organizations needed to learn how to go beyond "outreach" to deeper more meaningful community engagement. The course was designed to integrate community organizing tools into the day-to-day work of the cultural sector by offering strategies for sustained community building and audience development. The course curriculum went well beyond marketing and sales, to explore inclusive programming practices and culturally responsive curricula, as well as authentic opportunities for community participation, especially of access to culture for historically marginalized groups.[391]

Kent State University's "Five Principles of Social Justice," include access, equity, diversity, participation, and human rights. These social justice principles map almost perfectly to issues identified in an article in *Theater for Young Audiences* (Fall 2019).[392] "Beyond the Traditional," highlights the issues of accessibility, diversity, equity, and inclusion as of critical import to TYA theaters. This congruence suggests that learning more about the experiences of social justice activists could offer performing arts organizations useful guidance for current approaches to successful community engagement. One article—"From Assets to Agents of Change: Social Justice, Organizing, and Youth Development"—stands out as particularly relevant for the focus Junior Programs placed on preparing young people for activities related to protecting and preserving democracy. The authors state that "political participation has been the cornerstone of American democratic ideals," and they identify barriers to democratic participation as one of the greatest challenges facing young people today. They pose two questions that would have resonated with Junior Programs. First, "What role can youth play in forging a democratic society?" and second, "How can adults support sociopolitical development among youth?" The article cites numerous examples of the effective organizing of youth for social justice. These include the 1960s civil rights lunch counter sit-ins; South African youth protesting the Bantu educational system; a San Francisco protest of 6,000 young people calling out the underfunding of schools; and a protest against California Proposition 21 which attempted to try children as young as 14 as adults in the criminal justice system. The authors assert that participation in these kinds of actions is among the most effective ways for young people to learn how to be full citizens. They argue that such involvement not only serves to revitalize democracy by including the voices of those most directly affected, it also teaches young people critical and systemic thinking. It provides a positive sense of identity by enabling the youthful participants to see themselves as effective change agents able to transform toxic environments.[393]

I do not mean to imply that theaters for young audiences should be out organizing protests. However, if the performing arts is to be more than entertainment, it needs to have some increased level of direct experience with what is going on in the communities of which they are a part, especially in communities of color. The image of the young people in *Doodle Dandy* cheerfully riding Humphry Dumphry out of Springville on a rail may seem impossibly naive in comparison to the life of many of today's teenagers, especially those of color. Nevertheless, the importance of adults—and the performing arts—providing early opportunities for young audiences to experience a sense of agency remains. What that looks like—and how that should be actualized— are questions to be answered. Organizations such as TYA-USA and AATE are ideally positioned to partner with communities to find ways to support the direct involvement of young people in the dialogue required to answer those questions.

Reframing the Role of the Performing Arts in Addressing Racism

Considering the state of race relations at that time, the *Credo* Junior Programs articulated was a bold statement. It challenged the status quo by committing the company to productions that sought to normalize racial and cultural diversity as a democratic asset (e.g., *Reward of the Sun God, Emperor's Treasure Chest,* and *Marco Polo*). Junior Programs made the decision to tap the power of the performing arts to tell positive stories about various marginalized communities in ways that communicated the richness and strengths of diversity. They took this route rather than perpetuate the negative othering of those communities by the larger society. This made Junior Programs an important pioneer and leader in the long, uphill battle for the equality and inclusion required for a flourishing democracy. Junior Programs chose to tell stories congruent with America's highest aspiration—that of equality for all: for the urgent need to protect America's democracy, for the value of diversity, and for the inclusion and acceptance of those who were unlike the dominant white population.

However, their commitment was just a beginning. They were successful in keeping their ticket prices low so that children of all economic levels could attend. But there were hurdles—such as touring with a mixed-race cast—that Junior Programs was unable to overcome. Their efforts were not perfect in other ways as well: white authors wrote the scripts addressing racial and cultural differences. Their commitment to authenticity was filtered through a white lens, and the racial composition of their audiences was primarily white. Nevertheless, at that time, their specific and repeated focus on the social, cultural and racial inequities so deeply ingrained in the American culture provided the beginnings of an alternative.[394] Junior Programs' clear and unequivocal articulation of the need to reach *all* children, regardless of race, culture, religion, and class—and, importantly, linking these issues to the next generation's ability to protect and sustain democracy—places them in the category of pioneers and leaders. It set them on a new path as they worked to counter the divisive consequences of the country's history of social, economic, and artistic racism and the pernicious othering that helped keep it in place. Despite the many racial constraints affecting their operations, including those they were unable to overcome, Junior Program repeatedly commissioned productions that normalized other races, cultures, and ethnicities (*Reward of the Sun God; Emperor's Treasure Chest, Run, Peddler, Run,* and *Marco Polo*). Their CCSUs did not shy away from the inclusion of specific discussions about difficult issues. And with *Doodle Dandy,* they were not only willing to help children confront the problem of fascism's continuing attacks on democracy, they also were able to do so in an age-appropriate way which had their youthful audience "cheering for democracy" as enthusiastically as they would cheer for their favorite sports team.

Every day, we read of another threat to the ability of *all* Americans to cast their vote in elections, to freedom of speech, and to the freedom to teach and learn an accurate history of the United States, and to the hard-won promises of our constitution. The very ability of our government to operate in a democratic manner is being challenged by those who refuse to acknowledge the racist history of the nation, or who insist that its negative impacts no longer exist. Despite, or even because of, these attacks, recent scholarship has reflected a growing recognition of the importance of "critical race theory" (CRT).[395] For example, CRT research not only identifies the "joined-at-the-hip" relationship between historic redlining and the widespread racial discrimination that still occurs in housing—with its related educational segregation—but also reveals the literally "whitewashed" content of American history permeating the current educational system at every level. This current unwillingness to tell an honest story about the US history of enslavement, together with the systemic inequality in the way the nation's educational institutions are funded strongly suggests that as currently constituted, America's educational systems are unable to perform their critical role in educating the next generation to be sustainers of the equality and equity on which real democracy is based. The result is an often purposeful and systemic exclusion of people of color from many of democracy's most important benefits.

This "whitewashing" holds true for the racial history of much of the performing arts as well. On June 8, 2020, the long-festering racism in the performing arts exploded with the "We See You White American Theater Manifesto." This was a groundbreaking call for "transformative measures, guided by principles of self-determination, presence, joy, access, protection, transparency, and integrity in the spirit of independence from our colonialized past and present."[396] On July 10, 2020, a *New York Times* article titled "Theater Artists of Color Enumerate Demands for Change," characterized the Manifesto, if adopted, as resulting "in a sweeping restructuring of the theater ecosystem in America."[397] For years, there has been a broad range of mostly unsuccessful efforts to address issues of structural racism and inequity in the performing arts, but this document finally moved the issue to center stage, making it impossible for the field to look the other way. It pushed hundreds of theaters that had been paying little more than lip service to the problems to begin to seriously and thoroughly examine their organizational status quo. It was finally clear that they needed to identify concrete changes designed to dismantle the many institutional systems that have kept social, economic, and artistic racism tenaciously in place.

With the issuance of the manifesto, the current performing arts status quo has begun to splinter. Whether this splintering will be enough to crack open and reframe the way the performing arts are organized, thus enabling systemic changes to emerge and grow is still an open question. On the plus side, virtually every aspect of the performing arts and its various institutions has become a topic for discussion, reexamination, and rethinking. Whose stories get told? By whom? Who has access? What is the role of technology? How do the current performing arts business models hold racism in place? What is the relationship between performing arts organizations and their communities, be they white or communities of color? These are crucial questions to which we urgently need answers, but there is yet another important question that needs to be considered—one that Junior Programs asked eighty years ago: What role can/could/should/must the performing arts play in reframing the nation's conversation about race in a democratic society?

These questions need to be answered by each performing arts organization, and collectively by the TYA field as a whole. To answer such questions will require multiple partners—internally, from within the performing arts field, and externally, from those in the community as well as other disciplines such as systems change, non-arts education, community organizing, social justice, and the full range of African American, Latinx, Asian, and Native American studies. Without directly addressing such questions, the performing arts runs the risk of remaining trapped in its current paradigm, nibbling around the edges of non-systemic solutions. Einstein is purported to have said something to the effect of, "The problems that exist in the world today cannot be solved by the level of thinking that created them."[398] Learning how to reframe problems—how to pose the right questions, and how to successfully make the necessary *systemic* changes that would enable marginalized voices to mainstream their stories—becomes an essential but complex skillset. This requires a network of partnerships and an organizational and industry culture committed to continuous learning. Both partnerships and continuous learning were important parts of Junior Programs' strategy, and both need to be incorporated into today's strategies as well.

Yet in many ways, our nation is more divided on these issues than at any time since the Civil War. Imani Perry, the Black author of *South to America,* calls it the "changing same."[399] An alarming number of states are banning in-school discussions of racial issues, especially anything based on the recent scholarship that falls into the CRT category. The critical question now is one embedded in another article in the Fall 2019 issue of *TYA Today.* In "Beyond the Traditional," Shavonne T. Coleman, a performing artist and educator, highlighted issues of accessibility, diversity, equity, and inclusion. The discussion included several encouraging comments. Stephanie Ybarra, artistic director at Baltimore Center Stage quoted adrienne maree brown's book *Emergent Strategy,* saying, "Art is not neutral. It either upholds or disrupts the status quo." Ybarra went on to say, "we are either working toward justice or furthering injustice." Coleman added, "There is no personal shame in our country's historical structures, only in continuing to ignore it."[400] Assertions such as these, coupled with the 2020 police killing of George Floyd and numerous other Black men, women, and children in the years before and since, all point to overarching questions: What will the performing arts do about persistent and pernicious inequities? Is the current generation of performing arts practitioners willing to use the performing arts to disrupt the status quo and work actively toward racial justice?

One possible answer lies in understanding that *disruptions are opportunities*: when the structures keeping the status quo in place are loosened, the *possibility* of sustainable change increases. The status quo is exquisitely designed to maintain itself, so change is by no means inevitable or easy. However, when the norms of a culture no longer function effectively, as occurred during the COVID-19 pandemic, previously unimaginable new patterns in systemic arrangements suddenly become possible. Massive numbers of people working from home post-COVID is an example of one of those changes, and despite a predictable push to "return to the office," it seems unlikely that the old norm will ever fully reestablish itself. Unsurprisingly, working from home snowballed into an almost endless series of other formerly unimaginable changes. Most businesses have had to shift to include online ordering and home delivery; urban centers need to find new uses for their sparsely populated office buildings; and restaurants are unlikely to give up their outdoor spaces, despite the resultant decrease in parking spaces. Whether everyone likes or approves of these changes is not the issue. The fact is that new norms are being established *because* the old way of doing things was disrupted. COVID caused a massive shakeup, but the same dynamic is at work in smaller disruptions as well.

In essence, Junior Programs took advantage of the widespread disruptions caused by the Depression, the rise of fascism, the possibility of another world war, the shift in society's view of childhood, Dewey's new philosophy of education, the continued influx of immigrants, and the threat to democracy. Their *Credo* laid out their desired destination. They set a course and then proceeded to navigate in ways that identified or even created opportunities to move forward. This was evident in the scripts they commissioned, the research they did, and the relationships and partnerships they developed with a wide range of people possessing various forms of cross-cultural expertise. Today, utilizing the CRT lens, we can finally "see" the vast array of microaggressions, as well as larger institutional infrastructures that both create and maintain multiple forms of systemic oppression. The work that needs to be done is clearer than ever! In response to the "We See You White Theater Manifesto," many organizations have created or are in the process of creating plans to deal with the behavioral and structural changes they need to make. However, the challenge going forward is multi-dimensional. First, organizations must make sure that the plans focused on changes to their internal structures, policies, processes, and programs are effectively implemented and sustained. Second, changing individual organizations will not be sufficient. Collective change is necessary. Third, organizations such as TYA-USA and AATE need to position themselves to foster partnerships and a broad range of experiments among and between their members; and fourth, they need to partner with a range of social and racial justice advocacy organizations with the knowledge, experience, and expertise in how best to achieve sustainable anti-racist change. In other words, using the performing arts to help achieve the racial justice necessary for a thriving democracy will require strategic, broad-based collective effort from organizations like TYA-USA and AATE, as well as from individual theaters and their community partners. There is one more thing to remember: there are few professions as ideally placed as TYA in terms of the ability to connect with the next generation during their value-forming years, and equity, diversity, inclusion, and belonging are all values-based concerns. The status quo has been cracked open. Thus, despite the many difficulties involved, finding bold ways to address these issues is a major opportunity, one that can move the performing arts to center-stage.

Junior Programs' Artistic Innovations

With a social and artistic mission as innovative as the one they chose, Junior Programs understood that they would not be able to turn that mission into a reality if they did not change the way the performing arts were presented to children. There had been a scattering of Broadway productions like *Peter Pan* and various holiday spectaculars. These were available to a select number of children whose families could afford the ticket prices. There also were local or regional adult professional efforts such as the Goodman Children's Theater in Chicago, and Clare Tree Major's touring Threshold Players. However, the vast majority of performing arts productions for children had been either part of the Junior Leagues' early commitment to amateur adult theatricals, or part of the settlement house movement in which neighborhood children themselves took part in the productions. Those were—and are—all worthy undertakings. Junior Programs, however, believed the nation's children also deserved the best of professional theater.

In an interesting article about artificial intelligence, Kareem Abdul-Jabbar—six-time NBA champion, eight-time award winning Columnist of the Year, social activist, and philanthropist—defines innovation as seeing things in a new way, from

VII. THE JUNIOR PROGRAMS LEGACY   333

a different perspective, or from a reframed context. What artists of all kinds do, he says, is find new ways of seeing the world, new ways of expressing their vision, and from that perspective, develop new and transforming solutions—solutions that were literally invisible from the old vantage points.[401] Artists, then, by definition, are leaders. They help society focus on the needs of the future. Junior Programs would have agreed with Abdul-Jabbar's assessment. Their approach to almost every challenge was to step outside the comfort zone of the prevailing artistic expertise and question "the way it's always been done." This new perspective literally enabled them to see possibilities that had not previously been recognized. Opera for children? To most people, that was an absurdity. As was the idea of interesting children in ballet. Succeeding at those and other such undertakings required a constant willingness to question basic assumptions, to listen deeply, to take risks, and to experiment until they found an approach that eliminated the original problem. Both McFadden and Lancourt seemed to excel at this, and they never lost the flexibility of mind required for continuous learning.

Lancourt, responsible for Junior Programs' artistic decisions, and the success of each production utilized this approach to generate a steady stream of artistic innovations for all three companies. These innovations fall into four categories. First were those that made opera and dance accessible and fun for young audiences; second, was Lancourt's creative and seamless fusion of drama, dance, music and song; third, the commitment to authenticity as a way to make all productions more vivid and compelling; and fourth, the ability to mount touring productions that were qualitatively on a par with Broadway productions.

Making Opera and Dance Accessible

From the outset, Lancourt's position gave him the opportunity to use his musical and operatic expertise to re-envision opera in a way that would make it both accessible and enjoyable to children. In multiple interviews, he made it clear that he had no patience with operatic traditions that put an audience to sleep. With his eye on the needs of his youthful audience, and without compromising the musical line, he introduced appealing and amusing dramatic actions into the staging of the company's three operas. Dozens of reviews attest to his success at holding the children's attention. He also made sure the pace of the productions never lagged:

there would be no static arias—literally "showstoppers"—to interrupt the story line and slow things down. He intentionally hired singers who, in addition to their vocal talents, had significant acting skills, enabling them to bring their characters to life in vivid and nuanced ways. His decision to have the operas sung in English, unusual at the time, was deemed necessary to retain the children's attention, and many reviews noted the unusual clarity of the singers' enunciation. Similarly, he made the decision to forego even the semblance of an orchestra. While this was in part dictated by pragmatic logistical and financial concerns, he presciently determined that paring back the number of instruments would help his audience to better hear and appreciate the musical line. At the time, all these adaptations were new and untested. But for Lancourt, they were simply part of what needed to be done, and he brought an appealing mix of confidence and humility to the challenges he sought to overcome.

He was also responsible for another major innovation related to access—the integration of the role of the narrator, a character Junior Programs incorporated into all their operas and ballets as well as the company recordings of *The Bumble Bee Prince* and *Robin Hood*. Costumed in appropriate attire, the narrator sat at the side of the stage and told the story, making it easy for even the youngest audience members to understand what was happening. The popularity and effectiveness of this new role appears to have been universal. Three accomplished actresses alternated in the part, or as noted earlier, someone from the local community with acting experience might be asked to step in. In writing each of the narrator's scripts, Lancourt also made sure that there was a set of questions to be posed directly to the youthful audience. It was a simple device that was effective in keeping the children engaged. This added touch worked remarkably well, as the youthful audiences always answered with spontaneity and enthusiasm. In one interview, Lancourt commented that they (the audience) "never missed their cue."

From the development of the narrator's role, it was only a small additional step to the ballet company's creation of the "dance-play." Lancourt worked with Strawbridge to develop this new form, and much like training wheels on a child's bicycle, it made it easier for a child to strike a balance between the unfamiliar dance forms and the more familiar experience of listening to a story. In a paradoxical way, it not only helped make sense of what was happening on stage, it led to the beginning of an understanding of how one could tell a story without words.

VII. THE JUNIOR PROGRAMS LEGACY 335

From the outset, it was clear that Junior Programs did not do "tried and true." They seem to have seen opportunity everywhere. For example, most children already knew the story of *Hansel and Gretel,* and *Pinocchio.* Then why not use this familiarity to their advantage? How much easier it would be to usher a child into a new form—opera and ballet—with an old familiar tale. This steady stream of artistic surprises—large and small— kept their productions fresh and captivating, contributing to their continuing success.

The Synthesis of Story, Dance, and Song

Unwittingly, the company's penultimate production of *Marco Polo* turned out to be one of Junior Programs' most important artistic innovations. Due to the restrictions imposed by the impending war, they were no longer able to tour three companies. Faced with this challenge, Lancourt drew on all they had learned about theater for young audiences from their innovative, social and culturally themed plays, and from the several artistic innovations that had made their operas and ballets into crowd pleasers. The result was *Marco Polo,* a production that integrated the various performing arts disciplines—drama, dance, music, and song—to create a balanced and uniquely American form. The script he wrote addressed several serious issues—cultural and racial differences, the need for cross-cultural and religious tolerance, and even elements of familial strife. It combined acting, music, songs, and dances, so that each artistic discipline was used to advance the plot in an organic way. Singers sang, dancers danced, and actors acted, but everyone had lines to deliver that served to move the story inexorably forward. In 1941, such an artistic synthesis was unusual, having been "invented" by Jerome Kern and Oscar Hammerstein in their 1927 musical *Showboat*. Indeed, it was the popularity of *Showboat* that, in essence, created the form we now know as American musical theater. Whether Lancourt was consciously influenced by *Showboat* or not is unknown, but he had become sufficiently skilled in each of the performing arts to be able to achieve a similar synthesis in both *Marco Polo,* and *Doodle Dandy.* The latter was his most important story about what it takes to preserve democracy, and he told it with great effectiveness. Not a note or movement in the piece was superfluous, and through a series of dramatically integrated songs and dances, as one review put it, he had every child loudly cheering for democracy as the production moved the story to its happy conclusion.

The Commitment to Authenticity

The issue of authenticity is complex and often highly emotional, especially in the context of CRT. Accusations of cultural appropriation are often a significant part of today's dialogue on the subject, frequently generating heated discussions concerning who has the right to use or comment on various cultural expressions. However, in the 1930s and '40s, Junior Programs framed the issue as a means of providing a more positive and respectful alternative to Hollywood's negative stereotypes of people of color. As noted earlier, their concept of authenticity, while well intentioned, was, at best, underdeveloped—a far cry from today's understanding of what is or isn't authentic. Nevertheless, their version was an important step forward. From an artistic, religious, and cultural perspective, they were able to make reasonably accurate copies of authentic garments and *kachina* masks for *Reward of the Sun God*. Photographs indicate that the masks did contribute to Junior Programs' ability to present an exciting, intriguing, and fascinating picture of the Native American Hopi culture and religion. Similarly, they went to great lengths to ensure that the dances and costumes in *The Emperor's Treasure Chest*, created and supervised by several Brazilian cultural and governmental organizations, would captivate their young audience with its energy and unusual movements.

However, the dances for *Marco Polo* would likely present a problem today. Although St. Denis had been considered one of the leading authorities on Oriental dance, in reality she had been greatly influenced by her audiences' fascination with anything exotic. Her "Oriental" performances fed that appetite, but today, it is widely acknowledged that, while she was a major pioneer of modern dance, neither her dances nor the costumes could be considered authentic representations of the Indian, Chinese, or other Asian cultures. Nevertheless, according to the preponderance of newspaper reviews, even these imperfect attempts at authenticity went a long way toward capturing and holding the interest of Junior Programs youthful audiences, sparking their imaginations, and drawing them more deeply into the positive stories about a marginalized culture.

Another form of authenticity played an important role in Junior Programs' artistic choices. For several of their productions, we know that extensive historical research informed their decisions. Margaret Carlisle's years of research in England enabled Junior Programs to include numerous unfamiliar early English tunes and songs in *Robin Hood*. There was also the careful copy of an authentic medieval tapestry hanging in the Metropolitan Museum of Art used as a backdrop for *Robin Hood* that contributed to the ballet's effort to convey a sense of its medieval period. And Elie Siegmeister, composer for *Doodle Dandy*, had spent a lifetime researching early American songs. *The Brooklyn New York Eagle*, (Dec 20, 1942) said of his music for *Doodle Dandy*, "there are psalms of the Pilgrims . . . ballads of courting . . . sea chanteys, children's game songs, street cries and folk tunes . . . it is the stuff Americans have been humming, whistling, chanting, crooning, shaking a foot to or scratching a fiddle at ever since there has been an America," and it was the incorporation of these lively early American musical themes that contributed to the play's ability to connect with its young audience.

How the issue of authenticity will impact today's TYA choices is an open question. Like "telling the truth," it is part of building trust, a key ingredient of productive partnerships. That Junior Programs identified it as important is yet another indication of their desire to create a world on stage that portrayed marginalized communities in a positive way.

Sets to Fit Every Performance Space

One of Junior Programs' major achievements was the ability of their designers to create sets that were not only visually engaging, but flexible enough to be set up quickly and easily in an almost endless variety of performance spaces. There were school auditoriums and gymnasiums of varying sizes and shapes, and ease of access could be a challenge. However, it is clear from production photographs that the various designers for Junior Programs were up to the task and did not sacrifice splendor for adjustability. *Marco Polo* featured an almost life-sized gondola that moved across the rear of the stage in Act I. During Act II, Marco's travels from Italy to China were charted on an enormous, illuminated map as several shadow puppet figures were highlighted as they moved across the vast distances. However, by the time *Doodle Dandy* began to tour, it had become necessary to reimagine what a quality production would look like with only minimal scenery and a few props. Again, the designers were up to the task, creatively using visual projections to replace the usual scenery. As they listened to the audience responses and maintaining their characteristic learning mode to the very end, they quickly understood that the children's imagination easily filled in the blanks. That they were on the right track is confirmed in another article in the Fall 2019 issue of *TYA Today*. "Page to Stage" discusses the uses of new technologies and suggests that lighting needs to be "as flexible as possible," that sound technology needs to give aural suggestions, "so kid's imagination could fill in the gaps," and sets need to "use projections" to depict quickly changing scenes. The echoes and connections between Junior Programs and the present are unmistakable.[402]

Junior Programs artistic innovations were clearly a major factor in their success. However, by definition, successful innovations soon become old news. The legacy here is not in the specifics, but in the way they rolled with the punches. *They seemed never to struggle to hold back the need for change; rather they seemed to focus on being part of and shaping the change.*

The Legacy of Leadership

By definition, beginnings are imperfect, and outcomes are often incomplete. Learning is a process. Developing partnerships and relationships takes time. Breaking with the status quo is messy, often painful and scary, and is seldom linear. The challenge for today's performing arts companies, as it was for Junior Programs, is to make the break, to keep going, and *to be intentional about learning*—holding the desired outcomes as a *visible* guiding star. That is what Junior Programs did on every level for the entirety of their seven years—artistically, socially, educationally, and organizationally. Junior Programs possessed the boldness of the innocent, serving as pioneers and artistic leaders in the then virtually nonexistent field of adult professional children's theater. They approached their work with a fresh set of eyes and a bold and visionary set of guiding principles. When they deemed it necessary, they broke old molds, inventing new solutions whenever the old ways no longer served their needs.

There can be little question that they were pioneers and leaders in their field, not only for issues of access, equity, diversity, and inclusion but in the way they reached deep into the smaller cities and towns of America, planting some early seeds for today's network of regional children's theater. Given the current social and political scene, it seems worth considering not only their *Credo*, and sense of responsibility to the next generation as the future of democracy, but their many forms of engagement with local communities, and, above all, their belief that the performing arts should and could be a powerful element in all aspects of a child's education, especially in the arena of social justice. That their demise was a loss to the communities, the schools, and the children they served, as well as to the budding field of theater for young audiences seems clear. Yet almost a century later, what they were able to achieve offers a beacon of hope, an inspiration, and a set of principles to guide current and future efforts. Their *Credo* and mission are as important and relevant now as it was then. They understood the power of live performance to inspire and encourage children to learn, and they believed in the potential of the performing arts as a critical component for the flowering of democracy in a civil society. These important insights have never been more urgently needed.

It would be tempting to look at the current landscape and feel discouraged. We no longer have Junior Program's protection of innocence. We *know* how hard it is to change institutions and systemic structures. The reach of any individual geographically based theater is limited, and educational systems are struggling to provide even the basic building blocks of a twenty-first-century education. However, today, there are a growing number of individuals and institutions (theatrical and educational) engaged in exploring and addressing these issues, many with a far more sophisticated understanding of the complex problems and challenges we face than existed during the lifetime of Junior Programs. It is striking that every one of the current issues being discussed today was also of concern to Junior Programs, be it inclusivity, accessibility, democracy, social justice, community participation, respect for young people, engagement, artistic excellence, innovation, inspiration, pedagogical excellence, or the need for and involvement of trained performing arts professionals. The rediscovery of the Junior Programs story provides not only a vivid case example of an early effort to address these problems, but also one that was impressively successful in its contribution to a foundation for a new theatrical field—a nationwide Theater for Young Audiences.

Junior Programs was a pioneer in this work. It is for today's organizations, such as TYA-USA, AATE, and the many other performing arts organizations, to continue resolutely down the path forged by Junior Programs. While many of the issues remain the same, the specific solutions will have to take new forms and will require new structures, and this is as it should be. We cannot simply copy what they did. The virtual world forced on us by COVID may actually be an opportunity. When thinking about our "return to normal," we would do well to remember that Junior

Programs did not cling to or model itself on the past. Nor should today's performing artists!

Junior Programs' boldness, creativity, flexibility, and willingness to experiment are timeless, while their inventiveness, inclusiveness, leadership and many successes should serve as inspiration for other such initiatives. Junior Programs pushed open a door to a set of artistic, social, political, and educational opportunities. At that time, few understood that the performing arts had something unique to offer when attempting to solve major social concerns. McFadden called their work "an experiment." Lancourt called the work "an adventure." Both words offer an image of immense opportunities for TYA practitioners everywhere.

VIII. APPENDIX I
PARTIAL RECONSTRUCTION OF JUNIOR PROGRAMS TOURING SCHEDULE

Number of Performances: 1936–1943 2,016*
Number of Own Productions: 1,290
Maximum Number of Towns in one year: 220
Total states played in: 42 and Canada
Maximum Number of Opera Performances in One Year: 136
Maximum Number of Ballet Performances in One Year: 156
Maximum Number of Players Performances in One Year: 104

*This number includes single bookings of non-Junior Programs productions such as concerts, solo performances, etc.

A Partial Listing of Junior Programs' Tours States, Cities and Towns, Dates and Productions

Key:
HG – *Hansel and Gretel*
MP – *The Adventures of Marco Polo*
Jack – *Jack and the Beanstalk*
RH – *The Adventures of Robin Hood*
Emperor – *The Emperor's Treasure Chest*
Sun God – *Reward of the Sun God*
Pin – *Pinocchio*
BBP – *The Bumble Bee Prince*
Swineherd – *The Princess and the Swineherd*
RPR – *Run Peddler Run*
DD – *Doodle Dandy of the USA*
Puck – *The Adventures of Puck*

CITIES & STATES	DATES & PRODUCTIONS
Gadsden, AL	Nov. 8, 1939 – HG; Nov. 26, 1941 – MP
Montgomery, AL	Nov. 24, 1940 – Jack; n.d. – RH; Nov 18, 1941 – MP
Tuscaloosa, AL	n.d. – Emperor
Little Rock, AR	Nov. 7, 1937 – HG; 1937-8 – Sun God; 1937-8 – Pin
Bakersfield, CA	March 17, 1942 – MP
Chico, CA	March 4, 1940 - Jack
Los Angeles, CA	March 23, 1940 – BBP; 1941 – Emperor
Monterey, CA	Feb. 28, 1941 – ?
Oakland, CA	n.d. – Swineherd; n.d. – Emperor
Salinas, CA	March 16, 1942 – MP
San Francisco, CA	March 18, 1942 – MP
Bridgeport, CT	March 13, 1940 – Pin; Sept. 28, 1940 – RH; Nov. 10, 1940 – Jack; Oct. 8, 194? – MP
Danbury, CT	n.d. – H&G
Greenwich, CT	April 16, 1940 – RPR
Hartford, CT	1937-8 – Pin & HG; March 4, 1940 – Sun God; n.d. – RH; Jan. 21, 1942 – MP
New Haven, CT	April 22, 1937 – Pin; April 13, 1941 – Emperor
Thompsonville, CT	n.d. – HG; n.d. – Emperor
Waterbury, CT	1937-8 –Sun God; 1937-8 – Pin
Whitneyville, CT	April 21, 1941 – Emperor
Washington, DC	1937-8 – Sun God; 1937-8 – Swineherd; 1937-8 – BBP
Clearwater, FL	??
Jacksonville, FL	n.d. – Emperor; Dec. 3, 1941 – MP; Nov. 8, 1942 – DD
Panama City, FL	Jan. 29, 1941
Sarasota, FL	1939 – HG
St. Petersburg, FL	Nov. 22, 1940 – RH; May 28, 1940 – Swineherd; 1940-41 – BBP; n.d. 1940-41 – RPR; Dec. 4, 1941 – MP
Tallahassee, FL	March 9, 1941 – Emperor
West Palm Beach, FL	Nov. 20, 1941 – MP
Atlanta, GA	n.d. – Emperor
Bainbridge, GA	Feb. 3, 1941 – BBP
Columbus, GA	1937-8 – Pin; Feb. 10, 1939 – BBP; Oct. 29, 1940 – RH; Nov 8, 1942 – DD
Macon, GA	1937-8 – Pin; Jan 29, 1939 – HG; n.d. – Pinocchio; n.d. – RH
Savannah, GA	Feb. 5, 1939, Feb. 14, 1939 – ??

VIII. APPENDIX I PARTIAL RECONSTRUCTION TOURING SCHEDULE

CITIES & STATES	DATES & PRODUCTIONS
Ames, IA	n.d. – RPR
Burlington, IA	n.d. – H&G; n.d. – Jack; April 23-24, 1940 – RH; Oct. 1940 – Emperor
Waterloo, IA	n.d. – Jack
Elkhart, IN	n.d. – MP
Evansville, IN	April 14, 1940 – BBP; Jan. 26, 1941 – RH
Ft. Wayne, IN	Dec. 11, 1937 – HG; 1937-8 – Pin; n.d. – MP
Gary, IN	1937-8 – Sun God; 1937-8 – Pin; 1937-8 – BBP; n.d. – RPR
Indianapolis, IN	1936-7 - Pin; 1937-8 - Swineherd; Feb. 7, 1939 – HG; March 15, 1940 - BBP
Kokomo, IN	1936-7 – Pin
Richmond, IN	1937-8 – BBP
South Bend, IN	1936-7 – Pin; March 7, 1937 – Pin
Belleville, IL	Jan. 19, 1939 – ??
Bloomington, IL	1937-8 – Pin
Charleston, IL	May 8, 1941 – BBP
Chicago, IL	May 21, 1940 – BBP
Decatur, IL	1936-7 – Pin; 1937-8 – BBP; Nov. 3, 1940 – Puck
Dixon, IL	Sept. 28, 1940 – RH
East St. Louis, IL	1937-8 – Sun God; 1937-8 – Pin
Evansville, IL	Jan. 26, 1940 – RH
Joliet, IL	1937-8 – Pin
La Grange/Western Springs, IL	1940 – RH; n.d. – MP
Lake Forest, IL	Sept, 26, 1940 – RH; Feb. 21, 1941 – RPR; April 25, 1941 – Jack; Oct. 16, 1941 - MP
La Salle, IL	n.d. – BBP; n.d. – Emperor
Peru, IL	n.d. – Pin
Rockford, IL	Feb. 26, 1937 – Pin; Jan. 14, 1939 – HG
Springfield, IL	1936-7 – Pin
Waukegan, IL	1937-8 – Pin
Wheaton, IL	Oct. 21, 1940 – RH; Oct. 28, 1940 – RH; April 24, 1941 – RPR cancelled
Emporia, KS	Feb. 22, 1943 – DD
Topeka, KS	March 22, 1941 – Puck

CITIES & STATES	DATES & PRODUCTIONS
Ashland, KY	Feb. 11, 1939 – BBP
Hopkinsville, KY	Nov. 2, 1939 – HG
Lexington, KY	1937-8 – Pin
Louisville, KY	March 1941 – Emperor
Versailles, KY	1937-8 – Pin
Lafayette, LA	Feb. 25, 1942 – DD
New Orleans, LA	Dec. 7, 1940 – RH
Andover, MA	1936-7 – HG; 1936-7 – Pin; 1937-8 – Swineherd; 1937-8 – Sun God
Arlington, MA	1937-8 – BBP
Boston, MA	1936-7 – Pin; Dec. 28, 1942 – DD
Dedham, MA	1936-7 – HG
Hingham, MA	1936-7 – HG
Haverhill, MA	1936-7 – Pin
Lowell, MA	Jan 12, 1937 – HG; April 5, 1937 – Pin; 1937-8 – BBP
New Bedford, MA	n.d. – RH; April 12, 1940 – Pin; Nov. 8, 1940 – Jack; Oct. 3, 1941 – MP; Jan. 24, 1943 – DD
Newton, MA	Jan. 1942 – MP
North Adams, MA	1937-8 – Sun God
Salem, MA	Oct. 21, 1939 – ??
Springfield, MA	Oct. 17, 1937 – BBP
Wellesley, MA	Feb. 10, 1938 – BBP; April 30, 19?? – Emperor
Baltimore, MD	1937-8 – BBP; Dec. 12, 1939 – BBP; Dec. 28, 1940 – RH; Feb. 22, 1940 – Jack; Dec. 26, 1941 – MP
College Park, MD	Nov. 9, 1939 – ??
Fort Fairfield, MN	??
Adrian, MI	1937-8 – Sun God
Detroit, MI	1936-7 – Pin; March 13, 1938 – BBP
Elkhart, MI	n.d. – MP
Grand Rapids, MI	1937-8 – Pin
Highland Park, MI	Jan. 26, 1939 – HG
Kalamazoo, MI	1937-8 – Pin
Midland, MI	n.d. – Pin; n.d. – Jack
Mt. Clemens, MI	March 4, 1941 – RH
Mt. Pleasant, MI	n.d. – Emperor; Oct. 28, 194? – MP
Saginaw, MI	1937-8 – Pin; n.d. – RPR
Wyandotte, MI	n.d. – MP

VIII. APPENDIX I PARTIAL RECONSTRUCTION TOURING SCHEDULE

CITIES & STATES	DATES & PRODUCTIONS
Duluth, MN	June 7, 1940 – ??; March 21, 1943 – DD
Hibbing, MN	April 19 – BBP
St. Cloud, MN	Oct. 31, 1940 – RH
Virginia, MN	n.d. – MP; n.d. –-RH; Jan. 23, 1943 – DD
East St. Louis, MO	March 23, 1938 – Pin & Sun God
Jefferson City, MO	1937-8 – HG; n.d. – DD
Kansas City, MO	Nov. 13 1938 – ??
Logan, MO	Jan. 22, 1941 – Emperor; Jan 22, 1941 – RPR
Springfield, MO	1937-8 – HG; 1937-8 – Pin
Lincoln, NE	Feb. 21, 1943 – DD
Omaha, NE	n.d. – Emperor; Jan. 15, 1941 – RPR; Nov. 7, 1941 – MP; Feb. 7 & 19 1943 – DD
Concord, NH	1937-8 – BBP; 1937-8 – HG
Manchester, NH	1937-8 – HG; Feb. 8, 1938 – BBP
Natchez, MS	Feb. 6, 1941– Jack (matinee); Feb. 6, 1941 – BBP (evening)
Allandale, NJ	Jan 15, 1942 – MP
Atlantic City, NJ	1937-8 – Pin; 1937-8 – HG
Bayonne, NJ	1936-7 – Pin
Camden, NJ	April 3, 1943 – DD
Chatham, NJ	1936-7 – Pin; 1937-8 – BBP
Elizabeth, NJ	Dec. 11, 1940 – Jack; Jan. 28, 1941 – RH
Englewood, NJ	1936-7 – Pin; 1937-8 – BBP; 1937-8 – Sun God
Glen Rock, NJ	Jan. 4, 1940 – BBP
Maplewood, NJ	1937-8 – Pin; 1937-8 – BBP
Millburn, NJ	1937-8 – Pin
Montclair, NJ	1937-8 – Pin
New Brunswick, NJ	Dec 14, 1939 – ??
Nutley, NJ	1937-8 – Sun God
Plainfield, NJ	1936-7 – HG; 1936-7 – Pin; April 1938 – BBP; Dec. 26, 1941 – MP
Princeton, NJ	n.d. – RPR; May 19, 1942 – MP
Roselle, NJ	1936-7 – Pin
Ridgewood, NJ	Jan. 24, 1942 – MP
Trenton, NJ	1937-8 –Pin; 1937-8 – BBP; May 5, 1941 – Jack; n.d. – Emperor; April 2, 1943 – DD
Verona, NJ	1937-8 – Sun God
Westfield, NJ	1937-8 – BBP
West Orange, NJ	Jan 16, 1942 – MP

CITIES & STATES	DATES & PRODUCTIONS
Binghamton, NY	1937-8 – BBP; 1937-8 – Sun God; Feb 18 1941 – ??
Bronxville, NY	1937-8 – HG; 1937-8 – BBP
Brooklyn, NY	Dec. 31, 1937 – BBP; Feb. 4, 1940 – Jack; Sept 22, 1941 – MP
Buffalo, NY	1936-7 – Pin; 1937-8 – Swineherd; March 13, 1938 – BBP; 1937-8 – Sun God
Douglaston, NY	1936-7 – Pin; 1936-7 – BBP; 1936-7 – Sun God
Elmira, NY	1937-8 – Pin; Feb. 1, 1942 – MP; Jan. 25, 1943 –??
East Rockaway, NY	n.d. – RPR; Floral Park, NY – Jan. 12, 1939 – BBP
Florida Park, NY	Dec. 15, 1938 – BBP
Harrison, NY	Nov. 10, 1938 – BBP
Hempstead, NY	March 14, 1940 – Puck
Ithaca, NY	Oct. 21, 1942 – DD
Irvington, NY	1936-7 – Pin
Jamestown, NY	March 6, 1940 – BBP
Larchmont, NY	n.d. – MP
Mamaroneck, NY	Feb. 8, 1940 – H&G
Merrick, NY	1937-8 – Sun God
Mt. Vernon, NY	Jan 12, 1940; Oct. 1, 1940 – RH; n.d. – MP
Newburg, NY	1936-7 – Pin; 1937-8 – Swineherd; 1937-8 – Sun God
New Rochelle, NY	Dec. 1, 1937 – HG
New York City, NY	1937-8 – HG; Dec. 27, 30, 1937 – BBP; Nov. 11, 1940 – BBP; April 19, 1938 – Pin; 1937-8 – Sun God; Oct 21, 1942 & Dec. 27, 1942 – DD
Niagara Falls, NY	Feb. 17, 1940 – BBP
Orleans, NY	March 2, 1940 – BBP
Rockville Center, NY	Jan. 13, 1939 – BBP
Salamanca, NY	1936-7 – Pin
Scarsdale, NY	1937-8 – Sun God; Jan. 1940 – HG
Schenectady, NY	Jan. 24, 1942 – MP; Feb. 3, 1942 – DD
Syracuse, NY	March 24, 1938 – BBP; 1937-8 – Swineherd
Utica, NY	1936-7 – HG; Nov. 26, 1936-7 – Pin; 1937-8 – Swineherd
White Plains, NY	1936-7 – Pin
Woodmere-Hewlett, NY	1937-8 – Pin

VIII. APPENDIX I PARTIAL RECONSTRUCTION TOURING SCHEDULE

CITIES & STATES	DATES & PRODUCTIONS
Ashville, NC	1937-8 – Pin; Dec. 14, 1940 – RH; March 14, 1941 – Emperor
Charlotte, NC	Dec. 1939 – HG
Elizabeth City, NC	July 31, 1941 – MP
Greensboro, NC	1937-8 – Pin; Feb. 15, 1939; March 11, 1941 – Emperor; n.d. – DD
High Point, NC	1937-8 - Pin
Kinston, NC	Feb. 2, 1940 – Sun God
Leaksville, NC	Jan. 26, 1939 – BBP
Wilmington, NC	Dec. 1939 – H&G; n.d. RPR
Winston Salem, NC	1937-8 – Pin; Dec. 7, 1939 (cancelled); n.d. – BBP; Nov. 2, 1941 – MP; Oct. 22, 1940 – RH
Oklahoma City, OK	1937-8 – Sun God; 1937-8 – HG; 1937-8 – Pin
Tulsa, OK	1937-8 – Pin.
Ada, OH	n.d. – Emperor
Canton, OH	1937-8 – HG; 1937-8 – Pin
Cincinnati, OH	1937-8 – HG; 1937-8 – Pin; March 19, 1938 – BBP; Feb. 5, 1938 – Swineherd
Cleveland, OH	1937-8 – HG
Columbus, OH	1937-8 – Swineherd
Dayton, OH	1937-8 – BBP
East Liverpool, OH	1937-8 – Pin
Findlay, OH	Nov. 19, 1940 – Jack
Gallipolis, OH	1937-8 – Sun God; n.d. – "Pinocchio"
Mansfield, OH	1936-7 – Pin; 1937-8 – Sun God
Sandusky, OH	1936-7 – HG; 1936-7 – Pin; 1937-8 – Swineherd; 1937-8 – Sun God
Steubenville, OH	1937-8 – Pin
Youngstown, OH	Nov. 18, 1936 – HG
Albany, OR	Feb. 29, 1940 – Jack
Astoria, OR	n.d. – Jack
Eugene, OR	n.d. – Emperor; March 10, 1941 – Jack
Portland, OR	n.d. – Swineherd; April 25, 1941 – RH
Salem, OR	April 3, 1940 – BBP; n.d. – RPR; n.d. – Puck; March 1, 1941 – Jack

CITIES & STATES	DATES & PRODUCTIONS
Altoona, PA	1936-7 – HG
Allentown, PA	1937-8 – Pin; 1937-8 – BBP
Bradford, PA	1936-7 – Pin
Greensburg, PA	1937-8 – HG
New Castle, PA	1937-8 – HG; 1937-38 – Pin; 1937-8 – Sun God; Feb. 22, 1939 – BBP
Mt. Lebanon, PA	1936-7 – HG; 1936-7 – Pin; 1937-8 – Swineherd; 1937-8 – BBP; March 6 ,1940 – Jack
Pittsburgh, PA	1937-8 – Swineherd; 1937-8 – BBP
Radnor, PA	Jan. 26, 19?? – HG; n.d. – RH
Reading, PA	Oct. 6, 1940 – RH
Washington, PA	Jan. 1940 – HG
Williamsport, PA	Jan. 19, 1939; Jan. 29, 1939 – HG
Providence, RI	1936-7 – Pin; Nov. 1939, Jan. 26, 1941 – RH; Jan. 23, 1943 – DD
Greenville, SC	March 11, 1941 – Emperor
Columbia, SC	1941 – RH; fall, 1942 – MP; Jan. 24, 1943 – DD
Rock Hill, SC	1935-6 – HG
Aberdeen, SD	March 18, 1941 – RH
San Angelo, TX	March 13, 1943 – DD
Baytown, TX	??
Jackson, TN	n.d. – MP
Knoxville, TN	1937-8 – Pin
Memphis, TN	1935-6 – HG
Nashville, TN	Jan. 5, 1941 – BBP; Jan. 19, 1941 – RH; Nov 14, 1942 – DD
Ogden City, UT	Jan. 21, 1941 - RPR; March 15, 1943 – MP
Salt Lake City, UT	n.d. – Emperor; March 1942 – MP
Newport News, VA	Jan. 14, 1941 – BBP
Fredericksburg, VA	1937-8 – Pin; Feb 7, 1940 – RPR
Lynchburg, VA	1937-8 – Pin
Norfolk, VA	1937-8 – Pin
Richmond, VA	Feb. 24, 1940 – Swineherd; Jan. 18, 1941 – BBP
Roanoke, VA	1937-8 – Pin; Feb 19, 1939 – BBP

VIII. APPENDIX I PARTIAL RECONSTRUCTION TOURING SCHEDULE

CITIES & STATES	DATES & PRODUCTIONS
Charleston, WV	1936-7 – HG; 1937-8 – Pin
Fairmont, WV	1936-7 – HG; 1936-7 – Pin; 1937-8 – Swineherd; 1937-8 – Sun God; March 11 1938 – BBP; n.d. – RPR; n.d. – Emperor; Feb 23, 1941 – RH; Jan 30, 1942 – MP
Huntington, WV	Dec. 14, 1936 – HG; March 9, 1937 – Pin; 1937-8 – Swineherd; 1937-8 – Sun God
Morgantown, WV	Nov. 12, 1936 – H&G; March 15, 1937 – Pin
Parkersburg, WV	March 12, 1937 – Pin; 1937-8 – Swineherd; March 19, 1941 – RPR
Weirton, WV	
Wellsburg, WV	May 5. 1941– Puck
Wheeling, WV	n.d. – RH; 1936-7 – HG; Feb 28, 1937 – Pin; 1937-8 – Swineherd
Seattle, WA	Nov. 22, 1939 - Pin; April 5, 1940 – BBP; March 29, 1941 – Jack; 1941– Swineherd; Dec. 27, 194? – Emperor; Feb. 1, 194? – RPR; May 3, 194? – RH
Spokane, WA	April 29 & 30, 1941 – RH
Tacoma, WA	n.d. – RH
Wenatchee, WA	April 26, 1941 – RH
Yakama, WA	April 13, 1940 – BBP
Green Bay, WI	n.d. – BBP; Oct. 13, 1941 – MP
Kenosha, WI	1940 – RH
La Crosse, WI	May 23, 1940 – BBP; Sept. 27, 1940 – RH; Feb. 14/15, 1941– Emperor
Manitowoc, WI	Feb. 3, 1940 – SG; May 16, 1940 – BBP
Milwaukee, WI	n.d. – BBP; n.d. – DD
Monroe, WI	Feb. 1942 – MP; Nov. 14, 1942 – DD
Sheboygan, WI	May 6, 1940 – BBP
Wauwatosa, WI	n.d. – Emperor
Casper, WY	1938 – Sun God
Hamilton, CANADA	1937-8 – Pin

IX. BIBLIOGRAPHY

Primary Sources

Junior Programs, Inc. (JP) Scrapbooks. Billy Rose Theatre Division. New York Public Library for the Performing Arts, New York, NY

* Most of the newspaper sources that appear within the text are materials found in the JP Scrapbooks.

Saul Lancourt personal papers (property of the author).

Additional Sources

Abookire, Noerena, and Jennifer Scott McNair. "Children's Theatre Activities at Karamu House, 1915–1975." In *Spotlight on the Child: Studies in the History of American Children's Theatre*, edited by Roger L. Bedard and C. John Tolch, 69–84. New York: Greenwood Press, 1989.

Andersen, Hans Christian. "The Swineherd." 1842. http://hca.gilead.org.il/swineher.html.

Anderson, Carol. *White Rage: The Unspoken Truth of Our Racial Divide*. New York: Bloomsbury, 2017.

Beckwith, Dave, and Cristina Lopez. "Community Organizing: People Power from the Grassroots." Center for Community Change. comm-org.wisc.edu/papers97/beckwith.htm.

Bedard, Roger L., and John Tolch, eds. *Spotlight on the Child: Studies in the History of American Children's Theatre*. New York: Greenwood Press, 1989.

Berg, Charles Ramírez. "Stereotyping in Films in General and of the Hispanics in Particular." *Howard Journal of Communications* 2, no. 3 (1990): 286–300. https://doi.org/10.1080/10646179009359721.

Bigsby, C. W. E. *A Critical Introduction to Twentieth-Century American Drama: Volume One 1900-1940*. Cambridge: Cambridge University Press, 1982.

Blackhawk, Maggie. "The Indian Law that Helps Build Walls." *New York Times*, May 26, 2019. https://www.nytimes.com/2019/05/26/opinion/american-indian-law-trump.html.

Borwick, Doug. *Building Communities, Not Audiences: The Future of the Arts in the United States*. Winston-Salem, NC: ArtsEngaged, 2012.

Bosworth, Allan R. *America's Concentration Camps*. New York: W.W. Norton, 1967.

Caldbick, John. "Seattle Children's Theatre." HistoryLink. November 6, 2012. https://www.historylink.org/File/10239.

Carroll, Lewis. *Alice in Wonderland*. 1865, Amazon, 2021.

Chait, Richard P., William P. Ryan, and Barbara E. Taylor. *Governance as Leadership: Reframing the Work of Nonprofit Boards*. Hoboken, NJ: Wiley, 2005.

Charalambos, Vrasidas. "The White Man's Indian: Stereotype in Film and Beyond." *VisionQuest: Journeys Toward Visual Literacy* (January 1997): 63–70.

Clurman, Harold. *The Fervent Years: The Story of the Group Theatre and the Thirties*. New York: Hill and Wang, 1957.

"Community Organizing 101." NYC Cultural Affairs. https://www.nyc.gov/site/dcla/about/community-organizing-application.page.

Davis, Jed H., and Mary Jane Evans. *Theatre, Children and Youth*. New Orleans, LA: Anchorage Press, 1987.

Davis, Lisa Selin. "The Loneliest Land." *National Parks*, Spring 2015. npca.org/articles/942-the-loneliest-land.

de Beauvoir, Simone. *The Second Sex*. Translated by Constance Borde and Sheila Malovany-Chevallier. New York: Vintage, 2011.

Department of Dance. "Doris Humphrey." University of Washington. https://dance.washington.edu/people/doris-humphrey.

Dewey, John. "Creative Democracy—The Task Before Us." 1939. https://www.academia.edu/25643623/Creative_Democracy_The_Task_Before_Us.

Domínguez, Alberto, Susan Racho, and Nancy De Los Santos-Reza dirs., *The Bronze Screen: 100 Years of the Latino Image in Hollywood*. Latino

Entertainment Media Institute, 2002.

Dossett, Kate. *Radical Black Theatre in the New Deal*. Chapel Hill: University of North Carolina Press, 2020.

Eisinger, Nikki. "The Soul of an Indian: The Best Quotes on Nature and Spirituality from Charles Eastman, Ohiyesa." Glad.is, November 24, 2021. https://glad.is/blogs/articles/the-soul-of-an-indian-the-best-quotes-from-charles-eastman-ohiyesa?_pos=9&_sid=e9ad458d1&_ss=r.

Editors. "Kublai Khan." History.com, updated June 10, 2019. https://www.history.com/topics/asian-history/kublai-khan.

Engle Printing and Publishing. "Tire Rationing During World War II." Antiques and Auction News, June 22, 2018. https://antiquesandauctionnews.net/articles/Tire-Rationing-During-World-War-II/.

Fearnow, Mark. *The American Stage and the Great Depression: A Cultural History of the Grotesque*. Cambridge: Cambridge University Press, 1997.

"The Five Principles of Social Justice." Kent State University, July 30, 2020. https://onlinedegrees.kent.edu/political-science/master-of-public-administration/community/five-principles-of-social-justice.

Flanagan, Hallie. *Arena: The History of the Federal Theatre*. New York: Arno Press, 1980.

Foa, Roberto Stefan, and Yascha Mounk, "The Danger of Deconsolidation: The Democratic Discontent." *Journal of Democracy* 27, no. 3 (July 2016): 5–17. https://doi.org/10.1353/jod.2016.0049.

Foer, Joshua. "Butantan Snake Institute." Atlas Obscura. November 24, 2008. https://www.atlasobscura.com/places/butantan-snake-institute.

Franco, Joana. "Ruth St. Denis's Radha (1906): The West's Assumption of the East." Research proposal, December 2018, http://doi.org/10.13140/RG.2.2.10318.82247.

Frost, Leslie Elaine. *Dreaming America: Popular Front Ideals and Aesthetics in Children's Plays of the Federal Theatre Project*. Columbus: Ohio State

University Press, 2013.

Ginwright, Shawn, and Taj James. "From Assets to Agents of Change: Social Justice, Organizing, and Youth Development." *New Directions for Youth Development* 2002, no. 96 (2002): 27–46. https://onlinelibrary.wiley.com/doi/10.1002/yd.25.

Goldberg, Moses. *Children's Theatre: A Philosophy and a Method*. Englewood Cliffs, NJ: Prentice-Hall, 1974.

———. *TYA: Essays on the Theater for Young Audiences*. Louisville, KY: Anchorage Press Plays, 2006.

Gordy, Wilbur F. *American Leaders and Heroes: A Preliminary Text-book in United States History*. 1901. https://www.gutenberg.org/ebooks/35742.

Green, Jesse. "Let Us Tell You a Story: How Jewish People Built the American Theater as We Know It." *New York Times*, November 29, 2023. https://www.nytimes.com/interactive/2023/11/29/t-magazine/jewish-theater-antisemitism-maestro.html?unlocked_article_code=1.DU0.dIg2.vJjSlfLY69UX&smid=url-share.

Green, Laura. "Negative Racial Stereotypes and Their Effect on Attitudes Toward African-Americans." Jim Crow Museum, Ferris State University.63≠70 https://jimcrowmuseum.ferris.edu/links/essays/vcu.htm.

Green, Victor H. *The Negro Motorist Green Book*. 1949, http://www.autolife.umd.umich.edu/Race/R_Casestudy/Negro_motorist_green_bk.htm.

Henry, Tricia. "Perry-Mansfield School of Dance and Theatre." *Journal of the Society for Dance Research* 8, no. 2 (1990): 49–68. https://doi.org/10.2307/1290569.

Herts, Alice Minnie. *The Children's Educational Theatre*. New York: Harper & Brothers, 1911.

Hibri, Cyma. "Orientalism: Edward Said's Groundbreaking Book Explained." The Conversation, February 12, 2023. https://theconversation.com/orientalism-edward-saids-groundbreaking-book-explained-197429.

Hildebrand, David. "John Dewey." Stanford Encyclopedia of Philosophy, ed. Edward N. Zalta and Uri Nodelman, Fall 2023 ed., https://plato.stanford.edu/entries/dewey/.

Hill, Errol G., and James V. Hatch. *A History of African American Theatre*. Cambridge: Cambridge University Press, 2003.

History.com. "Chinese Exclusion Act." August 9, 2022. history.com/topics/immigration/chinese-exclusion-act-1882#.

"Home Is Where the Heart Is." Special issue, *TYA Today* (Fall 2019).

Horace Mann School. "A Long Tradition." horacemann.org/our-school/a-long-tradition.

Houghton Library. "Dorothy Coit King-Coit School and Children's Theatre Collection." Harvard University. https://hollisarchives.lib.harvard.edu/repositories/24/resources/8016

Jacob's Pillow. "Ted Shawn." https://www.jacobspillow.org/about/pillow-history/ted-shawn.

Johnson, Dale L., Jodi L. Allion-Bunnell, Teresa Hamann, and Donna McCrea. ""Frank B. Lindeman Memorial Collection 1885-2005," finding aid. Archives West. archiveswest.orbiscascade.org/ark:80444/xv81400.

Johnson, Richard C. *Producing Plays for Children*. New York: Richards Rosen Press, 1971.

Jones, Nicole Hannah, ed. *The 1619 Project*. New York: One World, 2021.

Kazacoff, George. *Dangerous Theatre: The Federal Theatre Project as a Forum for New Plays*. Xlibris Corporation, 2011.

Kendi, Ibram X. *How to Be an Antiracist*. New York: One World, 2019.

———. *Stamped from the Beginning: The Definitive History of Racist Ideas in America*. New York: Bold Type, 2016.

Lancourt, Joan. Review of *Broadway Goes to War* by Robert L. McLaughlin and Sally E. Parry. *Arts Fuse*, June 13, 2021. https://artsfuse.org/230647/book-review-broadway-goes-to-war-american-theater-during-world-war-ii/.

———. "What About the Children?" *Arts Fuse,* August 9, 2022. https://artsfuse.org/260179/theater-commentary-january-6-what-about-the-children/.

Lancourt, Saul. *Doodle Dandy of the U.S.A.* New York: Musette Publishers, 1943.

———. *The Bumble Bee Prince.* New York: Garden City Publishing, 1940.

———. *The Adventures of Marco Polo. Unpublished script, 1941.*

Launer, Pat. "The Theater's Queen of Green—and Contessa of Community Outreach." San Diego Metro, September 14, 2011. https://www.sandiegometro.com/2011/09/the-theater%e2%80%99s-queen-of-green-%e2%80%93-and-contessa-of-community-outreach/.

Lazarus, Joan. *Signs of Change New Directions in Theatre Education.* University of Chicago Press, 2012.

Levin, Neil W. "Elie Siegmeiser." Milken Archive of Jewish Music. https://www.milkenarchive.org/artists/view/elie-siegmeister.

Linder, Douglas. "Lynchings: By State and Race, 1882–1968." Famous American Trials: The Trial of Sheriff Joseph Shipp et al., 2000, http://law2.umkc.edu/faculty/projects/ftrials/shipp/lynchingsstate.html.

Manuel, Tiffany. *Strategic CaseMaking: The Field Guide for Building Public and Political Will.* CaseMade Press, 2020.

Matschat, Cecile Hulse. *Seven Grass Huts: An Engineers Wife in Central - and - South America.* New York: Literary Guild of America, 1939.

Maguire, Tom, and Karian Schuitema, eds. *Theatre for Young Audiences: A Critical Handbook.* London: UCL Institute of Education Press, 2012.

McCaslin, Nellie. *Historical Guide to Children's Theatre in America.* New York: Greenwood Press, 1987.

McFadden, Dorothy L. "Activities In Children's Theatre Abroad." *Junior League Magazine,* June 1937.

———. Autobiography (unpublished). 1985.

———. "Careers Sneak Up on Dorothy McFadden." *Morris County's Daily Record,* May 21, 1965.

———. "Entertainment In Your Community." *Journal of the American Association of University Women* (June 1939).

———. "Europe Challenges American Parents." National Parent-Teacher, June 1937.

——— "Guiding Our Children's Amusement Tastes." National Parent-Teacher, June 1941.

McLaughlin, Robert L., and Sally E. Parry. *Broadway Goes to War.* University Press of Kentucky, 2021.

Medina, Jennifer, Tim Arango, Dana Goldstein, and Louis Keene. "Los Angeles Teachers Strike, Disrupting Classes for 500,000 Students." *New York Times*, January 14, 2019, https://www.nytimes.com/2019/01/14/us/lausd-teachers-strike.html.

Miller, Arthur. *Death of a Salesman.* New York: Penguin, 1949.

Mountz, Alison. "The Other." In *Key Concepts in Political Geography*, edited by Carolyn Gallaher, Carl T. Dahlman, Mary Gilmartin, Alison Mountz, and Peter Shirlow, 328–35. Los Angeles: Sage, 2009. https://doi.org/10.4135/9781446279496.

Mowry, William Augustus, and Arthur May Mowry. *First Steps in the History of Our Country.* New York: Silver, Burdett, and Company, 1898. https://www.loc.gov/item/98001054.

Mussett, Shannon. "Simone de Beauvoir." Internet Encyclopedia of Philosophy, https://iep.utm.edu/simone-de-beauvoir/.

National Archives. "President Franklin Roosevelt's Annual Message (Four Freedoms) to Congress (1941)." US National Archives and Records Administration. https://www.archives.gov/milestone-documents/president-franklin-roosevelts-annual-message-to-congress.

National Park Service. "Edgar Lee Hewett." Salinas Pueblo Missions. Updated November 22, 2020. https://www.nps.gov/sapu/learn/historyculture/edgar-lee-hewett.htm.

Naylor, Larry L. *Cultural Diversity in the United States*. Westport, CT: Bergin & Garvey, 1997.

Nelson, John Louw. *Rhythm for Rain*. Cambridge, MA: Riverside Press, 1937.

Nevis, Edwin C., Joan Lancourt, and Helen G. Vassalo. *Intentional Revolutions: A Seven-Point Strategy for Transforming Organizations*. San Francisco: Jossey-Bass, 1996.

Office of the Historian. "The Neutrality Acts, 1930s." US Department of State. https://history.state.gov/milestones/1921-1936/neutrality-acts.

Ohl, Ronald E. "Sidonie Matsner Grueberg." Jewish Virtual Library, jewishvirtuallibrary.org/sidonie-matsner-gruenberg.

Olcott, Frances Jenkins. *Good Stories for Great Birthdays*. Boston: Houghton Mifflin, 1922. https://www.gutenberg.org/cache/epub/55592/pg55592-images.html.

Oluo, Ijeoma. *Mediocre: The Dangerous Legacy of White Male America*. New York: Seal Press, 2020.

———. *So You Want to Talk about Race*. New York: Seal Press, 2019.

Parker, Arthur C. *The Indian How Book*. New York: Dover, 1927.

Perry, Imani. *South to America: A Journey Below the Mason Dixon to Understand the Soul of a Nation*. New York: Harper Collins, 2022.

Phillips, Burr W. "Reading Textbooks which Teach Democracy." *Elementary School Journal* 41, no. 2 (October 1940): 155–56. https://www.journals.uchicago.edu/doi/10.1086/457872.

"Remarks by President Biden to Mark One Year Since the January 6th Deadly Assault on the U.S. Capitol." The White House, January 6, 2022. https://www.whitehouse.gov/briefing-room/speeches-remarks/2022/01/06/remarks-by-president-biden-to-mark-one-year-since-the-january-6th-deadly-assault-on-the-u-s-capitol/.

Richardson, Heather Cox. "Letters from an American," May 29, 2023. https://heathercoxrichardson.substack.com/p/may-29-2023.

River, Celeste. "Mountains in Memory: Frank Bir Bird Linderman, His Role in Acquiring the Rocky Boy Indian Reservation for the Montana Chippewa and Cree, and the Importance of that Experience in the Development of His Literary Career." Master's thesis, University of Montana, 1984. scholarworks.umt.edu/cgi/viewcontent.cgi?article=4052&context=etd.

Roberts, Dean W. "Highlights of the Midcentury White House Conference on Children and Youth." *American Journal of Public Health* 41, no. 1 (1951): 96–99. https://doi.org/10.2105/AJPH.41.1.96.

Rodin, Frank H. "Sight Saving Classes." *Western Journal of Medicine* 42, no. 6 (June 1935): 426–29. https://pubmed.ncbi.nlm.nih.gov/18743280.

"The Rotogravure Process." Library of Congress. https://loc.gov/collections/world-war-i-rotogravures/articles-and-essays/the-rotogravure-process/#:~:t

Ruane, Michael E. "A Brief History of the Enduring Phony Science that Perpetuates White Supremacy." *Washington Post*, April 30, 2019. https://www.washingtonpost.com/local/a-brief-history-of-the-enduring-phony-science-that-perpetuates-white-supremacy/2019/04/29/20e6aef0-5aeb-11e9-a00e-050dc7b82693_story.html.

Said, Edward W. *Orientalism*. 25th anniversary ed. New York: Vintage, 1979.

Schalk, Sami. "Self, Other and Other Self: Going Beyond the Self/Other Binary in Contemporary Consciousness." *Journal of Comparative Research in Anthropology and Sociology* 2, no. 1 (Spring 2011): 197–209.

Scholes, Percy A. *The Complete Book of the Great Musicians*. 1928. Ithaca: Yesterday's Classics, 2021).

"Seattle Junior Theatre Records, 1939–1984." Finding aid. Archives West. https://archiveswest.orbiscascade.org/ark:80444/xv69168.

"Seattle Theatre Archives: Collections of Theatre Companies." University of Washington Libraries. Updated February 9, 2023. https://guides.lib.uw.edu/research/theatrearchives/companies/list.

Shelton, Suzanne. *Divine Dancer: A Biography of Ruth St. Denis*. Garden City, NY: Doubleday, 1981.

Siber, Kate. "The 19th-Century Writer Who Braved the Desert Alone." Outside Online, January 22, 2019. https://www.outsideonline.com/culture/books-media/mary-austin-mojave-nature-writer/.

Teachers College. "A History of Anticipating—and Shaping—the Future." Columbia University, April 26, 2018. tc.columbia.edu/about/history/.

Umeda, Mihori. "Asian Stereotypes in American Films." *Zhongjing English Studies* 38 (2018): 145–71. https://chukyo-u.repo.nii.ac.jp/record/17211/files/102020380106umeda-chukyo-u.pdf.

Uyehara, Mari. "The Anti-Asian Roots of Today's Anti-Immigrant Politics." *The Nation*. August 9, 2021. https://www.thenation.com/article/politics/anti-asian-violence-labor/.

Vannest, Charles Garrett. Review of *The Growth of the American People and Nation* by Mary G. Kelty. *Elementary School Journal* 31, no. 10 (June 1931): 795–96. https://www.journals.uchicago.edu/doi/10.1086/456663.

Verderame, Carla L. Review of *The Gospel of the Redman* edited by Ernest Thompson Seton and Julia Seton. *Foreword*, August 18, 2009. https://www.forewordreviews.com/reviews/the-gospel-of-the-redman/.

Virginia Commonwealth University Libraires. "Junior Leagues." Social Welfare History Project. https://socialwelfare.library.vcu.edu/eras/civil-war-reconstruction/junior-leagues/.

Walker-Kuhne, Donna. *Invitation to the Party: Building Bridges to the Arts, Culture and Community*. New York: Theatre Communications Group, 2005.

Washington Parent. "Opera Provides Optimum Benefits for Children." March 1, 2021. https://washingtonparent.com/opera-provides-optimum-benefits-for-children/.

We See You, White American Theater. "Statement." https://www.weseeyouwat.com/statement.

Weaver, Robert B. The Past and Present in America," *Elementary School Journal* 42, no. 5 (January 1942): 393–94 https://www.journals.uchicago.edu/doi/10.1086/456663.

"Wei Ji: Opportunity in Crisis." Tai He Academy. Accessed April 3, 2024. https://taiheacademy.com/post/opportunity-in-crisis.

Wilkerson, Isabel. *Caste: The Origins of Our Discontents*. New York: Random House, 2020.

Wilmeth, Don B., and Christopher Bigsby, eds. *The Cambridge History of American Theatre: Volume II 1870-1945*. Cambridge: Cambridge University Press, 1999.

Wood, David, and Janet Grant. *Theatre for Children: A Guide to Writing, Adapting, Directing, and Acting*. Chicago: Ivan R. Dee, 1979.

ENDNOTES

1   "Wei Ji: Opportunity in Crisis," Tai He Academy, accessed April 3, 2024, https://taiheacademy.com/post/opportunity-in-crisis.

2   "Remarks by President Biden to Mark One Year Since the January 6th Deadly Assault on the U.S. Capitol," The White House, January 6, 2022, https://www.whitehouse.gov/briefing-room/speeches-remarks/2022/01/06/remarks-by-president-biden-to-mark-one-year-since-the-january-6th-deadly-assault-on-the-u-s-capitol/.

3   Arthur Miller, *Death of a Salesman* (New York: Penguin, 1949), 188.

4   "Biden Says Americans 'Can't Take Democracy for Granted Any Longer,'" *Washington Post*, November 2, 2022, https://www.washingtonpost.com/politics/2022/11/02/election-2022-latest-news/.

5   Roberto Stefan Foa and Yascha Mounk, "The Danger of Deconsolidation: The Democratic Discontent," *Journal of Democracy* 27, no. 3 (July 2016): 8, https://doi.org/10.1353/jod.2016.0049.

6   Seattle offers an example: in 1939, the Junior Programs, Inc., local sponsoring committee joined with the Seattle Junior League to form Seattle Junior Programs, Inc. Between 1939 and 1943, that organization brought seven Junior Programs, Inc., productions to Seattle. Since then, operating under a series of different names, there has been some form of children's theater in Seattle. John Caldbick, "Seattle Children's Theatre," HistoryLink, November 6, 2012, https://www.historylink.org/File/10239; "Seattle Theatre Archives: Collections of Theatre Companies," University of Washington Libraries, updated February 9, 2023, https://guides.lib.uw.edu/research/theatrearchives/companies/list.

7   Lewis Carroll, *Alice in Wonderland* (1865; Amazon, 2021), 95.

8   Nicole Hannah Jones, ed., *The 1619 Project* (New York: One World, 2021), 392, 466.

9   Leslie Elaine Frost, *Dreaming America* (Columbus: Ohio State University Press, 2013), 29–30.

10 Frost, *Dreaming America*, 31.

11 Frost, *Dreaming America*, 32.

12 Frost, *Dreaming America*, 34.

13 Quoted in Frost, *Dreaming America*, 34.

14 Quoted in Frost, *Dreaming America*, 35.

15 Frost, *Dreaming America*, 35.

16 Frost, *Dreaming America*, 28.

17 David Hildebrand, "John Dewey," Stanford Encyclopedia of Philosophy, ed. Edward N. Zalta and Uri Nodelman, Fall 2023 ed., https://plato.stanford.edu/entries/dewey/. See Section 5.3 Democracy Through Education.

18 Hildebrand, "John Dewey," Sec. 5.3 Democracy Through Education.

19 Hildebrand, "John Dewey," Sec. 5.3 Democracy Through Education.

20 Don B. Wilmeth and Jonathan Curley, "Timeline: Post-Civil War to 1945," in *The Cambridge History of American Theatre Vol. II*, ed. Don B. Wilmeth and Christopher Bigsby (Cambridge: Cambridge University Press), 54.

21 Alice Minnie Herts, "To Make Good Citizens - The Theatre for Children," *New York Times*, November 12, 1911, https://www.nytimes.com/1911/11/12/archives/-to-make-good-citizensthe-theatre-for-children-miss-alice-minnie.html.

22 Alice Minnie Herts, *The Children's Educational Theatre* (New York: Harper & Brothers, 1911), 59–67.

23 Nellie McCaslin, *Historical Guide to Children's Theatre in America* (New York: Greenwood Press, 1987), 11, emphasis added.

24 McCaslin, *Historical Guide to Children's Theatre in America*, 21.

25 McCaslin, *Historical Guide to Children's Theatre in America*, 177–78.

26 The company was successful and eventually took their productions "on the road," but they never achieved the breadth or scale of the Junior Programs Company tours.

27 McCaslin, *Historical Guide to Children's Theatre in America*, 112–13.

28 McCaslin, *Historical Guide to Children's Theatre in America*, 62–63.

29 McCaslin, *Historical Guide to Children's Theatre in America*, 65–66.

30 McCaslin, *Historical Guide to Children's Theatre in America*, 96.

31 McCaslin, *Historical Guide to Children's Theatre in America*, 127.

32 McCaslin, *Historical Guide to Children's Theatre in America*, 156-7.

33   McCaslin, *Historical Guide to Children's Theatre in America*, 206.
34   McCaslin, *Historical Guide to Children's Theatre in America*, 149.
35   McCaslin, *Historical Guide to Children's Theatre in America*, 22.
36   Joan Lancourt, "What About the Children?" *Arts Fuse*, August 9, 2022, https://artsfuse.org/260179/theater-commentary-january-6-what-about-the-children/.
37   Wilmeth, and Curley, "Time Line: Post-Civil War to 1945," 53, 58; John Frick, "A Changing Theatre: New York and Beyond," in *Cambridge History of American Theatre*, ed. Wilmeth and Bigsby, 213–17.
38   Wilmeth and Curley, "Timeline: Post-Civil War to 1945," 55–91.
39   Wilmeth and Curley, "Timeline: Post-Civil War to 1945," 55–84.
40   Wilmeth and Curley, "Timeline: Post-Civil War to 1945," 70–93.
41   Wilmeth and Curley, "Timeline: Post-Civil War to 1945," 68–94.
42   Cheryl Black and Anne Fletcher, "Moving the World toward Brotherhood," in *Experiments in Democracy*, Edited by Cheryl Black and Jonathan Shandell (Carbondale: Southern Illinois University Press, 2016), 84.
43   Wilmeth and Curley, "Timeline: Post-Civil War to 1945," 58–91.
44   Wilmeth and Curley, "Timeline: Post-Civil War to 1945," 74, 85, 88.
45   C. W. E. Bigsby, *A Critical Introduction to Twentieth-Century American Drama* (Cambridge: Cambridge University Press, 1989), 1.
46   Frick, "A Changing Theatre: New York and Beyond," 228.
47   Hallie Flanagan, *Arena: The History of the Federal Theatre* (New York: Arno Press, 1980), 381–431.
48   McCaslin, *Historical Guide to Children's Theatre in America*, 20.
49   Frick, "A Changing Theatre: New York and Beyond," 227.
50   Errol G. Hill and James V. Hatch, *A History of African American Theatre* (Cambridge: Cambridge University Press, 2003), 325.
51   Henry J. Elam, Jr., "The Politics of Black Masculinity in Theodore Browne's *Natural Man*, [1937]" in *Experiments in Democracy*, Edited by Cheryl Black and Jonathan Shandell (Carbondale: Southern Illinois University Press, 2016), 126.
52   Elizabeth A. Osborne, "Imagined Democracy," in *Experiments in Democracy*, Edited by Cheryl Black and Jonathan Shandell (Carbondale: Southern Illinois University Press, 2016), 173.

53 Frick, "A Changing Theatre: New York and Beyond," 225; Flanagan, *Arena*, 91, 97, 99, 105, 152, 154, 159, 230, 283, 289.

54 Flanagan, *Arena*, 73, 380–99.

55 Flanagan, *Arena*, 27, 91, 109, 150, 205.

56 Frost, *Dreaming America*, 43; Flanagan, *Arena*, 149, 283.

57 Frost, *Dreaming America*, 73–75.

58 Douglas Linder, "Lynchings: By State and Race, 1882–1968," Famous American Trials: The Trial of Sheriff Joseph Shipp et al., 2000, http://law2.umkc.edu/faculty/projects/ftrials/shipp/lynchingsstate.html.

59 Frost, *Dreaming America*, 73.

60 Frost, *Dreaming America*, 74.

61 Frost, *Dreaming America*, 91–92.

62 Frost, *Dreaming America*, 102.

63 Frost, *Dreaming America*, 115.

64 Brooks Atkinson, "'*The Revolt of the Beavers,*' or Mother Goose Marx," *New York Times*, May 21, 1937.

65 Flanagan, *Arena*, 200.

66 Flanagan, *Arena*, 342.

67 Dorothy L. McFadden, "Guiding Our Children's Amusement Tastes," *National Parent-Teacher*, June 1941, 32.

68 McFadden, "Junior Programs, Inc., Beginnings in Maplewood, N.J.," December 1985, in unpublished autobiography, 328.

69 "Purer Piping," *Time*, December 20, 1937 (Saul Lancourt personal papers).

70 National Music League Fund Raising Brochure, ca. 1934 (Junior Programs, Inc., Scrapbooks, Billy Rose Theatre Division, New York Public Library; hereafter JP Scrapbooks).

71 McFadden, unpublished autobiography, 328, 328a.

72 McFadden, "Corporation Facts," in unpublished autobiography, no page number.

73 "Purer Piping."

74 McFadden, marketing flyer, unpublished autobiography, 337.

75 "Careers Sneak Up on Dorothy McFadden," *Morris County's Daily Record*, May 21, 1965.

76 McFadden, "My Two Trips to Europe to See Performances for Children," in unpublished autobiography.

77 Dorothy L. McFadden, "Europe Challenges American Parents," *National Parent-Teacher,* June 1937.

78 McFadden, "Guiding Our Children's Amusement Tastes."

79 "Purer Piping."

80 Junior Programs *Pinocchio* program booklet, n.d., 2. (Saul Lancourt personal papers).

81 Programs from the 1930 Brooklyn Little Theatre list Lancourt as an actor and Assistant Stage Manager, and then Stage Manager; a 1932 program from The Children's Players list him as an actor and Lighting; a 1932 program from the Scarborough Players list him as an actor and Electrician; and a 1936 program from the Chautauqua Opera Association list him as Assistant to Mr. Valenti, the artistic director. (Saul Lancourt personal papers).

82 McFadden, unpublished autobiography, 329.

83 "A Christmas Gift to Youth," *Opera News,* December 22, 1941 (Saul Lancourt personal papers).

84 Junior Programs, Code of Entertainment formulated for Child Study Association of America, n.d. (JP Scrapbooks; Saul Lancourt personal papers). The James Russell Lowell quote at the end is from *To The Memory Of Hood.* According to All Poetry.com it speaks to the enduring social justice impact the deceased had on the lives of the oppressed. https://allpoetry.com/To-The-Memory-Of-Hood.

85 Junior Programs, Sixth Season Program Announcement (Saul Lancourt personal papers).

86 Hildebrand, "Art and Aesthetic Experience," in "John Dewey."

87 Heather Cox Richardson, "Letters from an American," May 29, 2023, https://heathercoxrichardson.substack.com/p/may-29-2023.

88 John Dewey, "Creative Democracy—The Task Before Us," 1939, https://chipbruce.files.wordpress.com/2008/11/dewey_creative_dem.pdf.

89 Wikipedia, s.v. "Timeline of Voting Rights in the United States," updated January 22, 2024, https://en.wikipedia.org/wiki/Timeline_of_voting_rights_in_the_United_States.

90 Alison Mountz, "The Other," in *Key Concepts in Political Geography*, ed. Carolyn Gallaher et al. (Los Angeles: Sage, 2012), 328–38.

91 Sami Schalk, "Self, Other and Other Self: Going Beyond the Self/Other Binary in Contemporary Consciousness," *Journal of Comparative Research in Anthropology and Sociology* 2, no. 1 (2011): 197–209.

92 Mountz, "The Other," 328.

93 Shannon Mussett, "Simone de Beauvoir," Internet Encyclopedia of Philosophy, https://iep.utm.edu/simone-de-beauvoir/.

94 Edward Said, *Orientalism*, 25th anniversary ed. (New York: Vintage, 1979), 184–90.

95 Wikipedia, s.v. "Orientalism," updated February 12, 2024, https://en.wikipedia.org/wiki/Orientalism.

96 Said, *Orientalism*, 94.

97 Cyma Hibri, "Orientalism: Edward Said's Groundbreaking Book Explained," The Conversation, February 12, 2023, https://theconversation.com/orientalism-edward-saids-groundbreaking-book-explained-197429.

98 Michael E. Ruane, "A Brief History of the Enduring Phony Science that Perpetuates White Supremacy," *Washington Post*, April 30, 2019, https://www.washingtonpost.com/local/a-brief-history-of-the-enduring-phony-science-that-perpetuates-white-supremacy/2019/04/29/20e6aef0-5aeb-11e9-a00e-050dc7b82693_story.html.

99 Ibram X. Kendi, *How To Be An Antiracist* (New York: One World, 2019).

100 Mihori Umeda, "Asian Stereotypes in American Films," *Zhongjing English Studies* 38 (2018): 154–60, https://chukyo-u.repo.nii.ac.jp/record/17211/files/102020380106umeda-chukyo-u.pdf.

101 Charles Ramírez Berg, "Stereotyping in Films in General and of the Hispanics in Particular," *Howard Journal of Communications* 2, no. 3 (1990): 286–300, https://doi.org/10.1080/10646179009359721.

102 Laura Green, "Negative Racial Stereotypes and Their Effect on Attitudes Toward African-Americans," Jim Crow Museum, Ferris State University, https://jimcrowmuseum.ferris.edu/links/essays/vcu.htm.

103 Vrasidas Charalambos, "The White Man's Indian: Stereotype in Film and Beyond," *VisionQuest: Journeys Toward Visual Literacy* (January 1997): 63–70.

104 Junior Programs, Inc., Annual Report, 1939–40 (Saul Lancourt personal papers).

105 Jesse Green, "Let Us Tell You a Story: How Jewish People Built the American Theater as We Know It," *New York Times*, November 29, 2023, https://

www.nytimes.com/interactive/2023/11/29/t-magazine/jewish-theater-anti-semitism-maestro.html?unlocked_article_code=1.DU0.dIg2.vJjSlfLY69UX-&smid=url-share.

106 Ijeoma Oluo, *Mediocre: The Dangerous Legacy of White Male America* (New York: Seal Press, 2020), 20–28.

107 Oluo, *Mediocre*, 20–28.

108 Alberto Domínguez, Susan Racho, and Nancy De Los Santos-Reza, dirs., *The Bronze Screen: 100 Years of the Latino Image in Hollywood* (Latino Entertainment Media Institute, 2002).

109 History.com, "Chinese Exclusion Act," August 9, 2022, http://history.com/topics/immigration/chinese-exclusion-act-1882#; Mari Uyehara, "The Anti-Asian Roots of Today's Anti-Immigrant Politics," *The Nation*. August 9, 2021, https://www.thenation.com/article/politics/anti-asian-violence-labor/.

110 Allan R. Bosworth, *America's Concentration Camps* (New York: W.W. Norton, 1967).

111 Lancourt's personal copy of the script for *The Adventures of Marco Polo*, n.d. (Saul Lancourt personal papers).

112 Typically, a practice of seven years of unpaid labor in return for payment of an individual's passage to America.

113 Wikipedia, s.v. "Philadelphia Nativist Riots," updated January 28, 2024, https://en.wikipedia.org/wiki/Philadelphia_nativist_riots.

114 Wikipedia, s.v. "*Studs Lonigan*," updated December 26, 2023, https://en.wikipedia.org/wiki/Studs_Lonigan.

115 Hill and Hatch, *History of African American Theatre*, 318.

116 Hannah-Jones, *1619 Project*; Ibram X. Kendi, *Stamped from the Beginning: The Definitive History of Racist Ideas in America* (New York: Bold Type Books, 2016).

117 Carol Anderson, *White Rage: The Unspoken Truth of Our Racial Divide* (New York: Bloomsbury, 2017).

118 A "sundown town" was a city or town in which signs were posted telling Black people that they needed to be "out of town by sundown."

119 Victor H. Green, *The Negro Motorist Green Book* (1949), http://www.autolife.umd.umich.edu/Race/R_Casestudy/Negro_motorist_green_bk.htm.

120 Hill and Hatch, *History of African American Theatre*, 231.

121 Hill and Hatch, *History of African American Theatre*, 235.

122 Hill and Hatch, *History of African American Theatre*, 238.

123 Hill and Hatch, *History of African American Theatre*, 231.

124 Hill and Hatch, *History of African American Theatre*, 226.

125 Hill and Hatch, *History of African American Theatre*, 309.

126 Hill and Hatch, *History of African American Theatre*, 318.

127 Hill and Hatch, *History of African American Theatre*, 331.

128 Joan Lancourt, review of *Broadway Goes to War* by Robert L. McLaughlin and Sally E. Parry, *Arts Fuse*, June 13, 2021, https://artsfuse.org/230647/book-review-broadway-goes-to-war-american-theater-during-world-war-ii/.

129 Robert L. McLaughlin and Sally E. Parry, *Broadway Goes to War: American Theater during World War II* (Lexington: University Press of Kentucky, 2021), 160.

130 Hill and Hatch, *History of African American Theatre*, 56, 78, 179–80, 226.

131 Hill and Hatch, *History of African American Theatre*, 331.

132 Saul Lancourt, *Doodle Dandy of the U.S.A.* (New York: Musette Publishers, 1943).

133 Tiffany Manuel, *Strategic CaseMaking: The Field Guide for Building Public and Political Will* (CaseMade Press, 2020), 67–77, 111–16, 206–9.

134 The cast for *Reward of the Sun God*: James Rawls–Hoya; Mary Hutchinson–Mana; Virginia True–Yampove, Cloud Mother, Mudhead; Roberta Seaman–Mother, Crow Mother; Barry Mahool–Chief, Sun God, Shalako; Norman Clark–Letayo, Cross-Legged Uncle, Mudhead; Viki Weldon–Posiwu, Arthur Aylesforth–Castille, Hand-Katchina, Old Man of the Water, Vi de Camp–Kokozhori; Percival Vivian & Charlotte Chorpenning–Director; Kenneth MacClelland–Scenery; Tora Nelson–Costumes; Irene Marmein–Dances; William Turner–Stage Manager; entire production under supervision of Saul Lancourt (Saul Lancourt personal papers).

135 John Louw Nelson, *Rhythm for Rain* (Cambridge, MA: Riverside Press, 1937).

136 Nelson, *Rhythm for Rain*, ix.

137 Nelson, *Rhythm for Rain*, vii.

138 Nelson, *Rhythm for Rain*, viii.

139 Maggie Blackhawk, "The Indian Law that Helps Build Walls," *New York Times*, May 26, 2019, https://www.nytimes.com/2019/05/26/opinion/american-indian-law-trump.html.

140 John Louw Nelson, *Reward of the Sun God,* unpublished story, MAI/Heye Foundation Records, Archive Center, Smithsonian Institution's National Museum of the American Indian, n.d.; "'Reward of the Sun God' Play All Children Will Like," *Free Press* (Kinston, NC), February 2, 1940 (JP Scrapbooks).

141 Nelson, *Reward of the Sun God,* 25.

142 Nelson, *Reward of the Sun God,* 30.

143 Nelson, *Reward of the Sun God,* 53.

144 Nelson, *Reward of the Sun God,* 86, 88–90.

145 Nelson, *Reward of the Sun God,* 92.

146 Nelson, *Reward of the Sun God,* 104–6.

147 At the age of sixty, Charlotte Chorpenning became artistic director of Chicago's Goodman Children's Theater from 1932 to 1952. During that time, she wrote at least 55 children's plays and became interested in analyzing audience responses, even training observers to collect audience data. Her book, *Twenty-One Years with Children's Theatre*, chronicles her tenure at the Goodman. *Twenty-One Years with Children's Theatre* (Children's Theatre Press, 1953).

148 Untitled pages from the Goodman Theatre, n.d. (Saul Lancourt personal papers).

149 The troupe of three sisters had appeared multiple times at Carnegie Hall, the New York Symphony and New York Philharmonic. Irene Marmein had directed numerous productions for the Schenectady Civic Players and the Schenectady Opera Company. Wikipedia, s.v. "Marmein Dancers," updated February 7, 2023, https://en.wikipedia.org/wiki/Marmein_Dancers.

150 Untitled pages from the Goodman Theatre, n.d. (Saul Lancourt personal papers).

151 The cast for *Run, Peddler, Run*: Barry Mahool–Gideon Small, Josiah Hicks; Viki Weldon–Abigail Small, Carlista Nichols; Anthony James–Captain Nicholas Oursell, Christopher Stubbins; Edythe Wood–Annie Pattison; Barney Brown–William Pattison, Fairlee Wist; Walter Draper–Titus Hurlbut, Rob Roy Higgins; Virginia True–Janto; Roberta Barclay–Hannah Snood; Robert Paddock, Theodore Fuchs–Scenery; Nettie Hopkins–Costumes; Ben Bunin–stage manager; entire production under the supervision of Saul Lancourt (Saul Lancourt personal papers).

152 Junior Programs *Run, Peddler, Run* marketing materials, n.d. (Saul Lancourt personal papers).

153 Junior Programs *Run, Peddler, Run* marketing materials, n.d. (Saul Lancourt personal papers).

154 Junior Programs *Run, Peddler, Run* marketing material, n.d. (Saul Lancourt personal papers).

155 Charlotte Perry cofounded the Perry Mansfield Performing Arts School and Camp in 1913. The camp, which still exists, was a magnet for many of the most influential modern dancers of that time. It offered an Isadora Duncan approach to dance and attracted notables such as Hanya Holm, Agnes de Mille, José Limón, and Merce Cunningham—all legendary names in the dance world. Perry viewed engaging children in the theater arts as not only a way to teach them how to use their bodies as an instrument of expression, but as a way to develop a range of skills that would make them more effective as adults. Wikipedia, s.v. "Charlotte Perry," updated September 28, 2023, https://en.wikipedia.org/wiki/Charlotte_Perry; Tricia Henry, "Perry-Mansfield School of Dance and Theatre," *Journal of the Society for Dance Research* 8, no. 2 (1990): 49–68, https://doi.org/10.2307/1290569.

156 Junior Programs *Run, Peddler, Run* marketing material, n.d. (Saul Lancourt personal papers).

157 Junior Programs *Run, Peddler, Run* marketing materials, n.d. (Saul Lancourt personal papers).

158 Junior Programs *Run, Peddler, Run* marketing materials, n.d. (Saul Lancourt personal papers).

159 The cast for *The Emperor's Treasure Chest*: Anthony James–Jose; John Rogers–Mateo, Policeman; Viki Weldon–Maria; Hana Karol–Silvana; William Boyer–Pedro; Roberta Barclay–Grandmother; Barry Mahool–Manuel Alvarez; Kenneth MacClelland–Scenery; Lillian Baume–Costumes; Josef–Masks; Elsie Houston–Dances, Songs; Ben Alexander–Stage Manager; Saul Lancourt–Director (Saul Lancourt personal papers).

160 Wikipedia, s.v. "Good Neighbor Policy and the 1939 World's Fair," updated December 6, 2023, https://en.wikipedia.org/wiki/Good_Neighbor_Policy_and_the_1939_World%27s_Fair.

161 Today, the idea that the United States should be a "melting pot" has been thoroughly discredited. The belief that an immigrant's goal, or the goal of any person of color, should be assimilation into the white, Eurocentric culture has become an anathema. At its core, it embodies the racist assumption that the white Anglo-Saxon culture is superior to all others. Nevertheless, the acknowl-

edgement by the *New Haven Register* that there was something significantly amiss in the American view of interracial relations indicates a step, however small it may now seem, toward a more accurate understanding of the problem.

162 Junior Programs believed that audience etiquette needed to be taught. In a 1940 news piece (unknown source, n.d.) Joop is described as "the personification of the perfect audience. He never needs a drink; he has no vocal cords [no giraffe does!] so he can't make a sound; and he has an accommodatingly long neck which enables him to see over the heads of others. The children loved and applauded him and then, under the direction of Mrs. Wismer at the piano, sang with zest their Joop song." According to the La Salle, Illinois, *Post Tribune* (May 2, 1940), "preceding the program, the children 'whooped it up for Joop' in the official Joop song, with Mrs. Hazel Bett as director and with Miss Sarah McConnell at the piano." Leading the audience in singing or providing musical accompaniment for the Joop Song was one of the many ways Junior Programs engaged members of the local community. Joop—a "J and a P with an oop in the middle"—appeared between the curtains before every performance, and his ear wiggling was translated by a cast member into funny hints about courteous audience behaviors. (Saul Lancourt personal papers); Junior Programs marketing material, n.d. (JP Scrapbooks).

163 The cast for *Marco Polo*: Don Keefer–Marco Polo; Barry Mahool–Nicolo Polo, Baron Achmath, company manager; Dale Lefler–Nicki, Tebet; Albert Gifford–Enrico, Choi-Chong, Guard; Charles Tate–Ching; Cecile Sherman–Christina, Aijurac; Dorothy Lysaght, Natalie MacDonald–Maddelena, Moliu; Richard Woodworth–Barto, Kublai Khan; Ben Alexander–Guard, Stage Manager; Ruth St. Denis–Choreography; Margaret Carlisle–Music; Kenneth MacClelland–Scenery; Lillian Baume–Costumes; Jacque Radunski–Piano; Charles Plotkin–Press; Saul Lancourt–Author, Director (Saul Lancourt personal papers).

164 It was pure coincidence, of course, but the opening battle between China's National Revolutionary Army and the Japanese Imperial Army took place at the Marco Polo Bridge in 1937. Wikipedia, s.v. "Marco Polo Bridge Incident," updated February 13, 2024, https://en.wikipedia.org/wiki/Marco_Polo_ Bridge_Incident.

165 Office of the Historian, "The Neutrality Acts, 1930s," US Department of State, https://history.state.gov/milestones/1921-1936/neutrality-acts.

166 Encyclopedia Britannica, s.v. "Kublai Khan," updated January 1, 2024, https://www.britannica.com/biography/Kublai-Khan.

167 Editors, "Kublai Khan," History.com, updated June 10, 2019, https://www.history.com/topics/asian-history/kublai-khan.

168 Wikipedia, s.v. "Kublai Khan," updated Februrary 23, 2024, https://en.wikipedia.org/wiki/Kublai_Khan; "Kublai Khan," China Culture, http://en.chinaculture.org/gb/en_aboutchina/2003-09/24/content_22894.htm.

169 Uyehara, "Anti-Asian Roots of Today's Anti-Immigrant Politics."

170 Uyehara, "Anti-Asian Roots of Today's Anti-Immigrant Politics."

171 William Vickery, "To The Schools: Using Junior Program Performances to Promote National Unity and Inter-Racial Understanding," n.d. (Saul Lancourt personal papers).

172 Walter Terry, "Saul Lancourt Presents Story of Marco Polo," *New York Herald Tribune,* December 28, 1941.

173 Joana Franco, "Ruth St. Denis's Radha (1906): The West's Assumption of the East," research proposal, December 2018, http://doi.org/10.13140/RG.2.2.10318.82247.

174 Junior Programs, *Marco Polo* press release, n.d. (Saul Lancourt personal papers).

175 The cast for *Doodle Dandy of the U.S.A.*: Sam Steen–Doodle Dandy; Barbara Gaye–Luck Star; Leon Kahn–Humphrey Dumphrey, The Clock; Alfred Allegro–Thomas Jefferson, Rush McNelton; Karal Shook, John Hurdle–Joel Barlow, The Sound Engineer; Mary Whitis Bell–Anne Hutchison, Elizabeth Drake; Michael Road, George Hoxie–Benjamin Franklin Budd, Narrator; Blake Ritter–Benjamin Franklin; Henry Fioro–Ballad Singer; Beman Lord–Michael Ridge; Elizabeth Shaw–Cordelia Cherry; George Spelvin–The Announcer; Ted Shawn–Dances; Elie Siegmeister–Music; Leo Kerz–Sets; Jacques Radunski–Piano; Saul Lancourt–Author and Director (Saul Lancourt personal papers).

176 "Leaders Acclaim 'Doodle Dandy' For Building Civilian Morale," Junior Programs press release, n.d. (Saul Lancourt personal papers).

177 "Leaders Acclaim 'Doodle Dandy' For Building Civilian Morale."

178 Barry Mahool, unknown source, n.d. (Saul Lancourt personal papers).

179 Saul Lancourt, "Writing For The Kids," *New York Times*, January 17, 1943 (Saul Lancourt personal papers).

180 The Four Freedoms formed the heart of Franklin D. Roosevelt's 1941 State of the Union address to Congress. In it, Roosevelt offered a rationale for abandoning the country's post-WWI isolationist stance, and for America's Lend-Lease program to aid the Allies in their war effort. The essence of his speech is contained in the following lines: "In the future days, which we seek to make secure, we look forward to a world founded upon four essential human freedoms. The first is freedom of speech and expression—everywhere in the world. The second is freedom of every person to worship God in his own way—everywhere in the world. The third is freedom from want—which, translated into world terms, means economic understandings which will secure to every nation a healthy peacetime life for its inhabitants—everywhere in the world. The fourth is freedom from fear—which, translated into world terms, means a world-wide reduction of armaments to such a point and in such a thorough fashion that no nation will be in a position to commit an act of physical aggression against any neighbor—anywhere in the world. That is no vision of a distant millennium. It is a definite basis for a kind of world attainable in our own time and generation." With Norman Rockwell's depiction of each of the Four Freedoms on the covers of the *Saturday Evening Post*, Roosevelt's articulation of America's moral core became enshrined in the collective psyche. National Archives, "President Franklin Roosevelt's Annual Message (Four Freedoms) to Congress (1941)," US National Archives and Records Administration, https://www.archives.gov/milestone-documents/president-franklin-roosevelts-annual-message-to-congress.

181 Jacob's Pillow, "Ted Shawn," https://www.jacobspillow.org/about/pillow-history/ted-shawn/; Wikipedia, s.v. "Ted Shawn," updated October 14, 2023, https://en.wikipedia.org/wiki/Ted_Shawn.

182 "Democracy Is Theme For Ballet," unknown source, n.d. (Saul Lancourt personal papers).

183 Ralph Warner, "Anti-Fascist Fantasy," *Daily Worker* (New York), December 30, 1942.

184 Neil W. Levin, "Elie Siegmeister," Milken Archive of Jewish Music, https://www.milkenarchive.org/artists/view/elie-siegmeister; Wikipedia, s.v. "Elie Siegmeister," updated November 4, 2023, https://en.wikipedia.org/wiki/Elie_Siegmeister.

185 "Siegmeister Provides Score for Music Play," *New York Herald Tribune*, October 18, 1942.

186 Lancourt, *Doodle Dandy of the U.S.A.*, 3.

187 Washington Parent, "Opera Provides Optimum Benefits for Children," March 1, 2021, https://washingtonparent.com/opera-provides-optimum-benefits-for-children/.

188 Dorothy L. McFadden, "Opera for the Very Young," *Opera News,* December 10, 1940, 24 (Saul Lancourt personal papers).

189 McFadden, "Guiding Our Children's Amusement Tastes," 32–33.

190 McFadden, "Guiding Our Children's Amusement Tastes," 33.

191 "Bringing the Land of Make-Believe to Young Audiences," *Musical America*, February 10, 1940, 146 (Saul Lancourt personal papers).

192 "Opera for Youngsters," *New York Times,* n.d. (Saul Lancourt personal papers).

193 Charles Plotkin, "School Audiences Applaud," unknown source, n.d. (Saul Lancourt personal papers).

194 John Torinus, *Press Gazette* (Green Bay, WI), n.d. (JP Scrapbooks).

195 Torinus, *Press Gazette.*

196 Torinus, *Press Gazette.*

197 "Opera for the Young," *Victor Record Review* 2, no. 10 (1940): 10 (Saul Lancourt personal papers).

198 McFadden, "Opera for the Very Young," 26.

199 McFadden, "Opera for the Very Young," 25.

200 McFadden, "Opera for the Very Young," 26.

201 The cast for *Hansel and Gretel*: Marion Selee–Hansel; Cecile Sherman–Gretel; Mary Bell–Mother, Witch; Marjorie Livingston, Selma Bojalad, Alma Milstead–Sandman, Dew Fairy; Tom Williams–Father; Kenneth MacClelland–Scenery; Howard Kubik, Esther Lundell–Piano; Barry Mahool–Narrator; Gregory Ashman–Musical Director; Saul Lancourt–Director (Saul Lancourt personal papers).

202 Junior Programs *Hansel and Gretel* press materials, n.d. (Saul Lancourt personal papers).

203 *Hansel and Gretel* libretto, n.d. (SaulLancourt personal papers).

204 Much of the casting for *Hansel and Gretel* was inherited from the NML's production with Saul Lancourt moving from stage manager to director. National Music League, Inc. program, n.d.; Brooklyn Academy of Music, program, n.d.; Junior Programs, Inc. program, n.d. (JP Scrapbooks; Saul Lancourt personal papers).

205 The cast for *The Bumble Bee Prince:* Alma Milstead–Good Sister Militrissa; Cecile Sherman–Bad Sister, Swan Princess; Marion Selee–Barbaricha; Tom Williams–Tsar Saltan; Patrick Henry, Albert Gifford–Tsarevich, Guard, Sailor; Howard Laramy–Messenger, Sailor; Bernice Zaconick, Kenneth MacClelland–Bumble Bee; Lanni Carvell, Howard Laramy–Narrator; Gregory Ashman–musical director; Ester Lundell, Jacque Radunski–piano; Kenneth MacClelland–Scenery; Josef, Georgia Anderson–Costumes, Masks, and Special Props; Saul Lancourt–Director (Saul Lancourt personal papers).

206 McFadden, unpublished autobiography, 336.

207 McFadden, unpublished autobiography, 336.

208 *The Bumble Bee Prince, A Junior Programs Book* (Garden City Publishing, 1940).

209 "A Suggestion to Local Choruses," Junior Programs Sponsoring Committee materials, n.d. (Saul Lancourt personal papers).

210 The cast for *Jack and the Beanstalk*: Alma Milstead–Jack; Howard Laramy–Giant, Tanner; Marion Selee–Mother, Butcher; Cecile Sherman–A Village Girl, Princess; Tom Williams, Ford Ogden–Cow; Albert Gifford–Jester, Harp; Kenneth MacClelland–Scenery; Christine–Costumes; Josef–Special Properties; Margaret Carlisle–Musical Direction; Saul Lancourt–Director (Saul Lancourt personal papers).

211 Wikipedia, s.v. "Louis Gruenberg," updated December 30, 2023, https://en.wikipedia.org/wiki/Louis_Gruenberg.

212 Wikipedia, s.v. "John Erskine (Educator)," updated December 31, 2023, https://en.wikipedia.org/wiki/John_Erskine_(educator).

213 Unfortunately, there was no information on how this, or any of the other "magical" effects (such as the transformation of the Tzarevich into a bumble bee) was actually achieved.

214 "Opera for the Young," unknown source, n.d. (Saul Lancourt personal papers).

215 The Chicago *Journal of Commerce* (Oct 11, 19??), the Madison, Wisconsin, *State Journal* (Nov 14, 1940), the *New York Times* (n.d.), the Cleveland, Ohio, *Press* (Jan 3, 1941), the West Virginia *Wheeling News Register* (n.d.), the *Berkshire County Eagle* (n.d.), the Newport News, Virginia, *Herald* (Dec 9, 1940), as well as in the Junior Programs season program announcements. For the 1941–42 season, they listed both the four sets of Victor Records—*Marco Polo* (8 sides with album, for $2.50), *Hansel and Gretel* (4 sides with album and

libretto, for $2.50), *Robin Hood* (3 sides with album and libretto, for $2.00), and *The Bumble Bee Prince,* (4 sides with libretto, $1.50)—and the Junior Programs Story Books—*Robin Hood, The Bumble Bee Prince,* and *Marco Polo*—all written by Saul Lancourt, and "profusely illustrated in color by Sheilah Beckett. As a child, I recall listening to the records over and over again, and the exquisite illustrations by Sheilah Beckett in the various books transported me into the world of the story. To this day, her illustrations still define my visual image of perfect fairy-tale fantasy.

216 McFadden, "Opera for the Very Young."

217 "Paderewski in California," unknown source, n.d. (Saul Lancourt personal papers).

218 Department of Dance, "Doris Humphrey," University of Washington, https://dance.washington.edu/people/doris-humphrey.

219 McFadden, unpublished autobiography, 340.

220 Junior Programs, Inc. Presents "Pinocchio," ""Pinocchio" Brought to Life," n.d., 3 (Saul Lancourt personal papers).

221 Edwin Strawbridge, "What Dancing Can Do for the Child," To Dancing Teachers, Junior Programs marketing materials, n.d. (Saul Lancourt personal papers).

222 Strawbridge, "What Dancing Can Do for the Child."

223 Strawbridge, "What Dancing Can Do for the Child."

224 For example: Sadness: Body depressed with down-drooping lines of head and shoulders; Egotism: Chest forced out and elbows sticking out wide; Timidity: toes turned in, body restless with hands shuffling needlessly; Ambition: Back pushed in; Self-Consciousness: Shoulders lifted; Interest: Head and body leaning forward; Ecstasy: Head lifted, entire body relaxed. Letty Lynn, "Pantomimes Help to Express Your Mood," *Sun,* Binghamton, NY, Feb 18, 1941 (JP Scrapbooks).

225 The cast for *Pinocchio*: Edwin Strawbridge–Pinocchio; Virginia Miller, Lisa Parnova, Frances Rands–Fairy with Blue Hair; Martha Picken, Lanni Caravell, Julia Vaughn–Narrator; William Miller, Cowden McCord–Gepetto; Harriet Donnelly, Hazel Yallowley, Marguerite deAnguera, Virginia Miller, Nanette Charise, Mila Ginia–A-B-C and Gold Pieces; Dale Lefler, Olaf–Cat; William Miller, Sam Steen–Fox; Hazel Yarrowley, Harriet Donnelly, Nanette Charise–White Mice; William Miller, Cowden McCord, Sam Steen–Dr. Owl, Lamp Wick; Dale Lefler–Dr. Crow; Mila Ginia, Nanette Charise–Playground

Children; Harriet Donnelly, Haxel Yallowley–Rope Dancer; Ray Harrison, Cowden McCord–Donkey Driver; Dale Lefler, Olaf–Donkey, Front Legs; William MacLeod, Frederick Spires–Donkey, Back Leg.; Walter Roach–Scenery; Willy Pogany, Elizabeth Parsons–Costumes; Bill Baird–Masks; Leo Polski–Piano; Saul Lancourt–Production Director. (*Standard-Times*, New Bedford, MA, Apr 12, 1940) (Saul Lancourt personal papers).

226 Flanagan, *Arena*, 283.

227 Flanagan, *Arena*, 365.

228 Houghton Library, "Dorothy Coit King-Coit School and Children's Theatre Collection," Harvard University, https://hollisarchives.lib.harvard.edu/repositories/24/resources/8016.

229 "Mrs. Mabel Wood Hill, Noted Composer, and founder of the Brooklyn Music School Settlement, Hudson River Music School, and New York Music School Settlement," *Brooklyn Daily Eagle*, March 3, 1954, https://www.newspapers.com/article/49524800/obituary-for-mabel-wood-hill/.

230 "Junior Programs Inc. Presents 'Pinocchio,'" n.d., 3 (Saul Lancourt personal papers).

231 "Junior Programs Inc. Presents 'Pinocchio,'" 4, 6.

232 "Junior Programs, Inc. Presents 'Pinocchio,'" 10.

233 The cast for *The Princess and the Swineherd*: Edwin Strawbridge–Prince; Lanni Caravell–Narrator; Virginia Miller–Princess; Francis Farnsworth, Hazel Yallowley, Marguerite DeAnguera–Ladies-in-Waiting; Cowden McCord, Sam Steen, Dale Lefler–King; Walter Roach–Scenery; Christine and Elizabeth Thompson–Costumes; Josef– Masks and Cooking Pot; Leo Polanski–Piano; Solomon Rokoff–Violin; Saul Lancourt–Director. The Cincinnati *Enquirer* (Jan 27, 1938) (Saul Lancourt personal papers).

234 McFadden, unpublished autobiography, 340.

235 "Junior Programs, Inc. Sends to Young Audiences Operas, Ballets, Plays, Concerts," 1940–41, 11 (Saul Lancourt personal papers).

236 "Junior Programs, Inc. Sends to Young Audiences Operas, Ballets, Plays, Concerts," 11. The 1940–41 marketing program booklet lists Pignatelli di Montecalvo as author of the *Princess and the Swineherd* script. Whether McFadden and Pignatelli di Montecalvo collaborated on the script, or whether there was a dance version and a narrators' version, or successive iterations is unknown.

237 Hans Christian Andersen, "The Swineherd," 1842, http://hca.gilead.org.il/swineher.html.

238 McFadden, unpublished autobiography, 340; "Junior Programs, Inc. Sends to Young Audiences Operas, Ballets, Plays, Concerts," 11.

239 "Junior Programs, Inc. Sends to Young Audiences Operas, Ballets, Plays, Concerts," 11.

240 The cast for *The Adventures of Puck*: Edwin Strawbridge–Puck; Virginia Miller–Titania; Martha Picken–Narrator; William Miller–Oberon, Beatle, Snug; Henry Ormond–Robert Starveling; Marguerite de Anguera–Flute, Moth, and Elf; William Cooper–Tom Snout, Mustardseed; Louis Vinai-Peter Quince, Cobweb; Barbara Gaye-Peaseblossom, Elf; Mila Ginia- Ef; Edwin Strawbridge–Choreography; Robert Rowe Paddock–Scenery; Henry Ormond, Christine Thompson–Costumes; Josef–Donkey's Head; Saul Lancourt–Production Director (Saul Lancourt personal papers).

241 Wikipedia, s.v. "*A Midsummer Night's Dream*, (Mendelssohn)" updated January 21, 2024 https://en.wikipedia.org/wiki/A_Midsummer_Night%27s_Dream_(Mendelssohn).

242 "Music For Ballet A Concert Favorite," Junior Programs press material, n.d. (Saul Lancourt personal papers).

243 *Dance Magazine* also noted that once the Junior Programs season was over, Strawbridge would teach at a summer school he opened in 1939 near Newnan, Georgia. He offered advanced work in "choreography, stagecraft and composition, to ten selected semi-professionals" who would stage twice weekly performances.

244 "Unique Costumes and Effects Feature Shakespeare Ballet," n.d. (Saul Lancourt personal papers).

245 "Unique Costumes and Effects Feature Shakespeare Ballet."

246 "Music for Ballet a Concert Favorite," Junior Programs press release, n.d. (Saul Lancourt personal papers).

247 Ellen McClellan Wilshire and Hugh B. Wood, "Junior Programs Appreciation Units to Accompany the Junior Programs Productions," 1940 (Saul Lancourt personal papers).

248 Wilshire and Wood, "Junior Programs Appreciation Units."

249 "Junior Programs, Inc. Sends to Young Audiences."

250 The cast for *Robin Hood*: Edwin Strawbridge–Robin Hood; Virginia Miller–Lady Marion; Martha Picken–Narrator; Charles Tate–Jester, Friar Tuck; Hen-

ry Oromond–Chamberlain, King Henry; William Cooper–Poacher, Little John; Louis Vinai–Bear, Tinker; William Miller–Sheriff; Barbara Gaye–Page, Lady-in-Waiting; Edwin Strawbridge–Choreography; Saul Lancourt–Book, Production Director; Marguerite Carlisle–musical arrangement, Robert Rowe Paddock–Scenery; , Christine and Sheila Barrett–Costumes; Josef–Masks;Leo Polski, Jack Radunski–piano.

251 George Kittredge, a major figure in Harvard's Modern Language Department and a Shakespearean scholar of note, was extremely eclectic in his literary tastes. His edition of Shakespeare was the standard college text well past his death. He was also responsible for bringing Chaucer to the college English curriculum, and his interest in folk tales and songs helped bring American folklore into the curriculum as well; and for many years, he taught courses in Icelandic, Norse, and German Mythology. Wikipedia, s.v. "George Lyman Kittredge," updated January 23, 2024, https://en.wikipedia.org/wiki/George_Lyman_Kittredge.

252 "Child Study Association Presents Edwin Strawbridge in Robin Hood," *Baltimore District*, December 28, 1940. Sadly, there was no information as to how these feats of marksmanship were actually performed onstage.

253 "The Story of the Blazing Yule," National Recreation Association, Junior Programs marketing materials, n.d. (Saul Lancourt personal papers).

254 St. Petersburg, FL, *Independent,* (Nov 1940); New York, *World Telegram,* (n.d.); Lake Forest, IL, *Lake Forester,* (n.d.); Montgomery, AL, *Advertiser,* (n.d.); *Musical America,* (Feb 10, 1940).

255 "Using Junior Program Performances to Promote National Unity and Inter-Racial Understanding," To The Schools, Junior Programs marketing material, n.d. (Saul Lancourt personal papers).

256 Joan Lazarus, *Signs of Change New Directions in Theatre Education* (Chicago: University of Chicago Press, 2012), 121.

257 "Plays and Operas Aid Cultural Plan," *New York Times*, November 20, 1938.

258 Horace Mann School, "A Long Tradition," horacemann.org/our-school/a-long-tradition.

259 Teachers College, "A History of Anticipating—and Shaping—the Future," Columbia University, April 26, 2018, tc.columbia.edu/about/history/.

260 The Educational Guidance Committee was composed of the following prominent educators: Dr. W. Carson Ryan Jr. (honorary chairman), University of North Carolina Department of Education; Dr. Hugh B. Wood (chairman),

University of Oregon; Dr. Paul Eddy (assistant chairman), Adelphi College President; Dr. Jean Betzner, Teachers College, Columbia University; Mrs. Ursula Bringhurst, New York University; Dr. Cecile Fleming, Teachers College, Columbia University; Mrs. Paula Goldwasser, Brooklyn Ethical Culture School; Rita Hochheimer, Bureau of Visual Instruction, NYC Public Schools; Dr. Frank J. O'Brien, Director of Bureau of Child Guidance, NYC; Lilla Belle Pitts, Teachers College, Columbia University; Ellen Steele Reece, Director of Rosemary Junior School, Greenwich, CT; Dr. Mary Reed, Teachers College, Columbia University; Dr. Ina Craig Sartorius, Horace Mann School, NYC; and Mrs. Rose Schwatz, classroom teacher, P.S. 191, Brooklyn, NYC. In May, 1939, the *New York City Motion Picture Herald* noted that a series of additional committee members were announced: Community Relations—Dr. Gary C. Meyers, honorary chairman; John W. Faust, chairman; Educational Guidance—Dr. W. Carson Ryan, Jr., honorary chairman; Dr. Hugh B. Wood, chairman; Music—Eugene Goossens, honorary chairman; Lee Pattison, chairman; Drama—Jane Cowl, honorary chairman; Margaret Anglin, chairman; and Radio—Mrs. Sidonie Matsner Gruenberg, honorary chairman; and Margaret Harrison, chairman. Also involved were the Teachers College of Columbia University, the Curriculum Project at the University of Oregon, the federal Office of Education, the Horace Mann School in New York, and representatives of the National Orchestral Association, National Music League, Child Study Association, and National Congress of Parents and Teachers (Saul Lancourt personal papers).

261 "Appreciation Units to Accompany the Junior Programs Productions for Primary, Intermediate, and High School Grades," Junior Programs press release to schools, n.d. (Saul Lancourt personal papers).

262 Junior Programs educational marketing brochure, 1940–41, 18 (Saul Lancourt personal papers).

263 McFadden, "Entertainment In Your Community."

264 McFadden, "Guiding Our Children's Amusement," 32–33.

265 In the absence of more complete CCSUs, wherever possible, I have annotated items in the existing bibliographies as a proxy that hopefully will provide a window into the breadth, depth, and tone of the materials they prepared.

266 Arthur C. Parker, *The Indian How Book* (New York: Dover, 1927).

267 National Park Service, "Edgar Lee Hewett," Salinas Pueblo Missions, updated November 22, 2020, https://www.nps.gov/sapu/learn/historyculture/edgar-lee-hewett.htm

268 *The Adventures of Marco Polo*, Suggested Unit Plan for Primary Grades, for Intermediate Grades, and for High School Grades, n.d. (Saul Lancourt personal papers).

269 *The Adventures of Marco Polo* CCSU Materials, n.d. (Saul Lancourt personal papers).

270 "Using Junior Program Performances to Promote National Unity And Inter-Racial Understanding," Junior Programs press release, n.d. (Saul Lancourt personal papers).

271 Ellen McClellan Wilshire and Hugh B. Wood, "Brazil: The Land of Opportunity, Appreciation Unit," Curriculum Bulletin, no. 27 (October 30, 1940): 3 (University of Illinois, Urbana-Champaign, Library).

272 Junior Programs CCSU materials, n.d. (Saul Lancourt personal papers).

273 "Directions for Playing the Indian Corn-Cob Game," Junior Programs supplement to *The Reward of the Sun God*, CCSU materials, n.d. (Saul Lancourt personal papers).

274 National Recreation Association (Formerly Playground & Recreation Association of America), n.d. (Saul Lancourt personal papers).

275 These sections also explored how they made fire, tipis, bark houses, canoes, war bonnets, traps, fishhooks, wampum, masks, buckskin, rawhide, baskets, and pottery, and how they drew their designs. There were also descriptions of how the Sun Dance and Ghost Dance were performed, how they danced with snakes, made trails, sent signals, tracked and eluded their enemies, swam under water, ran the gauntlet, went to war, scalped their foes, conducted adoptions, used eagle feathers, and how the war bonnet was made an honor sign.

276 National Park Service, "Edgar Lee Hewett."

277 In a preface to a commemorative edition (2005), Seton's daughter speaks to the possible misinterpretation, from a twenty-first-century perspective, of his use of the label "redman" in the title. However, in an August 18, 2009, review by Carla L. Verderame, she is of the opinion that despite the fact that "the sensibilities of the time in which the text was written have changed significantly. . . the spirit and intention of the text during its era are positive and thorough. Carla L. Verderame, review of *The Gospel of the Redman*, ed. Ernest Thompson Seton and Julia Seton, *Foreword*, August 18, 2009, https://www.forewordreviews.com/reviews/the-gospel-of-the-redman/.

278 Wikipedia, s.v. "Charles Eastman," updated February 16, 2024, en.wikipedia.org/wiki/Charles_ Eastman; Nikki Eisinger, "The Soul of an Indian: The Best

Quotes on Nature and Spirituality from Charles Eastman, Ohiyesa," Glad.is, November 24, 2021, https://glad.is/blogs/articles/the-soul-of-an-indian-the-best-quotes-from-charles-eastman-ohiyesa?_pos=9&_sid=e9ad458d1&_ss=r.

279   Lisa Selin Davis, "The Loneliest Land," *National Parks*, Spring 2015, npca.org/articles/942-the-loneliest-land.

280   In 2014, Austin was "rediscovered" by William Randolph Hearst, grandson of the newspaper magnate, who published a new edition of the book, accompanied by a collection of landscape photographs by Walter Feller. Kate Siber, "The 19th-Century Writer Who Braved the Desert Alone," Outside Online, January 22, 2019, https://www.outsideonline.com/culture/books-media/mary-austin-mojave-nature-writer/; Wikipedia, s.v. "Mary Hunter Austin," updated February 23, 2024, en.wikipedia.org/wiki/Mary_Hunter_Austin.

281   The book contains engaging stories about "How the Ducks Got Their Fine Feathers," "Why the Kingfisher Always Wears a War-Bonnet," "Why the Chipmunk's Back Is Striped," "Why Blackfeet Never Kill Mice," "How the Otter Skin Became Great 'Medicine,'" "Why the Mountain-Lion Is Long and Lean," "How the Man Found His Mate," "Why the Birch-Tree Wears the Slashes in Its Bark," and many other tales rich in fanciful characters.

282   Celeste River, "Mountains in Memory: Frank Bird Linderman, His Role in Acquiring the Rocky Boy Indian Reservation for the Montana Chippewa and Cree, and the Importance of that Experience in the Development of His Literary Career" (master's thesis, University of Montana, 1984), scholarworks.umt.edu/cgi/viewcontent.cgi?article=4052&context=etd; Dale L. Johnson et al., "Frank B. Lindeman Memorial Collection 1885-2005," finding aid, Archives West, archiveswest.orbiscascade.org/ark:80444/xv81400).

283   Wikipedia, s.v. "Clark Wissler," September 12, 2023, https://en.wikipedia.org/wiki/Clark_Wissler.

284   Wikipedia, s.v. "Lois Lenski," November 16, 2022, https://en.wikipedia.org/wiki /Lois_Lenski.

285   *Run, Peddler, Run* CCSU, n.d. (Saul Lancourt personal papers).

286   *Run, Peddler, Run* CCSU, n.d. (Saul Lancourt personal papers).

287   Members of the Educational Guidance Committee were librarian Celeste Barnes from Pierre, South Dakota, Nora Beust and Helen Macintosh from the federal Office of Education, Ina Craig Sartorius from New York's Horace Mann School, and Gretchen Westervelt of Columbia University (Saul Lancourt personal papers).

288 *Run, Peddler, Run* CCSU, n.d. (Saul Lancourt personal papers).

289 *Run, Peddler, Run* CCSU, n.d. (Saul Lancourt personal papers).

290 Hugh B. Wood, "Good Will Shows Proposed for Children of Americas," unknown source, n.d. (Saul Lancourt personal papers).

291 The schools were located in Trenton, NJ; Binghamton, NY; Salem, MA; and Thompsonville, CT in the Northeast; Fairmont, WV; Atlanta, GA; Tuscaloosa, AL; and Jacksonville, FL, in the South; La Salle, IL; Ada, OH; Mount Pleasant, MI; Wauwatosa, WI; and Omaha, NE in the Midwest; and Salt Lake City, UT; Oakland, CA; and Eugene, OR in the West.

292 Benjamin Fine, "Will Use Drama As School Help," *New York Times,* February 9, 1941 (Saul Lancourt personal papers).

293 Wilshire and Wood, "Brazil: The Land of Opportunity, Appreciation Unit."

294 Ellen McClellan Wilshire, "Maps and Films of Brazil Suggested," *The Emperor's Treasure Chest* CCSU material, n.d. (Saul Lancourt personal papers).

295 Wilshire and Wood, "Brazil: The Land of Opportunity, Appreciation Unit," 21–26.

296 William La Varre, "Hitler's Plan for South America," *American Language Arts* (Nov 1940) or W.B. Courtney's "What South America Thinks of Us," in *Colliers* (Nov 9, 1940). There was also *The People and Politics of Latin America* by Mary Wilhemine Williams (Boston: Ginn & Co., 1930) and *Brazil: A Study of Economic Types* by Joao Frederico Normano (Chapel Hill: University of North Carolina Press, 1936). See Wilshire and Wood, "Brazil: The Land of Opportunity, Appreciation Unit," 18–19, 24–25).

297 The Butantan Institute is still one of the largest biomedical research centers in the world. It accounts for more than 93% of serums and vaccines produced in Brazil, among them for diphtheria, tetanus, pertussis, hepatitis B, seasonal influenza, H1N1, and most recently COVID-19. Joshua Foer, "Butantan Snake Institute," Atlas Obscura, November 24, 2008, https://www.atlasobscura.com/places/butantan-snake-institute.

298 Ellen McClellan Wilshire and Agnes Fay, "Brazilian Songs Suggested," Junior Programs *The Emperor's Treasure Chest,*, n.d. (Saul Lancourt personal papers).

299 *The Adventures of Marco Polo* CCSU material, n.d. (JP Scrapbooks and Saul Lancourt personal papers).

300 "Using Junior Program Performances to Promote National Unity and Inter-Racial Understanding," To The Schools, Junior Programs marketing material, n.d. (Saul Lancourt personal papers).

301 Intrigued by his research for writing *The Adventures of Marco Polo*, in 1944 Lancourt wrote a forty-five-minute play for the Council For Democracy entitled *China Had A Washington*. The play, performed at the Demonstration High School of the New Jersey State Teachers College in Montclair, NJ, juxtaposed George Washington's leadership during the American Revolution, sparked by "taxation without representation," with Sun Yat-sen's leadership in China's battle against the Manchu dynasty and its oppressive taxes. The theme of the play was that the people of both countries wanted the same things: "eyes round or slant, All colors of skin . . . The dream's the same the world around." Everyone wants freedom—from oppression, and for a good life. (Saul Lancourt personal papers).

302 *The Adventures of Marco Polo* Appendix A, Suggested Unit Plan for Primary Grades, CCSU materials, n.d. (Saul Lancourt personal papers).

303 *The Adventures of Marco Polo* Appendix B, Suggested Unit Plan for Intermediate Grades, CCSU materials, n.d. (Saul Lancourt personal papers).

304 *The Adventures of Marco Polo* Appendix C, Suggested Unit Plan for High School Grades, CCSU material, n.d. (JP Scrapbooks).

305 "Notes on the Dances in Junior Programs' Play 'The Adventures of Marco Polo,'" Junior Programs Supplemental CCSU materials, n.d. (Saul Lancourt personal papers).

306 "Leaders Acclaim 'Doodle Dandy' for Building Civilian Morale, Junior Programs, Inc.," press release, n.d. (Saul Lancourt personal papers).

307 "Leaders Acclaim 'Doodle Dandy' for Building Civilian Morale, Junior Programs, Inc."

308 Lancourt, *Doodle Dandy of the U.S.A*, xi.

309 The bibliography was compiled by Muriel Schumacher of Albany Public Schools (Saul Lancourt personal papers).

310 Wilbur F. Gordy, *American Leaders and Heroes: A Preliminary Text-book in United State History* (1901), https://www.gutenberg.org/ebooks/35742.

311 Burr W. Phillips, "Reading Textbooks which Teach Democracy," *Elementary School Journal* 41, no. 2 (October 1940): 155–56, https://www.journals.uchicago.edu/doi/10.1086/457872.

312 William Augustus Mowry and Arthur May Mowry, *First Steps in the History of Our Country* (New York: Silver, Burdett, and Company, 1898), https://www.loc.gov/item/98001054.

313 Frances Jenkins Olcott, *Good Stories for Great Birthdays* (Boston: Houghton Mifflin, 1922), https://www.gutenberg.org/cache/epub/55592/pg55592-images.html.

314 Ellen Lewis Buell, review of *The Codfish Musket* by Agnes Danforth Hewes, *New York Times*, December 20, 1936, https://www.nytimes.com/1936/12/20/archives/the-codfish-musket-by-agnes-danforth-hewes-illustrated-by-armstrong.html.

315 The Solovox was a recent musical invention: a short, three-octave monophonic keyboard attachment designed by Alan Young of the Hammond Organ Company. It was stored on a sliding mount under a piano keyboard, with a knee-operated volume control. It was intended to accompany the piano with organ-type lead voices and was connected to an electronic sound generation box and speaker. It was made from 1940 to 1948 and used two vibrating metal reeds to modulate the oscillator frequency to create a vibrato effect. On the front of the instrument, below the keyboard, there were a series of large thumb-operated buttons for oscillator range (switchable up and down three octaves: soprano, contralto, tenor, and bass) vibrato, attack time, deep tone, full tone, first voice, second voice, brilliant, and a switch for selecting woodwind, string sound, or mute. It was able to create a range of string, woodwind, and organ-type sounds. Reverb, "Hammond Solovox," https://reverb.com/item/26859-hammond-solovox-40-s-early-monophonic—synth.

316 "Notes on the Music of "Doodle Dandy of the U.S.A.," *Doodle Dandy* CCSU materials, n.d. (Saul Lancourt personal papers).

317 "Doodle Dandy of the U.S.A.," Dramatists Play Service, n.d. (Saul Lancourt personal papers).

318 Performances began at Joan of Arc Junior High School in Manhattan on January 6, 7, and 8; January 11, 12, 13, and 14 at Brooklyn's P. S. 223 and 210; and on January 19 and 20 at P. S. 70 in the Bronx.

319 Examples included *Grimms' Fairy Tales*, illustrated by Hope Dunlap (Rand McNally, 1913), which included thirty-six stories with full-page color illustrations and large print, and *Grimms' Fairy Tales*, edited by Frances Jenkins Olcott and illustrated by Rie Cramer (Penn Publishing Company, 1922) with full-page illustrations.

320 Percy A. Scholes, *The Complete Book of the Great Musicians* (1928; Ithaca: Yesterday's Classics, 2021).

321 *Bumble Bee Prince* CCSU materials, n.d. (Saul Lancourt personal papers).

322 *Bumble Bee Prince* CCSU materials, n.d. (Saul Lancourt personal papers).

323 Table of Contents, *The Adventures of Puck* CCSU materials, n.d. (Saul Lancourt personal papers).

324 *Robin Hood* CCSU materials, n.d. (Saul Lancourt personal papers).

325 *An Economic and Social History of the Middle Ages* by J. W. Thompson (1928); *Scenes and Characters of the Middle Age* by E.L. Cutts; *Civilization During the Middle Ages* by C. B. Adams (1914); *The Medieval Village* by G.G. Coulton (1926); *Medieval Days and Ways* by Gertrude Hartman; *Life on the English Manor, 1150-1400* by H. S. Bennett; *Chivalry* by F. W. Cornish (1901); *Life on a Medieval Barony* by W. S. Davis (1923); *English Wayfaring Life in the Middle Ages* by J. J. Jusserand (1889); and *Knights Life in the Days of Chivalry* by W. C. Miller (1924).

326 The unit developed for the physical education or recreation department offered a suggested bibliography on archery, including *The Teaching of Archery* by Dave and Cia Craft, an illustrated *Student's Handbook of Archery* by Phillip Rounsevalle, instructions on how to make bows and arrows in *Bows and Arrows* by James Duff, and *Archery Tackle* by Adolph Shane. The bibliography also included books on tumbling: *Tumbling and Stunts for Youths and Men*, by Walter Wiltich and H. C. Renter; *Tumbling for Girls* by Marna Venable Brady; and *Tumbling, Pyramid Building, and Stunts for Girls and Women*, by Bonnie and Donnie Colteral. National Recreation Association, Recreation Bulletin Services, "The Tool Kit of the Community Recreation Worker," n.d. (Saul Lancourt personal papers).

327 National Recreation Association, n.d. (Saul Lancourt personal papers).

328 *Robin Hood* CCSU material, n.d.

329 "Music for Robin Hood," mimeographed page, n.d. (Saul Lancourt personal papers).

330 "Suggestions for Children's Participation in the Junior Programs 'Robin Hood' Ballet," Educational material, n.d. (Saul Lancourt personal papers).

331 The course included a series of four panel discussions in which outstanding authorities in the field of childcare would participate: The Child at Play—Mark McCloskey, Director of Recreation, Federal Security Agency; The Child at Home—Katherine Lenroot, Chief, Children's Bureau, US Department of Labor; The Child at School—Dr. Frank O'Brien, Associate Superintendent of Schools, New York City; and The Child and His [sic] Amusements. —Dorothy McFadden, President, Junior Programs, Inc.

332 Depending on the year, various documents place them at different addresses—37 W. 57th St.; 45 W. 57th St.; 221 W. 57th St; and 250 W. 57th St. Unfortunately, as many of the documents are undated, it is difficult to know when, why, and in what order each move occurred.

333 Presumably, as Junior Programs expanded to the West Coast, there would have been a field secretary responsible for that geography or some rearrangement of the geographic boundaries, but I found no further information on additions to the field staff in any of the collections.

334 Virginia Commonwealth University Libraires, "Junior Leagues," Social Welfare History Project, https://socialwelfare.library.vcu.edu/eras/civil-war-reconstruction/junior-leagues/.

335 McFadden, "Entertainment in Your Community," unpublished autobiography.

336 *Think Magazine*, March 1940; *Vogue Magazine*, August 1, 1940; "Dance for Children," *New York Herald Tribune*, January 12, 1941; John M. Patterson, "Culture for Your Children," *Good Housekeeping*, April 1940, 97, 236 (JP Scrapbooks).

337 The Seattle Junior Programs, Inc., continued to exist until the late 1970s when it became the Seattle Junior Theater. In August 1984 it merged with the Young ACT Company, a division of A Contemporary Theater (ACT). Caldbick, "Seattle Children's Theatre"; "Seattle Theatre Archives: Collections of Theatre Companies."

338 A Los Angeles reference to Joop the Giraffe, the Junior Programs mascot.

339 Sight-saving classes for visually impaired, but not blind, students were introduced in public schools in 1913. Classes had specially trained teachers, focused on oral teaching, use of large print books, typewriters and dark lead pencils for written materials, and better than normal lighting. See Frank H. Rodin, "Sight Saving Classes," *Western Journal of Medicine* 42, no. 6 (June 1935): 426–29, https://pubmed.ncbi.nlm.nih.gov/18743280/.

340 As noted earlier, there was no information available as to whether children of color were included, although in one audience photo (unknown source, n.d.), there is a picture of one child who appears to be Black (Saul Lancourt personal papers).

341 Junior Programs' Coloring Contest Press Release, n.d. (Saul Lancourt personal papers).

342 Rotogravure is a printing technology that increased the clarity and color of

printing, especially for photographs. It was frequently used for publications such as Sunday news supplements which featured many pictures. The process is still used today for commercial printing. "The Rotogravure Process," Library of Congress, https://loc.gov/collections/world-war-i-rotogravures/articles-and-essays/the-rotogravure-process/#:~:t.

343   The answers, contained in a news release or on the radio the next day, were "Freedom of speech; freedom of worship; freedom from fear; freedom from want; "Yankee Doodle;" Both were messengers: Mercury for the Greek gods and Doodle Dandy for "Freedom Incorporated"; Generally about a mile." *Doodle Dandy* marketing materials, n.d. (Saul Lancourt personal papers).

344   Junior Programs *Doodle Dandy* song writing contest press release, n.d. (Saul Lancourt personal papers).

345   The final report needed to contain contact information for officers and committee members; for all schools involved; for all patrons, hostesses, ushers, scout troops; for all newspapers, and magazines; and for all organizations involved in publicity. Also needed were lists of the programs, dates, hours, and auditoriums as well as those who received free tickets. Planned and actual budgets, including a breakdown of income per performance, advance and door sales, contributions, income per school/organization; and expenses with notes as to future possible savings are essential. Attendance records by performance, with notes on circumstances that may have influenced the numbers (e.g., weather or competing events) were needed. Also subcommittee reports with suggestions for improvements; meeting locations, dates, and meeting minutes; all press clippings, photos, fliers, sample tickets, or programs if used; records and notes of any ancillary events such as panel discussions, or speeches; a complete set of materials distributed for classroom use; copies of various forms used for communication to schools and parents; samples of drawings, letters, and exhibits of children's work; various letters of commendation; and a short report to be presented at various organizational meetings as a way to "sustain enthusiasm for the next season" (16).

346   "Junior Programs At Work," in "Junior Programs Sends Young Audiences Operas, Ballets, Plays, Concerts 1940-1941," marketing booklet (Saul Lancourt personal papers).

347   Barry Mahool, unknown source, ca. 1941–42 (Saul Lancourt personal papers).

348   McFadden, unpublished autobiography, 324.

ENDNOTES

349 McFadden, unpublished autobiography, 32?a.

350 Saul Lancourt, "Writing for the Kids," *New York Times*, December 20, 1942 (Saul Lancourt personal papers).

351 Gregory Ashman, a Ukrainian pianist who emigrated to the United States in 1921, was an accompanist and opera coach at the Julliard School of Music (Saul Lancourt personal papers).

352 New York *World Telegram*, n.d. (Saul Lancourt personal papers).

353 The decision to conduct additional periodic rehearsals for a production that has been on the road for some period of time is usually an indication of a commitment to quality. Over time, pacing and rhythm can slip, and unwanted mannerisms and shortcuts creep in; therefore, it is hardly surprising that, before returning to New York for a series of holiday matinees, Lancourt felt additional rehearsals would ensure that New York would see *Marco Polo* at its best.

354 McFadden, unpublished autobiography, 324.

355 "New Attractions Added; Touring Territory is Extended to Pacific," *New York Herald Tribune*, June 25, 1939 (Saul Lancourt personal papers).

356 *CBS Student Guide*, October 1940 (JP Scrapbooks)

357 Barry Mahool, unknown source, ca. 1941–42.

358 Letter from Lawrence Tibbett to Dorothy McFadden, January 17, 1940 (Saul Lancourt personal papers).

359 "Junior Programs Inc. Nearly Doubles in Scope Last Year - Reports Rapid Progress in Professional Entertainment for Juveniles," *Republican* (Springfield, MA), July 14, 1940 (Saul Lancourt personal papers).

360 In today's dollars, $15,000 is roughly $329,887, while $20,000 translates into roughly $424,000.

361 Junior Programs Annual Report, 1937–38 (Saul Lancourt personal papers; JP Scrapbooks)

362 Members of the National Sponsoring Committee included actresses Irene Dunne, Helen Hayes, and Peggy Wood, as well as opera stars and musicians Kirsten Flagstad, Rise Stevens, Lawrence Tibbett, Albert Stoessel, and Olga Samaroff Stokowski. The list also included Carleton Sprague Smith (head of the New York Public Library Department of Music), James Roland Angell (president of Yale University), George N. Shuster (president of Hunter College), W. Carson Ryan (education director of the Bureau of Indian Affairs),

John Erskine (Columbia University), Sidonie Matsner Gruenberg (director of Child Study Association of America), Alice V. Keliher, ("grandmother" of the Day Care Movement), Winifred Ward (founder of Children's Theatre of Evanston, Illinois), philanthropic activists Mrs. Herbert H. Lehman, Mrs. Kermit Roosevelt, and Anna Eleanor Roosevelt Halsted, scientists Raymond Lee Ditmars (herpetologist), Frank Michler Chapman (ornithologist), George Clyde Fisher (curator of the American Museum of Natural History), Morris Ernst (cofounder ACLU), Warfield T. Longcope (physician-in-chief of Johns Hopkins Hospital), William Pearson Merrill, Malcolm Endicott Peabody (Bishop of the Episcopal Diocese of Central New York), and James DeWolf Perry (Bishop of Rhode Island), Ruth Meisnest (Seattle social figure), Princess Constance Pignatelli, Mrs. Helenka Pantaleoni Jr. (head of Children's Theater Department of the Junior League of New York), and Alice Tully (Saul Lancourt personal papers).

363   The Music Advisory Board included the Cincinnati Symphony, the Metropolitan Opera, Los Angeles Symphony, National Music Council, National Federation of Music Clubs, Seattle Symphony, and the Los Angeles Opera. The Radio Advisory Board included the Child Study Association of America, Progressive Education Association, Library of Congress, Columbia Broadcasting Company, National Council of Women, and Ohio State University. The Drama Advisory Board included the Papermill Playhouse, Goodman Theatre, Columbia Broadcasting Company, Marionette Fellowship of Detroit, and Children's Theatre Press; and the Community Relations Advisory Board included the Service Bureau for Intercultural Education, National Recreation Association, Council for Democracy, American Association of University Women, International Federation of Catholic Alumnae, Parents' Magazine, Boys Clubs of America, Museum of Natural History, Campfire Girls, and Boy Scouts of America (Saul Lancourt personal papers).

364   "It's 1750th Performance — Celebration in 1941," marketing flyer (Saul Lancourt personal papers).

365   McFadden, unpublished autobiography, 349b.

366   Engle Printing and Publishing, "Tire Rationing During World War II," Antiques and Auction News, June 22, 2018, https://antiquesandauctionnews.net/articles/Tire-Rationing-During-World-War-II/.

367   The White House Conference on Children and Youth had been held roughly every ten years, beginning in 1909. It was hosted by the President of the

United States, and involved thousands of delegates from around the country devoted to improving the lives of children. Wikipedia, s.v. "White House Conference on Children and Youth," updated July 3, 2022, https://en.wikipedia.org/wiki/White_House_Conference_on_Children_and_Youth.

368 It is not beyond the realm of possibility that there were a number of former participants in the Junior Programs' story in attendance at this conference: an unrelated Google search serendipitously revealed that Sidonie Matsner Gruenberg, a member of the Junior Programs Board of Directors was a conference participant, and it is hard not to hear an echo of Junior Programs' mission in the conference themes related to preparing children to engage in the democratic practices of responsible citizenship. Ronald E. Ohl, "Sidonie Matsner Gruenberg,"Jewish Virtual Library, jewishvirtuallibrary.org/sidonie-matsner-gruenberg.

369 Dean W. Roberts, "Highlights of the Midcentury White House Conference on Children and Youth," *American Journal of Public Health* 41, no. 1 (1951): 96–99, https://doi.org/10.2105/AJPH.41.1.96.

370 McCaslin, *Historical Guide to Children's Theatre in America*, 28–29.

371 McCaslin, *Historical Guide to Children's Theatre in America*, 29–32.

372 McCaslin, *Historical Guide to Children's Theatre in America*, 33.

373 McCaslin, *Historical Guide to Children's Theatre in America*, 33–34.

374 TYA-USA membership list.

375 TYA-USA, https://www.tyausa.org.

376 Childrens Theatre Foundation of America, https://www.childrenstheatrefoundation.org.

377 Arts Education Partnership, https://www.aep-arts.org/.

378 "Mission, Vision, and Values," American Alliance for Theatre and Education, https://www.aate.com/mission-vision-values.

379 International Association of Theatre & Performing Arts for Children and Young People, https://www.assitej-international.org.

380 McFadden, "Europe Challenges American Parents," *National Parent-Teacher* XXXI, no. 10, (June 1937): 10–11, 28–30.

381 Letter from Lawrence Tibbett to Dorothy McFadden, January 17, 1940; John Martin, *New York Times,* June 23, 1940 (Saul Lancourt personal papers).

382 McFadden, "Europe Challenges American Parents."

383 Jessica Gelt, "Shocking Closure at L.A.'s Mark Taper Forum Reflects a Crisis at Regional Theaters Nationwide," *Los Angeles Times*, June 18, 2023, https://www.latimes.com/entertainment-arts/story/2023-06-17/center-theatre-group-closing-mark-taper-forum-public-dallas-theater, emphasis added.

384 Manuel, *Strategic CaseMaking*, 79-93.

385 Foa and Mounk, "The Danger of Deconsolidation."

386 Dan Merica, Kyung Lah, and Alberto Moya, "Democrats See Energy Behind Teachers Strikes as a Force in 2020," CNN, May 28, 2019, https://edition.cnn.com/2019/05/28/politics/2020-democrats-teachers-unions/index.html; Mitch Smith and Monica Davey, "Chicago Teachers Strike Longest in Decades, Ends," *New York Times*, October 31, 2019, https://www.nytimes.com/2019/10/31/us/chicago-cps-teachers-strike.html; Dana Goldstein, "West Virginia Teachers Walk Out (Again) and Score a Win in Hours," *New York Times*, February 19, 2019, https://www.nytimes.com/2019/02/19/us/teachers-strikes.html; Jennifer Medina et. al, "Los Angeles Teachers Strike, Disrupting Classes For 500,000," *New York Times*, January 14, 2019, https://www.nytimes.com/2019/01/14/us/lausd-teachers-strike.html.

387 See Edwin C. Nevis, Joan Lancourt, and Helen G. Vassalo, *Intentional Revolutions: A Seven-Point Strategy for Transforming Organizations* (San Francisco: Jossey-Bass, 1996); Richard P. Chait, William P. Ryan, and Barbara E. Taylor, *Governance as Leadership: Reframing the Work of Nonprofit Boards* (Hoboken, NJ: Wiley, 2005).

388 Wikipedia, s.v. "Partnership," updated March 26, 2024, https://en.wikipedia.org/wiki/Partnership.

389 Dave Beckwith and Cristina Lopez, "Community Organizing: People Power from the Grassroots," Center for Community Change, comm-org.wisc.edu/papers97/beckwith.htm.

390 Pat Launer, "The Theater's Queen of Green—and Contessa of Community Outreach," San Diego Metro, September 14, 2011, https://www.sandiegometro.com/2011/09/the-theater%e2%80%99s-queen-of-green-%e2%80%93-and-contessa-of-community-outreach/.

391 "Community Organizing 101," NYC Cultural Affairs, https://www.nyc.gov/site/dcla/about/community-organizing-application.page.

392 "The Five Principles of Social Justice," Kent State University, July 30, 2020, https://onlinedegrees.kent.edu/political-science/master-of-public-administration/community/five-principles-of-social-justice.

393 Shawn Ginwright and Taj James, "From Assets to Agents of Change: Social Justice, Organizing, and Youth Development," *New Directions for Youth Development* 2002, no. 96 (2002): 27–46, https://onlinelibrary.wiley.com/doi/10.1002/yd.25.

394 Cleveland's Karamu House was one of the few settlement houses with a major focus on the theater arts as an explicit means of bringing children of different races and cultures together, "fostering interracial appreciation through group work in arts projects." Noerena Abookire and Jennifer Scott McNair, "Children's Theatre Activities at Karamu House, 1915–1975," in *Spotlight on the Child: Studies in the History of American Children's Theatre*, ed. Roger L. Bedard and C. John Tolch (New York: Greenwood Press, 1989), 81.

395 Hannah-Jones, *1619 Project*; Kendi, *How To Be An Antiracist*; Kendi, *Stamped From the Beginning*; Anderson, *White Rage*; Wilkerson, *Caste*; Oluo, *So You Want to Talk about Race*.

396 We See You, White American Theater, "Statement," https://www.weseeyouwat.com/statement.

397 Michael Paulson, "Theater Artists of Color Enumerate Demands for Change," *New York Times*, July 10, 2020, https://www.nytimes.com/2020/07/10/theater/we-see-you-theater-demands.html.

398 "Albert Einstein Quotes," Brainy Quote, https://www.brainyquote.com/quotes/albert_einstein_385842.

399 Imani Perry, *South to America: A Journey Below the Mason Dixon to Understand the Soul of a Nation* (New York: Harper Collins, 2022), 138.

400 Shavonne T. Coleman, "Beyond the Traditional: Conversations of Inclusivity," *TYA Today*, Spring 2019, 46–47.

401 Kareem Abdul-Jabbar, Substack newsletter, January 17, 2023.

402 "Page to Stage," *TYA Today*, Fall 2019, 45.

ABOUT THE AUTHOR

Dr. Joan Lancourt had a forty-year management career combining work in the public, private, academic and not-for-profit sectors. Since then, Dr. Lancourt has devoted much of her energy and skills to working with and writing about the efforts of local and regional theater board leaders to increase the diversity of their audiences, boards, and staffs. Combining expertise from her work in sustainable community involvement and organizational change, she authored a three-part series in HowlRound Theatre Commons, an online hub for global theater conversations that encourage world-wide sharing of intellectual and artistic resources and expertise. The series "Why Boards Don't Need To Be Bored" is based on the experience of innovative theater boards across the country and focuses on the need for more generative board leadership, more strategic decision-making, and for deeper and more meaningful engagement of theater organizations in the diverse racial and ethnic communities they serve. Drawing on her experience as board chair of two theater companies as well as her experience as a community organizer, a manager in and consultant to national and international organizations, and as an executive coach for ten years in a Harvard Kennedy School professional leadership development program, Dr. Lancourt organized a series of workshops for board members from seven theaters. These workshops advocated for a significant increase in racial and age diversity at all levels of a theater's organization as well as in its audiences.

Dr. Lancourt received her MSW in community organizing from the UCLA School of Social Work and earned her PhD from The Heller School of Social Policy and Planning at Brandeis University. Always mission driven, she came to see research as an important way to tease out "lessons learned" from past experience, thereby enabling today's practitioners to use them to improve current practice. In her 1979 book, *Confront or Concede: The Alinsky Citizen Action Organizations*, she secured funding from the National Institute of Mental Health to examine and assess the effectiveness of the community organizing model created by the flamboyant community organizer Saul Alinsky. In 1996, with Ed Nevis of the Sloan School of Management, and Helen Vassallo, she co-authored the book *Intentional Revolutions: A Seven Point Strategy for Transforming Organizations,* which identifies critical success factors for making major, sustainable organizational change.

More Than Entertainment: Democracy and the Performing Arts is, in many ways, a synthesis of all she has learned along the way. Her story of Junior Programs, Inc. documents and strengthens our understanding of how the performing arts can be an important catalyst for transformational social change, as well as an effective and compelling way to normalize diversity—be it racial or otherwise. In a sense, the inclusion of a broad range of different perspectives and experiences is an essential ingredient of innovation and, therefore, a prerequisite for the creation of a more just and equitable world. As with her previous books, her extensive research documenting the life and times of Junior Programs, Inc. identifies numerous lessons from the past that are still relevant for today's theater leaders. And what better way to put those lessons into practice than for TYA theaters to form strong and stable partnerships with the communities and schools responsible for ensuring that the next generation of children internalize the democratic values and beliefs needed to guide and inform their life's journey.

Active in her local community to promote a range of social justice issues, and for several years chair of her town's Commission on Diversity, Inclusion and Community Relations, Dr. Lancourt's expertise, reflected in numerous articles and papers, ranges from mission-driven generative thinking and leadership development to strategic planning, design and management of structural and cultural change as well as the implementation of a broad range of new programs and policies.

Dr. Lancourt can be contacted at www.juniorprogramsbook.com website.

INDEX

access, 6, 49, 261, 307, 326
acting, 14, 173, 290, 334; *The Bumble Bee Prince*, 156; in opera, 142, 172–73
Actors' Equity, 45, 292, 303
Adventures of Marco Polo, The, 41, 47, 204, 296–97, 335; CCSU, 206, 212–13, 214; dance in, 105–6; development of, 94–95; reviews of, 104–5, 112–13, 116–17; set design, 106–8, 108–10; synopsis of, 98–104, 108–12
Adventures of Puck, The, 46; CCSU, 251–53; costume design, 188–89; development of, 186–87; music, 187, 189; reviews of, 190; set design, 189; synopsis of, 189–90
advisory boards, 30, 208, 304, 324, 390n363
American Alliance for Theatre and Education (AATE), 204–5, 311, 317, 327, 332
American Dream, 8, 64, 137
American Opera Company, 115, 142
anti-communism, 2, 8, 19
archives, xxi, 51, 211
arts: education, 215, 310; funding, 307–8. *See also* performing arts
Arts Education Partnership, 311
Ashman, Gregory, 153, 288, 389n351
Asia: immigrants from, 97, 226; prejudice toward, 57, 97; stereotypes of, 40, 57–58
assimilation, 3, 55, 64, 97, 370n161
Association of Junior Leagues of America, 11, 21, 45, 262, 266–67, 269, 275, 309–10, 323
audience: development, 1–2, 313, 314–15; diversity, 21; engagement, 134–35, 150; feedback, 44; participation, 270, 284
audiences: children as, 5, 62, 155–56, 283–84; and race, 58–59
authenticity, 75, 76, 84, 86, 105–6, 138, 327, 336–37

ballet: CCSUs, 211; and children, 177, 202; classical, 174; narrative (*see* dance-play); narrators in, 177
Biden, Joseph R., 3
Billy Rose Theatre Division, xxi, 51

Black: representation, 18, 58–59; stereotypes, 40
blackface, 18, 60, 61
Brazil, 86–88, 213–14, 224–33, 320
Broadway, xix, 13, 16
budgeting, 271, 272, 292. *See also* finances
Bumble Bee Prince, The, 46, 204; acting, 156; development, 288; music, 159; recording, 172–73; reviews of, 155–60; set design, 160; storybook, 172–73; synopsis of, 154–55

Carlisle, Margaret, 47, 191, 288, 336–37
casting, 290; and race, 59, 61, 116, 327
Catholicism, 54, 58
CCSU. *See* correlated curriculum study units
Center, Katherine, 78, 80, 221–22
child: development, 2, 9, 10, 41–42, 76, 77; education, 203; labor, 9, 10, 58
childhood, 2–3, 9, 10, 203, 316
children, 9–10; as audience, 5, 62, 155–56, 283–84; and ballet, 177, 202; dance for, 174–76; and democracy, 211, 321, 326; entertainment for, 21, 25–26, 47–48, 50, 139–40, 210; music for, 121, 292; and opera, 171–72, 208, 333–34; as performers, 78–80, 169–70, 203, 265, 267; respect for, 5, 6, 137, 257, 313–14, 314
Children's Education Theater (NY), 10–11
children's theater, 3, 309–10; professional, 11–12, 17, 311, 332. *See also* theater for young audiences
Children's Theater of Evanston, 11
Children's Theatre Foundation of America, 311
China, 57, 95–96, 116–117, 214, 235–38, 244, 372n168, 384n301; stereotypes of, 95
Chorpenning, Charlotte, 17, 75, 76, 288, 349n147
citizenship, 33, 36, 48, 57, 118, 120, 309, 321–22
civic: duty, 262; engagement, 4, 43; organizations, 45, 260–62, 279, 294, 323 (*see also* local, sponsoring organizations)
Civil War, 3
climate change, 3, 317, 319–20
Code of Entertainment, 30–31, 33
Coit, Dorothy, 179
colonial America, 222–23

coloring contests, 267, 275–77. *See also* publicity
Columbia University Teachers College, 206–7
commercial theater, 3, 13–14. *See also* Broadway
communism, 2
community, 49, 258, 288; cooperation, 269; engagement, 6, 43, 45, 64, 160–61, 314, 323–25, 325; involvement, 210, 262–63, 267, 294, 295, 322–23; organizing, 325–26; participation, 44; partnerships, 5–6
correlated curriculum study units (CCSUs), 5, 25, 42, 43, 205–7, 207, 211–12, 294–95, 319, 320; *The Adventures of Marco Polo*, 206, 212–13, 214; *The Adventures of Puck*, 251–53; art, 205, 215; ballet, 211; bibliographies, 212, 218; *Doodle Dandy of the U.S.A.*, 214; drama, 215; *The Emperor's Treasure Chest*, 206, 224–35; history, 214; home economics, 206, 215, 222; literature, 216; music, 213, 215, 223; opera, 143–44, 211; physical education, 206, 215; publicity, 259; reviews of, 215; *The Reward of the Sun God*, 206, 212, 214, 218–21; *Robin Hood*, 206, 213, 214, 253–57; *Run, Peddler, Run*, 80, 206, 214, 221–23; science, 206; shop class, 206, 215; social studies, 206, 213–14, 222–23
costume design, 84, 288–89; *The Adventures of Puck*, 188–89; *The Emperor's Treasure Chest*, 92–94; *Jack and the Beanstalk*, 168–69; *Pinocchio*, 183; *Robin Hood*, 195–96
COVID-19, 1, 314–15, 331
Credo, 2, 7, 30–32, 36, 64, 75, 173, 203, 272, 315–16, 327, 338–39
crisis, 1
critical race theory (CRT), 39–40, 58, 321, 328, 330, 331
Culminating Activities, 216, 218, 258, 319. *See also* correlated curriculum study units
cultural: appropriation, 75; diversity, 42, 212, 224–25; representation, 204

dance, 76. *The Adventures of Marco Polo*, 105–6; American, 162, 174; *Doodle Dandy of the U.S.A.*, 120–21; *Pinocchio*, 181–82; *Robin Hood*, 197, 199–200. *See also* ballet
dance-play, 46, 177, 187–88, 201, 334
democracy, 3–4, 33–35, 314, 315; and children, 211, 321, 326; in crisis, 1, 2; defending, 3–4, 63, 134, 316; and diversity, 34, 36, 50; and education, 10, 35, 321–22; future of, 118; history of, 221–22; inclusive, 3; and performing arts, 2, 4, 7, 31–33, 36, 48, 316–17, 329–30; portrayals of, 63; preserving, 2–4, 31, 33, 51, 53, 64, 132, 134, 137, 211, 312, 321–22, 335; and theater,

12, 17; values of, 4, 35, 317
Dewey, John, 10, 33, 34–36; educational philosophy, 48, 64, 174–75, 258 (*see also* child, development; childhood)
didacticism, 76, 105, 225
difference, 41, 62–63, 64, 68, 212, 324, 327
discrimination, 54; racial, 221, 328 (*see also* racism)
diversity, 4, 6, 36, 55, 203, 311, 326, 327; cultural, 42, 212, 224–25; and democracy, 34, 36, 50; and education, 42
Doodle Dandy of the U.S.A., xix–xx, 33, 37, 47, 63, 314; CCSU, 214; dance, 120–21; development of, 120; music, 121; reviews of, 132–35, 135–37; set design, 121–23; synopsis of, 124–32

education, 5, 6, 10, 42; arts, 215, 310; and democracy, 10, 35, 321–22; and diversity, 42; intercultural, 98, 204; and performing arts, 5, 42–43, 175, 202, 203–5, 257, 318–19; public, 320–21
educational: conferences, 210; materials, 270–71; partnerships, 5, 206–8, 321–22
Educational Guidance Committee, 41–43, 207, 217, 270, 294–95, 379n260
"educational theater," 11
empathy, 7, 74, 201
Emperor's Treasure Chest, The, 41, 56–57; CCSU, 206, 224–35; costume design, 92–94; development of, 86–87; music, 91–92; reviews of, 86–87, 92; synopsis of, 88–89
enslavement, 2, 3, 77, 320, 328
entertainment, 274, 302, 315–16; for children, 21, 25–26, 47–48, 50, 139–40, 210; popular, 14–15
equality, 327, 328–29
equity, 4, 6, 317, 326, 328–29; racial, 33
Erskine, John, 46, 163–64, 171

Farquhar, Marion, 153, 156
fascism, 2, 34, 36, 63, 328
FDR. *See* Roosevelt, Franklin Delano
Federal Theatre Project, 16–19; Children's Units, 17–18, 49–50; closure of, 19, 179; Negro Theater Units, 17, 60; regional units, 17
feminism, 38, 262
field secretaries, 44, 261, 262, 292–94
film, 14–15, 85, 258–59; popular, 40; and race, 15

finances, 264–65, 297, 303, 306
Flanagan, Hallie, 16, 19, 179
Four Freedoms, 120, 241, 247, 280, 281, 373n180
freedom, 35, 118, 121, 128, 240
funding, 302, 315; arts, 307–8
fundraising, 24, 303, 305–6. *See also* finances

games, 206, 212, 218–19, 254, 320
Good Neighbor Policy, 85–86, 223
Goodman Children's Theatre, 12, 75, 332
Great Depression, 2, 8, 15, 162
Gruenberg, Louis, 46, 162–64, 286–87, 299

Hansel and Gretel, 21–22, 46; recording, 172–73; reviews, 146, 148, 150–51; set design, 151; synopsis of, 146–48
Herts, Alice Minnie, 10–11
Hollywood, 14, 40–41, 56, 56–58, 212, 336. *See also* film
Hopi, 56, 67–76, 218, 336. *See also* Indigenous peoples
Horace Mann School, 206–7
House Un-American Activities Committee (HUAC), 19, 179
Hull House Players, 10
Humperdinck, Engelbert, 146

immigrants, 8, 10; Asian, 97, 226; children, 11; Irish, 54; Jewish, 54; Latinx, 55; representations of, 76–77
immigration, 2–3, 29, 36, 317, 370n161; Chinese, 57
inclusion, 6, 55, 63, 317, 326, 327
Indigenous peoples, 56, 213–15, 219–21, 319–20; stereotypes of, 40–41, 69, 74, 212. *See also* Native Americans
inequality, 3, 328
inequity, 3
innovation, 50, 332–33
International Association of Theatre and Performing Arts for Young People (ASSITEJ), 201, 204, 310, 311

Jack and the Beanstalk, 46; acting, 170; costume design, 168–69; libretto, 164, 171; music, 163–64; reviews of, 162, 163–64, 167–71; set design, 167, 169; singing, 170; synopsis of, 164–67

INDEX

January 6 US Capitol attack, 3, 317
Jim Crow, 36. *See also* racism
Joop the Giraffe, 98–99, 154, 264, 371n162
Junior League. *See* Association of Junior Leagues of America
Junior Programs, Inc.: Ballet Company, 46, 201–2; as booking agent, 23, 291–92; closure, xx, 6, 307; *Code of Entertainment,* 30–31, 33; collaboration with agencies, 44; collaboration with NML, 21–23; combination of companies, 47, 94–95, 295, 307, 335; company structure, 6, 20; *Credo,* 2, 7, 30–32, 36, 64, 75, 173, 203, 272, 315–16, 327, 338–39; Educational Guidance Committee, 41–43, 207, 217, 270, 294–95, 379n260; educational partnerships, 24, 206; finances, 306; founding, xix, 20–24, 22–23; mission, 20, 30; National Sponsoring Committee, 30; New York office, 44, 260, 261, 291; Opera Company, 46; organizational structure, 24, 27, 43, 44–45, 260–61, 295, 308; performers, 289–90; Players, 46; production costs, 303; recording adaptations, 172–73; storybooks, 172–73; touring, 46
Junior Programs Committees' Organization and Promotion Booklet, 268, 314
justice: racial, 316, 330; social, 7, 33, 325, 326

King-Coit School of Acting and Design, 11, 179
Kublai Khan: as character, 57, 101–4, 117; as historical figure, 96–97, 214, 236. See also *Adventures of Marco Polo, The*

labor, 15; child, 9, 10, 58; unions, 8, 29
Lancourt, Joan, xix–xx, 29
Lancourt, Saul, xix, 44–45, 50, 62, 286, 287, 314, 333–35, 365n81; biography, 27–30; as director, 140–41, 288, 289; partnership with Dorothy McFadden, 24, 28; as script writer, 63, 104, 120, 142–43
Latinx: immigrants, 55; stereotypes, 40, 56–57, 85–86
leadership, 269–70
liveness, 7, 217, 316
Living Newspaper, 16
local: news, 275, 277, 280, 285; performers, 160–61, 169–70, 265, 267, 271, 284, 294; schools, 207–8, 210; sponsoring organizations, xx, 5–6, 43–44, 287
local sponsoring committees, 260–62, 262–63, 314, 323; personnel, 269–70

MacClelland, Kenneth, 75, 106, 158, 288, 289
Mahool, Barry, 108, 120, 290–91

Major, Clare Tree, 11, 203, 332
Matschat, Cecile Hulse, 86, 288
McFadden, Dorothy, xix, 20–22, 44–45, 50, 139–40, 210, 262, 268, 286, 292, 302, 314; biography, 24–27; as fundraiser, 304; at the NML, 22–23; partnership with Saul Lancourt, 24, 28; as script writer, 184; as translator, 153; trips to Europe, 25–26, 153, 287, 312–13
membership campaigns, 266, 268
Mendelssohn, Felix, 187, 252
Midsummer Night's Dream, A, 186. See also *Adventures of Puck, The*
morale, 118, 123
Moscow Children's Theatre, 25, 153
music, 21, 68; *The Adventures of Puck,* 187, 189; appreciation, 141; *The Bumble Bee Prince,* 159; for children, 292; *Doodle Dandy of the U.S.A.,* 121; *The Emperor's Treasure Chest,* 91–92; *Jack and the Beanstalk,* 163–64; *Pinocchio,* 180; *The Princess and the Swineherd,* 184; *Robin Hood,* 191, 197
musical theater, 13, 335

narrative reparations, 38, 138, 144, 212
narrators, 161, 172, 177, 202, 290, 334; in opera, 142–43; *Pinocchio,* 182; *Robin Hood,* 198–99
National Endowment of the Arts, 310
National Music League (NML), 21
National Sponsoring Committee, 30, 304
national unity, 44, 63. *See also* morale
Native Americans, 36; culture, 219–21; stereotypes, 40, 56, 67, 68, 69, 218. *See also* Indigenous peoples
Nelson, John Louw, 67, 68, 69, 288
neoliberalism, 3, 321
New York City Association of Teachers of English, 11
New York Public Library, xxi, 51

off-Broadway, 14
off-off-Broadway, 14
O'Neill, Eugene, 14
opera, 139–41; accessibility of, 173; acting in, 142, 172–73; American, 162–63, 171, 173; canon, 162; CCSUs, 143–44, 211; and children, 171–72, 208, 333–34; in English, 143, 173, 334; librettos, 164; narrators in, 142–43; singers, 142, 144; staging, 140–41, 173; traditional, 142, 173

INDEX

optimism, 65
Orientalism, 39. *See also* stereotypes, Asian
"other," 37–39
othering, 3, 39–41, 42, 54, 76, 104, 204, 221

parents, 210–11
parent-teacher associations (PTAs), 22, 269, 274
partnerships, 330, 332; community, 5–6; with schools, 43, 269–70, 270–71
pedagogy, 4, 217
people of color, 39–40
performance venues, 281–83, 337–38
performers: children as, 78–80, 169–70, 203, 265, 267; local, 160–61, 169–70, 265, 267, 271, 284, 294; training, 216
performing arts: and democracy, 2, 4, 7, 31–33, 36, 48, 316–17, 329–30; and education, 5, 42–43, 175, 202, 203–5, 257, 318–19; and racism, 311, 327–32; racism in, 329. *See also* theater
Perry, Charlotte, 46, 79–80, 370n155
Picken, Martha, 182, 187, 188, 197, 198–99, 290
Pignatelli di Montecalvo, Constance, 185
Pinocchio, 46, 204; costume design, 183; dance in, 181–82; development of, 179–80; music, 180; narrator, 182; reviews of, 181–83; synopsis of, 180–81
playwrights, 13–14
Plotkin, Charles, 151, 208, 261
political polarization, 3, 317
popular: entertainment, 14–15; film, 40
previews, 291, 313
Princess and the Swineherd, The, 46; music, 184; reviews of, 186; script, 184, 185; synopsis of, 185–86
production costs, 272, 303–4. *See also* finances
professional: actors, 13; children's theater, 11–12, 17, 311, 332; performers, 303–4
professionalism, 274, 289
program choice, 53–54, 153, 271. *See also* season planning
PTA. *See* parent-teacher associations
public education, 320–21
publicity, 266, 272, 273, 273–75, 277–79, 298
Pushkin, Alexander, 153, 173, 249, 319

race, 39–40, 316; and casting, 59, 61, 116, 327; and film, 15
racial: equity, 33; justice, 316, 330; stereotypes, 55–56
racism, 3, 18, 37, 49, 55, 59–60, 315; in American theater, 60, 61; and performing arts, 311, 327–32; in performing arts, 329
radio, 15, 91, 280
regional theater, 2, 6, 14, 311, 315
rehearsals, 290–91. *See also* previews
representation, 212; Black, 18, 58–59; cultural, 204; immigrant, 76–77; Indigenous, 221
Reward of the Sun God, The, 41, 46, 56; CCSU, 206, 212, 214, 218–21; director, 75; publicity, 69–70; set design, 75–76; synopsis of, 70–74
Rhythm for Rain, 67–68
Rimsky-Korsakov, Nikolai, 153, 250
Robin Hood, 47; CCSU, 206, 213, 214, 253–57; costume design, 195–96; dance, 197, 199–200; development of, 191–93; music, 191, 197; narrator, 198–99; reviews of, 195–201; set design, 196; storybook, 172–73; synopsis of, 193–95
Roosevelt, Franklin Delano (FDR), 15, 85, 95–96, 162, 373n180
Run, Peddler, Run: CCSU, 80, 206, 214, 221–23; development of, 78–80; reviews of, 80, 81–84; synopsis of, 80–81

season planning, 271, 286–88. *See also* program choice
Seattle, WA, 263–64, 361n6
Seattle Junior Programs, Inc., 263–64
segregation, 49, 55, 59, 60, 328
Selee, Marion, 150–51, 155, 157, 170, 290, 299
Service Bureau for Intercultural Education, 97, 204, 214, 236, 390n363
set design, 288–89, 337–38; *The Adventures of Marco Polo*, 106–8, 108–10; *Adventures of Puck*, 189; *The Bumble Bee Prince*, 160; *Doodle Dandy of the U.S.A.*, 121–23; *Hansel and Gretel*, 151; *Jack and the Beanstalk*, 167, 169; *The Reward of the Sun God*, 75–76; *Robin Hood*, 196
settlement house movement, 203, 262
Shakespeare, William, 16, 186, 189–90, 215, 250, 251–52, 319
Shawn, Ted, 47, 120–21, 174, 288
Siegmeister, Elie, 47, 121, 288, 337
social: events, 280, 285, 305–6; justice, 7, 33, 325, 326
social studies, 213–14, 222

INDEX 405

speaking campaigns, 266, 270, 274, 280, 293
St. Denis, Ruth, 47, 104–6, 174, 239, 288, 336
stereotypes, 37, 44, 212, 336; Asian, 40, 57–58; Black, 40; Chinese, 95; Latinx, 40, 56–57, 85–86; Native American, 40, 56, 67, 68, 69, 218; racial, 55–56; racist, 13, 17–18
Strawbridge, Edwin, 46, 47, 174–77, 201, 301; as choreographer, 184; as dancer, 176, 181, 190

Tale of the Tsar Saltan, 153. See also *Bumble Bee Prince, The*
teachers, 5, 42, 205, 258, 271, 310
teaching artists, 42, 217, 258
theater: American, 162; commercial, 3, 13–14; and democracy, 12, 17; history of, 12; regional, 2, 6, 14, 311, 315. *See also* performing arts
theater for young audiences (TYA), xxii, 1–2, 7, 10–11, 204, 326, 339–40; history of, 7–8, 11–13. *See also* children's theater
Theatre for Young Audiences-USA (TYA-USA), 204, 311, 317, 327, 332
Threshold Players, 11, 203
ticket: prices, 16, 22, 264–65, 271, 272, 302, 303, 327; selling, 271, 272–73
touring, 6, 13, 46, 49–50, 263, 289, 292, 294, 296–297, 297; difficulties of, 307; and race, 59, 61; schedule, 298–302
Trump, Donald J., 317, 321
TYA. *See* theater for young audiences

University of Oregon, 208, 211, 224, 235, 251

values, 321, 332; democratic, 4, 35, 317
vaudeville, 13, 26, 60
Vickery, William, 97–98, 204, 214
violence: anti-Asian, 97; anti-Black, 60–61, 330
volunteers, 5–6, 24, 45, 260, 262, 302, 323
voting, 36, 328

Ward, Winifred, 11
Wei Ji, 1–2
white supremacy, 40, 41. *See also* racism
Wilshire, Ellen McClellan, 208, 232, 251, 253

Wood, Hugh B., 224, 234, 235, 251, 379n260
Works Progress Administration (WPA), 15. *See also* Federal Theatre Project
World War II, xx, 47, 118, 307

YouthARTS Development Project, 311